1972
The Supreme Court Review

1972

The

"Judges as persons, or courts as institutions, are entitled to
no greater immunity from criticism than other persons
or institutions . . . [J]udges must be kept mindful of their limitations and
of their ultimate public responsibility by a vigorous
stream of criticism expressed with candor however blunt."
—*Felix Frankfurter*

". . . while it is proper that people should find fault when
their judges fail, it is only reasonable that they should recognize the
difficulties. . . . Let them be severely brought to book,
when they go wrong, but by those who will take the trouble
to understand them."
—*Learned Hand*

THE LAW SCHOOL

THE UNIVERSITY OF CHICAGO

Supreme Court Review

EDITED BY

PHILIP B. KURLAND

 THE UNIVERSITY OF CHICAGO PRESS

CHICAGO AND LONDON

INTERNATIONAL STANDARD BOOK NUMBER: 0-226-46423-7

LIBRARY OF CONGRESS CATALOG CARD NUMBER: 60-14353

THE UNIVERSITY OF CHICAGO PRESS, CHICAGO 60637

THE UNIVERSITY OF CHICAGO PRESS, LTD., LONDON

To A. H. K.

In Memoriam

Oft in the stilly night
   E'er slumber's chain has bound me,
Fond memory brings the light
   Of other days around me.

—Thomas Moore

CONTENTS

DANIEL D. POLSBY

THE DEATH OF CAPITAL

PUNISHMENT? FURMAN v. GEORGIA

In its last decision day before adjourning the 1971 Term, the Supreme Court issued some 50,000 words of opinions striking down sentences of capital punishment in three cases.[1] Nine separate opinions, preceded by a short per curiam, were handed down. The question presented was whether the death punishment violated the Cruel and Unusual Punishment Clause of the Eighth Amendment. The answer: at least sometimes. What the Court held must be sought in five opinions of the majority, none of whose members joined the opinion of any other. The per curiam significantly speaks of "these cases"—the three petitioners before the Court—and states that as to them, carrying out the death penalty would constitute cruel and unusual punishment in violation of the Eighth and Fourteenth Amendments. By implication, most or all extant statutes in American jurisdictions that prescribe the death penalty are unconstitutional. And five hundred men and women theretofore condemned to suffer that punishment cannot now be legally hanged, shot, gassed, or electrocuted.

William Henry Furman, a commonplace sort of murderer, and Lucious Jackson and Elmer Branch, both run-of-the-mill rapists,

Daniel D. Polsby is a member of the bar of Minnesota and of the District of Columbia. Robert L. Palmer and Richard A. Allen helped the author by discussing with him a number of the issues raised in the *Furman* case. Nelson W. Polsby and David B. Cook read the first draft of this paper and made valuable suggestions and comments. Their generosity with their time and insights is gratefully acknowledged.

[1] Furman v. Georgia, 408 U.S. 238 (1972).

were at first bracketed with Earnest James Aikens, Jr., an extraordinarily vicious and unrepentant multiple rape-murderer. Aikens's case was to have been the centerpiece in the death penalty cases, for his case was by far the clearest of the four. If any convicted criminal deserved the death penalty, it was Aikens. But when the California Supreme Court decided in February of 1972 that the death penalty was offensive to a clause in the California Constitution which prohibits the use of cruel or unusual punishments,[2] Aikens's case was remanded to the California courts to give him the advantage of the new ruling.[3]

Furman v. Georgia was decided in the context of great ferment in the case law over the death penalty. In 1968, *Witherspoon v. Illinois*[4] had held that persons morally opposed to the use of the death penalty could not be excluded from capital juries unless their beliefs would prevent them from performing their public duties. Late in the 1970 Term, *McGautha v. California*[5] had held, first, that nothing in the Constitution required a capital jury to be instructed as to what specific standards it ought to apply in deciding whether to recommend the imposition of the death penalty, and second, that the Constitution and fundamental fairness did not require a bifurcation of capital trials into a guilt phase and a punishment phase.[6] A letter to the *New York Times* from several illustrious New York lawyers praising the *Furman* decision makes it clear that, as the letter puts it, "The Supreme Court decision did not just happen," but was the outcome of many years of feverish and co-ordinated work by the NAACP Legal Defense and Educational Fund, a number of academic lawyers, and "scores of attorneys across the country."[7]

The efforts of these crusaders seem all the more remarkable when one considers the cross-currents. The past few years have scarcely provided a tranquil environment for the nurture of new and more

---

[2] People v. Anderson, 6 Cal.3d 628 (1972), *application for stay denied*, 405 U.S. 903 (1972).

[3] Aikens v. California, 406 U.S. 813 (1972).

[4] 391 U.S. 510 (1968).   [5] 402 U.S. 183 (1971).

[6] This second issue was raised, not in *McGautha*, but in its companion case, Crampton v. Ohio, which the Court decided simultaneously with it. Crampton had also challenged the standardless charge to the jury.

[7] Letter from Francis T. P. Plimpton, Simon H. Rifkind, Samuel I. Rosenman, Orville H. Schell, Jr., and Cyrus Vance, 24 July 1972.

polished ideals of reverence for human life. On the contrary, besides the agonies of our overseas follies, we have had some violent new awakenings at home. Little by little, terms like "hijacking" and "piracy" have transpired from their former sanctuaries in Errol Flynn movies and begun to travel the domestic air routes. Political murders have taken a prominent place in the decision-making processes of our democracy. Hundreds of thousands of our citizens have turned to the use of heroin and so entrapped themselves in a recurring cycle of criminal activity. And the universities, which used to be viewed by outsiders as kinds of cloisters not of the real world, have at times seemed like veritable warehouses of violent lunatics.

In response to all of this, a new mytho-statistical player began to edge toward center stage of the American consciousness: the wife of a machinist in Dayton, Ohio—the model middle American, epitome of the Real Majority.[8] While the *haut monde* read Camus[9] and refined their thoughts on the sanctity of life, the machinist's wife read the newspapers and thought about how the world was going to hell.

It may be thought that the recent congressional legislation on air piracy[10] and presidential[11] and congressional[12] assassinations, all of which provide for the infliction of the death penalty, are creatures of the machinist's wife and her sentiments. The victory of the petitioners is unquestionably the more remarkable considering the sanguinary temper of the time.

This paper explores what the Supreme Court did in *Furman v. Georgia*. The exploration does not begin, however, from a neutral ground, since I am biased against the use of the death penalty. The question I ask is not whether *Furman v. Georgia* was rightly decided, but rather whether the Court has furnished any new or useful tools which might be used to help the unenlightened to see why the death penalty is cruel and unusual punishment. The analysis must begin, not with *Furman* itself, but with *McGautha v. California*, decided only thirteen months prior to *Furman*. For although it is not an Eighth Amendment case at all, the questions posed by

---

[8] See SCAMMON & WATTENBERG, THE REAL MAJORITY (1970).

[9] *Reflections on the Guillotine*, in CAMUS, RESISTANCE, REBELLION AND DEATH (1961).

[10] 49 U.S.C. § 1472(i) (1961).

[11] 18 U.S.C. § 1751.   [12] 18 U.S.C. § 351.

McGautha, as well as the way that the late Mr. Justice Harlan answered them for the Court, trench very closely upon the issue presented in *Furman*.

Early in the afternoon on February 14, 1967, Dennis McGautha and an accomplice, one Wilkinson, entered the business premises of Mrs. Pon Lock and robbed her at gunpoint of $300. Three hours later, the two bandits entered and robbed a store owned by Mrs. Benjamin Smetana. During the course of that robbery one of the two shot and killed Mr. Smetana. Although there was evidence tending to show that McGautha had fired the fatal shot, the point was not established conclusively. At length, both men were captured, tried, and convicted of two counts of armed robbery and one count of first degree murder. The jury, following California law, was left at large to affix such punishment as might seem to them best. Wilkinson's sentence was life imprisonment and McGautha was sentenced to die.

Upon appeal, McGautha urged that the practice of submitting the issue of punishment to the jury without articulate standards to govern the jury's consideration of that question violated due process of law. The case wound its way through mandatory appeals in the California courts[13] and arrived in the United States Supreme Court, where it was affirmed, 6 to 3.[14]

Justice Harlan was convincing in arguing that juries should take the punishment decision under submission without standards to guide the determination: it should be done this way because it must be done this way. Experience has shown that it is all but impossible "to identify before the fact those homicides for which the slayer should die."[15]

Petitioner had made a very subtle argument: by structuring the penalty-allocation processes as they did, the legislature must implicitly have made the determination that many, perhaps most, of those eligible to receive the death penalty should in fact be sentenced to prison. Since they have made that implicit determination, the legislatures should not be permitted to stop short and avoid specification of the criteria which distinguish those who should be permitted to live from those who should die. Harlan replied: "To

---

[13] People v. McGautha, 70 Cal.2d 770 (1969).

[14] McGautha v. California, 402 U.S. 183 (1971).

[15] *Id.* at 197.

identify before the fact those characteristics of criminal homicides and their perpetrators which call for the death penalty, and to express these characteristics in language which can be fairly understood and applied by the sentencing authority, appear to be tasks which are beyond present human ability."[16] Murders, murderers, and victims come in many different spots and stripes. General standards meant to guide discretion simply become, in the complex light of the real world, "meaningless boilerplate."[17] "In light of history, experience and the present limitations of human knowledge, we find it quite impossible to say that committing to the untrammeled discretion of the jury the power to pronounce life or death in capital cases is offensive to anything in the Constitution."[18]

McGautha did not, of course, decide the constitutionality of the death penalty. Its narrow holding is simply that if the death penalty is constitutional, then it is also constitutional to give the decision as to when to inflict it to the jury to decide according to its own untutored judgment. To say that *McGautha* did not decide an Eighth Amendment question, however, is not to say that *Furman*, as it was decided, is consistent with *McGautha*. I shall consider that question presently. But before looking into the *Furman* opinions, a short preliminary detour into the Supreme Court's cruel and unusual punishment jurisprudence seems warranted.

Three major themes run through the Eighth Amendment cases, whose thrust may be reduced to three questions which the Court has recurringly asked, in one way or another, in testing the constitutionality of a punishment: (1) Is the punishment grossly disproportionate to the offense? (2) Is the punishment barbaric in some absolute sense? (3) Were the intentions of the authorities in the infliction of the punishment humane or inhumane?

In *Wilkerson v. Utah*,[19] petitioner's sentence—public execution by musketry—was sustained. The Court conceded the difficulties of defining what a cruel and unusual punishment was, but stated that such a punishment would be one like torture or some such "in the same line involving unnecessary cruelty."[20] It was left unclear how one would distinguish necessary from unnecessary cruelty. *In re Kemmler*[21] suggested how the constitutional terms cruelty and unusualness might relate to one another. Petitioner, a murderer, was

---

[16] *Id*. at 204.

[17] *Id*. at 208.

[18] *Id*. at 207.

[19] 99 U.S. 130 (1878).

[20] *Id*. at 136.

[21] 136 U.S. 436 (1878).

sentenced to die in the electric chair, in the early days of that instrument's history. Among other claims, he asserted that electrocution was a cruel and unusual form of punishment. The Court noted with approval the conclusion of the state court that, although electrocution might be considered unusual because of its novelty, it was enacted by the legislature for humane reasons and was, in fact, an apparently instantaneous and painless death. Based on *Kemmler*, it would seem that a punishment may be increasingly unusual the less cruel it is. But the Court did not attempt to propose a general theory of the Eighth Amendment. Rather it remained consciously and ,cautiously aphoristic: "Punishments are cruel when they involve torture or a lingering death; but the punishment of death is not cruel, within the meaning of that word as used in the Constitution. It implies there something inhuman and barbarous, something more than the mere extinguishment of life."[22]

Weems v. United States[23] involved neither torture nor a lingering death. Petitioner was an American employee of the Philippine government who was convicted of falsifying an official document. For such an offense, Philippine law provided the punishment of *cadena temporal*, which involves imprisonment for at least twelve years and one day, in chains, at hard and painful labor, together with loss of civil rights, and perpetual surveillance. "No circumstance of degradation is omitted,"[24] said the Supreme Court: "Such penalties for such offenses amaze those who . . . believe that it is a precept of justice that punishment for crime should be graduated and proportioned to offense."[25] This Philippine punishment "has no fellow in American legislation."[26]

> Let us remember that it has come to us from a government of a different form and genius from ours. It is cruel and in excess of imprisonment and that which accompanies and follows imprisonment. It is unusual in its character. Its punishments come under the condemnation of the bill of rights, both on account of their degree and kind.[27]

The theme of proportionality has the leading place in the decision although it is never clear what standards the Court used to pin down the disproportion. Thus the "lingering death" notion advanced in *Kemmler* could be subsumed in a more general principle, that pen-

---

[22] *Id*. at 447.

[23] 217 U.S. 349 (1910).

[24] *Id*. at 366.

[25] *Id*. at 366–67.

[26] *Id*. at 377.

[27] *Ibid*.

alties both excessive in relation to the offense and harsh in themselves fall afoul the Eighth Amendment.

Louisiana ex rel. Francis v. Resweber[28] added another piece to the puzzle. Petitioner, duly convicted and sentenced to death, was prepared for execution, placed in the state's electric chair, and subjected to an electrical current. Through some mischance (if that is the right thing to call an accident which saves a man's life) the current was not of sufficient intensity to cause death. Francis was removed from the execution chamber, returned to prison, and a new execution date was set. He objected that subjecting him a second time to the electric chair and the psychological stress bound up in facing the moment of death would be cruel and unusual punishment. The Supreme Court disagreed. Mr. Justice Reed, speaking for four Justices, disposed of the Eighth Amendment issue by noting that the slip-up was non-negligent:[29]

> The cruelty against which the Constitution protects a convicted man is cruelty inherent in the method of punishment, not the necessary suffering involved in any method employed to extinguish life humanely. The fact that an unforseeable accident prevented the prompt consummation of the sentence cannot . . . add an element of cruelty to a subsequent execution.

Thus *Francis* emphasizes and somewhat broadens the notion, first raised in *Kemmler*, that the intentions of the authorities have a bearing on whether a punishment is cruel and unusual.

The most puzzling of this line of cases is *Trop v. Dulles*.[30] Petitioner, a native-born American, was convicted by court-martial of wartime desertion. Eight years later, after he had served a term in prison, he applied for a passport. The application was turned down on ground that petitioner had lost his citizenship and become stateless by reason of his conviction of the wartime offense. This consequence, found the Court, was cruel and unusual punishment. The opinion of Chief Justice Warren for the plurality bristles with quotable phrases: "The Amendment must draw its meaning from evolving standards of decency that mark the progress of a maturing society."[31] Denationalization "is a form of punishment more primitive than torture, for it destroys for the individual the political existence that was centuries in the development. The punishment

---

[28] 329 U.S. 459 (1947).
[29] *Id.* at 464.

[30] 356 U.S. 86 (1958).
[31] *Id.* at 101.

strips the citizen of his status in the national and international political community.[32] "In short, the expatriate has lost the right to
have rights."[33] Precisely what it was about denationalization that
the Chief Justice found unacceptable, however, is hard to fathom,
particularly in view of his concession that "even execution may be
imposed depending upon the enormity of the crime."[34] What does
denationalization do to a man that killing him does not also do, only
worse?[35] The plurality nowhere joins issue with the dissenting contentions of Justice Frankfurter that denationalization is not, in such
a case, a punishment in the Eighth Amendment sense at all, and that
even if it were, it could hardly be thought of as a fate worse than
death.[36]

The sense of *Trop* is that denationalization is not a constitutional
consequence to impose on one who has broken the law. Although
certain passages of the Warren opinion suggest that excessiveness,
in the *Weems* sense, also played a part, the language of the opinion
more clearly suggests that a broader holding was intended. An additional contribution of *Trop* to the lore is that the prohibition of
the Eighth Amendment may fall not only upon sentences pro-
nounced by a court but also upon more remote consequences of
law-breaking as well. This aspect of *Trop* adumbrates the approach
of some of the Justices in *Furman* by suggesting that the Eighth
Amendment is broad enough that, on one of its boundaries, it
bumps into the doctrine of due process. Mr. Justice Brennan's concurring opinion in *Trop*,[37] which completed the majority, high-
lights this fact. He wrote: "We must inquire whether there exists
a relevant connection between the particular legislative enactment
and the power granted to Congress by the Constitution."[38] Following the relevant-connection test, Brennan thought that expatriation of a deserter was beyond the power of Congress. His analysis was premised on the idea that expatriation was explainable only
as punishment, and that as punishment it was inefficient; this in turn
sapped the interest of Congress in having such a statute at all. Especially in view of the fact that other, unquestionably valid means
of deterring wartime desertion were available, "the requisite rational relation between this statute and the war power does not ap-

---

[32] *Ibid.*   [33] *Id.* at 102.   [34] *Id.* at 100.

[35] Or "better"—depending upon your values and your point of view.

[36] 356 U.S. at 114, 124–25.   [37] *Id.* at 105.   [38] *Ibid.*

pear."[39] The Eighth Amendment was nowhere mentioned in Mr. Justice Brennan's opinion.

The last of the cases finding a cruel and unusual punishment, and in many ways the most interesting of all, is *Robinson v. California*.[40] California made it an offense to be addicted to the use of a narcotic drug. This, said the Court, was not constitutional. The law did not "even purport to provide or require medical treatment," and furthermore, the prohibition of the law fell upon being addicted, a status, rather than on an act:[41]

> To be sure, imprisonment for ninety days [the statutory period] is not, in the abstract, a punishment which is either cruel or unusual. But the question cannot be considered in the abstract. Even one day in prison would be cruel and unusual punishment for the "crime" of having a common cold.

The Court took note of the possibility of a person becoming addicted innocently—even a newborn infant might be addicted because of its mother's use of narcotics—and held that a law which would send a person to prison "even though he has never touched any narcotic drug within the State or been guilty of any irregular behavior there"[42] could not be upheld.

Obviously important to the *Robinson* Court was the fact that this state law did not have any apparently remedial objectives. *Robinson* can easily be read to leave it open to a state to make it a criminal offense for a person, knowing himself to be an addict, to fail to seek treatment for the addiction. If read this way, *Robinson* picks up and resonates the "humane intentions" theme expressed in *Kemmler* and to some extent in *Francis*. Also important was the fact that no act was required to trigger the criminal liability. This aspect of the holding, stated in the Court's opinion and emphasized by Justice Harlan's concurrence,[43] suggests that the old common law requirement of an *actus reus* may have constitutional stature. Although it was unnecessary for *Robinson* to spell out the full implications of its holding, even the narrowest reading of the case must acknowledge that the Court's cruel and unusual punishment theory had taken another step by accepting the principle that the Court would not only review a punishment for disproportion but

---

[39] *Id.* at 114.
[40] 370 U.S. 660 (1962).
[41] *Id.* at 667.
[42] *Ibid.*
[43] *Id.* at 678.

would look beyond to the thing sought to be prohibited to determine whether, in Eighth Amendment terms, that thing could be made a crime at all.[44]

In sum, the pre-*Furman* cruel and unusual punishment cases do not state a comprehensive theory of the Eighth Amendment. But they do contain the seeds of two fundamentally distinct approaches to the Eighth Amendment whose growth is on vigorous display in the five opinions of the *Furman* majority. For convenience, I call these approaches, to distinguish between them, the analytical approach and the normative approach. These two views of the Eighth Amendment are not everywhere distinct, but they do have quite different characteristics. The tendency of the former theory is to use the Eighth Amendment as a sort of collection point for other, established constitutional theories, such as due process and equal protection. The normative tendency is rather to view the Eighth Amendment as posing a core question of values which are *sui generis* in the Constitution—values which relate not to questions of fairness and equality, but to such things as mercy and charity. Illustrative of the former approach would be cases like *Francis* and *Robinson* and Mr. Justice Brennan's concurring opinion in *Trop.*

---

[44] Following upon *Robinson* was the intriguing case of Powell v. Texas, 392 U.S. 514 (1968), which rejected an Eighth Amendment challenge to the conviction of a chronic alcoholic for public drunkenness. Mr. Justice Marshall, for four Justices, questioned the value of characterizing the compulsive consumption of alcohol as a disease and noted that, in view of the fact that no generally accepted therapy for alcoholism exists, it would be difficult to maintain that society's use of the criminal process in coping with certain aspects of alcoholism is never rational. *Robinson* was distinguished on the ground that the statute there imposed a criminal penalty without the requirement of an *actus reus*. In *Powell*, on the other hand, being drunk in public was not a status but an act.

Mr. Justice White joined the majority in affirmance, but did not assent to the most vital sections of Marshall's analysis. White was sympathetic to the notion that drinking is not really voluntary behavior for an alcoholic; but he was nevertheless able to uphold the conviction because it was not for drunkenness, but *public* drunkenness. Even if Powell could bring himself under *Robinson* on the ground that this consumption of alcohol, and consequent intoxication, was not voluntary, there was no showing whatever that this compulsion forced Powell to be drunk in public rather than in some private place.

Mr. Justice Fortas's dissenting opinion, joined by three other Justices, is premised on the disease concept of alcoholism, and requires acceptance of the unconfirmable but not necessarily improbable fact that petitioner was powerless to avoid the forbidden behavior.

This branch of Eighth Amendment theory is thus left in shadow. Five members of the *Powell* Court were prepared to accept, at least in principle, some version of the notion that acts which (although distinct from automatic activity) are characterized as not fully voluntary cannot give rise to criminal liability. Such was not, however, the holding of the Court. The future of a general constitutional theory of criminal responsibility, based on *Robinson* and the Eighth Amendment, is in considerable doubt.

Illustrative of the latter are the plurality opinion in *Trop* and that of the Court in *Weems*. The analytic view of the Eighth Amendment was taken in *Furman* by Justices Douglas, Stewart, and White; the normative approach by Justices Brennan and Marshall. Each view of cruel and unusual punishment has strengths and weaknesses of its own.

"We are now imprisoned in the *McGautha* holding," says Mr. Justice Douglas.[45] He must mean that a certain range of procedural objections to the imposition of the death penalty are now foreclosed, but the statement has a ring to it reminiscent of a magician's promise that there is nothing in his hat. And sure enough: "It would seem to be incontestible that the death penalty inflicted on one defendant is 'unusual' if it discriminates against him by reason of his race, religion, wealth, social position, or class, or if it is imposed under such a procedure that gives room for the play of such prejudices."[46] And: "[I]t is 'cruel and unusual' to apply the death penalty—or any other penalty—selectively to minorities whose members are few, who are outcasts of society, and who are unpopular, but whom society is willing to see suffer though it would not countenance general application of the same penalty across the boards."[47] The major principle thus stated, Douglas supplies the minor premise: "One searches the chronicles in vain for the execution of any member of the affluent strata of our society."[48] The upshot Douglas likens to the ancient Hindu system of increasing the severity of punishments in inverse proportion to the social status of the defendant. Two things combine to make this so—the way the legal process imposes the death penalty allows wide play for discretion; and the rich man can afford to hire adequate counsel while the poor man must be satisfied with whatever he gets.[49] Citing *Yick Wo v. Hopkins*,[50] Douglas implies that death-penalty statutes belong to that species of laws which, although fair on their face, are

---

[45] 408 U.S. at 248. [46] *Id*. at 242.

[47] *Id*. at 245. This is very like the contention made in Goldberg & Dershowitz, *Declaring the Death Penalty Unconstitutional*, 83 HARV. L. REV. 1773, 1790 (1970): "A penalty . . . should be considered 'unusually' imposed if it is administered arbitrarily or discriminatorily."

[48] *Id*. at 251–52. The "chronicles," of course, do not ordinarily contain references to whether or not a defendant is drawn from the affluent strata of society; so the vanity of searching them could perhaps be explained innocently.

[49] *Id*. at 255. [50] 118 U.S. 356 (1886).

enforced unfairly. "Whether a mandatory death penalty would . . . be constitutional is a question I do not reach."[51]

In other words, punishments which are imposed in violation of equal protection of the law are "cruel and unusual" in the Eighth Amendment sense. But whether death per se is a cruel and unusual punishment, because it is barbaric, or inconsistent with the evolving standards of decency which mark the progress of a maturing society, Douglas did not say.

Just how vexing Douglas found his imprisonment within the *McGautha* holding is a topic whose discussion I defer. But it is worth pausing for a moment to consider other aspects of Douglas's argument, and whether they do not stir up as many problems as they resolve. Cruelty and equality, as constitutional values, are both elusive. And Douglas defines one in terms of the other. It is crucial to his argument that we accept that rich defendants can hire excellent lawyers to fend off the electricians, while poor defendants cannot. Yet this unequal bargaining stance with respect to the world is not something peculiar to the capital case. Good lawyers are almost always to be preferred to mediocre ones, whether the charge is first degree murder or reckless driving. Thus what is really suggested by the Douglas position is a sort of Sixth Amendment case—a trial is not really a fair trial unless it is defended with some minimum degree of ingenuity. A Sixth Amendment solution—remanding for a new trial—would also seem thriftier and more responsive to the problems which Douglas identifies than casting out the form of punishment because over the long road the procedures which lead to its imposition are believed to work invidiously.

In this particular case, it is difficult to maintain that the poverty of these petitioners prevented them from getting adequate lawyering, since the appellate argument was handled by Professor Anthony G. Amsterdam of the Stanford Law School, supported by hordes of colleagues and cohorts, including Jack Greenberg and the NAACP Legal Defense and Educational Fund. (Usually, in capital cases, defendants have had the benefit of experienced trial counsel.) On the other hand, it could be fairly maintained that that common ramification of not having enough money—low social status—is an even more insidious determiner of penalty outcomes than differences in lawyering that money can buy. A study conducted

---

[51] 408 U.S. at 257.

by Stanford law students suggested penalty "juries are lenient toward white-collar defendants," and speculated that this might be
due to their occupational status alone, or perhaps that "white collar
defendants exhibit subtle patterns of behavior and appearance which
impress the jury favorably."[52] Even if this is a correct conclusion,
what are the constitutional implications? One possibility is that in
certain cases, juries are rigged. If that is the case, the proper remedy
is to dismiss the indictment or information. If, however, everything
possible has been done to make the jury fair, then either the jury's
decision must be accepted as just (if rational), or the use of juries to
allocate justice must be discarded. In other words, once it has been
decided to use a jury, it has also been decided to accept characteristics
which are thought to inhere in the common run of citizens—conceiv-
ably including a true rendering of community standards which may
work to the disadvantage of persons of lower status. In short, Douglas's argument boils down to one of two propositions: (1) The
poverty of these defendants prevented them from getting adequate
lawyers—which is in this instance plainly incorrect. (2) The low
social status of defendants prejudiced the jury against them, a bias
which is (a) invidious if all possible steps were not taken to prevent
bias, or (b) inevitable if no conceivable steps could have ameliorated
the bias. If 2(a) is accepted, then what is wanted is a new trial. If
2(b) is accepted—and unconstitutionality is nonetheless found—then
what is wanted is a new world, where worldly advantages do not
prove advantageous. No matter how Douglas's argument is interpreted, therefore, it seems to me very inadequate for producing an
Eighth Amendment rationale.

Mr. Justice Stewart argued that, although there is obvious plausi-
bility to the claim that the death penalty is per se unconstitutional,
under the *Ashwander* principle,[53] the question is not reached. The
Court decides a question whose context is limited to punishment
statutes which give the court or jury leeway to impose a lesser penalty than death. A mandatory punishment statute would present
another, and a distinct, question. By framing their punishment statutes so as to make murder and rape punishable by a sentence less
than death, the state signifies that the use of the death penalty is

---

[52] 21 STAN. L. REV. 1297, 1379 (1969).

[53] Ashwander v. T.V.A., 297 U.S. 288, 341, 346 (1936) (concurring opinion of
Brandeis, J.).

not "necessary." And a punishment is "cruel" if it goes beyond what a legislature believes to be necessary. The punishment of death is also "unusual" in the sense that it is seldom imposed. And beyond these considerations, a punishment may be thought of as cruel and unusual when those selected to die constitute a seemingly random handful of a much larger number of men and women who, just as deserving of death, received only prison sentences. For the few selected to die, the punishment of death is cruel and unusual "the same way that being struck by lightning is cruel and unusual."[54]

The metaphor of being struck by lightning is splendidly ingenious, and makes a persuasive point. But on second thought, it also contains a serious weakness. Being struck by lightning is cruel because it is painful and unusual because it seldom happens—but is it unconstitutional? Put another way—can there be any reason to accuse a state of arbitrariness in passing out sentences of death if the process cannot be shown to have been operated unfairly in producing this result? If it is assumed that government has taken every available step in keeping human unfairness out of the process, what remains may still be unfair—but unfair, not in the sense of "invidious"—rather, unfair in the way that the world is unfair; unfair in the sense that it is unfair for a person to be struck by lightning.[55]

Mr. Justice White was also disturbed by the fact that it is difficult to state a rational rule for who gets sentenced to death and who does not. He conceded that no matter how infrequently the punishment of death is invoked, those who receive it do not, of their own merit, deserve better. On the other hand, insofar as the punishment is not regularly invoked, its potential as a deterrent to the potential crimes of others is reduced.[56] And as the general deterrence mechanism is

---

[54] 408 U.S. at 309.

[55] "It was well known by experience to the nations which employed elephants in war, that, though by the terror of their bulk, and the violence of their impression, they often threw the enemy into disorder, yet there was always the danger in the use of them, very nearly equivalent to the advantage; for, if their first charge could be supported, they were easily driven back upon their confederates, they broke through the troops behind them, and made no less havoc in the precipitation of their retreat than in the fury of their onset." 21 Johnson, THE RAMBLER, May 29, 1750. It is the same with arguments, Dr. Johnson reminds us: sometimes the strongest ones are, if turned around, the most self-destructive.

[56] White's position at this point is not consistent with currently accepted learning theory. If it is conceded that the threat of punishment, generally, is a deterrent to criminal behavior, it seems extremely unlikely that a partial reinforcement schedule destroys, or even greatly compromises the credibility of the threat. Indeed, for all anyone knows, the

degraded, to that extent the moral justification for the use of the punishment is compromised.[57] White then supplies the factual premise that quickens the argument: the punishment of death is imposed so infrequently that its capacity to produce law-abiding behavior in persons other than defendants is much reduced. That being so, the imposition of death begins to seem pointless: "A penalty with such negligible returns to the State would be patently excessive and cruel and unusual punishment violative of the Eighth Amendment."[58] The jury has so effectively fulfilled its role of mitigating the harshness of the law that "capital punishment within the confines of the statute now before us has for all practical purposes run its course."[59]

Mr. Justice Brennan's approach to the Eighth Amendment was very different from that of Justices Douglas, Stewart, and White. Although not less interested than the others in such values as arbi-

---

very intermittent execution of criminals may well be the thriftiest and most rational way to administer the death penalty, since intermittent executions may well be all that is necessary to keep the threat of death operating at its maximum deterrent potential.

Partial reinforcements are discussed in HILGARD, ATKINSON, & ATKINSON, INTRODUCTION TO PSYCHOLOGY 200 (5th ed., 1971): "In the typical experiment, a pigeon learns to peck at a lighted disc mounted on the wall and receives access to a small quantity of grain as its reinforcement. Once this conditional operant is established, the pigeon will peck at a high and relatively uniform rate, even if it receives only an occasional reinforcement." In the experiment which Hilgard et al. used for illustration, the pigeon produced 6,000 responses in an hour, with only twelve reinforcements. See generally Berger & Lambert, Stimulus-Response Theory in Contemporary Social Psychology, 1 HANDBOOK OF SOCIAL PSYCHOLOGY 81 et seq. (Lindsey & Aronson eds., 1968).

It could be soundly argued, of course, that it is dubious morality to "make an example of A"—that is, to use A's misbehavior as the occasion for chastening B. This problem is ventilated by Prof. Andenaes in The Morality of Deterrence, 37 U. CHI. L. REV. 649 (1970). White, however, concedes both the morality and the utility of this system. 408 U.S. at 312.

The 1930 British Select Committee took under advisement a suggestion, kindred to my objection above, which, however, does not rely on newfangled theories of human behavior: "Sir John Anderson, of the Home Office, claimed for the present system the cumulative advantage of a double deterrency—the deterrent of the capital sentence plus the deterrent of imprisonment, for it may be one or the other. In reply to the question, whether a man would be deterred more by a life sentence or by Capital Punishment, he said:—'As I have already said, I think it is impossible to generalise. I think there are some people who, if they thought about it, would be more deterred by the associations of the gallows; but I think it is fair to make the point that as the law now stands you get the advantage, such as it is, of both deterrents.' " REPORT FROM THE SELECT COMMITTEE ON CAPITAL PUNISHMENT 24–25, ¶99 (1930).

[57] Similar thoughts are advanced by Sidney Hook in The Death Sentence, in BEDAU, ed., THE DEATH PENALTY IN AMERICA 146 (1964).

[58] 408 U.S. at 312.   [59] Id. at 313.

trariness and discrimination, these were only partial concerns that
went into a much more complicated construction. In the last analysis, Brennan did not want to know whether a punishment is arbitrarily inflicted: he wanted to know what a cruel and unusual
punishment is. He began his long quest with an apology: what the
Eighth Amendment is supposed to require by way of government
conduct is obscure and elusive, but the Eighth Amendment places
on the courts a duty to find a form for the amorphous language of
the Constitution. The history of the cruel and unusual punishment
language in the Constitution does not give satisfactory guidance.
Two conclusions emerged for Brennan in light of the history of the
adoption of the clause: First, the framers were concerned with the
exercise of legislative power. Second, we cannot know for sure
what the framers thought cruel and unusual punishments were.[60]

Looking at the evolutionary character of the Cruel and Unusual
Punishment Clause, Brennan restated the inquiry thus: Does a particular penalty "subject the individual to a fate forbidden by the
principle of civilized treatment guaranteed by the [Clause]?"[61] "A
punishment is 'cruel and unusual' . . . if it does not comport with
human dignity."[62] Brennan stated a cumulative four-part test which,
if it did not actually tell what is consistent or inconsistent with
human dignity, at least advanced considerations closely related to
the interest in being free of cruel and unusual punishments.

First: A punishment which imparts, by its extreme severity,
drastic physical or psychic pain falls into a suspect category. This
criterion is not normally enough to warrant calling a punishment
cruel and unusual—but it could be. On this criterion alone, for example, the rack or thumbscrews would be forbidden, as too painful
per se. Furthermore, argued Brennan obscurely, the infliction of
these punishments treats a human being as nonhuman, as if an "object to be toyed with and discarded."[63]

Second: A state may not arbitrarily inflict a severe punishment.

---

[60] Apparently, the framers' concern was with intrinsically barbaric penalties. The
language of the clause, however, is taken from the 1689 English Bill of Rights, whose
authors were concerned more with selective application of penalties than with their
inherent harshness. Granucci, *"Nor Cruel and Unusual Punishments Inflicted": The Original
Meaning*, 57 CALIF. L. REV. 839 (1969).

[61] 408 U.S. at 270, quoting Trop v. Dulles, 356 U.S. 86, 99 (1958) (plurality opinion
of Warren, C. J.).

[62] 408 U.S. at 270.   [63] *Id.* at 273.

Whenever A is treated differently from B, there must be a reason for it.

Third: A severe punishment must not be unacceptable to contemporary society. What society finds acceptable and unacceptable for these purposes must be determined by custom and usage, and not merely by reference to the community's stated, official norms. That the death penalty is authorized by the legislature as punishment for certain crimes does not in itself establish contemporary society's acceptance.[64]

Fourth: A punishment must not be excessive. The infliction of a severe punishment is pointless and unnecessary when some less severe punishment would accomplish the same penal objectives. Following on this analysis, Brennan concluded that the death penalty must fall.

First, he pointed out that death is a unique penalty.[65] This uniqueness he subdivided into three parts—painfulness, finality, and enormity. No other punishment imposes so much physical and mental anguish; no other aims at the deliberate infliction of physical pain;[66] and no other punishment is so final in the sense that, once inflicted, it is irreversible.[67] If it were not for the traditional acceptance of

---

[64] *Id.* at 279.

[65] *Id.* at 286. "It is the universal experience in the administration of criminal justice that those charged with capital offenses are granted special considerations." Griffin v. Illinois, 351 U.S. 12, 28 (1956) (dissenting opinion of Burton and Minton, JJ.).

[66] It is highly debatable that, in inflicting a sentence of death, a state aims at the infliction of physical pain. The idea of electric chairs and lethal gas is to remove as much pain as is possible from the execution, and the cases have stressed this point.

[67] All penalties are irrevocable in the sense that, once suffered, they cannot be unsuffered. This logical fact—and that is all it is—was the occasion of one of George Bernard Shaw's most entertaining diatribes: "[T]he . . . deliberate infliction of malicious injuries which now goes on under the name of punishment [should] be abandoned; so that the thief, the ruffian, the gambler, and the beggar, may without inhumanity be handed over to the law, and made to understand that a State which is too humane to punish will also be too thrifty to waste the life of honest men in watching or restraining dishonest ones. That is why we do not imprison dogs. We even take our chance of their first bite. But if a dog delights to bark and bite, it goes to the lethal chamber. That seems to me sensible. To allow the dog to expiate his bite by a period of torment, and then let him loose in a much more savage condition (for the chain makes a dog savage) to bite again and expiate again, having meanwhile spent a great deal of human life and happiness in the task of chaining and feeding and tormenting him, seems to me idiotic and superstitious. Yet that is what we do to men who bark and bite and steal. It would be far more sensible to put up with their vices, as we put up with their illnesses, until they give more trouble than they are worth, at which point we should, with many apologies and expressions of sympathy, and some generosity in complying with their last wishes, place them

capital punishment, says Brennan, he would have to go no further to declare such punishment cruel and unusual.

Second, Brennan considered arbitrariness: [68]

> When the punishment of death is inflicted in a trivial number of the cases in which it is legally available, the conclusion is virtually inescapable that it is being inflicted arbitrarily. Indeed, it smacks of little more than a lottery system. . . . No one has yet suggested a rational basis that could differentiate . . . the few who die from the many who go to prison.

But Brennan did not rely on this factor in isolation: he simply found it weighty enough to go into the balance.

Third, Brennan concluded that contemporary society has overwhelmingly rejected the use of the death penalty. The history of the penalty in the courts and legislatures has been, he argued, one of progressive restriction. And "when an unusually severe punishment is authorized for wide-scale application but not, because of society's refusal, inflicted save in a few instances, the inference is compelling that there is a deep-seated reluctance to inflict it."[69]

Finally, Brennan looked to excessiveness: "When there is a strong probability that the state is arbitrarily inflicting an unusually severe punishment that is subject to grave societal doubts, it is likely also that the punishment cannot be shown to be serving any penal purpose that could not be served equally well by some less-severe punishment."[70] Brennan then reminded us that the deterrent capacity of the death penalty is a very important consideration in deciding whether it is excessive. And whatever deterrent advantages death might have over imprisonment must be heavily discounted by the

---

in the lethal chamber and get rid of them. Under no circumstances should they be allowed to expiate their misdeeds by a manufactured penalty, to subscribe to a charity, or to compensate the victims. If there is to be no punishment there can be no forgiveness. We shall never have real moral responsibility until everyone knows that his deeds are irrevocable, and that his life depends on his usefulness. Hitherto, alas! humanity has never dared face these hard facts. We frantically scatter conscience money and invent systems of conscience banking, with expiatory penalties, atonements, redemptions, salvations, hospital subscription lists and what not, to enable us to contract-out of the moral code. Not content with the old scapegoat and sacrificial lamb, we deify human saviors, and pray to miraculous virgin intercessors. We attribute mercy to the inexorable; soothe our consciences after committing murder by throwing ourselves on the bosom of divine love; and shrink even from our own gallows because we are forced to admit that it, at least, is irrevocable—as if one hour of imprisonment were not as irrevocable as any execution!" SHAW, MAJOR BARBARA 47–48 (Penguin ed. 1959).

[68] 408 U.S. at 293.   [69] *Id.* at 300.   [70] *Ibid.*

slowness of the processes leading up to an execution, and by the unlikelihood that an execution will ever take place.

To the argument that the death penalty is necessary, or useful, to manifest the community's outrage at the rapist or murderer, Brennan replied: "There is no evidence . . . that utilization of imprisonment rather than death encourages private blood feuds and other disorders."[71] Furthermore: "[W]hen the overwhelming number of criminals who commit capital crimes go to prison, it cannot be concluded that death serves the purpose of retribution more effectively than prison."[72] Brennan concluded this part of the analysis by suggesting that the death penalty is more likely to brutalize community norms of desirable conduct than to reinforce them.

It is difficult to respond articulately to Brennan's cumulative four-part test, for the test is manifestly atmospheric. No one—Brennan least of all—would pretend that it can be applied mechanically, like instructions in a box of Tinker Toys. Yet to say that the test is emotive and hortatory is not to say it is meaningless. It is still possible to ask whether Brennan's opinion brings home some heretofore unappreciated truth about cruel and unusual punishment.

I begin with the statement that a cruel and unusual punishment is one that affronts human dignity. This formula affords no means of distinguishing cruel and unusual punishment from punishment in general. All punishment affronts human dignity. That, in some sense, is one of its important purposes. So long as the criminal process is used to label intolerable behavior as intolerable and to castigate those who have stepped out of bounds, it is inevitable that the sensibilities of whoever suffers at the hands of justice will smart. No one will question this statement who has ever sat, red-faced, in the back seat of a police car while a policeman wrote him a speeding citation. The question, therefore, is not whether human dignity is affronted, but whether it is affronted in a way or to an extent which is impermissible. I take it that a punishment that impermissibly affronts human dignity is cruel and unusual. Thus we must seek further for the distinguishing characteristics of cruel and unusual punishments.

---

[71] *Id.* at 303. The REPORT OF THE BRITISH SELECT COMMITTEE ON CAPITAL PUNISHMENT (1930) answered the prediction that lynch law would follow the abolition of capital punishment with a placidness which we can only envy: "Such courses are alien to the genius and habits of the British people." REPORT at p. 55.

[72] 408 U.S. at 304.

Consider arbitrariness. Does it follow "inescapably" that a punishment is being inflicted arbitrarily (and therefore impermissibly) when it is "inflicted in a trivial number of the cases in which it is legally available"? It seems to me as inherently plausible that juries, judges, and governors of states conduct themselves with deliberation and caution so as to err on the side of mercy, reserving their ultimate punishment for those whose transgressions are most clearly established and seem to them most revolting. This explanation if it is accurate (and no one knows whether it is) is not arbitrariness but the antithesis of arbitrariness.

Then what of the notion that society has rejected the use of the death penalty, because it is morally disgusted by it. This contention fails, not because it is mistaken, but because it is left unsupported. To be sure, the penalty of death is infrequently imposed. An entirely valid inference from this bare fact would be, not that the society has repudiated the penalty, but that it wishes to reserve its use to a small number of cases. A reluctance to impose a penalty is not necessarily the same as its repudiation. Reluctance may spring from moral revulsion; but it may just as commonly proceed from a humane and heartfelt sorrow.

Finally, Brennan is on shaky ground in asserting that death is an excessive punishment to satisfy the legitimate penal purposes of the legislature. He said, "it cannot be concluded that death serves the purpose of retribution more effectively than prison." The trouble is that most state legislatures and Congress have so concluded: Why can't they? In certain contexts, excessiveness could be argued with some assurance, for some penal purposes refer to societal benefits that are relatively subject to measurement. One purpose of punishment is the deterrence of misbehavior in other persons. The death penalty cannot be shown to serve this penal purpose more effectively than long sentences of imprisonment; perhaps it could rightly be said that a legislature could not believe the contrary. But retribution—also heretofore a legitimate penal purpose—is simply not subject to measurement. One cannot, just by looking at a punishment, tell whether it is excessively retributive. In order to make a judgment that a punishment is unduly retributive, one would need a general theory about how much retribution is "enough." Brennan's opinion only hinted at a criterion by observing that most capital criminals are sentenced to prison. But that fact, if it is advanced as a general theory, only begs the question: life in prison was enough retribution for those convicts who were sentenced to life imprisonment—why should it be enough for those as to whom the elaborate processes of justice have decreed death? Brennan did not say.

Mr. Justice Marshall's argument was as ambitious as Brennan's and has certain similarities to it. As did Brennan's, Marshall's argument turns on two essential assertions: that the death penalty is excessive, and that society, having found it repugnant, has repudiated its use in fact. He began by focusing on the interrelation between the purposes to be served by criminal punishment in general and the values to be served by the Cruel and Unusual Punishment Clause. Four reasons were given why a punishment might be held cruel and unusual. First, punishments which amount to torture are clearly forbidden. Second, a punishment that is novel, in the sense of never having been used in connection with a given crime, may be unconstitutional, although it is likely that a novel punishment which is less painful than a traditional one may well be accepted in its place.[73] Third, a penalty may be unconstitutional because it is excessive in the context of an allowable legislative purpose. Noting that the Eighth Amendment prohibits "excessive" bail and "excessive" fines, Marshall reasons that the entire thrust of the Eighth Amendment is "against 'that which is excessive.' "[74] Fourth, a punishment may be unconstitutional, although proportionate to the offense and connected to a valid legislative purpose, if it is abhorrent to popular feeling. Marshall conceded the first and second of these reasons and based his result on the third and fourth.

To decide whether death is an excessive or unnecessary penalty, Marshall considers six reasons why a legislature would choose it at all: retribution, deterrence of misconduct by other persons, prevention of future misconduct by the convict, encouragement of guilty pleas, eugenics, and economy. (The last three are given short shrift by Marshall and need not be discussed here.)

Retribution, says Marshall, is a much misunderstood interest, because it is very easy to confuse the question "Why do we punish?" with the question "What justifies punishment?" The moral premise that lies on the threshold of our punishing A is that A shall have broken some law. Lawbreaking is the sine qua non of punishment. But the fact that retribution triggers a justification for punishment

---

[73] See, *e.g.*, *In re* Kemmler, 136 U.S. 436 (1890).

[74] 408 U.S. at 332.

does not mean that it may be the state's sole aim in punishing. Retaliation is an intolerable goal in a free society. "If retribution alone could serve as a justification for any particular penalty, then all penalties selected by the legislature would by definition be acceptable means of designating society's moral approbation [*sic*][75] of a particular act."[76] "But the Eighth Amendment is our insulation from our baser selves," says Marshall. "Retribution for its own sake is improper."[77]

"The most hotly contested issue regarding capital punishment is whether it is better than life imprisonment as a deterrent to crime."[78] After reviewing the available data, Marshall concludes: "Despite the fact that abolitionists have not proved non-deterrence beyond a reasonable doubt, they have succeeded in showing by clear and convincing evidence that capital punishment is not necessary as a deterrent to crime in our society."[79]

Prevention of future misconduct on the part of a murderer is not a very important interest, Marshall believes, because murderers, predictably, behave themselves after their convictions. Generally they are model prisoners, with low rates of recidivism upon their ultimate release from prison. And although it may be possible to distinguish, for the purpose of this interest, between a murderer who is likely to be dangerous in the future and the commonplace, run-of-the-mine spouse-shooter, prediction of future dangerousness is something juries are never asked to do.[80]

---

[75] "Reprobation" was probably intended.

[76] 408 U.S. at 344. This entire statement is a non sequitur. It does not follow that if retribution is an allowable interest, then the lid is off on every form of brutality.

[77] *Id.* at 345.   [78] *Ibid.*   [79] *Id.* at 353.

[80] There is no reason why a jury could not be asked to estimate probable future dangerousness, but such a consideration is not only never mentioned, it is commonly forbidden. In McGautha v. California, 402 U.S. 183, 190–91, n.4: "The penalty jury interrupted its deliberations to ask whether a sentence of life imprisonment meant that there was no possibility of parole. The trial judge responded as follows: 'A sentence of life imprisonment means that the prisoner may be paroled at some time during his lifetime or that he may spend the remainder of his natural life in prison. An agency known as the Adult Authority is empowered by statute to determine if and when a prisoner is to be paroled, and under the statute no prisoner can be paroled unless the Adult Authority is of the opinion that the prisoner when released will assume a proper place in society and that his release is not contrary to the welfare of society. A prisoner released on parole may remain on parole for the balance of his life and if he violates the terms of the parole he may be returned to prison to serve the life sentence.'

" 'So that you will have no misunderstandings relating to a sentence of life imprisonment, you have been informed as to the general scheme of our parole system. You are

Putting all these considerations into the balance, Marshall concluded that the legislature could have no rational basis for imposing the death penalty: "There is no rational basis for concluding that the death penalty is not excessive."[81] This seems to say, not that the death penalty is unconstitutional because it is irrational, but that it is cruel and unusual, and it would be irrational to believe the contrary.

Furthermore, even if it were not excessive, capital punishment would be unconstitutional because "the people" find it "morally unacceptable."[82] Marshall distinguished between people being shocked at the mere mention of a thing, and being shocked by the informed reality, as experienced in the light of full information. Most people are not shocked by the casual thought that some bad people might be put to death; but "American citizens know almost nothing about capital punishment."[83] If they did, they would surely be convinced that the death penalty is unwise. And because they would not accept, morally, a punishment so severe unless it could be defended in utilitarian terms, if they only knew how weak the utilitarian arguments were, the people would reject the use of the death penalty.

Like Brennan, Marshall ran aground on the difficulty of verifying the assertion that the people, or society, find the death penalty abhorrent. Marshall approached the problem by appealing to the distinction between "knowing" and "appreciating," between cognitive knowledge and affective knowledge concerning the death penalty. He concluded that if people knew the death penalty more closely, they would be revolted.[84] But there are two defects in this

---

now instructed, however, that the matter of parole is not to be considered by you in determining the punishment for either defendant, and you may not speculate as to if, or when, parole would or would not be granted. It is not your function to decide now whether these men will be suitable for parole at some future date. So far as you are concerned, you are to decide only whether these men shall suffer the death penalty or whether they shall be permitted to remain alive. If upon consideration of the evidence you believe that life imprisonment is the proper sentence, you must assume that those officials charged with the operation of our parole system will perform their duty in a correct and responsible manner, and that they will not parole a defendant unless he can be safely released into society. It would be a violation of your duty as jurors if you were to fix the penalty at death because of a doubt that the Adult Authority will properly carry out its responsibilities.' " App. 224–25.

[81] 408 U.S. at 359.   [82] *Id*. at 360.   [83] *Id*. at 362.

[84] In *People v. Anderson*, where the California Supreme Court invalidated capital punishment under the California Constitution, a clever technique was used for showing that people are against executions. Although conceding that public opinion polls and the existence of legislation set up a prima facie case for the acceptance of the death penalty, the California Court said that the relevant public to look to was the public which is

argument. First, it necessarily conceded that people are *not* re-volted—it only says that they would be. Second, it would make this revulsion or abhorrence sufficient in itself to strike down the death penalty, and I do not think it can be made to do this as Marshall argued the case. For there are a number of things we do not wish to think about that are disgusting and perhaps revolting but that we may also acknowledge as necessary. Enemas, the vivisection of monkeys, cleaning up outhouses, all are disgusting and abhorrent, but they may also be necessary. Imprisonment is abhorrent—people would find it so if they knew more about it—but it is hardly, in itself, cruel and unusual punishment. In order to complete Marshall's argument, therefore, he needed the concept of excessiveness. A punishment is cruel and unusual if it entails something which society finds abhorrent, and if it cannot be defended as proportionate to the offense.

And here again, Marshall foundered where Brennan did. For the root value question whether the additional retribution implicit in the death penalty justifies its use[85] is left untouched by his argument. He could not escape this problem by invoking the statement that retribution in itself is illegitimate, because even if that were accepted, it could not be maintained that the death penalty does not serve the objective of deterrence—it could only be maintained that it does not serve this objective better than long sentences of imprisonment. And so the puzzle why the death penalty is cruel and unusual punishment was left unsolved.

I have called the Douglas-Stewart-White approach to the Eighth Amendment "analytic" to distinguish it from the "normative" approach of Brennan and Marshall. I want now to extol the virtues and suggest the vices of each position. For the analytic approach, its chief virtue is at the same time its chief vice: it avoids the core normative question whether the "evolving standards of decency that mark the progress of a maturing society" have now risen high enough to wash the death penalty away. This avoids the sort of

---

actually involved in the carrying out of executions: "among those persons called upon to actually impose or carry out the death penalty it is being repudiated with ever increasing frequency. . . . What our society does in actuality belies what it says with regard to its acceptance of capital punishment." 6 Cal.3d at 648. If it is accepted that deeds cancel words as barometers of sentiment and belief, then it seems unassailable that one ought to look to those people who have an opportunity to act and thus betray their true feelings.

[85] Marshall conceded that the death penalty is a more severe punishment than life imprisonment. 408 U.S. at 345.

constitutional judging against which Mr. Justice Black, with no little reason on his side, used so eloquently to rail: "[T]he natural law theory of the Constitution degrade[s] the constitutional safeguards of the Bill of Rights and simultaneously appropriate[s] for this Court a broad power which we are not authorized by the Constitution to exercise."[86] But whatever the analytic approach gains in avoiding subjective and impressionistic sallies into the shadow world of language, it also fails to meet Mr. Justice Brennan's implicit objection that the Eighth Amendment—whatever it means—must mean something, and, indeed, must mean something different from the other provisions of the Constitution.

The arguments of Justices Douglas, Stewart, and White seem rather intent on avoiding, if possible, that core question. Rather, they prefer to emphasize the use of the Eighth Amendment as a tool for testing whether the penalty of death is evenhandedly applied. Why they should have done this is obscure in view of the fact that existing doctrines of equal protection (which was the emphasis of the Douglas opinion) or due process of law should have furnished more than adequate ground for striking down the death penalty, once the factual premises which these three Justices proffer (relating to the arbitrariness or irrationality of the penalty's use, or in Douglas's case, to its use on despised or dispossessed minorities) are accepted. To view the Eighth Amendment in those terms deprives it of a dimension which is latent in almost all of the previous cases, particularly in the *Weems* case and in the Warren opinion in *Trop*—as an independently potent moral force which is at the disposal of the least dangerous branch of government and which may be used to make the most dangerous branch a little less so.

There is another objection to reading the Eighth Amendment as a due process phenomenon, an objection either less or more serious than the first depending on the worth one attaches to the values residing in, and penumbral to, the doctrine of *stare decisis*. *Furman v. Georgia*, as it was decided by Justices Douglas, Stewart, and White, is not consistent with *McGautha v. California*, as it was decided by the Court. This is not to say that the bare holdings of both cases cannot be made, with the assistance of symbolic logic, to coexist. It only says that the rationale of *McGautha* should have laid to rest the due process objections to the use of the death penalty

---

[86] Adamson v. California, 332 U.S. 46, 70 (1947). (Black, J., dissenting.)

and left only the core normative question with which Justices Brennan and Marshall attempted to grapple. Consider, for example, the following key passage from the Douglas opinion in *Furman*:[87]

> We cannot say from the facts disclosed in these records that these defendants were sentenced to death because they were Black. Yet our task is not restricted to an effort to divine what motives impelled these death penalties. Rather we deal with a system of justice that leaves to the uncontrolled discretion of judges and juries the determination whether defendants committing these crimes should die or be imprisoned. Under these laws no standards govern the selection of the penalty. People live or die depending upon the whim of one man or 12.

Justice Stewart, in a similar vein, thought that the Eighth Amendment "cannot tolerate the infliction of a sentence of death under legal systems that permit this unique penalty to be so wantonly and freakishly imposed."[88] And Justice White, although more measured in his language, similarly invoked the concept of irrationality: "[T]he death penalty is exacted with great infrequency even for the most atrocious crimes and . . . there [can be] no meaningful basis for distinguishing the few cases in which it is imposed from the many in which it is not."[89] And White makes it clear that his result was compelled by "what judges and juries do in exercising the discretion so regularly conferred upon them."[90]

Yet, Justice Harlan had written in *McGautha*, with the concurrence of Justices Stewart and White: "States are entitled to assume that jurors confronted with the truly awesome responsibility of decreeing death for a fellow human will act with due regard for the consequences of their decision."[91] And: "In light of history, experience, and the present limitations of human knowledge, we find it quite impossible to say that committing to the untrammeled discretion of the jury the power to pronounce life or death in capital cases is offensive to anything in the Constitution."[92] Why Justices Stewart and White found the due process arguments unconvincing in *McGautha* but persuasive in *Furman* is an unusual riddle. Perhaps, in *Furman*, with twenty-five score human lives in their hands, they were unable to appreciate the virtues of consistency. If that is

---

[87] 408 U.S. at 253.

[88] *Id.* at 310.

[89] *Id.* at 313.

[90] *Id.* at 314.

[91] 402 U.S. at 208.

[92] *Id.* at 207.

the explanation, I suppose civilized men ought not to find their actions wholly censurable.

There is a final difficulty with the Douglas-Stewart-White approach, which suggests a profound contradiction that lies at the heart of their view of the Eighth Amendment. All three Justices take the position that what makes the punishment of death cruel and unusual under existing statutes is the possibility that some or most criminals sentenced to capital punishment may not be executed. Could it be that a punishment imposed under a system of unmitigated harshness would be less cruel? It is implicit in the approach of these Justices that the cruelty of a harsh punishment may be exacerbated by institutionalizing avenues of mercy.[93] Two logical possibilities are suggested: Either (1) mandatory death penalties would also be cruel and unusual, or (2) executing large numbers of people, on a continuous basis, without offering hope of mercy or mitigation, would not be cruel. It is worth noting that the constitutionality of mandatory death penalties is still open and may one day be before the Court.

The "normative" approach of Brennan and Marshall, because it goes to the core question, does not run afoul of *McGautha*, nor is it subject to criticism for treating the Eighth Amendment as superfluous. But it does have pitfalls of its own. Crucial to the arguments of both Brennan and Marshall are two notions, that the death penalty be accepted as both excessive and abhorrent to society. As I have already suggested, it will not do to separate these concepts, because members of society may abhor many things they acknowledge as necessary; presumably the Constitution would strike down only those punishments which were both abhorrent and unnecessary. But to start the judiciary in the business of second-guessing legislative judgment about excessiveness per se takes the first step on a slippery slope. Where does the inquiry end? The Court has sat in judgment on proportionality before, of course, the *Weems* case being the classic example. But there the Court explicitly undertook to measure a punishment against a crime: "Such penalties for such offenses amaze those who . . . believe that it is a precept of justice that punishment for crime should be graduated and proportioned to of-

---

[93] It appears, said the Chief Justice, "that the flexible sentencing system created by the legislatures, and carried out by juries and judges, has yielded more mercy than the Eighth Amendment can stand." 408 U.S. at 398.

fense."[94] In *Furman*, Brennan and Marshall essayed to measure a punishment against their judgment of what was necessary irrespective of the crime involved. If it is to be the practice of the courts to say, in the abstract, how much punishment is "enough," how, in reason, is the Chief Justice's trenchant question to be answered?[95] "I know of no convincing evidence that life imprisonment is a more effective deterrent than 20 years' imprisonment, or even that a $10 parking ticket is a more effective deterrent than a $5 parking ticket. In fact, there are some who go so far as to challenge the notion that any punishments deter crime." In the last analysis, the Brennan-Marshall showing boils down to a submission that society is revolted by, and rejects as unnecessary, the use of the death penalty. As to that normative question, neither Justice produced a very convincing showing that society is as absolutist as they say.

Hovering over the Brennan-Marshall approach, and to a lesser extent over that of the others, is an implicit notion of federalism which bodes very little cheer to those who value that form for American government. All of the majority opinions—and most especially Brennan and Marshall's—rely in one way or another about what "society" or "the people" think or do. Consistently, "society" is treated as if it were a transnational entity. An older view of our system of government, which I mention even though it is beginning to sound quaint, conceives of citizens of several states, each state, for certain purposes, a sovereign and a society unto itself. So long as the crucial matter of fact is taken to be what "society" thinks or does, I can think of no reason, a priori, why the relevant society to look to ought not to be the people of each separate state. If the

---

[94] 217 U.S. at 366–67.

[95] 408 U.S. at 396.

Mr. Justice Marshall answered this point, but he is much less than convincing. "THE CHIEF JUSTICE asserts that if we hold that capital punishment is unconstitutional because it is excessive, we will next have to determine whether a 10-year prison sentence rather than a five-year sentence is also excessive, or whether a $5 fine would not do equally well as a $10 fine. He may be correct that such determinations will have to be made, but, as in these cases, those persons challenging the penalty will bear a heavy burden of demonstrating that it is excessive. These cases arise after 200 years of inquiry, 200 years of public debate and 200 years of marshaling evidence. The burden placed on those challenging capital punishment could not have been greater. I am convinced that they have met their burden. Whether a similar burden will prove too great in future cases is a question that we can resolve in time." *Id.* at 360 n.141. Whatever the past 200 years has produced in the way of evidence suggesting that the death penalty is not a superior deterrent, and however hot the debate may have waxed, nothing has been discovered in that period of time, or is ever likely to be discovered, which will tell us whether the death penalty—or any penalty—is an appropriate social response to crime.

people of Minnesota abhor the death penalty, for example, and find
it unnecessary, then let them abolish it. As a matter of fact, they
did, some fifty years ago. But why, for purposes of establishing
constitutional norms, the feelings of the "society" of citizens of
Minnesota ought to control what is cruel and unusual punishment
in South Carolina does not seem to me obvious. Similarly, no one
would deny that:[96]

> If a statute that authorizes the discretionary imposition of a
> particular penalty for a particular crime is used primarily
> against defendants of a certain race, and if the pattern of use
> can be fairly explained only by reference to the race of the
> defendants, the Equal Protection Clause of the Fourteenth
> Amendment forbids continued enforcement of that statute in
> its existing form. Cf. *Yick Wo* v. *Hopkins,* 118 U.S. 356
> (1886); *Gomillion* v. *Lightfoot,* 364 U.S. 339 (1960).

But even if it is established that Arkansas, for example, hangs only
its Negro murderers and rapists,[97] that fact would logically furnish
no Eighth Amendment justification for why Montana could not
hang its white murderers and rapists. Thus when, for example, Justices Stewart and White speak of the rarity of the imposition of the
death penalty, it does not seem to me evident why the experience
of Rhode Island (which seldom employed the penalty of death) is
necessarily germane to the experience of Florida or Georgia (which
employed that penalty quite frequently).

   In other words, I find it difficult to see why Douglas's showing that
the death penalty is unconstitutional does not require him to show
that in every state the penalty is used to single out the despised and
dispossessed; or why Stewart and White's argument does not logi-

---

[96] *Id.* at 389 n.12. The Burger opinion was joined by each of the other three dissenters.

[97] See discussion in Maxwell v. Bishop, 398 F.2d 138, 142 *et seq.* (8th Cir. 1968),
vacated, 398 U.S. 262 (1970). Unfortunately for social science, the phenomenon of
execution has not been common enough for any confident conclusions, of nationwide
generality, to emerge as to whether a convicted person's race, per se, makes his execution
more or less likely. How importantly a defendant's race figures into what punishment he
gets is probably subject to regional differences. Careful scholars, in a number of limited
studies of capital punishment, have found that in some states, race does appear to play
an illegitimate role in post-conviction dispositions. See, *e.g.,* Wolfgang, Kelly, & Nolde,
Comparison of the Executed and the Commuted among Admissions to Death Row, 53 J.
Crim. L. Crim. & P.S. 301 (1962); Bedau, *Death Sentences in New Jersey, 1907–1960,*
19 Rutgers L. Rev. 1 (1964); Koeninger, *Capital Punishment in Texas, 1924-1968,* 15
Crime & Del. 132 (1969); Note, *Capital Punishment in Virginia,* 58 Va. L. Rev. 97
(1972). *A Study of the California Penalty Jury in First-Degree-Murder Cases,* 21 Stan. L.
Rev. 1297 (1969), did not find race a measurable factor in the decision to levy the death
penalty. It must be remembered, however, that only the penalty phase of first degree
murder trials was examined.

cally require confining the finding of unconstitutionality to those states where it can be shown that the penalty is visited only on a random handful of potentially eligible convicts; or why, under Brennan and Marshall's view, reference be made to the standards of decency and the notions of necessity of the people of particular states, rather than to the supposed views of the nation as a whole.

Without by any means exhausting the difficulties in the majority approaches to cruel and unusual punishment, I believe I have suggested enough problems to show what a formidable essay it is to create a prohibition of the death penalty out of the Eighth Amendment. The normative approach to the death penalty depends heavily on the notion that public opinion is against it; but legislatures have enacted, and continue to enact, capital punishment statutes, and public opinion polls consistently show the public pretty much evenly divided over the question whether the death penalty ought to be used.[98] But before discarding the normativist position as based on faulty premises, it is perhaps worth inquiring whether, when asked if they favor or oppose abolition of the death penalty, people give usable responses. The death penalty issue is, after all, one of the most emotional of social topics. I will examine some of that emotionalism presently; in the meantime, it seems to me at least plausible, if it is not likely, that when the person in the street—our friend the machinist's wife—is asked about abolition of the death penalty, what her answer means is that she is not in favor of coddling criminals and is not soft on crime. That she might thus confuse the issues is not unexpected, for clear thinking is generally a casualty when tempers rise. Conceding that many people in the United States are in favor of the death penalty—and maybe even the majority—it seems to me nevertheless probable that, as Mr. Justice Marshall says, capital punishment would have far fewer proponents if it were more generally understood how little instrumental advantage it brings into the world. The "most hotly contested issue"[99] in the capital punishment debate—whether the death penalty is a superior deterrent to serious crime—ought to be the coldest issue. The really hot issue—whether the extra retributive power of the punishment of death is morally justifiable—is almost never discussed at all. This fact surely has a hidden meaning. Why is the debate always conducted in utilitarian terms, never in moralistic

---

[98] See BEDAU, note 57 supra, at ch. 5. Long after this article was written, the electorate of California voted by referendum to restore the death penalty.

[99] 408 U.S. at 345.

ones? The following summary can do little more than suggest the divisions of the battle. I begin by sketching the statistical argument that indicates that the death penalty is not a superior deterrent to serious crime.

It is important at the outset to draw the boundaries of the argument. The question whether capital punishment ought to be a social response to serious crime is not necessarily the same question as whether punishment of any kind is an appropriate response to any crime. There may be a fair number of people who would favor social protection and individual rehabilitation as the sole aims of the criminal law. Such people would write off all punishment-qua-punishment, including death, as a form of cruelty. But it is hardly necessary to win the argument that all punishment is cruel. The core of the argument is that the death penalty may be justified morally only on the hypothesis that it is the best deterrent to serious crime, and that systematic observation throws this hypothesis deeply into doubt.

The feeling that death is not the most effective deterrent to serious crime has been building for a long time. In 1836, the second report of the Royal Commission on Criminal Law observed:[100]

> It is a matter of ordinary observation that the fear of death, however strong when the event is near and certain, has no proportionate influence when the event is remote and uncertain. Daily experience proves that men are constantly induced to engage in the most hazardous occupations without regard to peril of life.

More recent observers have treated the subject more systematically. Figures of several different kinds have been gathered in order to find out whether the death penalty is superior to long imprisonment as a deterrent to serious crime. There are serious threshold problems. Not all states keep crime statistics in the same way. Apparently no states distinguish between "capital murder" and other criminal homicides. In order to find out whether the death penalty is a better deterrent to murder than a long prison sentence, we must first assume that the homicide rate is an adequate index of the capital murder rate. Sellin argues that it is,[101] and there seems to be no good reason to contest this assumption.

---

[100] REPORT OF THE ROYAL COMMISSION ON CRIMINAL LAW 19 (1836).

[101] SELLIN, THE DEATH PENALTY 22 (1959). This report is the most widely used critique of the comparative data. It was published as an appendix to A. L. I., MODEL PENAL CODE (Tentative Draft No. 9) (1959).

Bedau[102] states six hypotheses that have been formulated over the past generation to test the proposition that death is a superior deterrent to prolonged imprisonment for the crime of murder:

(1) Death penalty jurisdictions should have a lower annual rate of criminal homicide than abolition jurisdictions.

(2) Jurisdictions that abolished the death penalty should show an increased annual rate of criminal homicide after abolition.

(3) Jurisdictions that reintroduced the death penalty should show a decreased annual rate of criminal homicide after reintroduction.

(4) Given two contiguous jurisdictions differing chiefly in that one has the death penalty and the other does not, the latter should show a higher annual rate of criminal homicide.

(5) Police officers on duty should suffer a higher annual rate of criminal assault and homicide in abolition jurisdictions than in death penalty jurisdictions.

(6) Prisoners and prison personnel should suffer a higher annual rate of criminal assault and homicide from life-term prisoners in abolition jurisdictions than in death penalty jurisdictions.

Bedau's claims for these hypotheses are quite modest. First, he concedes that the six hypotheses, taken together, may not be enough to dispose of the superior deterrence question. Second, he concedes that the data which have been produced to test these hypotheses, have not been, nor could they be, subjected to tests of statistical significance.[103] Thus, although we have evidence, we do not know how good it is. Third, he concedes that in order to test these six hypotheses against existing figures, certain additional assumptions, themselves unproved, may, to one degree or another, have to be relied upon:[104]

> One must assume that . . . homicides as measured by vital statistics are in a generally constant ratio to criminal homicides, [that] the years for which the evidence has been gathered are representative and not atypical, [that] however much fluctuations in the homicide rate owe to other factors, there is a nonnegligible proportion which is a function of the severity of

---

[102] Bedau, *Deterrence and the Death Penalty: A Reconsideration*, 61 J. Crim. L. Crim. & P.S. 539, 544 (1970).

[103] I believe this is so because the instances of executions are simply too few to permit such tests to be made.

[104] Bedau, note 102 *supra*, at 545.

the penalty, and . . . [that] the deterrent effect of a penalty
is not significantly weakened by its infrequent imposition.

In spite of these difficulties, it is possible to look at the existing
evidence relating to the six hypotheses and conclude that, if they
have not been "disproved," at least they have been badly under-
mined. For accepting the inherent infirmities in the evidence, and
the fact that the statistics cannot be milked for certainties, the existing evidence is nevertheless quite extraordinary.

1. Death penalty jurisdictions do not have a lower rate of criminal homicide than abolition jurisdictions. On the contrary, although
the level of homicide death rates varies among groups of states,
"within each group of states having similar social and economic
conditions and populations, it is impossible to distinguish the abolition states from the others."[105]

2. Jurisdictions that have abolished the death penalty show a
generally stable criminal homicide rate, rather than an increasing
one.

The *Report of the British Royal Commission on Capital Punishment* stated the American experience:

In Iowa, capital punishment was abolished for a six-year period
between 1872 and 1878. Between 1865 and 1872, there was an annual average of four murder convictions; during the abolition
period, the average jumped to nine; following reintroduction of the
death penalty, the seven-year average jumped again, to thirteen
convictions.

In Kansas, where capital punishment was abolished in 1887 and
restored in 1935, the annual average homicide rate for the last five
years of the abolition period was 6.5 per 100,000; the five-year
average following reintroduction dropped to 3.8.

In Colorado, where capital punishment was abandoned in 1897
and restored in 1901, the five-year average of murder convictions
preceding abolition was 15.4, compared with an annual average of
18 during the abolition period and 19 for the five years following
reintroduction.

In Washington, where capital punishment was abolished in 1913
and restored in 1919, the rate of first degree murders per 100,000 of
population steadily increased from 1902 to 1942; and during the
decade 1942 to 1952, the rate took a precipitous drop. The fact of

---

[105] SELLIN, note 101 *supra*, at 34. Sellin concludes, "The inevitable conclusion is that
executions have no discernible effect on homicide rates." *Ibid*. See also REPORT OF THE
ROYAL COMMISSION ON CAPITAL PUNISHMENT 350–52 (Cmd. 8932 1953).

abolition did not seem to disturb the trend of increase, leading to the notion that it did not affect it.

In Oregon, where capital punishment was abolished in 1914 and restored in 1920, the homicide rate increased slightly following re-introduction of capital punishment. The figures, although clearly inadequate to be conclusive, are at least suggestive: the homicide rates for 1912–19 were, average, 4.45 per 100,000; for the years 1919–28, the average was 4.7 per 100,000.

In South Dakota, which abolished capital punishment in 1915 but restored it in 1939, the average homicide rate for the last five years of the abolition period was 1.4 per 100,000, and it also averaged 1.4 for the first five years of the restoration period.

In Tennessee, which abolished in 1915 and restored in 1917, no adequate figures exist.

In Arizona, which abolished in 1916 and restored in 1918, there were 24 homicides in the year before abolition, 23 homicides the first year of abolition, 53 homicides the second year of abolition, and 24, 25, and 35 the three years following reintroduction.

In Missouri, which abolished capital punishment in 1917 and restored it in 1919, the homicide rates for 1912–15 were 9.07 per 100,000; for 1916–19 the rates were 10.52; and for 1919–28, the rates were 11.1.

More recent experience has enhanced the conclusion that capital punishment does not affect murder rates. Glenn W. Samuelson, reporting on Delaware's 3½-year experience with abolition, states that the criminal homicide rates were actually slightly lower during abolition than during the periods before and after.[106]

Although the data suffer obvious deficiencies, it is interesting to observe that all of them point in the same direction—that the amount of criminal homicide committed in a jurisdiction is not associated with whether there is a death penalty there.

3. The third hypothesis—that restoration of the death penalty ought to depress the rate of criminal homicide—was apparently borne out by the experience in Kansas and Arizona and contradicted by the experience in Iowa, Washington, Colorado, Oregon, South Dakota, Missouri, and Delaware.

4. The comparisons between contiguous jurisdictions which, although demographically and socio-economically similar, differ as to whether they have a death penalty, all tend to disprove the notion

---

[106] Samuelson, *Why Was Capital Punishment Restored in Delaware?* 60 J. CRIM. L. CRIM. & P.S. 148 (1969).

that the existence of capital punishment would produce a different homicide rate in similar and contiguous jurisdictions.[107]

5. Sellin has studied the effects of the death penalty on police safety and reports that the rate of homicides committed on policemen generally reflects the homicide rate of the state rather than the state's policy vis-à-vis capital punishment.[108]

Cumulatively, the statistical evidence strongly suggests that the death penalty does not function as a greater deterrent to serious crime—or at least criminal homicide—than long sentences of imprisonment. The evidence, as Bedau, Hook,[109] and others state—and as all might as well concede—does not "prove" the nondeterrence of the death penalty or that the death penalty is not a superior deterrent to life imprisonment. But superior deterrence is, in light of the evidence, definitely placed in doubt. And since almost all contemporary retentionists are utilitarians at heart, whose position on the death penalty depends very greatly on the intact survival of the best-deterrent theory, it is important to understand the nature of the response which they make to the statistical arguments.

It is not, I think, inappropriate to begin with the statement of the apotheosis of crime-busting. J. Edgar Hoover thought that its superior deterrent potential both justified and made necessary the penalty of death. "To abolish the death penalty would absolve other [traitors and murderers] from fear of the consequences for committing atrocious crimes."[110] Hoover discounted the statistical arguments against capital punishment, not on the ground that these are irrelevant to the core normative question, but on the ground that the statisticians are without integrity:[111]

> Some who propose the abolishment of capital punishment select statistics that "prove" their point and ignore those that point the other way. Comparisons of murder rates between

---

[107] See ROYAL COMMISSION ON CAPITAL PUNISHMENT, note 105, at 350–53.

[108] SELLIN, note 101 *supra*, at 52, *et seq*. To my knowledge, hypothesis 6 has not been explored, probably because the reported rate of assaultive crimes by life-term prisoners, whether in abolitionist or retention states, is so low as to preclude the possibility of meaningful inferences. The REPORT FROM THE SELECT COMMITTEE ON CAPITAL PUNISHMENT (1930) made two responses to the problem of unruly inmates: first, that there is every incentive for a life-termer to behave himself, because there is always the hope for eventual—albeit conditional—liberation, which continued misbehavior would rule out. Second, the principal danger would come from the "violent and insubordinate, or morose and sullen type; but convicts of a similar character are being dealt with now." P. 57.

[109] Hook, note 57 *supra*, at 148.

[110] Hoover, *Statements in Favor of the Death Penalty* in BEDAU, note 57 *supra*, at 131.

[111] *Id*. at 134.

the nine states which abolished the death penalty and the forty-one states which have retained it either individually, before or after abolition, or by group are completely inconclusive.

The professional law enforcement officer is convinced from experience that the hardened criminal has been and is deterred from killing based on the prospect of the death penalty.

Thus far, Hoover's argument is entirely utilitarian. But when he strays into biblical exegesis, one might hope that at last he will face the core question. Alas, he does not:[112]

> Misguided do-gooders frequently quote the Sixth Commandment, "Thou shalt not kill," to prove that capital punishment is wrong. This Commandment in the twentieth chapter, verse 13, of Exodus has also been interpreted to mean: "Thou shalt do no murder." Then the twenty-first chapter, verse 12, says, "He that smiteth a man, so that he die, shall be surely put to death." We can no more change the application to our society of this basic moral law in the Old Testament than we can change the meaning of Leviticus 19:18: "thou shalt love thy neighbor as thyself," which Jesus quoted in the New Testament.
>
> To "love thy neighbor" is to protect him; capital punishment acts as at least one wall to afford "God's children" protection.

It is odd that with the unvanquishable word of the fierce and moralistic Hebrew God on his side, Hoover would choose to recede, not to the question whether it is right that the evil should suffer, but rather to the utterly different question whether, when we inflict

---

[112] *Id.* at 133–34. There is no point in undertaking a lengthy rebuttal, but neither can the arguments that Hoover makes be permitted to pass without comment. No one suggests that murderers and traitors be absolved of the consequences of their crimes. Hoover's characterization of the abolitionist position in those terms is nonsense. Hoover also impugns the integrity of certain unnamed abolitionists, who argue their position from statistics which favor it but ignore the statistics which "point the other way." He does not tell us where to look for the statistics that do point the other way.

Finally, Hoover's chief proof of the superior deterrent power of the death penalty is that "the professional law enforcement officer is convinced" of it. This appeal to "experience" is not, of course, any different from the arguments which abolitionists make from statistics, since the data reflect nothing but experience. Hoover does not say precisely what experience professional law enforcement officers have that leads them to their conclusion about the deterrent superiority of the death penalty. What he probably means is that professional law enforcement officers, through continuous contact with criminals, entertain no romantic illusions about there being no such thing as a bad boy and would just as soon see such people killed. They may be right, but that is not the same proposition as that the death penalty is a superior deterrent.

the death penalty we are behaving efficaciously in affording protection to God's children.

The confusion between the proposition that the death penalty deters and the proposition that it is appropriate is a fairly stable feature of retentionist argument. It is displayed with unselfconscious starkness in the brief of Evelle Younger, attorney general of California, in the *Aikens* case,[113] which was argued to the Court and taken under submission prior to the California Supreme Court's decision in *People v. Anderson*. The following excerpt illustrates the point:[114]

> The studies upon which petitioner relies conclude that the death penalty exerts no discernible influence on the rate of homicides. The truism that one may prove almost anything with statistics is a circumstance that makes one particularly concerned, in a matter as fraught with strong feelings as the desirability of the death penalty, that the statistician be totally objective and free of bias.
>
> Aside from the shadow which this caveat casts across the findings of non-deterrence, or more accurately the absence of findings of deterrence, a question arises as to the efficacy of the statistical approach in an area as imbued with imponderables as the question of human motivation toward criminal conduct. Social and economic conditions, such as population pressure, unemployment rate, influx of racial and ethnic minorities, in addition to such factors as the efficacy of local law enforcement, climate and weather, and the number of attractive crime targets, must all play a significant role in determining the number of homicides (particularly robbery-homicides) committed in a given jurisdiction in a given period of time. The existence of so many influential factors, not susceptible of measurement and correlation, impugns the statistical methodology upon which petitioner places so much reliance. Clearly, the existence of these variables precludes a meaningful comparison between general undifferentiated murder statistics and a single proposed causal factor, that of the existence of the death penalty in the particular jurisdiction.
>
> Secondly, the steady increase in homicides across the nation, presumably caused by a multitude of social and economic factors, naturally tends to cover up the perceptible deterrent effects of the death penalty which might appear in the antiseptic conditions of a social laboratory.

This startling argument must be recapitulated to avoid misunderstanding. It contains in essence four statements:

---

[113] Note 3 *supra*. [114] Respondent's brief, pp. 77–79.

1. Perhaps the statisticians are dishonest.

2. The possibility that the statisticians are dishonest casts a shadow across their results.

3. There are all sorts of relevant things about criminal motivation that are imponderable and unmeasurable.

4. The fluctuations in the homicide rate cover up the effect of the death penalty.

Pending stronger evidence of the dishonesty of Messrs. Bedau, Sellin, Samuelson, *et al.*, than the fact that their conclusions are not to Mr. Younger's liking, I prefer not to discuss points 1 and 2. The fourth point seems to me to make no sense, so I will not attempt to discuss it beyond noting that it is apparently a mistake. Fluctuation in the homicide rate irrespective of the imposition of the death penalty suggests simply that the death penalty is not an important determinant of the homicide rate. This point, which Younger most wishes to refute, he seems, in his confusion, to concede. But Younger's third point requires more explication. It contains two parts: first, the factual statement that the death penalty is a better deterrent than long imprisonment; second, the assertion that this factual statement cannot be verified.

What kind of factual statement is that? Verification—the criterion of confirmability—is an integral part of every statement that purports to be factual. A statement purporting to be descriptive of something in the world is not, in the ordinary sense, a factual statement unless it admits, at least in principle, of verification. Conversely, unverifiable statements are generally of two kinds—mystical or normative. An example of a mystical statement is: "Every time we turn our backs the moon turns into green cheese, but when we peek, it changes back into dust and stone." A value statement is something like: "Chocolate is the tastiest flavor." Neither of these statements is "wrong" in any absolute sense; they are simply unconfirmable, and thus do not belong to the world of factual statements. What Younger fails to acknowledge about the studies that he hates is that they actually provide controls for the imponderables which he fondles by the technique of matching. It must be assumed that these imponderables, whatever they are, work similarly before and after a state abolishes capital punishment. Does the "climate"[115] in North Dakota vary with abolition?

---

[115] "Climate" is one of the "imponderables" mentioned in the Younger brief, at p. 77. See text *supra*, at note 114.

I think we can safely put to one side the notion that Younger believes that the invisible hand of a poltergeist is fouling the data. What is left, I submit, is this: that the declaration that the death penalty is a superior deterrent to serious crime, in spite of evidence to the contrary, amounts to nothing more than the expression of a value preference that, whether the penalty is a superior deterrent or not, it ought to be used.[116]

A priori, I can find nothing wrong with this value preference. It may be flinty and stern, but it does not seem to me necessarily barbaric, that someone might believe that certain criminals ought to be put to death, the inhuman brutality of their crimes being so great as to outrun all possibility of forgiveness or amends. But if the argument is to rest upon straight moralistic dogma, rooted in a steely Calvinistic premise, why should it dress itself up in the disguise of a utilitarian argument instead? Why should not the argument be allowed to stand or fall on its own merit?[117] One answer

---

[116] Examples of this confusion could be multiplied. One other instance is the brief *amicus curiae* of the State of Indiana, filed in the *Furman* case. *Amicus* acknowledged that "The deterrent effect of the death penalty is a vital consideration in discussing the necessity of its retention." Brief, p. 10. It continued: "It is the contention of a vast majority of prosecutors that the deterrent effect of capital punishment is significant. Forgetting for the moment the wealth of evidence available to substantiate its deterrent effect, we should rely more on the practitioner instead of the academic reformer. We should believe the person who deals with the accused murderer in the real-life situation, rather than the person who has analysed what he would or should have done in a clinical psychological vacuum." Amicus brief, p. 10.

The argument continued: "The statistics used to minimize the deterrent effect of capital punishment categorically omit the essential variables that would have, otherwise, given these statistics some meaning. One of the most glaring omissions from the statistical standpoint is the input of common sense." *Id*. at 13.

There is more, but these excerpts serve to illustrate essentially the same features that appear in the Hoover and Younger arguments. First, the slighting reference to the opponent, an "academic reformer" operating in a "clinical psychological vacuum" and not really in touch with "the real life situation." Second, the converse argument—the appeal to the experience of those persons who are in touch with the "real-life situation," the "vast majority of prosecutors." Finally, the assertion that the statistics do not really mean anything because they go against "common sense," that universally applicable datum which never needs confirmation. Nowhere in this brief is the "wealth of evidence" which demonstrates the superior deterrent power of capital punishment revealed. Indeed, at one point the brief almost confesses that there could be no such evidence, by quoting with approval the statement of Judge Hyman Barshay: "The death penalty is a warning, just like a lighthouse throwing its beam out to sea. We hear about the shipwrecks, but we do not hear about the ships that the lighthouse guides safely on their way. We do not have proof of the number of ships it saves, but we do not tear the lighthouse down." *Id*. at 14–15.

[117] "I cannot praise a fugitive and cloistered virtue, unexercised and unbreathed, that never sallies out and sees her adversary, but slinks out of the race, where that immortal

may be that retentionists would be ashamed to admit to having such values. If so, surely it is relevant to a judgment whether death is a cruel and unusual punishment.

In nineteenth-century England, it is said that persons found disguised in the public roads were hanged[118]—not because there is something inherently criminal about disguise, but because anyone who goes abroad in disguise is undoubtedly up to no good. There is an earthy wisdom in that assumption, and I submit that it applies as well to ideas as it does to people: when you find them in disguise in a public place, they are up to no good. Depend upon it.

I began by asking, not whether *Furman* was rightly decided, but whether the Court had made a persuasive case for the proposition that the death penalty is cruel and unusual punishment. I think my arguments suggest that, unless I misunderstand what the Court did, they failed to make a very persuasive case. And perhaps my own observations have added no more to the majority's case than a suggestion why it is impossible to get a retentionist to discuss his reasons with sense, consistency, or even civility. The long-term impact of *Furman* may be limited. To be sure, it represents another step in the rationalization of standards of government conduct. But this is not a novel development. And the way that the *Furman* majority presented itself to the world—five separate opinions with none commanding the concurrence of any Justice other than its author—seemed almost deliberately calculated to make this judgment of dubious value as a precedent when, for example, a state decides to enact a compulsory death penalty for first-degree murder or rape or kidnapping. What the Court did was to save the skins of more than five hundred men and women who would otherwise, in little dramas of indescribably obscene morbidity, have been taken from their places of confinement and ritualistically put to death. Certainly, for me, that was a decent and humane thing for the Court to have done. But in terms of reasoned judgments, the majority Justices in *Furman* did not have one of their finest hours.

---

garland is to be run for, not without dust and heat." MILTON, AREOPAGITICA 18 (G. Sabine ed. 1951).

[118] REPORT FROM THE SELECT COMMITTEE ON CAPITAL PUNISHMENT, note 108 *supra*, at p. 6, ¶ 15.

RALPH K. WINTER, JR.

POVERTY, ECONOMIC EQUALITY, AND

THE EQUAL PROTECTION CLAUSE

According to the legend, the Supreme Court is a stabilizing instrument of government, an institution which provides continuity and
which, while not impervious to change, alters the direction of its
judgments gradually and gracefully, unlike the "political" branches,
which make sharp and sudden turns after periodic elections. The
sophisticated, knowing of, among other things, the maneuvering
within and outside the Court which led to its dramatic reversal in
stance on the constitutionality of the Civil War Legal Tender Acts,[1]
aware of Mr. Justice Roberts' constitutional U-turn on March 29,
1937,[2] and having observed at first hand the Warren Court's rejection of earlier decisions at a "volume and speed . . . never . . . witnessed before,"[3] have never really accepted the myth. They are thus
ready to believe that the most far-reaching effect of the cliff-hang-
ing election of 1968 will be in the affairs of the ostensibly least
political branch and that, as a result, we are at a watershed in the
history of the Court. With the retirement of Chief Justice Warren
and several of his colleagues, and their replacement by men thought
to hold a "conservative judicial philosophy," it is predicted the
Court will play a more passive role as a constitutional arbiter. What

Ralph K. Winter, Jr., is Professor of Law, Yale University.

[1] See JACKSON, THE STRUGGLE FOR JUDICIAL SUPREMACY 41–44 (1941).

[2] Id. at 207–13. But see KURLAND, ed., FELIX FRANKFURTER ON THE SUPREME COURT
516 (1970).

[3] KURLAND, POLITICS, THE CONSTITUTION, AND THE WARREN COURT 91 (1970).

the Warren Court left unfinished, it is thought, will remain unfinished, or at least be held in abeyance, until another President and another watershed—be they near or far—once again establish the Court as the vanguard of the forces for social and political change.

It would be well at this time to reflect upon where it was the Warren Court and its champions seemed to be going when that funny thing happened in 1968. The conventional wisdom, after all, may be wrong. Presidents have been surprised before by their appointments to the Court and the force of precedent and the momentum of an idea may in any event overwhelm the predispositions of individual jurists. But even if the Court does turn from the goals staked out by the Warren Court, now is an appropriate time to reassess these goals, and, in particular, to reassess the role of the Equal Protection Clause. For as one "Court" is replaced by another, that provision remains in an exposed position, poised on the one hand to become the spearhead of a social and economic revolution, yet vulnerable on the other to a considerable reduction in constitutional significance.

This is the first of two articles reassessing the constitutional role of the Equal Protection Clause. It will deal with the use of the Clause as a device to reduce economic inequality and to alleviate poverty. The second article, which it is hoped will appear next year, will undertake an overall reassessment of the role of that constitutional provision, and will discuss its history and the permissible judicial extrapolations from that history. In particular, it will focus on the classifications affected by the Clause, the function performed by the norm of equality, and the scope of the requirement that the provision apply only to "state action."

I take up the economic inequality issue separately for several reasons. It is a legal issue of major contemporary significance; it marks the present high-water mark of equal protection. It is also a social and political issue which vexes many groups in the society and is the source of considerable discontent and unrest. The fundamental gravity of this issue for lawyers, however, has not led, in the journals of the profession, to an even minimally adequate discussion, much less full-blown debate, of the economic implications for the society or the institutional significance for the Supreme Court.

As the era of the Warren Court came to a close, the champions of judicial activism had gathered their forces for a constitutional assault on the distribution of income, a campaign, which, if successful, might ignite a social and political revolution rivaling that begun in *Brown v. Board of Education*[4] and intrude on the affairs of the elected branches in a fashion exceeding the judicial invalidation of the New Deal before 1937. This gathering of forces is, of course, no isolated phenomenon brought on by a fascination with the intricacies of constitutional law. Rather it is part of a more general movement—or malaise—which insists that the distribution of income in the United States is unfair, that a redistribution is called for, and that the persistence of economic inequality—or at least substantial inequality—is neither necessary nor humane. As is the case with many movements which find the political process inhospitable or slow, many of those clamoring for redistribution see in the Court an apt, or at least accessible, instrument of government for bringing it about. Theoretical cover is to be found in judicial doctrines of "substantive equal protection" which will permit the Court to identify "fundamental interests" or "just wants" which government is constitutionally obligated to fulfill for those who cannot afford them.[5]

This article takes the position that such a use of the judicial power is absolutely wrong. In terms of conventional constitutional interpretation, it may fairly be said that it not only finds no support in the language or discernible purpose of the Equal Protection Clause but fairly flies in their face. In terms of a sensible division of functions between the Court and the elected branches, moreover, it resembles more a call for partial rule by junta (of between five and nine men) than for an acceptable interpretation of the structure of the Constitution. To those who find such conclusions unduly harsh, it should be said they are no slap in the face of the advocates of substantive equal protection, who openly and candidly reject conventional legal criteria, as well as the democratic political process, in their quest for validation by "tomorrow's history."[6] Rarely has advocacy of a major constitutional doctrine been accompanied by less in the way of conventional constitutional argument and more in the way of fervor over its assumed wisdom as public policy. Rarely, moreover, has the wisdom of constitutional doctrine as public policy been so dependent on unspecified and untested assumptions.

---

[4] 347 U.S. 483 (1954).

[5] See Karst & Horowitz, *Reitman v. Mulkey: A Telophase of Substantive Equal Protection*, 1967 SUPREME COURT REVIEW 39.

[6] *Id.* at 79.

I. ALLEVIATING POVERTY AND REDUCING ECONOMIC INEQUALITY THROUGH THE EQUAL PROTECTION CLAUSE

A. THE LAW REVIEWS

Development of a theory of equal protection looking to the reduction of economic inequality began, it may fairly be said, when the "state action" doctrine was reported to have died under suspicious judicial circumstances. After extensive funeral ceremonies in the law reviews,[7] state action was consigned by the Warren Court's academic supporters to a grave in the Potter's Field of unmourned doctrinal constraints.

The state action doctrine itself, stated in a flat, unelaborated form, is derived from the language of the Fourteenth Amendment and seeks to distinguish between those actions of state government which the Amendment subjects to constitutional scrutiny and the conduct of private individuals which it does not. The existence of any such limitation is a major barrier to the development of a constitutional obligation to reduce economic inequality since, in the lexicon of everyday conversation at least, that inequality seems largely the result of private rather than governmental action. As a result, some disposition has to be made of the state action issue before substantive equal protection can be expanded to a scope which corresponds to the size of the problem for which it is said to be the solution.

Occasioning the many academic funerals for state action were decisions of the Supreme Court, among them: *Shelley v. Kraemer*,[8] which held that state judicial enforcement of a restrictive covenant between private parties was state action subject to (unfavorable) constitutional scrutiny; and *Reitman v. Mulkey*,[9] which invalidated a California constitutional amendment forbidding, *inter alia*, open housing legislation. Because so much private conduct relies upon either judicial enforcement or governmental tolerance, it was quite natural that these decisions would stimulate much learned comment

---

[7] *E.g.*, Horowitz, *The Misleading Search for "State Action" under the Fourteenth Amendment*, 30 S. CAL. L. REV. 208 (1957); Van Alstyne & Karst, *State Action*, 14 STAN. L. REV. 3 (1961); Henkin, *Shelley v. Kraemer: Notes for a Revised Opinion*, 110 U. PA. L. REV. 473 (1962); J. Williams, *The Twilight of State Action*, 41 TEXAS L. REV. 347 (1963); Silard, *A Constitutional Forecast: Demise of the "State Action" Limit on the Equal Protection Guarantee*, 66 COLUM. L. REV. 855 (1966); Black, *"State Action," Equal Protection, and California's Proposition 14*, 81 HARV. L. REV. 69 (1967).

[8] 334 U.S. 1 (1948).   [9] 387 U.S. 369 (1967).

on the quality of the opinions delivered, the merits of the results they reached, and the position they would occupy in a developing and meaningful concept of state action. And indeed they did. The opinions were widely—almost universally—condemned as inadequate explanations of the results they reached. These results, on the other hand, were just as widely applauded by academic commentators who seized the opportunity to try their hand at hypothetical opinion-writing and at synthesizing a concept of state action.

However analytically sound the opinions may have been, the attempt at synthesis was an avowed failure. Most commentators, having concluded that the results reached by the Court were dead right, found themselves unable to fashion a meaningful limiting role for a state action requirement. They thus felt called upon to recommend that the search be called off and that state action be abandoned as a meaningless and potentially harmful constraint on constitutional development. The recommendation was strongly worded and accompanied by no little derisive rhetoric. In this large and remarkably one-directional body of literature, one finds it said that state action is a "novel preoccupation" of judges,[10] the subject of a "misleading search,"[11] "a slogan from 1883,"[12] and a concept on which "the sun is setting."[13]

The main theme underlying this incapacitation of usually fertile imaginations is simple enough. All societal relationships require a governmental definition of rights and duties between individuals. When the state defines and enforces a right or duty, it has "acted." When it rules that there is no right or duty, it has also "acted." Thus, whether the state acts affirmatively to enforce a private decision or merely tolerates the making of a private decision matters not, for in either case it is the state which is making the private decision "good." The relevant constitutional inquiry is, therefore, not whether there is state action—there always is, except where the state lacks constitutional power to regulate—but whether the conduct involved violates the commands of the Fourteenth Amendment. And where the conduct does not pass constitutional muster, the state must either cease the unconstitutional activity—enforcing contracts, the laws against trespass, etc.—or, where the tainted activity persists because of governmental tolerance, provide affirmative relief—education, housing, a lawyer, etc.

---

[10] Van Alstyne & Karst, note 7 *supra*, at 4.

[11] Horowitz, note 7 *supra*, at 208.

[12] Black, note 7 *supra*, at 95.

[13] Williams, note 7 *supra*, at 389.

There are variations on the main theme, because even if state action is a hopeless enigma, it by no means follows that the Fourteenth Amendment should be read as a comprehensive code of social and economic conduct. One way of bridging the gap between discovering that state action is meaningless and finding that equal protection is all-encompassing is to appeal to the intent of the framers and argue that a meaningful concept of state action—something short of a broad reading of *Shelley v. Kraemer*—will emasculate the Amendment and thwart the good purposes of those who enacted it. This argument, however, is best delivered with a knowing wink, because few would seriously contend that at the very moment laissez-faire and Social Darwinism were about to peak, the framers even had an inkling that they were drafting a constitutional rule of such all-embracing scope that it compels governmental intervention in the name of economic equality, a constitutional war on poverty as it were. Resort is thus had to a second variation which holds that constitutional mandates live, grow, and change with the society (or some elements of society), "reflecting differences in prevailing philosophy and the continuing movement from *laissez-faire* government toward welfare and meliorism."[14] The state action requirement can thus be disposed of (as practical constraint anyway) because, to use Professor Henkin's memorable and revealing pronoun, "we"[15] think it is too constraining, as well as too enigmatic.

Once governmental tolerance of private conduct is established as state action, the next step is fairly obvious. Thus, Professors Karst and Horowitz:[16]

> [Un]constitutional inequities may arise from the impact of a classification by government that fails to compensate for significant differences in classes that are not themselves the direct product of governmental action—that is, a state can deny equal protection of the laws by treating unequals equally. There may, in fact, have been no formal governmental classification in the traditional sense at all, but only a toleration by government of private conduct that has produced the inequality. To rectify these denials of equal protection the state may be required, if one wishes to put it this way, to perform an "affirmative duty." Since total equality as a governmental goal is both impossible and undesirable, some selection must be made of the areas in which equality is to be imposed by the judiciary

---

[14] Henkin, note 7 *supra*, at 494.

[15] *Id.* at 488–89.   [16] Karst & Horowitz, note 5 *supra*, at 58.

in the name of the Constitution. The selection to date has been largely based on the Supreme Court's identification of fundamental interests, interests that carry relatively high priorities for the development of the nation's underdeveloped sectors.

The "identification of fundamental interests" will presumably entail a consideration and evaluation of various "needs" or "wants" in an effort to determine which are so "fundamental" as to call for a constitutional obligation to fulfill them when the individual cannot do so himself. But rather than attempt to spell out a theory of social justice which will serve to identify "just wants," the academic proponents of this use of the Equal Protection Clause have treated the "identification of fundamental interest" as a clerical detail to be handled on an ad hoc basis by the Court. The concept of "just wants" thus deserves further description.

The "just wants" theory appeared in an important article by Professor Frank I. Michelman which served as the foreword to the *Harvard Law Review*'s review of the Supreme Court's 1968 Term.[17] This was an explicit attempt to develop a theoretical framework within which elaboration of a governmental "duty to protect against certain hazards . . . endemic in an unequal society"[18] can take place. It is claimed to have usefulness in defining the affirmative duties to be imposed under what I have called substantive equal protection. A "just want" can be identified, Michelman said, by two distinctive characteristics. First, it is a want that "justice requires shall not go involuntarily unfulfilled."[19] Second, every person ranks the want "higher on his list of priorities than any other,"[20] except presumably other "just wants." To permit the want to go unfulfilled involuntarily is thus an injustice directly related to the lack of wealth, for had the individual access to the means, he would immediately satisfy it.

The claim to have a "just want" fulfilled does not, however, depend upon a showing that the society's institutional arrangements governing the distribution of income are unjust. If it did, it might well be met with the argument that government can reasonably be obligated only to insure that these arrangements are such that every individual has, over time, a fair opportunity to earn an income ade-

---

[17] Michelman, *On Protecting the Poor through the Fourteenth Amendment*, 83 HARV. L. REV. 7 (1969).

[18] *Id*. at 9.   [19] *Id*. at 30.   [20] *Ibid*.

quate to such needs, rather than affirmatively to provide for them upon a showing that they are at a particular moment involuntarily unfulfilled. "[J]ustice requires *more* than a fair opportunity to realize an income which can cover these needs or insure against them—requires, to be sure, absolute assurance that they will be met when and as felt, free of any remote contingencies pertaining to effort, thrift, or foresight."[21]

Recognition of such claims by no means entails equalization of income, for Michelman is aware that redistributions of income without regard to "effort, thrift or foresight" carry with them the risk of "incentive effects." Borrowing from Professor Rawls, he holds that inequalities are permissible when:[22]

> they are necessary to a system which assures to those who turn out to occupy society's least advantageous positions a better situation than they could reasonably expect under . . . equal shares. In particular, such inequalities might be just insofar as they were necessary to incentives and market allocations thought to make the economy more efficient and productive than it could otherwise be.

"Just wants" are then identified by assuming the role of one who has no idea what his economic station is likely to be and who accepts the necessity for incentives and free markets in maximizing productivity. What risks would he say everyone should be insured against and what needs would he say ought not go unfulfilled "as and when they accrue"? Thus are "just wants" identified.

B. THE UNITED STATES REPORTS

The development of substantive equal protection as a device to alleviate poverty and reduce economic inequality has not seen as steady and deliberate a progression in the Supreme Court as in the academic journals. At times the Court has been ahead of the commentators in developing such doctrine and, at the level of decisional language at least, the cases seemed for a time inexorably headed in that direction. In the last three years, however, the trend of decisions has been less hospitable to judicial intervention in the name of economic equality and a reexamination of the constitutional rationale of some of the earlier decisions may be in the offing. What follows is a sketch of the case law, as it now stands, with some

---

[21] *Id*. at 14.   [22] *Id*. at 15.

speculation as to possible future lines of development. Those who follow the Court closely might well skip the next two subsections.

1. *State action.* The academic commentators who view the state action limitation as meaningless or harmful are not without support in the case law, in particular in three decisions which antedated the accession of Governor Warren to the Chief Justiceship. *Marsh v. Alabama,*[23] holding that a company-owned town exhibiting all the indicia of a subordinate political unit was a town for purposes of the state action doctrine, was quickly dwarfed in constitutional significance two years later when *Shelley v. Kraemer* was decided. Even in subsequent cases it is hard to find a broader, more unlimited statement for a majority of the Court than Chief Justice Vinson's assertion that state judicial enforcement of a private restrictive covenant is "state action . . . in the full and complete sense of the phrase."[24] Five years later, the demise of state action seemed about complete. In *Terry v. Adams,*[25] the Court found state action in the operation of the Jaybird Democratic Association, an all-white Texas political group which held private primary elections to determine which candidates it would endorse in the official Democratic primary. Because white voters abided by the decision of the Jaybird primary—that is, Jaybird candidates always won or were unopposed in the official elections—the official primary and general election seemed to the Court "no more than perfunctory ratifiers" of the vote in which blacks were excluded.[26] Because multiple opinions were delivered, it is difficult to attribute any one legal theory or version of the facts to the Court. Nevertheless, a receptive mind can easily read the case to find state action in the state's toleration of the private, all-white Jaybird elections. Indeed, Mr. Justice Black's opinion, joined by two other Justices, explicitly stated: "For a state to *permit* such a duplication of its election processes is to permit a flagrant abuse of those processes to defeat the purposes of the Fifteenth Amendment."[27]

An interim period followed during which the decisions added little, one way or the other. In *Burton v. Wilmington Parking Authority,*[28] the Court found state action in the discriminatory conduct of a restaurateur who leased space on the first floor of a

---

[23] 326 U.S. 501 (1946).

[24] 334 U.S. at 19.

[25] 345 U.S. 461 (1953).

[26] *Id.* at 469.

[27] *Ibid.* (Emphasis added.)

[28] 365 U.S. 715 (1961).

municipally owned parking garage. Emphasizing that state action may be found "[o]nly by sifting facts and weighing circumstances"[29] and "only in the framework of the peculiar facts or circumstances present,"[30] the majority opinion went on to list so many relevant "facts" and "circumstances" that one can confidently say only that the rule of the case probably applies to Wilmington, North Carolina, as well as to Wilmington, Delaware.

For a time, *Reitman v. Mulkey* seemed more significant. Because it invalidated a California constitutional amendment which, *inter alia*, forbade open housing legislation, the decision might be interpreted as condemning state tolerance of certain kinds of private conduct. Subsequent commentators, notably my colleague Professor Charles L. Black, Jr., supplied a different rationale for the decision—one which the Court adopted in a subsequent but on the facts *a fortiori* case[31]—which would eliminate *Reitman*'s potential impact on the state action requirement. In his words, the *Reitman* rule provides:[32]

> where a racial group is in a political duel with those who would explicitly discriminate against it as a racial group, and where the regulatory action the racial group wants is of full and undoubted federal constitutionality, the state may not place in the way of the racial minority's attaining its political goal any barriers which, within the state's political system taken as a whole, are especially difficult of surmounting, by comparison with those barriers that normally stand in the way of those who wish to use political processes to get what they want.

That rationale, if accepted as the teaching of *Reitman*, consigns the state action question in the case to a minor role, for no one would contend that the placing of the extra political barrier was anything but a fully governmental act.

The *Sit-in Cases*,[33] raising the issue whether trespass convictions of civil rights demonstrators seeking to integrate various public accommodations constituted state action, were inconclusive, since a majority of the Justices would not be marshaled on either side of the question. This inability to perform the *coup de grace* on state action was significant, particularly since this was a "Court" which

---

[29] *Id.* at 722.   [30] *Id.* at 726.

[31] James v. Valtierra, 402 U.S. 137 (1971).

[32] Black, note 7 *supra*, at 82.

[33] *E.g.*, Bell v. Maryland, 378 U.S. 226 (1964).

was not squeamish about reaching and deciding constitutional issues. More significantly, in *Evans v. Abney*,[34] for the first time in eighty-seven years, a majority of the Court directly held in a case involving racial discrimination that state action was not involved. The very fact of such a ruling is of importance in view of the unsympathetic hearing the Court had given such claims in the past and of the universal condemnation of the very concept by academic commentators. On the facts, it is rather startling, for it is hardly the paradigm case in which to end an eighty-seven-year legal drought. *Abney* involved, not a private household, not a club with truly limited membership, not a discriminatory bequest involving only probate clearance, but a piece of land which for virtually half a century had been a municipal park. Left in trust to the city of Macon, Georgia, by United States Senator A. O. Bacon, for the express purpose of being a park for whites only, Baconsfield had in the clearest possible way served as a public facility operated by a political subdivision of the state of Georgia. After it became clear that federal constitutional law would not permit continued municipal operation of a segregated park, the Georgia courts appointed private trustees to run the park according to the bequest. The Supreme Court overruled the judgment, holding that Baconsfield was a "public institution subject to the command of the Fourteenth Amendment, regardless of who now has title under state law."[35] After further proceedings, the Georgia courts held that the racial separation clause was an inseparable part of the trust grant which could not be stricken so the park might operate on an integrated basis. The trust thus failed and Baconsfield reverted to the senator's heirs. On appeal, the Supreme Court affirmed.[36]

Mr. Justice Black's opinion is remarkable for its failure to apply the *Burton* test of "sifting facts and weighing circumstances" for, quite apart from the judicial intervention necessary to decree reversion of the trust, there was a long history of governmental involvement which seemed to weigh with the Court not at all. In distinguishing *Shelley v. Kraemer*, the Court noted that affirmative enforcement of a discriminatory scheme was not involved, since the effect of the Georgia rulings was to eliminate the park, a result which fell as heavily on white people as on black.

---

[34] 396 U.S. 435 (1970).

[35] Evans v. Newton, 382 U.S. 296, 302 (1966).   [36] 396 U.S. at 446.

Mr. Justice Black also emphasized that what was involved was the application of "normal principles of construction to determine the testator's true intent."[37] Nevertheless, the "true intent" so determined was that no park at all is better than an integrated park and the holding that Georgia is free to determine and give effect to that intent strongly implies, indeed, *a fortiori* insists, there is a broad range of social and economic conduct which, however discriminatory or unequal its impact, may be "tolerated" by a state without contravening the Fourteenth Amendment. This conclusion is buttressed by the decision in the 1971 Term in *Moose Lodge No. 107 v. Irvis*,[38] which held that state regulation of the sale of liquor did not so implicate the state in the affairs of a private club with a liquor license that the Fourteenth Amendment applied to its discriminatory practices. The Court also held, however, that a liquor board regulation requiring private clubs to adhere to their own discriminatory constitutions and by-laws was unconstitutional under *Shelley*.

While the precise role and overall dimensions of the state action requirement thus remain somewhat unclear, one can fairly say that it is a living doctrine that litigants must satisfy if they are to pursue Fourteenth Amendment claims successfully. This certainly implies that substantial changes in existing law are necessary before wholesale affirmative duties in the way of reducing economic inequality or alleviating poverty can be imposed on the states by judicial action. On the other hand, where the state is acting affirmatively— bringing criminal actions, providing housing, making welfare payments, furnishing educational facilities, etc., the state action requirement does not constrain the Court from imposing requirements that look to the reduction of economic inequality.

2. *The substance of equal protection.* Traditional equal protection analysis involves two principal doctrinal categories.[39] In the first, the Court identifies state regulation as touching upon a "fundamental interest," or invoking a "suspect classification," and then subjects the regulation to a searching scrutiny to insure that it is justified by a "compelling state interest." The second category embraces all other interests or classifications. State regulation there will

---

[37] *Ibid.*   [38] 407 U.S. 163 (1972).

[39] See generally *Developments in the Law, Equal Protection*, 82 HARV. L. REV. 1065 (1969).

pass constitutional muster if some "reasonable basis" for it is shown. Thus, substantive equal protection in the name of the reduction of economic inequality will have a bite only when: (*a*) a "fundamental interest" is adversely affected because of impecuniousness, or when a classification based on wealth is said to be "suspect," and (*b*) the very heavy burden of justification by demonstrating a compelling state interest is not met. When the Court invokes the first category, the burden is almost impossible to meet. If the Court invokes the second category, the constitutional challenge is far more difficult, since some "reasonable basis" for the state regulation can usually be shown.

The line between the valid and invalid is anything but bright. In *Skinner v. Oklahoma*,[40] for example, a statute permitting sterilization of certain habitual criminals was invalidated because it touched the fundamental interest of procreation and invidiously distinguished between various crimes, *e.g.*, larceny and embezzlement. But in *Kotch v. Board of River Port Pilot Commissioners*,[41] the state's right to deny pilots' licenses to qualified persons because they were not related by blood to existing pilots was upheld. So too in *Railway Express Agency v. New York*,[42] where the Court upheld a traffic regulation forbidding truck owners from selling advertising space on their trucks as a distracting hazard to other drivers but permitting them to advertise their own business in precisely that way. These all but invisible distinctions led my colleague Professor Robert H. Bork to observe recently, "[T]he differing results cannot be explained on any ground other than the Court's preferences for particular values."[43]

Be that as it may, the approach is easily adapted to the creation of a number of equal protection issues out of the problem of economic inequality. An important line of precedents, and the one with the oldest lineage, involves the rights of indigent defendants in state criminal proceedings. Under *Griffin v. Illinois*,[44] a state must provide a free transcript to those defendant-appellants who cannot afford one. In equal protection terms, the cases can be rationalized as involving a legal distinction between rich and poor touching on

---

[40] 316 U.S. 535 (1942).   [41] 330 U.S. 552 (1947).   [42] 336 U.S. 106 (1949).

[43] Bork, *Neutral Principles and Some First Amendment Problems*, 47 IND. L.J. 1, 12 (1971).

[44] 351 U.S. 12 (1956).

a fundamental matter, the interest in a fair trial and appeal. Since the state prosecuted the case and then failed to offer the means necessary to an effective appeal, it can be argued that a line has been drawn between the rich, who can provide their own means, and the poor, who cannot. Such decisions are obviously useful in seeking to undo other inequalities resulting from disparate economic circumstances, since, apart from initiating the prosecution, the only act of the state has been the failure to provide affirmative aid. Beyond that, this line of cases is important in that the relief they offer seems to be minimum protection—a transcript to the indigent— rather than equality—a transcript to all.

The second line of precedents involves voting rights, the most important decision being *Harper v. Virginia Board of Elections*,[45] which invalidated the poll tax. Mr. Justice Douglas's opinion is rather unclear both as to underlying judicial philosophy and the exact reasoning relied on to reach the result of the case. In one paragraph, he seems about to embrace the so-called Realist's view of a living, growing, changing, malleable Constitution; "we have never been confined to historic notions of equality. . . . Notions of what constitutes equal treatment for purpose of the Equal Protection Clause *do* change."[46] In the very next paragraph, however, he employs rhetoric smacking suspiciously of strict constructionism: "Our conclusion . . . is founded not on what we think governmental policy should be, but on what the Equal Protection Clause requires."[47] On the merits of the case, the opinion is not much better. The right to vote is a fundamental interest. The poll tax draws a line based on wealth. Such lines are "traditionally disfavored."[48] Wealth, moreover, is "not germane to one's ability to participate intelligently in the electoral process."[49] Therefore, a poll tax of $1.50 is unconstitutional. On the economic inequality issue alone, the *Harper* opinion defies overall critical analysis by the simple device of massive abandonment of the tools of the trade. In the words of Professor Cox, "[I]t expressly or impliedly repudiates every conventional guide to legal judgment."[50] *Harper* radically departs from the criminal procedure cases by commanding absolute

---

[45] 383 U.S. 663 (1966).

[46] *Id.* at 669.   [48] *Id.* at 668.

[47] *Id.* at 670.   [49] *Ibid.*

[50] Cox, *Constitutional Adjudication and the Promotion of Human Rights*, 80 HARV. L REV. 91, 95 (1966).

equality—no tax for all. By doing so, it employs a radically different approach to the problem of economic inequality and for no particular reason which finds expression in the opinion.

Some of the notions seemingly underlying *Griffin* and *Harper* have found their way into cases involving the constitutionality of state procedures governing civil proceedings. In *Boddie v. Connecticut*,[51] in an opinion by the late Justice Harlan, the Court held that a state may not insist upon payment of various court costs as a condition of instituting divorce proceedings in the face of a factual showing that the particular parties cannot pay them. Although the decision relied solely upon the Due Process Clause, resort to *Griffin* as a precedent was found necessary and much of the language has a familiar ring, *e.g.*, "no necessary connection between a litigant's assets and the seriousness of his motives in bringing suit."[52] And in *Lindsey v. Normet*,[53] the Court returned to an Equal Protection rationale in holding unconstitutional an Oregon requirement that a defendant tenant wanting to appeal an adverse judgment in an eviction action post twice the rental value of the premises from the initiation of the action until final judgment. The statute provided that if the judgment was affirmed, the landlord would receive twice the accrued rents without regard to actual damages. The Court, in an opinion by Mr. Justice White, held these provisions unconstitutional as to all tenant-appellants, not just those financially unable to post a bond, on the grounds that they discriminated between tenant-appellants and other kinds of appellants, between rich tenant-appellants and poor tenant-appellants, and, although the opinion is unclear on the point, between landlords and tenants.

The most important decision in this line of cases may be the invalidation of welfare residency requirements in *Shapiro v. Thompson*.[54] The ostensible rationale of the case—treating migrant indigents and resident indigents differently inhibits the exercise of the constitutional right of interstate travel—is certainly unsatisfactory. Under the Court's theory, it is not a "suspect" rich/poor classification under attack but a migrant-poor/resident-poor distinction. That distinction, however, touches upon the right to interstate travel in a way that may suggest more is at stake than residency

---

[51] 401 U.S. 371 (1971).   [53] 405 U.S. 56 (1972).

[52] *Id.* at 381.   [54] 394 U.S. 618 (1969).

requirements. For one thing, it seems to endanger any number of programs operated by state governments for state residents, *e.g.*, lower tuition in state schools, educational loan programs, etc. For another, the inhibition imposed on travel by residency requirements is a dollar sacrifice in public assistance benefits, precisely the same inhibition inherent in a system of differing state programs. Thus, when state A offers benefits of $20 a week and state B offers benefits of $100, travel from B to A is similarly inhibited by a sacrifice in public assistance benefits. *Shapiro* would seem to leave state B, moreover, with several alternatives other than abandonment of residency requirements. It might reduce all benefits to $15 (or does that also inhibit travel?). Or B might well offer benefits of only $20 to migrants from A, thus neutralizing the inhibition imposed by residency requirements.

One feels impelled to search for alternative rationales for *Shapiro*. One such is that the distinction is in fact not migrant-poor/resident-poor, but well-off-poor (or comparatively so)/not-so-well-off-poor. Because the means to "subsist" is a fundamental interest, it might be argued, the state cannot permit an individual to go without such means when others have them. Equal protection, therefore, compels a state to provide the means equal to a subsistence norm. Residency requirements are invalid because what the state presently provides residents is evidence of the minimum norm in that state. If that is indeed what *Shapiro* is all about, state B then must pay to migrants what it pays to residents and, carrying the underlying principle to its logical end, the adequacy of payments in all states is subject to constitutional scrutiny.

That such an idea lurks for some in *Shapiro* is reflected by a statement by Mr. Justice Marshall (who concurred in *Shapiro*) in dissenting from the Court's sustaining of maximum welfare grants in *Dandridge v. Williams*.[55] The ostensible classification at stake in that case was large-family-poor/small-family-poor, yet in arguing for stringent constitutional scrutiny of the setting of maximums on welfare grants, Justice Marshall emphasized that what was involved were not "interests that have more than enough power to protect themselves in the legislative halls" but "the literally vital interests of a powerless minority."[56] Because the classification ostensibly

---

[55] 397 U.S. 471 (1970). Brennan, J., the author of *Shapiro*, concurred in Marshall's dissent.

[56] *Id.* at 520.

under challenge—small family/large family—does not seem the product of overreaching by a powerful political majority, this remark strongly suggests that Justices Marshall and Brennan viewed the case differently and were less concerned over distinctions among the poor than between the poor and the rest of society. They might, for instance, view grants to small families as evidence of the subsistence norm and call for proportional increases for larger families.

The Marshall proposition was offered in dissent, however, because subsequent to *Shapiro,* the Court veered discernibly away from at-large intervention in the name of economic equality. In the case challenging maximum welfare grants, *Dandridge v. Williams,* Mr. Justice Stewart, writing for the majority, gave short shrift to the equal protection challenge. "In the area of economics and social welfare, a State does not violate the Equal Protection Clause merely because the classifications made by its laws are imperfect. If the classification has some 'reasonable basis,' it does not offend the Constitution."[57] The choice of that test over the "compelling state interest" standard was, of course, the kiss of death for the constitutional challenge. And, last Term, in *Lindsey v. Normet,*[58] the Court held that a tenant has no constitutional right to withhold rent pending litigation of alleged wrongdoing by his landlord. Finally, in the same Term, in *Schilb v. Kuebel,*[59] the Court upheld the Illinois bail statute against an equal protection challenge. It was argued in that case that because the state retained 1 percent of unsecured bail bonds for costs, the statute discriminated against those without the means to obtain secured bail bonds. The decision was inconclusive on the economic inequality issue because it relied on a number of different considerations, including the Court's view that the unsecured bond, 1 percent retention and all, would be more attractive to the wealthy than putting up extensive security.

Most significant, perhaps, is the decision in *James v. Valtierra,*[60] which upheld a California constitutional provision conditioning the construction of low-rent public housing projects upon approval by referendum in the particular municipality. In holding that the case was not governed by prior decisions invalidating similar requirements where racial issues, *e.g.,* fair housing ordinances, were involved,[61] the decision can be read to hold that poverty is not a "sus-

---

[57] *Id.* at 485.

[58] See note 53, *supra.*

[59] 404 U.S. 357 (1972).

[60] 402 U.S. 137 (1971).

[61] See note 31 *supra,* and accompanying text.

pect" classification like race. More than any other decision, therefore, *James* seems directly to reject equal protection as a path to the reduction of economic inequality.

C. THE FUTURE

A fair evaluation of both the views of the commentators and the existing case law would be that the law is well along the road toward substantive equal protection as a vehicle of income redistribution, although both as to the state action requirement and the substance of equal protection the Court has stepped back at critical times. Nevertheless, the penumbra of the Clause has expanded to the point that it is questionable whether it can be contained in the face of demands for more coherence in the body of law. So long as the Court continues to engage in the ad hoc process of recognizing "fundamental interests," the number of interests can be endlessly expanded through argument by analogy, which in turn depends almost entirely on the value preferences of individual Justices.

The principal constraint on doctrinal expansion is the continued viability of the state action requirement, for under present case law it would appear that some form of state action other than tolerance of private conduct must affect a fundamental interest before Fourteenth Amendment considerations will have an impact. Although this imposes a constraint on judicial intervention in the name of the reduction of economic inequality, government regulation is nevertheless so pervasive that the Court has plenty of room for further doctrinal expansion if it so chooses.

Thus, in *Serrano v. Priest*,[62] the California Supreme Court was able to move from *Brown* (education is a fundamental interest) and *Griffin* (no discrimination on basis of wealth) to the proposition that financing public education through local property taxes violates the Equal Protection Clause because it disadvantages persons in poorer school districts. As Professor Philip Kurland noted in a pre-*Serrano* article,[63] the logic of this argument in terms of established precedent is considerably stronger than many others which succeeded with the Warren Court. Indeed, if anything, the California Court shrank from the logic of precedent by failing to take the next step and to compel statewide equal per student expenditures on the basis of the reapportionment cases.

---

[62] 5 Cal.3d 584 (1971).

[63] Kurland, *Equal Educational Opportunity: The Limits of Constitutional Jurisprudence Undefined*, 35 U. CHI. L. REV. 583, 588 (1968).

The decisions in *Dandridge* and *James* (ignored by the *Serrano* Court) have made only cosmetic changes. For it is the very process of identification of "fundamental interests" that eliminates the constraint on doctrinal development, because that analysis calls upon the Justices to look solely to their own policy preferences for a constitutional standard. This uncontainability is well demonstrated by a recent decision that was publicized as driving yet another stake in the heart of the new equal protection. In *Lindsey v. Normet*,[64] the Court upheld that part of an Oregon statute which provides, absent security for rent, for a quick trial (two to six days after the complaint) in eviction proceedings and limits the triable issues in such actions to whether the rent was paid or the tenant had held over. Excluded from consideration were defenses such as the landlord's failure to repair and other claims such as back rent, although such matters can be the subject of independent actions. The Court's opinion contained the usual rhetoric stating that the "Constitution has not federalized the substantive law of landlord-tenant relations . . . and does not provide judicial remedies for every social and economic ill."[65]

On the other hand, the majority accepted the host of reasons offered against the validity of the double-bond provision: that it discriminated between tenant-appellants and other appellants under Oregon law, between well-off tenants who can afford the bond and poor tenants who cannot, and against tenants generally because it deters appeals and obviates the necessity of the landlord proving damages. The odd thing about the case is that all the reasons for striking down the double-bond provision are equally true of the provisions—quick trial, elimination of issues—upheld by the Court. They also discriminate between tenant-defendants and other defendants under Oregon law, against poor defendants who have a defense but no money for a bond, and against tenants generally because they compel an independent action to raise issues such as a failure to repair. The Oregon statute was an integrated procedure designed to enable landlords to litigate the issue of possession and to counter the routine tactic of delay by tenants in the face of eviction proceedings. Thus the quick trial, the simplification of issues and, because an appeal may cost a tenant with free legal services nothing and yet extend his possession of the premises, the double

---

[64] See note 53 *supra*, and accompanying text.

[65] 405 U.S. at 68, 74.

bond. Indeed, the immediate trial itself was upheld partly on the grounds that only simple factual issues are involved, yet that would seem plainly to suggest that only an infinitesimal number of cases would involve truly appealable issues, a point wholly ignored in the opinion's discussion of the invalidity of the appeal bond.

The variable can only be explained as a judicial preference for one kind of regulation of landlord-tenant relations over another. The rhetoric quoted above might well be amended in the following way: "The Constitution has not federalized *all* the substantive law of landlord-tenant relations . . . and does not provide judicial reme-·dies for every social and economic ill, only those which offend us to a particular degree."

This is by no means to say, however, that all the decisions discussed are wrong, for it may well be that grounds other than an economic inequality rationale are available to support them. Professor Robert H. Bork has suggested, for example, that the Court distinguish between inherent rights and rights derived from particular governmental processes.[66] The voting cases and the decisions in the field of criminal procedure are, in his view, better analyzed as creating rights in the individual in order to protect the integrity of constitutionally sanctioned processes than as inherent rights stemming from some ill-defined notion of fundamental rights or suspect classifications. *Harper* might thus be viewed as a Guarantee Clause decision involving "rights derived from the requirements of our form of government,"[67] while the criminal procedure decisions, such as *Griffin*, can be seen as a reflection of the needs of an adversary system of criminal justice, gleaned from the procedural overtones of Due Process and other Amendments having implications for criminal procedure. No claim is made that every precedent can be rationalized in those terms or that this way of thinking about them brings self-evident standards into focus. Nevertheless, it is a framework which poses the issues in a more meaningful way than whole cloth abstractions such as "fundamental interests," and which, as I shall argue, pulls the Court up short of an ill-advised assault on the distribution of income. Looking at *Harper* as a right-to-vote issue rather than a poverty decision, for example, illuminates the reason for invalidating the poll tax for everyone, not just those who can't afford $1.50. Similarly, if what is at stake in *Griffin* is insuring

---

[66] Bork, note 43 *supra*, at 17–19.   [67] *Id*. at 19.

that the adversary system of criminal justice operates at a certain level of efficiency, not the elimination of economic inequality, the minimum protection result seems understandable.

Nevertheless, the distinction between inherent and derived rights is of no help in rationalizing cases like *Shapiro* or some of the decisions involving civil procedure. *Boddie* perhaps can be legitimately viewed as involving the procedural overtones of the Due Process Clause, but the double rental bond upset in *Lindsey* seems very much to have been a substantive regulation of the landlord-tenant relationship designed to aid landlords to regain wrongfully withheld premises. As such, it is one more decision embodying an approach which invites further expansion.

II. A Skeptical View of Income Redistribution

As has been said, proponents of the reduction of economic inequality are modest in the claims they press by way of conventional legal argument. Unfortunately, they also spend precious little effort in an economic analysis of income redistribution. Professors Karst and Horowitz,[68] for example, could not be more candid about the fact that their argument rests almost entirely on their faith in the wisdom of the policies they urge, yet they curiously decline to discuss the merits of these policies in any detail.

The ability to avoid what seems a critical link in their chain of argument stems from two assumptions which, it should be said in their defense, are also found in much of the nonlegal literature calling for income redistribution and a restructuring of the economy along egalitarian lines. The first assumption is that there are discernible values of an egalitarian nature calling for the reduction of economic inequality. Thus, the suggestions in the legal literature that there are "fundamental interests" or "just wants" which society must fulfill finds a counterpart in nonlegal writings which assert that some jobs are too undesirable to hold or that there is some income line of transcendent importance below which exists "poverty."[69] The assumption that such values exist, however, is doubtful, for, as I shall argue, we live in a world of limited resources and infinite wants, and issues concerning the allocation of those resources are susceptible only of "least worst" solutions.[70]

---

[68] See note 5 *supra*, and accompanying text.

[69] See generally Piven & Cloward, Regulating the Poor (1971).

[70] Economics jargon is "more worse" than legal jargon.

The second assumption stems from the confluence of two great themes of contemporary American liberalism, the pursuit of equality and the reduction of poverty. Civil rights legislation, the women's movement, proposals for revamping the educational system, and the like, all find one source of their appeal in the widespread desire to make equality a governing principle of our society. That the reduction of poverty should appear as a major goal of those actively advocating equality seems to have been as natural as the operation of the law of gravity, for keepers of the liberal faith rarely view the reduction of income inequality and the elimination of poverty as distinct, much less inconsistent, goals. To them inequality of income is the cause, and its elimination the cure, of poverty. This assumption is also very doubtful, however, for the perceived inequality is in large part the result of the operation of a price system which performs important functions in allocating resources to productive uses in producing wealth for all. If the reduction of inequality were to inhibit the performance of these functions, the result might well be to affect the total wealth of the society adversely and to increase poverty in an absolute sense.

What follows is a statement of my misgivings about the utility of egalitarian values in analyzing the poverty issue and my fears as to the implications of a coerced redistribution for the economic well-being of the society and the freedom of its citizens. Although the statement is argumentative, I would be content if the issues it raises merely gained recognition as being relevant. The legal profession badly misunderstands how unformulated the theoretical case for redistribution is and the inadequacy of the empirical support on which it rests. As a result, much of the discussion, in both the academic journals and judicial reports, has been misdirected, if not wholly beside the point.

A. THE CASE FOR TOTAL EQUALITY OF INCOME[71]

Analysis must begin with a discussion of the case for the absolutely equal distribution of income,[72] even though no one in the

---

[71] I do not discuss the distribution of wealth because wealth is merely the capitalization of the stream of income and the argument made here applies equally to it. An accurate discussion of the wealth issue would be more difficult, because of the need to take human capital into account.

[72] See, e.g., BLUM & KALVEN, THE UNEASY CASE FOR PROGRESSIVE TAXATION (1952); DE JOUVENEL, THE ETHICS OF REDISTRIBUTION (1951); LERNER, THE ECONOMICS OF CONTROL (1944); ROBBINS, NATURE AND SIGNIFICANCE OF ECONOMIC SCIENCE (1935).

"real world"—apart from those who hold the view that every inequality is the result of an unjust exploitation—seems seriously at-
tracted to such a radical restructuring. Nevertheless, the call "equal
X for all" does crop up frequently in sloganeering, and judicial
decisions such as *Harper* and *Lindsey* (on the economic inequality
rationale at least) seem moved by a similar spirit. Much of the distaste for inequality, moreover, seems based on assumptions about
the validity of the claims made for absolute equality.

The case for equality goes as follows. At dawn on the D day of
the Genesis, there is a fixed stock of goods to be divided among a
fixed number of individuals. Distribution must occur at once and
the way in which the goods are distributed can thus have no effect
on the size of present or future stockpiles. Individuals do not have
identical preferences for the goods involved. Some think five
widgets are as satisfying as one gadget. Others get the same satisfaction from ten gadgets as from one widget. They also get very
different satisfaction from goods which are not in the stockpile.
Some crave material accumulation while others enjoy long periods
of silent contemplation. Only one thing do they have in common:
each additional unit of any particular thing—a material good or
contemplation—is of less utility to them than the preceding unit of
that same thing. Their behavior, in short, is governed by the law
of diminishing marginal utility.

Because the utility of a good diminishes as the quantity possessed
increases, total satisfaction in the society might seem to be maxi-
mized by an equal distribution, since the value of an additional unit
to a man who has only a few exceeds the loss of one unit to one
who has many. The difficulty is that while each individual is governed by the law of diminishing marginal utility, we cannot assume
that the utility of a specified number of goods to each individual
is the same. The man with many widgets may place so much more
value on them than the man with only a few that a move of only
one unit toward equality would in fact reduce total satisfaction.

There are many ways around this problem. First, we might assume that the utility of the good to all individuals is roughly similar.
Although such an assumption may be no more heroic than the
D day–fixed stockpile assumptions—also unreal but critical to the
argument—it seems rather contrary to what we know about people's tastes. In any event, it can be shown that, given our lack of
knowledge about the utility functions of particular individuals (ex-

cept that they diminish at the margins), equal distribution is less worse than a random distribution. (The argument assumes that unequal distributions based on personal characteristics favor those in power or that any criteria other than randomness and equality are wrong.) In a random distribution, it may be assumed that roughly half the deviations from equality would increase total satisfaction by giving those with higher utility functions a larger share of the distribution, while roughly half would decrease satisfaction by overendowing those with less capacity for enjoying the things distributed. It can be shown, however, that the total of the losses entailed in random mistakes of the latter kind will exceed the gains brought about by the former.[73] That being the case, an equal distribution may be said to be less favorable than its alternative, a random distribution.

This formulation of the case for equality—and I believe it the best available—is sound but so narrow as to be quite inapplicable to any actual society. On D day, there is no knowledge as to the preferences of individuals for and between goods in the fixed stockpile and the distribution cannot affect the quantum of goods available. We are always at $D + n$, however, and at that time our information is considerably better, sufficiently so that a satisfaction-maximizing alternative to equal or random distributions appears. Because individuals in the society have very different utility functions, the trading of goods (with or without chits called money, although very inefficient trading in the latter case) will take place. Widgets and gadgets will be traded (bought and sold), and, to the extent that society imposes time-consuming obligations (if we assume a fixed stockpile, it may be a ritualistic task such as showing a flag), those who find satisfaction in extensive contemplation will offer some of their goods (money) in exchange for one of their acquisitive fellow's performing the function, thus increasing the time available for contemplation.

When we demand "equal widgets—or food or clothing or contemplation—for all," we are saying that no trading is to be permitted, for by definition trading produces a condition of inequality. Some people will have more widgets, some more gadgets, some a lot of time for contemplation. Equality entails uniformity and that can be attained only at the cost of a sacrifice of the individual benefits from trading.

---

[73] The detail of the proof can be found in LERNER, note 72 *supra*, at 30 *et seq.*

If such exchanges are to be permitted, however, there is no reason not to permit trading for new goods and services. Parties may find it to their advantage to hire someone to manufacture new and better widgets and gadgets or to engage a broker to seek out the best deals. The contemplative, moreover, will exchange the opportunity to engage in this "profitable" trading for the leisure which gives them satisfaction. In the absence of trading for the manufacture of new goods, the stockpile will be depleted, unless a dominant power coerces individuals to make replacements.

None of this trading can take place, however, without producing further conditions of inequality. Once there is trading of goods (money) for the performance of productive functions, some people will be richer than others, some will be poorer. The very act of trading suggests, however, that even the poorest are better off with the existence of money than in its absence; otherwise they would not trade. Equality will be attainable only by prohibiting that trading and by sacrificing tomorrow's stockpile, unless a dominant power (including, to be sure, an ethos) coerces its manufacture. Equality of money income, for example, merely destroys money's usefulness as a medium of exchange. Producers would barter rather than sell, since any money they earn is irrelevant to their share in the stockpile. That of course would increase transaction costs enormously and correspondingly reduce production (trading).

If equality is really the goal, of course, barter would also have to be prohibited. Unless totalitarian control were then turned to, rather an inequality itself, primitive, but equal, living conditions, if not wholesale starvation, would be the result.

It should be emphasized that the collapse of the case for equality at $D + n$ is not simply the result of weighing the various gains and losses in total satisfaction against the norms of equality. The argument for equality did not establish the intrinsic worth of that value. Rather, it demonstrated that in the presence of two conditions—ignorance of the utility functions of individuals and a fixed stockpile of goods—equality of distribution was more likely to produce a greater total satisfaction than a random distribution. Since no one to my knowledge has ever suggested a random distribution anyway, opting for equality is surely a classic "least worst" solution justified only by the peculiar conditions surrounding its choice. Those conditions are eliminated at $D + 1$, however, for trading by its nature produces information about individual utility functions and the diminishing of the stockpile creates a need for further production.

At D + *n*, one can opt for equality only by pursuing two quite heroic routes. The first is to argue that the trading leads to net losses in total satisfaction because of market imperfections or the like. Those who view every economic inequality as evidence of exploitation seem to take that view, however hallucinatory it may be. The other route is to establish equality as such a transcendent goal that the sacrifices in material well-being, which a flat prohibition on trading entails, are worth enduring. The argument, in short, is that the elimination of inequalities is worth making everyone, including the poorest, worse off. For my part, I do not believe either route has been successfully traversed.

It would be well to emphasize that this discussion concerns only the case for absolute equality of income and that market imperfections, externalities or paternalistic goals other than equality (*e.g.*, protection of incompetents) may still be looked to justify more limited redistributions. Nevertheless, it demonstrates that equality is by no means a value of established intrinsic worth in the resolution of economic issues. To some extent, moreover, even limited redistributions may seriously interfere with productive "trading" and the gains anticipated must be weighed against the costs of that interference. A number of complex problems also arise when the redistribution takes the form of the provision of goods and services (in kind) to the poor rather than the transfer of cash, problems which ought to be dealt with before turning to the more general issue of the impact of a redistribution of income on the functions performed by a price system.

B. REDISTRIBUTION OF INCOME THROUGH THE PROVISION OF
   GOODS AND SERVICES TO THE POOR

1. *Professor Michelman and "just wants."* If economic inequality is to be reduced by providing the poor with certain goods and services—legal services, education, nutrition, housing, etc.—the threshold task would seem to be the establishment of standards by which it can be determined which things are to be provided in what quantities to which people without incurring costs that outweigh the contemplated benefits. Standards seem necessary no matter which agency of government undertakes to direct the distribution, although, as I shall argue, they seem an imperative if constitutional adjudication is to be the primary mechanism by which it is brought about. Not only do they provide direction and coherence to the

distribution, but they also serve to justify the undertaking as something more than a narrow interest group program. If there are no discernible standards other than the subjective judgment of those with political power, it can hardly be contended that this method of income redistribution is an ethical or moral imperative or that, at least in the absence of conventional legal criteria, it is constitutionally required. Indeed, one might better argue that it is the existence of such standards, and their discernment, which leads to the creation of the constitutional duty, rather than the other way around. The Michelman analysis is thus important because he stands alone among those who advocate use of the Equal Protection Clause to reduce economic inequality, in having undertaken this essential task. A critical examination of that analysis will serve to expose the underlying difficulties.[74]

There are a number of criticisms which can be leveled at the Rawlesian aspects of the Michelman analysis, which are beyond the scope of this article. For the issue addressed here is the extent to which the concept of "just wants" can be used to particularize government's obligation to provide certain goods and services to the poor. The usefulness of the Michelman analysis in that respect, however, is obscured by an initial ambiguity.

It is unclear whether the determination of "just wants" proceeds by way of unearthing a societal consensus or by the application of the idiosyncratic notions of the governmental officials involved. If the concept has merit, it would seem that a consensus on society's part as to its content must exist. Otherwise, it would be misleading to assert that "justice requires" the fulfillment of a want when the fact is only that certain individuals holding official positions require it. Nor can one, in the absence of a consensus, usefully speak of the involuntary unfulfillment of a "just want" because of a lack of wealth. Otherwise, large numbers of the better-off might legitimately look to government for the fulfillment of "just wants" because they had spent their income on things they quite honestly valued more while a number of poorer persons who held the same view of "just wants" as the officials—and disposed of their income accordingly—would receive nothing. The concept must, therefore, reflect an existing societal consensus, both to justify attributing to it the role of a requirement of "justice" and to begin to tie it in some way to an intelligible concept of poverty.

---

[74] See text *supra*, at notes 17 *et seq.*

The usefulness of the "just wants" concept also depends heavily upon the amount of information available. "Justice" cannot, for example, require government to provide for certain wants in the absence of a great deal of information about the wealth of the society involved. All "just wants" make claims on the resources of society, claims which, in any sensible economic terms, must be viewed as costs. The permissible range of costs, however, is subject to finite limits. They cannot exceed the resources of the society and, putting aside for the moment the incentive problem raised by any redistribution, they cannot, by definition, be so great as to leave the wealthier members of society worse off than the recipients of the governmental largess. Furthermore, because it is conceded there are incentive problems and because there is not a valid case for perfect equality of justice, the maximum costs must be less than would bring about an equal distribution of income.

Information is also necessary to establish the minimum costs of the fulfillment of "just wants." The concept would hardly be worthy of exposition in the *Harvard Law Review* if it were tied to the possibilities of income redistribution within the poorest society on the planet, for the goods and services involved would be so meager as to be inconsequential in a society such as the United States. Presumably, therefore, the wealthier the society, the more abundant its concept of "just wants." The minimum costs to be borne must also increase as the wealth of a particular society increases, and a considerable amount of information about the wealth of the society is necessary for that additional reason.

How or at what rate these costs are to increase is not explicitly faced by the Michelman analysis, although his argument by its very terms seems to provide the answer. Inequalities may be tolerated, we are told, only so long as they are necessary to guarantee a better position for those occupying the worst position in the society. Redistribution, therefore, would seem to be called for until it brought about incentive effects which made everyone, including the worst off, poorer. Apart from the problem of the feasibility of such a test, it has the merit of tying the concept of "just wants" to the wealth of the society and of relating it to poverty or relative deprivation. Unfortunately, it also generates serious doubts as to its meaningfulness.

Once it is recognized that the search for "just wants" begins, not with the "needs" of the poor, but with the possibilities of income redistribution without negative incentive effects, a number of disquieting conclusions follow. First, if there is a consensus as to "just wants," there is no need to provide them in kind rather than in cash to the poor. The existence of the consensus gives us assurance that cash will be expended on the very things government would provide, and most would probably agree that efficiency would be furthered by a direct distribution of money. So viewed, the Equal Protection Clause, instead of calling for the identification of fundamental interests" which must be protected, seems to dictate the establishment of some kind of negative income tax.

Consider for example the problem of providing legal services to the poor. If there is a consensus that part of the redistributed income should go toward the purchase of legal counsel, we can expect that an appropriate percentage of a cash distribution will be put to that use. To be sure, not all recipients will need legal counsel at a particular time, but they will nevertheless purchase insurance against that risk, and a "rule" guaranteeing the right to counsel regardless of one's means can be disposed of as superfluous. Disagreement with this conclusion must rest on reasons which themselves exclude legal counsel as a "just want." First, there may be no such consensus and the poor will in fact frequently choose not to insure against the risk of needing counsel. Cash is thus not a substitute for actual legal services. And, second, the cost of providing legal counsel to the poor cannot be met out of the funds available without either sacrificing "just wants" of a higher order or causing impermissible incentive effects.[75] In either or both cases, "justice" cannot be said to "require" counsel as the fulfillment of a "just want," and, moreover, the very process of the judicial identification of fundamental interests to be protected against impecuniousness seems, in terms of "just wants" analysis, either superfluous—cash will achieve the same result—or wrong, because of absence of consensus or negative incentive effects.

Once one determines that the quest for "just wants" begins, not with the needs of the poor, but with a quantifiable amount of income to be redistributed, yet another conclusion—this one fatal to

---

[75] The cost of such insurance would, of course, be enormous because of the "moral hazard." Since the insured has substantial control over the frequency of his involvement in litigation, the very existence of insurance greatly enhances the probabilities that litigation will occur. As the text will develop, the moral hazard also exists when free legal services are made available to the poor.

the argument—follows: There is in fact no consensus among either the poor or the better-off as to what goods and services should be purchased with that sum; there are in short no "just wants." To be sure, a pool might well determine that virtually everyone "wants" adequate housing, nutrition, legal counsel, law and order, quality education, and so on, just as it is the case that those who presently receive benefits from the government "want" them. The relevant inquiry has not been made, however; namely, are the designated goods valued more by the recipients than all other items of an identical or lesser cost? The answer seems to be, "plainly not." If, for example, cash was distributed to the poor so that each had exactly the amount necessary to purchase the designated goods, it seems extremely unlikely that expenditures would follow a uniform pattern, for the tastes of poor consumers no less than rich consumers are likely to vary widely. Of course, if government distributes goods and services, everyone "wants" them because that choice is between something and nothing. Once cash is distributed, however, a very different choice is presented and diversity is to be expected.[76] So long as income redistribution is to take the form of goods and services rather than cash, therefore, it must be recognized that whatever standards are employed to determine the goods and services to be distributed must be found in the will of those commanding the distribution and not in the tastes of the recipients or in a consensus of society.

2. *Designating minimum needs and identifying the poor.* If economic inequality is to be reduced through the provision of goods and services to the poor, there must be an official determination at the threshold of what the poor "need." This task is easier when the redistribution is designed to remedy market failure or to provide for a designated incompetent group. Similarly, when a noneconomic goal, such as the preservation of an efficientt adversary process, is at stake, the range of choice is narrowed. In these cases, the nature of the good or service is frequently obvious, and the principal inquiry is focused on the cost/benefit ratio. When the reduction of economic inequality is the goal, on the other hand, both the nature of the goods and services to be provided and the cost/benefit ratio are at issue.

A determination of the minimum "needs" of the poor must begin

---

[76] The poor as a whole in fact spend their income on as wide a range of goods and services as the better-off. STIGLER, THE THEORY OF PRICE (1946).

with the reason why in kind distributions are chosen over cash payments. This conviction is quite the opposite of a belief in a societal
consensus, for it holds that the poor will not, in fact, spend cash on
the items they really "need" and that, therefore, these must be provided in kind if the poor are to have them.[77] People holding this
conviction believe that poverty is a cultural condition which cannot
be remedied by money alone and that cash payments are inadequate
to help the poor become self-supporting.

This insight does not, however, establish guidelines as to the
poor's minimum needs. We live in a society in which life styles
differ among generations, racial and ethnic groups, and geographical
areas. What is "good" for the poor is simply not a matter on which
there is general agreement, though this is often obscured by the
correct but misleading observation that the poor "want" what is
offered. At bottom is the fact that the evil for which a cure is being
sought is not absolute but relative deprivation, and there is simply
no finite list of goods and services which can provide the cure. What
seems called for is the imposition of the cultural beliefs of the officials mandating the distribution, not a shocking proposition to one
whose legal training coexisted with the Warren Court, but surely
one which casts the undertaking in a different moral light.

Thus, although income redistribution in the form of the provision
of goods and services parades as an egalitarian undertaking, it has
a distinctive elitist cast—noblesse oblige if you will—because it necessarily entails regulating the life style of the poor. Again, the reason the goods and services route is chosen is precisely the belief
that the values of the poor are largely incorrect and that cash would
not be expended on their "real" needs. It assumes, in short, that the
poor lack judgment as well as income. It assumes also that the governmental organ determining the needs of the poor has proper
judgment.

It is easy to overlook this aspect of in kind redistributions because it is quite true that the poor "want" the goods and services
distributed by government and that these items are not in any sense
forced upon them. Nevertheless, by hypothesis, the poor do not
place a value on these goods and services equal to their cost in resources expended and would, if permitted, trade them for items

---

[77] See, *e.g.*, Aaron & von Furstenberg, *The Inefficiency of Transfers in Kind: The Case of
Housing Assistance*, 9 WESTERN ECON. J. 184 (1971).

which they—the poor—believe to be more desirable. Otherwise cash payments would suffice.

Those who advocate in kind redistribution minimize the intrusion on the life style of the poor in their conviction that goods and services received from the government do not in reality foreclose the poor from obtaining items they desire. The fact that the government provides goods on which the poor place a value less than the cost to society in resources expended does not, they seem to think, compel the poor to forgo items which they value more. It would seem, however, that this is not necessarily the case. To decree that the poor must have access to a particular good or service will necessarily make claims on society's resources and may divert resources from other employment. This may quite plausibly make the poor's access to other and more valued goods and services more difficult by making the resources entailed in their employment more scarce. If that is the case, in kind distributions are indistinguishable from direct coercion of the poor in the hope of imposing a life style upon them.

Having decreed what goods and services are to be provided, the officials involved must then determine the point at which redistributions entail incentive effects. Redistributions beyond that point (by the Michelman definition used here) will leave everyone, including the poor, worse off and can be justified, if at all, only by the argument for equality. Only after identifying the amount available for redistribution, therefore, can the best attainable mix of those goods and services which the poor "need" be determined.

The final threshold task is to insure that those who can in fact afford to provide themselves with the designated "mix" do not look to government to do it for them, some way in short to identify the poor in an official sense. No matter how tempting it may be to declare that everyone ought to have his "needs" fulfilled without regard to "effort, thrift, or foresight," only a society bent on self-destruction or a radical change of economic and political structure would create incentives for individuals or families deliberately to avoid private provision of those items which the society itself has officially declared to be minimum needs. Yet unless government provision of such items is denied to those who earn income sufficient to provide them on their own, just such incentives will be created. On the other hand, any such line seems, by its very nature, likely to undermine the moral authority of the very concept of minimum needs or to create irresistible pressures in the direction of equality regardless of incentive effects.

The volume demanded of any good or service varies with its price. At high prices, less is purchased than at low prices. When government makes a good or service available at zero or near zero price to a portion of society, that portion will tend to purchase more of the good than if they had to pay a market price, even if they had sufficient cash to cover the cost. (Remember again that the reason for providing the good or service is that a cash distribution will go to other things.) What this means is that the poor are likely, under an effective in kind distribution scheme, to have some or many of the designated minimum needs fulfilled to a greater degree than those who can afford them but choose to use their money in a different fashion. Once the government draws the line at ability to pay—and if it doesn't draw it there, the problems will be worse, not better—it leaves the provision of minimum needs to individual choice, and one can anticipate that some will choose to forgo fulfillment of the need for other gratifications. In the case of some goods or services, the number who go without can be quite large.

Consider the provision of legal services to the poor. Where a zero price exists for those who cannot afford such services, the recipients never balance the potential gain of contemplated litigation against the cost, for, to them, there is no cost. Those who can afford to purchase legal services, however, must make such a judgment and, depending on the stakes, will often decide the game is not worth the candle. I strongly doubt that many persons paying a lawyer find it worthwhile to indulge in prolonged but hopeless resistance to eviction proceedings or in doomed petitions for rehearings over small stakes, while I also suspect that just such proceedings are often routinely undertaken on behalf of the beneficiaries of free legal services.

Providing minimum needs to the poor, therefore, may in short create a new inequality: the better-off forgoing items received free by those designated as poor. The fact that some do without fulfillment of their officially established minimum needs must cast doubt on the wisdom of providing such needs to the designated poor in the hope of reducing economic inequality, since new inequalities which seem no more justifiable are thereby created. One can seek to avoid this attack by arguing that the provision of legal services or what have you be extended so that the new inequality is eliminated. That, however, creates incentives for those who could and would purchase legal services to avoid doing so and in effect abandons the minimum needs rationale for that of equality.

Neither the designation of the poor nor the cataloguing of their minimum needs are thus self-evident tasks, even for those guided by an optimal quantity of righteous indignation. Both tasks call for threshold judgments which are derived almost entirely from the subjective, cultural biases of officialdom. They are, moreover, arbitrary in the sense that many items included in the list of minimum needs will be relatively indistinguishable from many which are excluded and many persons designated as officially poor will in terms of worldly assets seem little different from those left to make do on their own. Providing minimum needs to one portion of the community, moreover, may quite plausibly entail the creation of new inequalities which themselves seem no more tolerable than those government undertook to eliminate. At bottom is the fact that reducing economic inequality by providing minimum needs (where other goals are at stake, of course, other considerations apply) is not based on a coherent underlying theory. Because the minimum needs enterprise abandons equality and circumvents the tastes of the poor, it rests on nothing but highly subjective judgments as to relative deprivation.

3. *In kind redistributions: costs and benefits.* Even if in kind redistributions for the purpose of reducing economic inequality were based on a coherent theory, one might still question the ultimate value to society of such a program, for it is quite plausible that the costs far exceed the benefits.

Let us say initially that the costs to society are that amount of taxes the better off pay to support the redistribution ($\$V_t$) and the benefit is the value received by the poor as the poor perceive it ($\$V_r$). Even if there are no transfer costs and the poor receive goods and services in a market value equal to $\$V_t$, $\$V_t$ *must always exceed* $\$V_r$. To reiterate, the principal reason for resorting to in kind rather than in cash distributions is that the poor will expend cash on a mix of goods and services which in the eyes of the representatives of society do not fulfill their minimum needs. $\$V_r/\$V_t$, therefore, is always less than 1. But $\$V_r/\$V_t$ is not all that determines the cost/benefit ratio of in kind distributions. In fact, goods and services of a market value equal to $\$V_t$ cannot be transferred directly to the poor, for there always are substantial transfer costs (TC). These

include establishment of a bureaucracy to procure and distribute
the goods and services as well as to police their use. Also allocable
to the redistribution (particularly when the Constitution is resorted
to) is the cost of the litigation needed to adjudicate individual claims
to goods and services. These costs include the time expended by the
court bureaucracy as well as those representing the litigants and the
litigants themselves.

The $\$V_t$, therefore, can never be transferred directly to the poor
but will be reduced in absolute terms by the size of the TC. Therefore, not only do the poor place a lower dollar value on the goods
and services they receive than does the market, but that dollar value
is always less in absolute terms than that paid by the better-off in
taxes. Our numerator will reflect this fact if we change it to $\$V -$
TC_r.

The denominator also does not reflect the true cost of redistribution to the better-off, for the amount they pay in taxes is only
part of the cost to them. Providing goods and services to the poor
requires the expenditure of resources which might otherwise be put
to other uses. (Being saved for future employment is an economic
use.) The increased demand for these resources will tend to increase
their price, thus forcing those who are better off to pay more for the
services they purchase. Thus, a program to provide housing will increase the demand for lumber, concrete, carpenters, etc., and raise
the price for competing claims on their services. The denominator
should thus reflect a possible increase in the costs of various goods
and services to the better off by reading $\$V_t + IP$.

If, then, the relevant cost/benefit ratio is the ratio of the benefits
received by the poor (in their eyes) to the cost to the better-off,
$\$V - TC_r/\$V_t + IP$, that ratio is not only always less than 1 but
considerably below it, perhaps 0.5, or, in extreme cases, 0.05. One
must be cautious in assessing the impact this gap between taxes and
perceived benefits to the poor may have on a society's total satisfaction, for it will surely vary from society to society. Nevertheless, to
say that total satisfaction can in fact be decreased by in kind redistribution may drastically understate the result in some societies. If
the gap is large enough, everyone—better-off and poor—will feel
cheated, and dangerous antagonisms between groups may be created. To some extent, this may be the case in the United States
today. One must also be cautious in making generalizations about
the divisions which afflict American society, but in the midst of a

wide and expensive range of programs providing goods and services to the poor we hear in strident terms how many "middle Americans" feel they are too heavily taxed and how many of the poor believe they are receiving too little. One may well query whether substantial in kind distributions are not an extremely risky method of income redistribution in a society rent by those particular divisions and antagonisms.

Some will challenge this analysis on the grounds that the definition of the benefits received is too narrow in that it assumes no increase in satisfaction among the better-off at seeing their less fortunate brethren receive a larger share of the economy's bounty. In responding to the counter point that confiscatory tax measures seem rather inappropriate vehicles for permitting taxpayers to indulge themselves in the pleasures of philanthropy, holders of this conviction resort to a classic "free rider" argument. Poverty, they say, is not a matter of individual deprivation but a widespread societal condition calling for wholesale remedies. Such remedies are beyond the power of any single individual, no matter how wealthy and charitable, and are attainable only by the concerted action of all the better-off. Voluntary concerted action is difficult to generate, however, since any one contribution is by itself meaningless and individuals will withhold their donation in the absence of firm assurance that others will contribute in the amounts necessary. The better-off, therefore, although willing and anxious to do their bit, are checkmated by the mutual fear that each will withhold his contribution. Therefore, the confiscatory tax is necessary to the success of the philanthropic venture.

This is an argument neither to be scorned nor embraced. There can be no question that many well-to-do persons do get pleasure at helping their fellow man. How many get how much pleasure, however, is not easily determined, if determinable at all. The answer will, moreover, vary with the size of the gap between taxes and perceived benefits. Donor willingness to give one dollar so that the poor get a value (to them) of eighty-five cents is likely to be greater than when one dollar results in fifteen cents of benefit. As the gap widens, one would expect more and more of the better-off to decide that the charity is not worth the cost. Donor pleasure, therefore, is no automatic answer to the analysis above, since it too depends upon the size of the gap.

One may also query why those whose profession it is to seek votes behave unanimously as though the better-off are predominantly against substantial income redistribution. More pertinent to this article is the further query why, if the well-to-do, or relatively so, are anxious to make the sacrifices necessary to such a redistribution, is it necessary to turn to the Court to compel it? Surely the democratic branches of government would not fail to respond to a measure strongly favored by the poor as well as the better-off and surely it is not the active opposition of the potential recipients of governmental gratuities which makes it necessary to resort to the judicial branch. Unless virtually all informed opinion on political attitudes in the United States is absolutely wrong, it is simply not the case that the better-off members of the society are predominantly in favor of substantially increasing the financial burdens on themselves for the purpose of redistributing wealth.

The belief that in kind redistribution of income will increase total satisfaction in the society thus rests on an extremely shaky foundation, and this is so quite apart from the probability of incentive effects. That probability, however, is quite high, particularly where those whose incomes are taxed are concerned. To have a substantial effect at the receiving end, enormous expenditures are required, because in kind redistributions have high bureaucratic costs and are viewed by the poor as being worth less than their actual costs. It would seem, therefore, that such distributions should not be undertaken unless the anticipated benefits are also great. In terms of the goal of the reduction of economic inequality, however, these benefits seem rather meager in comparison with cash payments, particularly since the decision as to which goods and services are to be distributed or who is to receive them is little more than the subjective judgment of those in power. Where other goals are sought, such as maintaining the viability of the adversary system of justice or protecting a group from their own incompetency, e.g., children, different considerations come into play and other benefits are to be weighed against the costs. Those other goals, however, must be viewed on their own merits and are, except for occasional mention to remind the reader that there are alternative rationales for various programs, beyond the scope of this article.

C. REDISTRIBUTING INCOME: THE COSTS

Discussions of the redistribution of income commonly treat the problem as one of periodically taking the money from group A and giving it to group B, A becoming poorer by the amount taken, B becoming richer by an identical sum.[78] Although provision is made for individuals to move from A to B to A, it seems to be assumed that total income will remain unchanged over time and that all that is involved is a series of transfers which have no effect on the economic system other than to make A poorer and B richer. These assumptions are almost surely wrong. In fact, such transfers must have side or secondary effects to be weighed in evaluating the desirability of income redistribution.

There is no reason to believe that many of the burdens of individual taxation cannot be in part "passed on" to other groups in the economy, such as consumers or complementary factors of production. If, for example, we posit that there are highly paid occupations known as "coordinators of production," one result of a highly progressive tax might be that only higher salaries would attract a sufficient number of talented persons into these positions. The extra cost might then be "passed on" to those who purchase the product or, since a relative increase in the cost of one factor will tend to decrease the price of complementary factors, result in a wage decrease to production workers. I do not pretend to predict precisely what result will occur other than to say the assumption that the burden will fall only on the higher paid is simply unfounded. A redistribution will indeed take place but the result may be to take income from C, possibly an even poorer group, and thus to create more inequality rather than less.

The possibilities of income redistribution are also limited by the ability of employers and employees to make arrangements which for income substitute in kind rewards which are difficult to isolate and tax, for example, fancy offices, French chefs to provide lunches, more pleasant surroundings, eased workloads, and so on. There are a myriad of such devices which serve the reward function (inefficiently except as tax avoidance devices) but are exceedingly difficult to tax and thus are not available for redistribution. Because wages can go "underground," the estimates as to the amounts available for redistribution are thus easily overestimated in advance of the fact.

The most important doubt about the wisdom of substantial income redistributions stems from the question of how the functions

---

[78] See GREEN, NEGATIVE TAXES AND THE POVERTY PROGRAM 15–33 (1967).

of a price or wage system in labor markets are to be performed if these systems are modified so as to produce more equality. Although this is commonly referred to in discussions of income redistribution as the incentive issue, it must be made clear at the outset that the function of a price or wage system is to do more than insure that sweat forms on brows. Even if the assertions of some advocates of income redistribution that there is no long-run trade-off between income and leisure are true—and those seem almost flagrantly unrealistic—they by no means account for all the functions performed by a wage system. In labor markets the wage system allocates labor to productive kinds of employment and to productive geographic areas, as well as helping to govern the trade-off between leisure and income. It induces people to enter the most valued occupations in the most valued industries and to move to those geographical areas in which their labor is most productive.

Productivity depends on a mechanism by which the amount of effort expended by individuals, the kind of work they do and the areas in which they do it, is determined. If, for example, society decides that housing is more important than hula hoops, there must be a way to attract people from the hula hoop industry to the construction industry. Similarly, if a particular area exhausts its natural resources, it is essential to have a mechanism to give people an incentive to move to areas where their effort would be more productive. The performance of these functions is critical to any economy, for unless they are performed in a relatively efficient fashion, the elimination of poverty is simply not possible.[79]

This is elementary economic analysis, but analysis central to the issue. The alternatives to a wage system are custom or governmental control of job allocation.[80] Tribal custom seems rather unrealistic in a nation of over two hundred million heterogeneous persons. Governmental control, on the other hand, seems both inefficient, given the number of individual job decisions which must be made, and a threat to personal freedom. A regime that controls the job opportunities of individuals has all the power necessary to totalitarian political control.[81] And, for all that, history rather plainly

---

[79] Aid to a "depressed" area may well have the impact of prolonging the depression by creating a nonproductive dependence upon it. DRUCKER, THE AGE OF DISCONTINUITY 117–18 (1969).

[80] GROSSMAN, ECONOMIC SYSTEMS 13–15 (1967).

[81] See FRIEDMAN, CAPITALISM AND FREEDOM 7–21 (1962).

demonstrates that government control is no guarantee even of relative equality. A wage system, on the other hand, seems more efficient and less coercive.

Proponents of redistribution rarely discuss what will perform the allocative function in labor markets if the price system is tampered with, although the issue is at the heart of whether our goal is equality or making the poor better off in an absolute sense. If the goal is to better poor people in an absolute sense, every indicator we have demonstrates that increasing economic growth and productivity are the quickest route.[82] I take it to be a fact that the American economic system has been more successful than any other system in bettering its poor people. I also take it to be a fact that there is no example of a developed society equalizing income and relieving poverty at the same time. By any relevant standard, therefore, the American economic system has been a major success in the elimination of poverty.[83] Thus it is that the *New York Times* reports that this country faces an enormous problem of illegal immigration—perhaps two thousand people per day—caused precisely because the economic opportunities in this country are so much greater than in other countries.[84] Indeed, to the extent that those who vigorously advocate income redistribution rest their case on moral grounds, it would seem they are hard pressed not to call for redistribution on an international scale, which would have the effect of compelling what we call the poor in the United States to give up part of their income.[85]

The point is that a good case can be made for the proposition that the economic improvement of people in an absolute sense requires inequality of income and that the goals of equalizing income and reducing poverty are simply inconsistent. I suspect that a historical study of times of prosperity and times of recession or depression would find that income was far more equal when the level of economic activity was low than when it was high. It may well be that

---

[82] BATCHELDER, THE ECONOMICS OF POVERTY 90 (1966); Tobin, *On Improving the Economic Status of the Negro*, 94 PROC. AMER. ACAD. ARTS & SCI. 878 (1965).

[83] Even so-called "radical economists" concede the decline of poverty in absolute terms. See GORDON, ed., PROBLEMS IN POLITICAL ECONOMY 237–44 (1971).

[84] New York Times, Oct. 17, 1971, pp. 1, 5.

[85] It has been said that in fact "Black Harlem is one of the world's wealthiest communities—fifth or so in per capita income of all communities outside of North America and Europe," and "what is considered 'poverty' in the United States . . . is considered great wealth almost everywhere else." DRUCKER note 79 *supra*, at 123.

if equalization of income is really the right goal for American society to pursue, we should begin to look upon The Depression as a
Golden Era.

Nor are the possibilities of income redistribution nearly so large
as seems to be assumed by many, for far more than the very wealthy
would be significantly affected by any such undertaking. In 1969,
for example, the wealthiest 10 percent of families in terms of income
(before taxes) received 29 percent of the total income. If, somehow,
the highest tenth's share of the total income was taxed to the point
that it equaled the share of the second highest tenth, 16 percent,
(and everyone in the new top 20 percent received the average income of that group) and the excess 13 percent was distributed
roughly among the poorest 45 percent of families, the lowest family
income would probably have been no more than $7,000 and the
highest somewhere in the vicinity of $16,500.[86] All this is before
any taxes (but for the 100 percent tax on everything over around
$16,500) to pay for any of the functions of government. If pro-
gressive taxes were then levied for defense, police, schools, and the
like, working or not working, or working at one job rather than
another, or working in one area rather than another would make
little difference indeed to individual incomes.

At the high end of the income scale, the effect of a substantial
redistribution might well be similar to a brain drain, for such redistribution would affect the professional people and coordinators
and directors of production most heavily.[87] To the extent that the
productivity of such people was adversely affected, other factors
of production would also tend to produce and thus to earn less. It
is an obvious but all too often forgotten fact that reducing the productivity of one factor of production will tend to reduce the productivity and earnings of complementary factors. Ruth and Maris
hit more home runs because Gehrig and Mantle followed them in
the batting order. A failure of leadership can doom any human en-
deavor for all involved and, for exactly the same reason, a lessening

---

[86] The figures are "eyeballed" from table 504, *Share of Money Income Received by
Family Units*, THE AMERICAN ALMANAC, THE STATISTICAL ABSTRACT OF THE UNITED
STATES 317 (1972). Of course they are not precise or intended to be so. My purpose is
only to give a ballpark idea of what the possibilities of redistribution are or, rather,
are not.

[87] See the figures on median income by occupation in THE AMERICAN ALMANAC, note
86 *supra*, at 320. Every median in five figures is in the category of either "professional,
technical," or "Managers, officials or proprietors."

of the productivity of coordinators and directors of production will result in a lessening of the earnings of groups such as production workers. The paradox which so many cannot accept is that the rewards received by recipients of large incomes are necessary to the maintenance of the lower incomes of others in the economy.

At the low end of the income scale, a substantial redistribution of income might also affect the poor adversely. Some might be deterred not only from seeking employment but also from seeking to better themselves by making themselves more productive. It is difficult to predict the extent of any such impact, but it is an observable fact that opportunities such as vocational training are advertised to the poor as ways of earning more money. A redistribution of income would seem naturally to affect that particular incentive. This is worthy of emphasis because the elimination of poverty in the United States seems generally to have been the result, not of governmental action, but of individual members of the society making themselves more productive. It would be tragic irony to retard this successful war on poverty.

Concern over incentive effects in labor markets is thought by many to be exaggerated because job decisions are often based on a myriad of factors other than anticipated income. Market theory not only does not deny the influence of nonmonetary considerations but affirms it. Indeed, what distinguishes a market system from tribal custom, caste assignment, or bureaucratic decision is that it permits the individual to trade off income for other nonmonetary rewards, the income forgone being the cost to the community of the reduced production. Individuals have different tastes for different aspects of work and possess skills of differing value to the society. The allocation of jobs, therefore, involves, from the worker's point of view, not only income but leisure, keeping busy, intellectual stimulation, a sense of social responsibility, geographical location, power, status, work neighbors, investment in training, future opportunities, responsibility, emotional stress, physical effort, family satisfaction, and so on and so on. All of these things can be traded off against each other and against income. What this means is that a wage system in labor markets is particularly vulnerable to any governmental action affecting compensation, because that is the sole means of inducing the particular production desired by society, all other aspects of the job calculus being producer-oriented. To repeat, this is not to say there will be no production, but only to say that what is produced will not, to the extent we approach equality, be what society wants to consume but what it finds satisfying to produce. A society desperate for housing, for example, will face frustration unless carpentry is considered a desirable occupation.

It is no answer, therefore, to assert that salary is not the only incentive. The point is that in the absence of an omnipotent, coercive bureaucracy, tribal custom, or caste assignment, income is the sole signal inducing the production of what the society values. Confusion has long surrounded this rather uncomplicated point because defenders of capitalism have exaggerated the efficiency of free markets in producing goods. In fact, given the range of trade-off choices, they are efficient only in the presence of a culture with a strong work ethic, or strong anti-leisure ethic, and then seem so only because the bureaucratic approach to work allocation is by comparison enormously inefficient. Of the alternatives, the free market is, ironically, most consistent with a hippie culture or voluntary communal arrangement, for the failure to reward for nonproduction is no more a penalty on the hippie than his lack of production is a penalty on society. What is involved is a free exchange. Communist societies are not so tolerant. Work there tends to be a legal obligation as well as a means of political control.

Any measure which either guarantees income or reduces the rewards offered by the market, therefore—and a redistribution of income to employables does both—will induce people to seek more in the way of psychic or nonmonetary return (or avoidance of harm) from work. To the extent market rewards are limited, people on the margin will find the teaching of law more attractive than its practice, four years of medical school not worth the effort, political activity more attractive than business, and jobs with a "social purpose" (ideologically satisfying) more rewarding than commercial positions. And if income is guaranteed at the bottom of the income scale, those at the margin there will find vocational training unnecessary, part-time outside work in the familiar hills more attractive than factory work in an urban area, and more and more jobs too demeaning to take. Indeed, we may well ask whether the heavy tax burdens imposed during the last generation have not in part resulted in precisely such phenomena.

The extent to which productive activity will be reduced depends on the size and effectiveness of the redistribution. Nevertheless, we may underestimate the allocative or wealth-producing aspects of the price system in labor markets because people are both creatures of habit and place great value on the familiar. Redistribution is unlikely to produce an immediate, drastic effect, for large numbers of people will continue for a time to work at their normal pace and to keep the jobs they have. (This latter effect is by no means desirable in a dynamic economy.) But, as critics of the market have stressed, there are many other incentives in the job calculus—all producer-oriented—and these will gain strength as time passes. The effect of redistribution, therefore, may be gradual and easily concealed, since what would have happened but for the redistribution can never be proved.

At bottom, the difficulty is that redistribution focuses on one item in the job calculus: money. But money has purchasing power only because others want to acquire it. Limit the right to acquire it and you reduce its purchasing power. Redistribution thus seems more a device to destroy money's value as a medium of exchange than to reduce poverty. The case for redistribution may well be little more than the case for barter.

Two objections frequently leveled at such arguments must be dealt with. The first ties the fear of incentive effects to the idea of consumer sovereignty and attempts to discredit the former by attacking the latter. It is thus argued that income inequality cannot be justified on grounds of consumer satisfaction since that satisfaction itself involves the very same inequality. The answer is simply that the incentive issue is separate and independent of notions of consumer sovereignty. No matter who determines what is to be produced, there must be a mechanism to allocate labor to those ends. So even if we replace free consumers with a government bureau or Ralph Nader, there is still a need for a mechanism to allocate labor to those things it or he directs.

The second objection picks up the free rider argument discussed above in connection with in kind redistributions and argues that the donors as well as the donees desire income redistribution. Since those who are taxed want to contribute to the cause, it is said, an incentive effect will not result. The free rider argument, however, cuts exactly the other way. We concluded above that we need confiscatory taxes to offset the mutual fear that others will not contribute their share because no individual contribution is large enough to diminish poverty perceptibly. For the same reason, however, even the most generously inclined taxpayers will react to increased taxes as though they were indifferent to the destination of the extra revenue, since the increment they will be called upon to pay in taxes is too little to have a perceptible effect on poverty. The generosity of the donor, therefore, is irrelevant to the incentive effect upon him.

D. CONCLUSION

As a general proposition, equalization of income and helping the poor in an economic sense seem inconsistent objectives. The former seems counterproductive to the very growth and productivity of the economy, which is critical to the latter. As a result, a general and substantial redistribution of income can be undertaken only after equality has been chosen as a transcendent purpose overriding the material well-being of the society. In my judgment, advocates of equality are light years from establishing the transcendence of that goal.

To reject general and substantial redistributions, however, is not to reject all redistributions. There may or may not be pools of income that can be heavily taxed without adversely affecting the functions performed by a price system in labor markets or treading upon widely held notions of justice. Nevertheless, the existence and location of these pools of income must be based on more than the intuition of those who have for so long viewed income redistribution as a first article of faith. And any expectations that such pools will yield large sums ought to be dispelled.

Similarly, there are individuals in the society who are hopelessly unemployable both in existing capacity to work and in potential for future betterment. Redistribution to them may have an incentive effect on the donor group but there is no fear of an adverse effect on the donees. The same may also be largely true of one-shot, temporary payments that do not generate dependence or reliance. There are difficulties here, of course, since transfer payments are often difficult to terminate and it is not easy to insure that they will not be foreseen and relied upon.

In any case, redistribution calls for selective and particularized judgments, a problem to be dealt with at the retail rather than wholesale level. It is plainly a venture to be embarked upon without great expectations, much less the conviction that it is the road to a povertyless society.

III. The Supreme Court, Economic Inequality, and the Equal Protection of the Laws

I turn back to the ultimate issue: the role of the Equal Protection Clause and the Supreme Court in the struggle over economic inequality in the United States. Two main topics arise under this question, the first being the thrust of conventional legal criteria such as the history of the Fourteenth Amendment and its language, the second addressing a number of institutional considerations relating to the constitutional functions of the Court. The latter issue is itself focused on two questions, namely, whether the problem of economic inequality yields itself to regulation by rules of law fashioned through constitutional adjudication and the extent to which the Court may, in the absence of supporting conventional legal criteria, impose its will on the elected, political branches of government.

A. CONVENTIONAL LEGAL CRITERIA: HISTORY AND LANGUAGE

It was noted earlier that this is the first of two articles reappraising the role of the Equal Protection Clause. In the second article I intend to present a detailed exposition of my views of that role based largely on the history of its enactment and what seem to me to be the permissible judicial extrapolations from that history.

Since advocates of the reduction of economic inequality through substantive equal protection make no serious claim to historical support, it will suffice here to confirm in brief fashion that their modesty in advocacy is fully justified. The Fourteenth Amendment was enacted at a point in American history when notions of laissez-faire and Social Darwinism were about to peak and when a number of states (not all Southern) had passed Black Codes severely restricting the legal rights of blacks and imposing substantial legal burdens upon them. The Amendment was not designed to reduce inequality in the society generally or to serve as a device by which government might be compelled to take steps to bring about economic equality. Neither the men involved nor the spirit of the times favored social or economic equality, much less the notion that government had responsibilities to rework society along egalitarian lines. Quite the contrary, equality was invoked in the Amendment out of the fear of government and as a device to neutralize governmental (and a narrow range of centralized private) power by compelling it to maintain legal equality when classifications based on race (or racelike matters) were employed. Had the utterly different philosophy entailed in notions of income redistribution by government been thought of as having anything whatever to do with the purpose of the Amendment, it is safe to say that it simply would have failed of passage.

Much the same can be said of the Amendment's language, although the conclusions are a shade less definite. "No State shall . . . deny to any person within its jurisdiction the equal protection of the laws." From that language proponents of substantive equal protection derive constitutional principles reducing economic inequality in the society. On its face, the provision seems remarkably ill-suited to that task, for, to the extent economic inequality is a problem, it is a national problem. But the Equal Protection Clause is in terms directed strictly to the conduct of states toward persons within their jurisdiction. If the Equal Protection Clause requires absolute equality—of income or housing or education or anything— the equality thus brought about seems to be equality within each state, not between them. Persons in the richer states will fare better than persons in the poorer states, as indeed they presently do even under *Serrano* and *Shapiro*. What all this accomplishes, apart from encouraging further migration for the purpose of receiving increased public services, is by no means clear. Indeed, there is no guarantee even that the quantum of inequality (if measurable) will not be increased, rather than diminished, by such measures.

If equality is not the goal, but simply minimum protection as to "just wants" or "fundamental interests," it still seems an utterly foolish division of responsibilities to make the identification of these wants or interests a matter for the federal judiciary and leave their fulfillment to the states. The content of these concepts must be related to the wealth of the societal unit involved, but what the citizen of Connecticut views as "basic" housing may well seem a luxury to one in Arkansas. Even notions of subsistence vary widely between the states. Is the Court to adopt the norms of a rich state or a poor state? If the former, how do the poor states pay the cost of providing what are essentially "extras" to their citizens? If the latter, how much can be accomplished in the way of reducing inequality in the richer states? Perhaps the Court ought to fashion an economic norm for each state. But even assuming it was equal to what seems an impossible task, the problem of wide inequalities between the states would remain.

To my knowledge, not a single nonlegal writer on the issue of economic inequality has suggested this sort of division of governmental responsibility. Rather, all seem agreed that if a serious redistribution of income is to take place—whether through direct cash payments or in kind provision of goods and services—the national government is the only appropriate governmental organ to carry it out.

Other aspects of the Amendment are less preclusive than the fact that it is directed to the states rather than the federal government. Nevertheless, they are still suggestive of a purpose far short of the all-embracing scope required by the proponents of the constitutional redistribution of income. The words "No State" and "of the laws" can, I suppose, be read to include all forms of governmental tolerance and thus all forms of private, but regulable, conduct. They seem, however, rather odd choices to that end because they specifically direct attention to formal governmental action. Such emphasis strongly suggests an intended limitation on the scope of the Amendment.

The word "equal" appears on its face more apt to the advocated purpose, for as Professor Cox has noted, "Once loosed, the idea of Equality is not easily cabined."[88] Nevertheless, Professor Kurland has correctly observed that "its expansionist tendency may be due to its uses as rhetoric rather than as an idea. And the rhetoric is subject to use, if not capture, by anyone on any side of the question."[89] Equality as an idea is in fact not particularly useful, since it is intolerably constraining, for, like virginity, it admits of no degrees. Equality in the provision of "just wants" or the protection of "fundamental interests" means that no person may have more in the way of provision or protection than anyone else, no matter what he is willing to sacrifice in exchange for it. It means equal education, equal housing, equal food, and so on. Few thus go the whole equality route, for it brings the tension between egalitarian notions of justice and the value of individual freedom to the breaking point by promising to suppress vast areas of valuable idiosyncratic behavior. In fact, the rhetoric of equality in stump speeches or stump opinions is really an expression of distaste for inequality rather than

---

[88] Cox, note 50 *supra*, at 91.   [89] KURLAND, note 3 *supra*, at 165.

an insistence on uniformity and it is that distaste which "once loosed ... is not easily cabined." Even Karst and Horowitz, having milked equal protection dry, abandon "total equality" as "impossible and undesirable,"[90] while Professor Michelman makes explicit that what is at stake in his analysis is "minimum protection," not equality.

The language of the Equal Protection Clause thus seems at best very badly suited, at worst plainly hostile, to the objectives of equality under discussion. The words "No State," "of the laws," and "equal" itself, all must in effect be abandoned as superfluous or meaningless. Indeed, were language the only guide to interpretation, there hardly seems more reason to put the Equal Protection Clause to this intended use than the initial statement of constitutional purpose ("to form a more perfect Union," etc.), or the Ninth Amendment. As a matter of history or language, therefore, focusing on the Equal Protection Clause smacks of random selection, or the content to be given to the law derived from it comes entirely from other sources.

B. IDENTIFYING FUNDAMENTAL INTERESTS

Examination of the process by which the Court is to identify and fulfill fundamental interests in order to reduce economic inequality raises serious question whether it may appropriately be assigned this task. In effect, the identification and fulfillment of fundamental interests is the judicial counterpart to the executive or legislative in kind redistributions. Such programs are, as has been discussed, fraught with difficulties. When the Court undertakes to command the distribution of goods and services to the poor, however, it faces a number of additional problems peculiar to its institutional nature which other branches of government do not confront. Courts have difficulty delegating authority since they have no direct control over the other branches of government and must themselves act through rules of law rather than the exercise of executive or administrative discretion. Given the issue before us, these rules are rules of constitutional law and must be consonant with three requirements imposed by the nature of the judicial process.

First, the rule must be based on a considered rationale embodying a principle which the Court is willing to apply in all similar cases.

---

[90] See note 16 *supra*.

This is the requirement that principles of constitutional law be neutrally applied, a point different from the claim that they must also be neutrally derived, the latter issue going to the relationship of the Court to the political branches.[91] I do not take the neutral application requirement to be seriously controverted. It accords with traditional notions of elemental justice and does no more than proscribe individual arbitrary decisions and require that judicial action be founded on informed opinion.

Second, the rule must effectuate the principle efficiently, that is, without great costs in the way of harmful side effects.

Third, the rule must be relatively precise. In the absence of some precision, similar factual situations will not necessarily yield similar legal results, and there is no assurance that like cases will be treated alike by lower courts. Relative precision also seems essential given the underlying goals of reducing economic inequality and helping the poor. These goals are not well-served by rules which in effect redistribute income more or less randomly. They also call for rules that permit relatively efficient and inexpensive enforcement. The costs of litigation and administration are transaction costs attributable to the redistribution, and in effect part of the redistribution itself. Since there is a limited sum available for redistribution—that amount which does not bring about disincentive effects—the legal rules must not entail such extensive litigation that little if anything is left in the way of benefits to be received by the poor. This is not the objection frequently raised in opposition to the extension of existing legal doctrine, namely, that courts will be flooded with litigation. That objection goes only to the quality of judicial administration. The present concern is that the costs of enforcing the rule will nullify the purpose of the rule itself by creating incentive effects which will in the event leave the most disadvantaged worse off. Again, if this consideration is not taken into account, it would seem that an equality rather than minimum need rationale is being employed.

In many areas of law a tension exists between these requirements. Tailoring rules so that they may be efficiently applied and like cases can easily be treated alike looks in the direction of rules that limit the discretion of the decision maker. Narrowing his discretion saves time and resources and diminishes the possibilities of resort to

---

[91] See Bork, note 43 *supra*.

impermissible considerations. Tailoring rules to embody policies that are derived from complex rationales and which avoid harmful side effects, on the other hand, may call for intricate and subtle formulas leaving considerable discretion in application in the hands of the decision-making tribunal.

Reconciling these conflicting pressures may or may not be possible, depending on the kind of human conduct law is seeking to affect and its intended social consequences. Consider for example the reapportionment problem. Putting aside for the moment the question what the underlying principle is, adoption of a one-man, one-vote rule greatly enhances the chances that like cases will be treated alike because it reduces the number of criteria for judgment of legislative apportionment plans. Since the criteria—under a strict one-man, one-vote rule, there would be but one criterion—are few and easily discernible, the enforcement tribunal has so little discretion that inconsistent decisions are virtually impossible. The cost of enforcement is also limited because such a rule can be applied without complicated trials. As one moves to rules permitting other factors to be considered along with voting equality—history and geography, for example—discretion increases and each case tends to be an individualized problem. Whether like cases are being treated alike is less easily determined because no one can say with certainty which cases are actually alike in relevant facts. Impermissible matters can more easily be considered because the reasons for a decision become less scrutable as the number of relevant factors to be taken into account increases. Generally, the cost of enforcement will be higher as one departs from rules of thumb to more discretionary standards because litigation becomes more complicated and perhaps more frequent.

On the other hand, it may well be questioned whether a strict one-man, one-vote rule adheres to the underlying principle, whether it be compelling state legislatures to justify apportionments on a "rational" basis, the vindication of an individual right to equal voting power, or the guarantee of majority rule.[92] Egregious gerrymandering is by no means inconsistent with a one-man, one-vote rule, and compelling periodic reapportionment inevitably invites resort to partisan considerations. Continued use of the single-mem-

---

[92] See generally, BICKEL, THE SUPREME COURT AND THE IDEA OF PROGRESS 151 *et seq.* (1970); DIXON, DEMOCRATIC REPRESENTATION (1968).

ber district, moreover, wipes out any guarantee of majority rule, since the political complexion of a legislative body is determined by which individuals receive a majority—no matter what size—in each district and not by the underlying total popular vote. It would thus appear that administrative considerations were thought by the Court to outweigh vindication of any of the plausible underlying principles at stake in the reapportionment issue. For that reason also, perhaps, the actual principle employed by the Court has always been obscure.

A one-man, one-vote rule thus can be justified only after determining that its administrative benefits outweigh its failure to effectuate fully any or all of the policies which called for judicial intervention in the apportionment area. Nevertheless, fashioning legal rules in reapportionment cases is child's play compared to what a court must undertake if it is to fashion a constitutional command that a designated minimum of goods and services be distributed to the poor. There is no coherent theory upon which constitutional principles can be derived and the number of potentially relevant considerations seems almost as unlimited as the information available to the Court is meager. The tension between the demands of administrative considerations and the claims imposed by the alternative underlying objectives, moreover, is so great that one may seriously doubt whether constitutional law is not too circumscribed a regulatory device to accommodate these conflicting considerations in a satisfactory manner.

When the Court identifies "fundamental interests" which the state may not allow to go unfulfilled because of an individual's impecuniousness, it is engaged in the provision of goods and services to the poor. Where the goal of this distribution is the reduction of economic inequality, in kind distributions seem, as discussed above at length, fraught with such great difficulties in comparison with direct cash payments that considerations of major importance alone justify resort to them. The reasons for the judicial choosing of the in kind route, however, are anything but compelling, for they seem mainly the result of accidents in legal doctrine. The "fundamental interest" rationale has existed at least since *Skinner* and is the handiest doctrinal device around. To the extent that the state action doctrine lives, moreover, a wholesale constitutional assault on economic inequality is impossible and judicial action seems limited to cases involving the affirmative exercise of governmental power affecting a "fundamental interest." Finally, there may well be the fear that judicial resort to cash payments would leave the Court overly exposed to the charge that it was willfully ignoring the Constitution for its own views of how the United States should be governed.

Whatever the merits of the considerations that led the Court to choose this route, its difficulties increase as it faces the task of identifying the goods and services that must be provided as fundamental interests. Its range of choice is limited in comparison with the capabilities of other branches so long as state action lives, since judicial intervention then can be no more than a reaction to steps taken by other organs of government. It may be argued, however, that the Court is as institutionally capable of identifying the minimum needs of the poor (within its narrowed range of choice) as any other organ of government, since the judgments involved are wholly subjective and the Court's views are as good as anyone's. I have trouble with this, for two reasons. First, absent an explicit constitutional directive, the Court ought to act only on a principle which is discernible and can be neutrally applied in similar cases. When it decides that, say, housing is a fundamental interest and recreation is not—thus denying the worthiness of the possible trade-off if cash were distributed—its decision should be based on such a principle. Clearly, however, it is not; what is called for is the ad hoc exercise of idiosyncratic fiat. Second, I strongly doubt that, if the society decided upon the wholesale provision of goods and services to the poor, more than a few eccentric souls would suggest entrusting the Court with such responsibilities. In fact, where government has engaged in such enterprises, other organs of government have been chosen. Resort to the Court is advocated here, not because of its institutional superiority, but because it is an accessible means of circumventing the democratic branches.

The institutional difficulties of using the judicial process for these purposes become clearer as we work further into the problem. Redistribution calls for selective and particularized judgments, judgments which require both more information and more flexibility than courts have. To begin with, the Court cannot know—or even make an intelligent guess—what income is available for redistribution without causing a disincentive effect. To be sure, other branches of government also have inadequate data, but those other branches at least can be flexible and change their estimates while the Court at best must make a semipermanent decision. This lack of information may well be thought to be fatal. An overestimate is no harmless error, since by hypothesis the most disadvantaged will be made worse off, albeit more equal. Income redistribution, moreover, is not by any means the sole responsibility of the judiciary. In determining the amount available for redistribution, the Court would presumably have to take into account present and future taxation and spending by all other branches of government, state and federal. Income redistribution calls for a coordinated governmental effort, a task for which the judicial process is ill suited.

Litigation also seems an inappropriate way to determine the proper mix of goods and services. Each case is likely to involve a claim of entitlement to a particular item. What claims will in the future come before the Court and how they will be resolved cannot be known when the initial claims are adjudicated. Yet the goal is a single mix of goods and services, a package which by definition cannot be put together through a process of random, isolated decisions. More legal services mean less housing, education, etc., and shaping the content of the entire package entails the weighing of various "needs" against one another, a process which seems virtually the opposite of that actually employed by the Court.

After a determination of the mix and estimation of the total cost, the next step is to institute carefully calibrated tax laws which avoid disincentive effects to the degree possible by tapping income which seems subject to confiscation without reducing productivity. Again a flexible institution of government able to fashion finely tailored rules and change them quickly seems to be called for. And again the Court seems anything but that institution.

Definition of minimum needs in a general way and estimation of the income available for redistribution is only preliminary to what may be the most difficult task of all, fashioning rules of constitutional law effectuating these determinations. As a result of a good deal of political sloganeering we have come to assume that we are saying something very meaningful when we talk about "housing," "education," etc. In fact, it is a considerable task to fashion a nationwide or even statewide rule which defines with any precision the content of these words. It is here that the tension between the need for rules which facilitate adjudication and the need for rules which effectuate policy is greatest. Housing as a term certainly encompasses a number of physical specifications as to matters such as bricks and mortar, but there must be adjustments to climate and the relative availability of various kinds of construction materials. That is, however, only the beginning. Also important to "housing" is location, character of neighborhood, control of one's life style, control of one's environment, whether one owns or rents and on what terms, etc.[93] A number of these considerations will frequently conflict. My right to live my life style may well be thought by my neighbor to encroach upon his, and vice versa. For such conflicts, there seems to be no easy means of accommodation through rules of constitutional law. Each of these matters may well be of considerable importance, moreover. It is difficult to see how a Court can reject considerations such as location and character of neighborhood without in fact depriving substantial numbers of the poor of "adequate" housing and without in fact creating perceived inequalities quite as vexing as those the rules are designed to eradicate.

The Court attempting to fashion such a rule, therefore, finds itself in a dilemma. Having rejected the market, it is now faced with the myriad of decisions that the market makes. This invites litigation from virtually every potential recipient of governmental services because each may genuinely believe that he is entitled to something that the government has not offered him. To avoid this result, the Court will most likely seek some sort of rule of thumb, like one-man, one-vote, so that the cost of litigation will not exhaust the money available for the goods and services themselves. It may thus hold that every officially designated poor person is entitled to a certain dollar input in housing. That seems reasonable, since it fixes upon the one measurable factor involved. On the other hand, dollar input is so rough a measurement that one can seriously question its evenhandedness. There are enormous variations in costs between areas and it simply is not the case that equalizing dollar input would have much relationship to equality or to meeting the perceived needs of the poor. It might thus plausibly lead to the reduction of government housing in some areas, just as the effect of *Shapiro* may ultimately be to reduce the rate of welfare payments.

This is the case with any number of questions involving potential "fundamental interests." The *Serrano* decision stopped at this very point and carefully avoided ruling that equal per student expenditures in each school district were to be required. Again, equalizing dollar input seems an apt and accessible rate—if not compelled by

---

[93] See Michelman, *The Advent of a Right to Housing: A Current Appraisal*, 5 HARV. CIV. RIGHTS L. REV. 207 (1970).

the reapportionment decisions—but again cost variations, differences in community-value placed on education, variations in need, and the diversity of views as to proper educational policy would seem to call for anything but that rule. In fact, there are many areas in the nation in which such a rule would lead to the reduction of expenditures in the school districts which served the poor. On the other hand, a rule which permits inquiry into the actual quality of public education in each district may turn the Court into a national school board.

Much the same can be said of virtually all goods and services that government might undertake to provide. A rule which takes into account all variations in taste, cost, and need ignores the value of relatively precise guidelines which permit like cases to be treated alike and reduces the transaction costs of litigation in adjudicating claims to the designated goods and services. Rules consistent with those criteria, however, seem very ill adapted to the underlying purpose of the enterprise, namely, the reduction of economic inequality. Once the decision is made to distribute goods and services rather than cash, economic inequality is more than a matter of income difference between individuals and involves the myriad of decisions involving the intermixture of taste and price which the market makes so noiselessly and costlessly or which are presently made by government on a decentralized basis. The equalization of dollar input is no substitute for those mechanisms.

It is also important that, when the Court fashions a rule providing goods and services, that it not do so in a way that creates harmful side effects. The problem that arises when legal services are provided free and are thus "purchased" by persons who would not expend cash upon them was discussed earlier. Unless a court can find a way to limit the provision of legal services to situations in which the recipient places a value on the possible judgment equal to the cost of the services provided, harmful side effects cannot be avoided. One such side effect is that previously mentioned: many who are not recipients of free legal services let their "need" for a lawyer go unfulfilled because they prefer other items. This, of course, creates an inequality as difficult to justify as the inequalities that were to be eliminated by the provision of the services themselves. But there is also another side effect. Consider the case of free legal services "purchased" to litigate landlord-tenant matters. Where the services are free, a client will request that they be put to any use of value no matter what the cost. For example, it may be possible to invoke legal procedures which put off eviction for two or three months even though there is no real defense to the eviction action. Whereas a person who pays a lawyer would rarely find the extension of possession of sufficient value to offset the legal costs, a recipient of free services almost always will. The ultimate effect, however, may be an increase in the cost of rental property to the poor and thus be counterproductive in terms of the underlying enterprise of reducing economic inequality. The Court seemed unaware of these problems, however, when, in *Lindsey v. Normet,* it struck down part of statute which may have been designed to mitigate just such effects, without giving any consideration to these very real problems.

C. WEALTH AS A SUSPECT CLASSIFICATION

It has been argued that wealth should be assimilated to race as a suspect classification. It is not necessary at this point to wrestle with the problem of precisely what legal result is called for when a classification is labeled "suspect." It may be the equivalent of a conclusive declaration that the statute is invalid; it may call for a searching scrutiny of the motive behind the legislation; it may create a presumption of the statute's invalidity rebuttable only by a showing of a "compelling state interest"; or it may simply shift the burden of demonstrating some legitimate legislative interest to the state. For our purposes, it is enough to say it casts serious constitutional doubt upon the legislation involved.

It would be well at the outset to establish what it is about race that makes it a suspect classification. There is, of course, the history of racial slavery in the United States and, in particular, the clear intent of the framers of the Fourteenth Amendment to invalidate the Black Codes. Those codes, and a disgracefully large amount of legislation in subsequent years, invoked race as a classification in a way which was intended to operate, and did operate, to discriminate against black people. Race is thus the basis of a stereotype which served as a systematic vehicle of governmental discrimination. Moreover, it is not a stereotype with a pretense at being related to individual merit, even though it is, for the frosting on the cake, unalterable by the individual.

Viewed in these terms, wealth seems by no means assimilable to race. This is so whether we view the issue as classification based on poverty, as in *Griffin* (a free transcript for those who can't afford one) or wealth generally, as in *Harper* (a free vote for all). In either case, the history of the Amendment would seem to cut the other way for there is no evidence that the framers were concerned with the distribution of income.

Unlike race, moreover, poverty is not absolutely unalterable for all those afflicted by it. The history of this nation is a history of virtually all of its people bettering themselves economically and, for the vast majority, becoming well-to-do or middle-class. Indeed, if income inequality performs the function of increasing productivity at all, income redistribution is then as likely to retard people from bringing themselves out of poverty as it is to cure the evil itself. Beyond that, it cannot be said that poverty has been used like race as the basis for systematic legislative discrimination. There simply has not been any legislation invoking a poverty classification even remotely resembling the widespread, official, racial segregation of schools and other facilities. To the contrary, there is an enormous amount of legislation which, whatever its actual effect, was said—and was intended by most of its supporters—to help the poor. Hour and wage legislation, legislation protecting collective bargaining, social security, the farm program, the creation of the Office of Economic Opportunity, fair employment laws, manpower training programs, unemployment compensation, public assistance, public housing, public education, subsidified health care, etc., have all had as their rationale at one time or another the need to help the poor. In 1970, roughly 47 percent of all governmental expenditures (15 percent of GNP) was allocable to social welfare.[94] Finally, to the extent low income is related to low productivity—and it is to a large extent—poverty is not entirely unrelated to individual merit. One need not adopt productivity as the sole criterion of merit to say that poverty resulting from low productivity is far different from legal exclusion from public facilities because of one's race.

In any event, there is no transcendent income line below which is poverty. The talk we hear of a poverty line refers to an administrative determination by the Social Security Administration, not divine revelation. The fact is that any person who has less material income than someone else will feel relatively deprived. Even if we were capable of raising the income of the bottom 20 percent of the

---

[94] The American Almanac, note 86 *supra*, at 271.

population to that of the lowest income in the twenty-first per-
centile, we would still have a "poverty problem," because the problem is one of relative rather than absolute deprivation. Thus it is
that even as the most disadvantaged in the society have had their
lot bettered rather steadily, learned commentators nevertheless
speak of those in poverty as being the lowest 20 percent in the population and use the words "getting better" to mean "more equal."[95]
This is not to say that one should be indifferent to the plight of
those in the lowest 20 percent or that we should ignore their welfare. It is very much to say, however, that the poverty problem is
a relative inequality problem rather than some sort of absolute
affliction.

Nor is it sensible to think of wealth classifications generally as
being suspect. That, of course, abandons the relief of poverty as a
goal—the president of General Motors would get a free transcript
along with Mr. Griffin—and turns to the even less supportable target
of complete equality.

D. THE COURT, ECONOMIC INEQUALITY, AND THE POLITICAL BRANCHES

A major theme in the scholarship of constitutional law is the relationship of the Supreme Court, its members appointed for life, to
the political branches, their members elected for a fixed term in
partisan elections. The principal issue is the identification of the appropriate constraints on the power of judicial review and the resulting spectrum of opinion is large and varied. At one end is the
view that the Court must hew closely to the language and specific
intent of the Constitution in order to insure that the least democratic
branch does not encroach on the powers of elected representatives.[96]
Opinions more in the middle call for the "neutral derivation"[97] of
constitutional principles or view the Court as "an institution charged
with the evolution and application of society's fundamental principles."[98] At the other end are what might be called the super-realists
(a term most definitely used for identification rather than descriptive purposes). The only constraint on the exercise of judicial
power they recognize is that it should be employed to the end of

---

[95] GORDON, note 83 *supra*, at 241–42.

[96] ERVIN, ROLE OF THE SUPREME COURT: POLICYMAKER OR ADJUDICATOR? 8 (1970).

[97] See Bork, note 43 *supra*.

[98] BICKEL, THE LEAST DANGEROUS BRANCH 109 (1962).

validation by "tomorrow's history,"[99] which is to say, of course, that they recognize no constraint at all, except possibly the need to avoid today's impeachment.

The use of the Equal Protection Clause to reduce economic inequality is not difficult to locate along this spectrum. Having no basis in the history or language of the Amendment and lying well outside what seems the core area of judicial competence, it finds sustenance solely in its alleged wisdom as public policy. Whatever its wisdom, however, it is the kind of policy one concerned with institutional competence would leave to the judgment of the legislative branch.

One area in which legislatures seem institutionally superior to other branches of government is in the representation of interest groups. Indeed, the device of the bicameral legislature seems principally designed to maximize that very function. The reduction of economic inequality, however, seems a classic issue calling for the resolution of the claims of competing groups. Who is to be taxed and how, who is to receive what, and how much sacrifice should society make in the name of equality, are precisely the kind of questions legislatures seem most suited to resolve. To be sure, there may, or may not, be good reason to believe that one interest group is more worthy or deserving than another but it is precisely that judgment, if any, which ought to be the routine grist of the political mill. It is simply impossible for all interested groups to be represented on a body such as the Court and, worse, quite likely that the Court will not even be able to identify the groups with the most at stake.

It is for these reasons, I should think, that most students of constitutional law believe the Court's vigorous use of notions of substantive due process to upset economic regulation earlier in the century to be a misuse of the power of judicial review. Substantive equal protection, however, in principle and practice suffers from quite the same defects and has itself created some uneasiness even among its proponents. For that reason, we witness the tragicomic phenomenon of both Justices and commentators nervously seeking to distinguish between what they are doing and the rejected and reviled substantive due process of another era. "Regulation of business or industry" is said to differ from "[t]he administration of public welfare assistance."[100] And we are told that state "economic

---

[99] See note 6 *supra*.   [100] 397 U.S. 471, at 485.

regulation" is to be distinguished from state imposed "distinctions
. . . that run against the poor."[101] Such subtleties, however, are almost patently artificial. All economic regulation involves the allocation of scarce resources and the distribution of income. One may
prefer one kind of regulation leading to a particular allocation and
distribution over another kind, but the judgment must be based on
personal value preferences— the need or worthiness of a group to be
helped or the relative lack of merit of one to be injured. These must
then be applied in the light of one's judgments as to the need for,
effect and feasibility of, regulation—judgments about market failure,
effect on incentives or on other government policies, etc. In constitutional principle the issues are indivisible. Consider a state minimum wage law. Invalidation of such a law by the Court would
surely be considered an illegitimate exercise of substantive due
process because what is involved is labeled the "[r]egulation of
business or industry." Many believe such laws help the poor. Most
economists, I should think, however, would disagree and hold that
such laws, while they help some persons, price the poor and other
disadvantaged groups, *e.g.*, teenagers and blacks, out of the job
market.[102] Spelling out a "suspect classification"/"fundamental interest" argument to invalidate such a law would be child's play to
a judge whose policy preferences impel him in that direction.

All intervention in the market is subject to similar analysis. Some
of the migrant poor no doubt receive short-run help as a result of
Shapiro v. Thompson; other groups, often no better off, will no
doubt suffer because of the increased claims on public budgets and
public services, the strains which an influx of migrants seeking public welfare place on society, and the economic and industrial ripples
caused by increased taxation. No one really knows who will gain
or suffer in the long run by invalidating regulations designed to prevent the concentration of the poorest and most troubled people of
our society in particular areas. Only judgments based on preferences
for various groups and one's view of the social and economic impact of particular policies can provide an answer. Such judgments

---

[101] Karst & Horowitz, note 5 *supra*, at 75.

[102] Brozen, *The Effect of Statutory Minimum Wage Increases on Teen-Age Employment*,
12 J. LAW & ECON. 109 (1969); Brozen, *Minimum Wage Rates and Household Workers*, 5
J. LAW & ECON. 103 (1962); PETERSON & STEWART, EMPLOYMENT EFFECTS OF MINI-
MUM WAGE RATES (1969); Stigler, *The Economics of Minimum Wage Legislation*, 36
AMER. ECON. REV. 358 (1946); Tobin, note 82 *supra*, at 889–90.

were the basis of substantive due process. The earlier decisions were not made by men who sought to protect a particular class purely for the sake of protecting it. They held a view of political economy which led them to believe that they were effectuating policies which made everyone, including the least fortunate, better off. Their mistake was to use their power as judges to deprive the political process of control over these policies. Substantive equal protectionists are on all fours in this respect. Make no mistake about it, *Lochner v. New York*[103] is alive and well in *Shapiro v. Thompson*.

It may be fairly said then that only those who view judicial review as being without any constraint save that dictated by the pursuit of validation by "tomorrow's history" can view the Court's intervention into questions of the distribution of income without alarm. For if there are constraints on the Court, if we are to maintain any sensible sort of institutional division of labor in the name of either competence or the democratic political process, it would seem that the line must be drawn to exclude income redistribution by judicial fiat. Thus it is that any observer concerned about maintaining constraints on judicial power is likely to view further intervention by the Court in the name of the reduction of economic inequality more as a seizure of power than a legitimate exercise of judicial review.

----

[103] 198 U.S. 45 (1905).

MARY CORNELIA ALDIS PORTER

JOHN MARSHALL HARLAN

THE ELDER & FEDERAL COMMON LAW:

A LESSON FROM HISTORY

Some years ago Judge Henry Friendly noted that the ink spilled since *Erie*[1] had "become a small lake" and wondered if "more could be usefully said."[2] The question was surely rhetorical. As long as the federal courts continue, for some reasons that are better than others, to create and apply federal common law, debate over the correctness and propriety of the decisions will continue.[3] That is one matter. Another, and one which has received less attention, was the tendency of the Warren Court to create federal common law not only when clearly or faintly called for by the Constitution, federal statutes, or treaties, but because the majority, especially in civil liberties and reapportionment cases, were inclined to increase the authority of the national government at the expense of the

Mary Cornelia Aldis Porter is Associate Professor and Chairman of the Political Science Department, Barat College.

[1] Erie R.R. v. Tompkins, 304 U.S. 64 (1938).

[2] Friendly, *In Praise of Erie—and of the New Federal Common Law*, in BENCHMARKS 156 (1967).

[3] The literature is extensive. For summaries and discussion of the cases, see Friendly, note 2 *supra*; Note, *The Competence of Federal Courts to Formulate Rules of Decision*, 74 HARV. L. REV. 1084 (1964); Note, *The Federal Common Law*, 82 HARV. L. REV. 1512 (1969). For the Supreme Court's latest expansive word on the subject, see Illinois v. City of Milwaukee, 406 U.S. 91 (1972).

states.[4] The Rules of Decision Act[5] has, in other words, been given short shrift simply because it got in the way of other and more pressing judicial pursuits. This casual use of means employed to achieve desired ends[6] was, of course, characteristic of the Warren Court, and it is perhaps not too surprising that more convincing reasons have not always been offered for the disregard of *Erie*.

Whether this trend, if continued by the Burger Court, signifies a real retreat from *Erie* and thereby a return to *Swift v. Tyson*[7] is a question only the future can answer. Surely no one, not even *Erie's* critics,[8] would wish a repeat of the confusions, inequities, uncertainties, and disruptions to the federal system occasioned by *Tyson*.[9] What has perhaps been forgotten is that *Tyson*, somewhat in the manner of *Mapp v. Ohio*[10] or *Reynolds v. Sims*,[11] manifested a theory of judicial power and represented a judicial frame of mind. All the natural law trappings—individual liberty, the sacred rights of property, the benign effects of commerce unfettered by the heavy hand of regulation, and an impartial judiciary resistant to raw political power and passions[12]—marched hand-in-hand with *Swift v. Tyson*.[13] Had the decision not already been established, the post–Civil War Court would surely have had to invent it.

That *Tyson* might be revived, however absent-mindedly, to serve a more contemporary master should give pause. The avowed objective of that decision, uniformity by judicial fiat in the common and, particularly, commercial law, was not only unattainable, the decision had quite the opposite effect. The Court, in pursuit of this will-o'-the-wisp, created a legal monstrosity: unworkable, untenable,

---

[4] For a discussion of this point, see KURLAND, POLITICS, THE CONSTITUTION, AND THE WARREN COURT chs. 3 & 4 (1970).

[5] 28 U.S.C. § 1652.

[6] The critical literature is extensive. See, *e.g.*, BICKEL, THE SUPREME COURT AND THE IDEA OF PROGRESS (1970).

[7] 16 Pet. 1 (1842).

[8] The great defense of the Story position is to be found in 2 CROSSKEY, POLITICS AND THE CONSTITUTION ch. 25 (1953).

[9] Justice Brandeis, in his *Erie* opinion, canvassed the literature and discussed the difficulties that *Tyson* created. 304 U.S. at 72–77.

[10] 367 U.S. 643 (1961).

[11] 377 U.S. 533 (1964).

[12] For a discussion of the Court's adherence to natural law precepts, see HAINES, THE REVIVAL OF NATURAL LAW CONCEPTS (1930).

[13] On Justice Story and natural law, see DUNNE, JUSTICE JOSEPH STORY AND THE RISE OF THE SUPREME COURT (1970), esp. ch. 32.

and, finally, ridiculous. What follows is a synoptic account of that history, with emphasis upon the jurisprudence of John Marshall Harlan the Elder, whose haphazard and reckless uses of the *Tyson* doctrine spawned much of the difficulty.

Harlan served on the Court for almost thirty-four years.[14] He was the only Justice during his tenure to protest the Court's relegation of the black man to second-class citizenship,[15] and the only Justice who thought the Bill of Rights applied to the states by way of the Fourteenth Amendment.[16] His position in these cases has been almost fully vindicated.[17] He was the only Justice to serve during the entire era of the first laissez-faire Court.[18] He lived to see that

---

[14] Harlan was born in 1833. He was appointed to the Court by Hayes and was on the bench from 10 Dec. 1877 until his death on 14 Oct. 1911. He served for 33 years, 10 months, and 25 days, a term of office exceeded only by his mentor, Chief Justice Marshall, his colleague Stephen Field, and Hugo LaFayette Black, in many ways Harlan's successor.

[15] See Civil Rights Cases, 109 U.S. 3 (1883); Louisville, N.O.&.T.R.R. v. Mississippi, 133 U.S. 587 (1890); Plessy v. Ferguson, 163 U.S. 537 (1896); Giles v. Harris, 189 U.S. 474 (1903) (joined by Brewer and Brown); James v. Bowman, 190 U.S. 127 (1903) (joined by Brown); Berea College v. Kentucky, 211 U.S. 45 (1908).

[16] Hurtado v. California, 110 U.S. 516 (1883); O'Neil v. Vermont, 144 U.S. 323 (1892) (joined by Field); Maxwell v. Dow, 176 U.S. 581 (1900); Twining v. New Jersey, 211 U.S. 78 (1908); Patterson v. Colorado, 207 U.S. 454 (1907).

[17] Brown v. Board of Education, 347 U.S. 483 (1954), ended the "separate-but-equal" reign of *Plessy*. While the Court has not fully incorporated the Bill of Rights in the Fourteenth Amendment, the elder Harlan's views no longer warrant Frankfurter's labeling of Harlan as "an eccentric exception." Adamson v. California, 332 U.S. 46, 62 (1947). On the extent to which the Court, especially the Warren Court, has vindicated Harlan, see Abraham, *John Marshall Harlan: A Justice Neglected*, 41 Va. L. Rev. 871 (1955); Bartosic, *The Constitution, Civil Liberties and John Marshall Harlan*, 46 Ky. L.J. 407 (1958); Beth, *Justice Harlan and the Uses of Dissent*, 49 Am. Pol. Sci. Rev. 1085 (1955); Canfield, *Our Constitution Is Color Blind: Mr. Justice Harlan and the Modern Problems of Civil Rights*, 32 U. Mo. Kan. City L. Rev. 292 (1964); Watt & Orlikoff, *The Coming Vindication of Mr. Justice Harlan*, 34 Nw. L. Rev. 13 (1949); Waite, *How Eccentric Was Mr. Justice Harlan?* 38 U. Minn. L. Rev. 173 (1953); Westin, *John Marshall Harlan and the Rights of Negroes*, 70 Yale L.J. 637 (1957).

[18] With the exception of 2 Warren, The Supreme Court in United States History (1937), the standard histories of the Court assume a pro-business, particularly pro-railroad, bias on the part of the majority. See, *e.g.*, Kelly & Harbison, The American Constitution chs. 19 & 20 (3d ed. 1963); McCloskey, The American Supreme Court ch. 5 (1969); Swisher, American Constitutional Development chs. 18–23 (1954). For more specialized considerations of the character of the Court of this era, see Jacobs, Law Writers and the Courts (1954); Paul, Conservative Crisis and the Rule of Law (1960); Twiss, Lawyer and the Constitution (1942). My own reservations about labeling Justices according to their economic predilections are not relevant here. A careful examination of the records of the Justices considered to be the most ardent exponents of laissez faire—Brewer, Field, and Peckham—indicates some of the perils of overly facile characterization.

Court adopt his earlier dissents,[19] support rulings of the earliest national regulatory agency, the Interstate Commerce Commission,[20] and uphold government prosecutions brought under the Sherman Act.[21] With the adoption of the Sixteenth Amendment, two years after his death, the "American people" heeded the charge, delivered in his *Income Tax Case* dissent, that they "could not too soon amend their Constitution."[22] Despite the length of his service, his prodigious output,[23] and the prophetic nature of his dissents, the literature on this great Justice is still inexplicably meager and largely devoted to civil rights and civil liberties cases.[24] Perhaps Alan Westin's long-promised and eagerly awaited biography will accord Harlan the recognition and honor that is long overdue.

What follows need in no way detract from the laurels Harlan so patently has earned. Despite what may at first appear to be internal contradictions, his contribution to the pre-*Erie* federal common

---

[19] Texas & P. R.R. v. I.C.C., 162 U.S. 197 (1896); I.C.C. v. Alabama Midland R.R., 168 U.S. 144 (1897); I.C.C. v. Brimson, 154 U.S. 447 (1894); I.C.C. v. Cincinnati, N.O. & T.P. R.R., 167 U.S. 479 (1897); United States v. Delaware & Hudson R.R., 213 U.S. 366 (1904); United States v. E. C. Knight Co., 156 U.S. 1 (1895); Anderson v. United States, 171 U.S. 604 (1898); Hopkins v. United States, 171 U.S. 578 (1898); Board of Trade v. Christie, 198 U.S. 245 (1905).

[20] After the passage of the Hepburn Act, 34 Stat. 584 (1906), the Court purported to limit itself to review only points of law and not facts as found by the I.C.C. Illinois Central R.R. v. I.C.C., 206 U.S. 441 (1907); I.C.C. v. Illinois Central R.R., 215 U.S. 452 (1910); I.C.C. v. Chicago & Rock Island R.R., 218 U.S. 88 (1910). These opinions were delivered by Harlan. On the question of the scope of review of the I.C.C.'s determination of facts, see DICKINSON, ADMINISTRATIVE JUSTICE AND THE SUPREMACY OF LAW 167–84 (1927). Harlan frequently dissented when he thought the courts to be entering the realm of administrative competence. See Pennsylvania Ref. Co. v. Western N.Y. & Pa. R.R., 208 U.S. 208 (1908); United States v. Delaware & Hudson Co., 213 U.S. 366 (1904).

[21] The Holmes "stream of commerce" doctrine, Swift & Co. v. United States, 196 U.S. 375 (1906), provided the rationale for overruling the *E. C. Knight* case, note 19 *supra*.

[22] Pollock v. Farmer's Loan & Trust Co., 158 U.S. 601, 674 (1895). For a description of Harlan's vigorous dissent in that case, see Farrelly, *Justice Harlan's Dissent in the Pollock Case*, 24 So. CALIF. L. REV. 175 (1951).

[23] One count came up with this tally: Harlan participated in 14,226 cases; wrote 745 majority or plurality opinions, 100 concurring opinions, and 155 dissenting opinions; dissented without opinion 161 times and joined 82 dissenting opinions of others. Gordon, John Marshall Harlan: Various Aspects (1963) (unpublished ms.).

[24] See note 16 *supra*; *John Marshall Harlan (1833–1911): A Symposium*, 46 KY. L.J. 46 (1958). Justice Henry Brown, Harlan's colleague on the bench for fifteen years, provided some useful insights. Brown, *The Dissenting Opinions of Mr. Justice Harlan*, 46 AM. L. REV. 324 (1912).

law was part and parcel of a comprehensive jurisprudence. His objectives, much like those of the Warren Court,[25] were generous, compassionate, and rooted in a staunch devotion to the ideals of democracy. But, much in the manner of the Warren Court, the loftiness of Harlan's purposes was not always matched by careful use of precedent, meticulous reasoning, or intelligible directives.

I. HARLAN'S JURISPRUDENCE

Harlan was first and foremost a nationalist, and his nationalism, the result of a Kentucky Whig upbringing and fortified by what might almost be called a conversion to Radical Republicanism,[26] was capacious enough to absorb Populist, Progressive, and orthodox Republican ideology. He was, on economic matters, at once a liberal and a conservative. His protests against Court-imposed obstacles to national reform measures abound with references to the "greed,"[27] "selfishness," and "audacity" of corporations which demanded nothing less than that "the whole population of America pay tribute to them."[28] "The dominion of aggregated wealth,"[29] he charged, "threaten[ed] the integrity of our institutions"[30] as it "sought" to fashion another kind of "slavery" upon the nation; "slavery that would result from aggregations of capital in the hands of a few individuals and corporations controlling for their own advantage exclusively, the entire business of the whole country."[31]

And yet, in roughly analogous state cases, Harlan made a sub-

---

[25] See Cox, THE WARREN COURT (1968).

[26] Harlan learned his Whiggery from his father and his father's good friend, Henry Clay. That party's Civil War death agonies sent Harlan briefly into the Know-Nothing party, whose credo he later denounced, the Constitutional Unionist party, the Democratic party, in protest against passage of the Thirteenth Amendment and the 1866 Civil Rights Act, the Conservative Union party, and, finally, the Republican party. In 1876, he led the Kentucky delegation to the Republican Convention and, at a crucial point, swung his state's votes to Hayes. He was neither the first nor the last Supreme Court Justice to earn his post through party convention machinations.

Harlan and his family had owned a few house slaves, all of whom, it is said, were well cared for. His attitude toward emancipation and the Civil War Amendments changed as he witnessed the rise of the Klan, the outbreak of violence against the blacks, and the refusal of Democratic officials to control the problem.

[27] Texas & P. R.R. Co. v. I.C.C., 162 U.S. 197, 252 (1896); United States v. E. C. Knight Co., 156 U.S. 1, 44 (1895).

[28] United States v. E. C. Knight Co., 156 U.S. 1, 43 (1895).

[29] Pollock v. Farmer's Loan & Trust Co., 158 U.S. 601, 685 (1895).

[30] United States v. E. C. Knight Co., 156 U.S. 1, 44 (1895).

[31] United States v. Standard Oil, 211 U.S. 1, 83 (1911).

stantial and creative contribution to laissez-faire jurisprudence. He was not only with the majority in all instances in which the Court invalidated, on the Fourteenth Amendment due process grounds, state established rates, but he earlier and unsuccessfully urged his brethren to do the same on Contract Clause grounds.[32] He delivered the greatly castigated opinion in *Smyth v. Ames*,[33] formulating a rule for publicly established rates which would allow investors a "fair return" on a "fair value" of the road's property. That decision marked a culmination point for Harlan. Earlier he had fretted over the effects which reform-minded state legislatures and regulatory commissions would have upon the investment market. Would builders and backers of the railroads have undertaken such vast exertions and "risked . . . immense sums" had they thought profits would depend, not on their own, but on some public official's estimation of the road's property?[34] Similarly, he expressed alarm over the value of securities of privately owned gas, water, and electric companies if proposed and ruinously competing municipal plants went into operation.[35]

He voiced this theme—that investors should not be left to the mercies of local majorities—early in the state and municipal bond repudiation cases. Dissenting with Field, he angrily brushed aside the Eleventh Amendment claims that, for a while, made it constitutionally possible for states to scale down their debts and to escape paying their contractual obligations to the holders of state bonds.[36]

---

[32] Stone v. Farmer's Loan & Trust Co. 116 U.S. 307, 341 (1885).

[33] 169 U.S. 466, 546–47 (1898). The opinion has been subjected to a surfeit of criticism, much of it encapsulated in the literature referred to in note 18 *supra*. See also Goddard, *The Evolution and Devolution of Public Utility Law*, 32 MICH. L. REV. 577 (1934). See Brandeis on the "laborious" and "baffling" task of finding the "present value" of public utility property, in Missouri *ex rel*. Southwestern Bell Tel. Co. v. Commission, 262 U.S. 276, 291 (1923), and Frankfurter's reference to the "hodge-podge" of the *Smyth* rule, in F.P.C. v. Hope Natural Gas Co., 320 U.S. 591, 627 (1944).

[34] Stone v. Farmer's Loan & Trust Co., 116 U.S. 307, 341 (1885). In Ruggles v. Illinois, 108 U.S. 526 (1883), Harlan concurred separately on the ground that the rates established by the Commission were reasonable even as the company viewed the question. He disagreed with that portion of Chief Justice Waite's opinion that rejected the railroad's claim that its charter gave it the exclusive right to fix rates. The majority here relied on an inalienable police power to amend such charter rights; Harlan depended on the immunity from change afforded to "contracts."

[35] New Orleans Gas v. Louisiana Light Co., 115 U.S. 650 (1885); New Orleans Waterworks v. Rivers, 115 U.S. 674 (1885).

[36] Antoni v. Greenhow, 107 U.S. 769, 801 (1882); Louisiana v. Jumel, 107 U.S. 711, 746 (1883); *Ex parte* Ayers, 123 U.S. 443, 501 (1887).

He utilized *Swift v. Tyson* to preserve the worth of municipal bonds issued to finance railroad construction. The liberal Harlan, wise to the knavish ways of railroad promoters[37] and acutely sensitive to agrarian discontents, adamantly insisted (even on the rare occasions when the majority relented)[38] that debt-ridden, impoverished, and rebellious communities impose the levies necessary to pay the interest on the bonds.[39] And this even where the promised line or spur, the payment for which the bonds were issued, was not constructed;[40] where elected officials and railroad promoters, in collusion, arranged for the issuance and sale of bonds for a road which they knew full well would never materialize;[41] and where local officials would not collect the taxes, preferring jail to the obedience of court orders.[42]

There can be no doubt that Harlan regarded the investment market, especially in public utilities, as an integral component of

---

[37] Harlan joined Swayne in dissent from the Court's ruling that the Government could not recover losses on loans made for railroad construction and dissipated by the *Credit Mobilier* scandal. United States v. Union Pac. R.R., 98 U.S. 569 (1879). Harlan also upheld homesteaders against claims made upon their lands by the railroads, Nelson v. Northern Pac. R.R., 188 U.S. 108 (1903), and dissented from the affirmation of patent awards to the railroads, Northern Pac. R.R. v. Smith, 171 U.S. 260 (1898).

[38] Thompson v. Allen County, 115 U.S. 550, 561 (1883); Meriwether v. Garrett, 102 U.S. 472, 521 (1880) (joining Strong's dissent). For a description of the desperate efforts made by communities to relieve themselves of their indebtedness, see Westin, *The Supreme Court, the Populist Movement, and the Campaign of 1896*, 15 J. POL. 3, 7–9 (1953).

[39] Harlan sternly ordered that the taxes be collected in an Illinois town where there were "no funds in the treasury . . . [and] the revenue of the city, . . . after meeting its necessary and current expenses and other demands . . . will be insufficient to pay [the] judgment." Mayor of Quincy v. United States, 113 U.S. 332, 335, 336 (1884).

[40] Kirkbridge v. Lafayette County, 108 U.S. 550 (1883); American Life Ins. Co. v. Bruce, 105 U.S. 328 (1881); Brooklyn v. Aetna Ins. Co., 99 U.S. 372 (1879).

[41] Brooklyn v. Aetna Ins. Co., 99 U.S. 372 (1879); Tipton County v. Rogers Locomotive Co., 103 U.S. 523 (1880).

[42] In Thompson v. Allen County, 115 U.S. 550, 561 (1884), Harlan dissented alone when the Court ruled that a county court could not, as a last resort and in the face of local intransigence, collect the necessary taxes. When federal court orders of mandamus to pay interest on bonds held by state courts to have been illegally or fraudulently issued were disobeyed, jail sentences were imposed on as many as one hundred local officials. See Warren, *Federal Court Interference with State Court Orders*, 43 HARV. L. REV. 345, 351–52 (1930); WENDELL, RELATIONS BETWEEN STATE AND FEDERAL COURTS 159 (1949). This took place before Harlan's appointment. As late as 1893, however, three Missouri judges went to jail when they refused to order the collection of taxes on bonds which they had previously invalidated. See Westin, note 38 *supra*, at 8. Harlan would certainly have sustained these sentences.

interstate commerce, and, in the cases mentioned, as coming under the protection of the Commerce Clause. But it was not the Commerce Clause that was applied. The reliance was on the Due Process Clause of the Fourteenth Amendment,"[43] the Contract Clause,[44] a highly restrictive view of the Eleventh Amendment, and the doctrine of *Swift v. Tyson*. In other cases dealing ostensibly with only intrastate commerce, but which Harlan thought involved burdens upon commerce among the states, he did much the same thing— maintaining that the Equal Protection Clause of the Fourteenth Amendment prohibited state imposition of special conditions for doing business and special taxes upon foreign and out-of-state firms.[45] He persuaded the Court that the Fourteenth Amendment guarantee of "liberty of contract" prohibited state interference with the interstate sales of insurance contracts.[46]

His vision and his grand design emerged: Harlan had an unshakable faith in the beneficent possibilities of American capitalism,

---

[43] Harlan was not so rigidly pro-utility company as some of these decisions would suggest. When sustaining municipally established water rates, he repeated a warning issued in *Smyth v. Ames*, 169 U.S. at 544, that "a railroad corporation maintaining a highway under the authority of the state" may not "fix its rates solely to its own interest and ignore the rights of the public." The public should not be expected to pay for errors of management; the property "may have cost more than it ought to have cost, and its outstanding bonds . . . may be in excess of the real value of the property." San Diego Land Co. v. National City, 174 U.S. 739, 758 (1899). Harlan joined in a large number of cases upholding publicly established rates on the ground that the public utilities had overvalued their property and were seeking excessive returns on the original investments. See San Diego Land Co. v. Jasper, 189 U.S. 439 (1903); Stanislaus v. San Joaquin Canal & Irr. Co., 192 U.S. 201 (1903); Minneapolis & St. L. R.R. v. Minnesota, 186 U.S. 257 (1902).

[44] As the movement for municipal ownership grew, Harlan rejected claims by privately owned utilities that they had been granted exclusive franchises. The *Charles River Bridge* doctrine was utilized to reject claims of implied monopoly. See Charles River Bridge v. Warren Bridge, 11 Pet. 420 (1837). Companies and their investors who were unaware of the inalienability of the police power and implied reservations were out of luck. Lehigh Valley Water Co. v. Easton, 121 U.S. 388 (1887); Stein v. Bienville Water Supply Co., 141 U.S. 74 (1891); Knoxville v. Knoxville Water Co., 212 U.S. 1 (1909). Dissenting in Vicksburg v. Vicksburg Water Co., 202 U.S. 453, 473 (1906), Harlan said that the rights of stockholders were secondary to the "duty to protect the public health, safety and morals."

[45] He was in dissent in Fidelity Mutual Life Ins. Co. v. Mettler, 185 U.S. 308, 328 (1902); Security Mut. Ins. Co. v. Prewitt, 202 U.S. 246, 258 (1906); Fire Assurance Ass'n of Philadelphia v. New York, 119 U.S. 110, 120 (1886); New York v. Roberts, 171 U.S. 358, 666 (1898).

[46] Allgeyer v. Louisiana, 165 U.S. 578 (1897), adopted the position taken by Harlan in dissent in Hooper v. California, 155 U.S. 648, 659 (1894).

possibilities which he saw threatened both by corporate venality, and by short-sighted local government. Congress had acted upon only one aspect of the problem, thereby placing the remainder of the burden upon the judiciary. To be equal to the task the federal courts were obligated to stretch to the utmost all their constitutional, statutory, and judicially created powers. Justice Story's interpretation of § 34 of the Judiciary Act of 1789,[47] was just such a power or, more accurately, combination of powers.

II. Swift v. Tyson and the Municipal Bond Cases

By the time of Harlan's appointment, *Swift v. Tyson*[48] had already been stretched a long way. It will be remembered that Story had there asserted that the "laws of the several states" to be followed as the "rules of decision" in diversity cases referred to state court construction of state statute law. But, because judge-made law was not itself law but "only evidence of what the laws are," the federal courts were free to exercise independent judgment on the common law.[49] Actually, Story, whatever his hopes for an overarching commercial law administered by the federal courts,[50] narrowed the scope of his holding. First, he noted that since the New York law concerning promissory notes was not settled, the Court lacked precedent to which it would give its "most deliberate attention and respect."[51] He added that the Court, in common-law cases, would accept "long established local custom having the force of laws."[52] Second, he placed real property law beyond the reach of the federal courts. The only freedom of decision staked out exclusively for the federal courts was the law of negotiable instruments, historically not confined to a particular forum, but "belonging to the whole commercial world."[53] The question how this might be affected by state statutes and state court construction was left open. But presumably, under the Rules of Decision Act, federal courts would be required to adhere to state court rulings even here.

Within a few years the Court had extended the ruling of *Swift* and ignored Story's qualifications of it. Independent judgment was exercised over various forms of what Story had called "ordinary

---

[47] 1 Stat. 92 (1789).

[48] 16 Pet. 1 (1849).   [51] 16 Pet. at 19.

[49] *Id.* at 18.   [52] *Ibid.*

[50] See Dunne, note 13 *supra*.   [53] *Ibid.*

contracts,"[54] over contracts connected with questions of land law,[55] and even over state statutes. The holdings in the last category were somewhat dubious;[56] *Greene v. Neal*,[57] left inviolate by Story and tested by time, was still the leading precedent. Here the Court even reversed itself in order to conform to the latest of several state court statutory constructions. Even so, by 1864 the Court, relying on the authority of *Tyson* had, to all intents and purposes, bestowed upon itself the power to create federal common law, state court construction of state statutes to the contrary notwithstanding. The stage was set for the leading municipal bond case, *Gelpke v. Dubuque*,[58] its progeny, and the mischief which would ensue.

In *Gelpke*, suit was initiated by out-of-state bondholders after the Iowa Supreme Court had first sustained tax levies as being for a "public purpose" within the meaning of the state constitution but then, responding perhaps to the plight of the hard-pressed taxpayers, reversed itself, declaring the bonds to be void.[59] This, announced Swayne for the Court, although repeating the observation that judges only discover but do not make law,[60] amounted to a violation of the Contract Clause. Miller protested in vain that the prohibition of the Contract Clause could only refer to legislative acts.[61] Cognizant, no doubt, of the difficulties of the Contract Clause, Swayne, writing for the majority, shifted his reliance to *Tyson*.

[54] *Ibid.*; Carpenter v. Providence Washington Ins. Co., 16 Pet. 494 (1842); Lane v. Vick, 3 How. 464 (1845); Chicago v. Robbins, 2 Black 418 (1862).

[55] Lane v. Vick, 3 How. 464 (1845); Chicago v. Robbins, 2 Black 418 (1862); Yates v. Milwaukee, 10 Wall. 497 (1870).

[56] Rowan v. Runnels, 5 How. 134 (1847), might be *sui generis* because of its connection with the slavery controversy. In Williamson v. Berry, 8 How. 495 (1850), the Court, in order to save the beneficiaries of a will "from their own folly," disregarded a New York statute. See WENDELL, note 42 *supra*, at 140. In Watson v. Tarpley, 18 How. 517 (1855), the Court refused to follow state codification of commercial law. But this decision was not "followed in other cases." Burns Mortgage Co. v. Fried, 292 U.S. 487, 495 (1934).

[57] 6 Pet. 291 (1832).   [58] 1 Wall. 175 (1864).

[59] There was probably a large element of expedience in the reversals. But the quality of the judges of the state courts mitigates against accepting so simplistic an explanation. Dillon of Iowa, Cooley of Michigan, Dixon of Wisconsin must rank high indeed in the pantheon of American jurists. For a discussion, see FAIRMAN, MR. JUSTICE MILLER 216 (1939); WENDELL, note 42 *supra*, at 143–50.

[60] See Rand, *Swift v. Tyson v. Gelpke v. Dubuque*, 8 HARV. L. REV. 328 (1895).

[61] On Miller's dissents in *Gelpke* and other bond cases, see FAIRMAN, note 59 *supra*, at ch. 9. Both Fairman and Wendell, while critical of the decisions in the bond cases, made the point that the bondholders had every right to believe in the validity of their bonds despite the schemes from which they derived.

The bonds, he remarked, were commercial paper. But while he passed over the qualifications that Story had proposed, he did not declare the absolute universality of the common law of negotiable instruments, regardless of state law.[62] This alone would have been a long step, and Swayne himself had only recently, and ringingly, reaffirmed *Greene v. Neal.*[63] But the Taney Court, in cases challenging the legislative withdrawal of the tax-exempt status of banks, had exercised its independent judgment to differ with Ohio court rulings that the grants of immunity did not constitute contracts within the meaning of the federal Constitution.[64] That determination made, the Court ruled that legislative impairment had indeed occurred.[65] Seizing on this, Swayne rushed full steam ahead. Where contractual obligations were concerned, the Court would not, "simply because a state tribunal [had] erected the altar and decreed the sacrifice," blindly follow suit, and thereby "immolate truth, justice and the law."[66] The difficulty here was that jurisdiction in the Ohio bank cases was based on the presentation of a federal question, not diversity of citizenship. The horrid deeds which Swayne attributed to the state court had, in reality, been committed by the legislature. And *Tyson,* which after all had reference to diversity jurisdiction,[67] was only peripheral to the rulings. Miller did not comment upon the jurisdictional tangle which the Court had made

---

[62] Taken together with Story's expansive view of the law of negotiable instruments, note 53 *supra,* and the holding of Watson v. Tarpley, 18 How. 517 (1885), note 56 *supra,* Swayne's brief reference to the bonds as commercial paper had wide-ranging implications. See Olcott v. Supervisors, 16 Wall. 678 (1872), note 73 *infra.* Dunne thinks that Justice Daniels' opinion in *Watson v. Tarpley* was "a most significant vindication of Story's views and vision." DUNNE, note 13 *supra,* at 414. Daniels was a strong advocate of states' rights and was not much admired for it by Story. *Ibid.*

[63] Leffingwell v. Warren, 2 Black 599 (1863).

[64] In Piqua Branch of the State Bank v. Knopp, 16 How. 396 (1853), and Ohio Life Ins. Co. v. Debolt, 16 How. 416 (1853), the Court exercised independent judgment to decide the existence of the contract and then ruled that the contract was not impaired. In the *Debolt* case, Taney had said that the Contract Clause is a limitation on the legislature only and not on the courts.

[65] Dodge v. Woolsey, 18 How. 331 (1885); Mechanics' & Traders' Bank v. Debolt, 18 How 380 (1855); Jefferson Branch Bank v. Skelly, 1 Black 436 (1861). See WRIGHT, THE CONTRACT CLAUSE OF THE CONSTITUTION 73, 74, 156 (1938).

[66] 1 Wall. at 206, 207.

[67] In Indiana *ex rel.* Anderson v. Brand, 303 U.S. 95 (1938), decided in the 1937 Term just before *Erie,* the Court exercised its independent judgment to determine the existence of a contract alleged to be legislatively impaired.

for itself.[68] The ground of the holding remained mysterious. The Court subsequently held that *Gelpke* was not based on the Contract Clause,[69] but it can hardly be based upon *Tyson* either. While the reasoning was unclear, the Court's, and particularly Swayne's, determination to guarantee the value of the bonds was not.[70] If one means was constitutionally and/or legally inadequate, another would do. If neither would suffice separately, both might make it together. The doctrine of *Gelpke v. Dubuque* was one that would take the Court "a good while to explain."[71]

More, and worse, was to come. Shortly thereafter the Court announced its freedom, where contract rights were at stake, to disregard the first[72] as well as consistent state court constructions of statutes.[73] Thus *Gelpke*, even though the questionable Contract Clause basis of that ruling was not strictly applicable, enabled the Court, in subsequent bond cases, to exercise its independent judgment wherever it chose. At one point the Justices skirted close to a declaration that negotiable instruments were unaffected by any manner of state law. Here, although the bonds had been issued prior to a judicial determination as to their constitutional invalidity, the Court ruled that a presumption of legality rendered the question whether the taxes were for a valid public purpose one of "general law."[74]

By that point the Court had almost, but not quite, lost sight of the disparate nature of *Tyson*, the Ohio bank cases, and *Gelpke*. Logically, and in keeping with the self-imposed mission to preserve the worth of these securities, it would have been neater, and certainly more sensible, for the Court to hold that in cases involving a pledge of public credit, it would determine the validity of bonds

---

[68] See PEPPER, THE BORDERLAND OF FEDERAL AND STATE DECISIONS 36 (1889).

[69] Tidal Oil Co. v. Flanagan, 263 U.S. 444 (1924). The Contract Clause basis of Gelpke was reasserted by Chief Justice Waite in Douglas v. Pike County, 101 U.S. 677 (1879).

[70] Miller described Swayne as "an extremist in upholding all negotiable bonds and especially Rail Road Securities." FAIRMAN, note 59 *supra*, at 233–34.

[71] Holmes, dissenting, in Muhlker v. New York Street R.R., 197 U.S. 544, 573 (1905).

[72] Butz v. Muscatine, 8 Wall. 575 (1896). The Court relied upon Jefferson Branch Bank v. Skelly, 1 Black 436 (1861), but its reliance was misplaced since that case involved legislative impairment.

[73] Olcott v. Supervisors, 16 Wall. 678 (1872), followed in Pine Grove v. Talcott, 19 Wall. 666 (1874). These cases are discussed in FAIRMAN, note 59 *supra*, at 217.

[74] Olcott v. Supervisors, 16 Wall. at 690 (1872).

for itself, state law notwithstanding. As it was, the Court had boxed itself in, and refused jurisdiction when resident bondholders claimed judicial impairment of contractual rights.[75] This meant, at least in the municipal bond cases, that federal law could only be raised when jurisdiction obtained because of the diversity of the parties. After 1868, it would, of course, have been possible to claim that this particular form of repudiation was, within the meaning of the Fourteenth Amendment, a deprivation of property without due process of law.[76] But, by then, matters were too far gone to resort to this rationalization.

In addition to its failures to recognize the jurisdictional confusions, the Court seemed unaware that *Gelpke* had modified *Tyson* beyond recognition. Whatever distinctions Story had made and whatever he had left unsaid about negotiable instruments and state statutes, *Tyson* was believed to hold that federal courts were free to exercise independent judgment at common law, but not when state court rulings on positive state law (statutes and constitutions) provided the rules of decision to govern the case. Admittedly, upon occasion, this qualification had been overlooked. But *Gelpke* pushed even further by justifying rejection of the accepted version of § 34. The primary reason was that, in cases involving contracts within the meaning of the federal Constitution, the federal courts were not bound by the latest state court construction of state law, where that law had been the object of conflicting rulings. Another justification for the exercise of independent judgment was that these inconsistent rulings amounted to taking the law out of the category of positive law and placing it in the category of unsettled law, as New York law had been unsettled when Mr. Swift took Mr. Tyson to court. That being the case, the Contract Clause disappeared from sight. A final rationale for the freedom of the federal courts in diversity cases would be that all negotiable instruments are the special preserve of the federal judiciary—a doctrine which the Court had once come close to stating.[77]

---

[75] Railroad Co. v. Rock, 4 Wall. 177 (1867); Railroad Co. v. McClure, 10 Wall. 511 (1871).

[76] "The suggestion has been made that the Court might be induced to treat the retroactive application of the overruling state decision as a deprivation of property without due process of law—a possibility which . . . did not exist in 1864, and which as yet is not supported in the jurisprudence of the Court." FAIRMAN, note 59 *supra*, at 220, citing Shulman, *The Demise of Swift v. Tyson*, 47 YALE L.J. 1336, 1351 (1938).

[77] Olcott v. Supervisors, 16 Wall. 678 (1872).

The second consideration is of more consequence. *Tyson* had asserted that the Rules of Decision Act obligated the federal courts to accept state court construction of positive state law. *Gelpke* held that the federal courts were not so bound. *Gelpke*, thus, rejected this dictum in *Tyson*, and both cases could not, as they so often were, be relied upon together where the issue was not one of common law.

None of this daunted Harlan. With the *Gelpke* Contract Clause principle lurking in the background, he utilized *Tyson* to justify overruling state court holdings that bonds were defective because of invalidity of elections or mode of issuance,[78] or because the tax levies themselves were contrary to statutory and/or constitutional provisions.[79] Harlan often disagreed when the majority held against the bondholders,[80] and objected to the majority's confirmation of a state court holding that authorization to borrow for municipal purposes did not include the power to issue bonds.[81] Because "enormous" amounts of capital had been invested upon the assumption that the power to borrow implicitly included the power to issue negotiable instruments, the decision would "produce incalculable mischief."[82] A natural-law note was sometimes struck. "Principles of justice" demanded that "only the clearest and most satisfactory proof" could convince the Court that all was not as it should be after the bonds had been "issued under corporate seals," "put on the market," and "passed into the hands of innocent shareholders."[83]

These opinions, however unsupportable, did not go beyond the

---

[78] Town of Roberts v. Bolles, 101 U.S. 119 (1880); Lewis v. Board of County Commissioners, 105 U.S. 739 (1882); Citizens' Loan Co. v. Perry County, 156 U.S. 689 (1895).

[79] Gunnison County v. E. H. Rollins & Sons, 173 U.S. 255 (1899).

[80] Nesbitt v. Riverside, 144 U.S. 610 (1891); Litchfield v. Ballou, 114 U.S. 190 (1895); Wells v. Supervisors, 102 U.S. 262 (1880). Harlan, on occasion, joined majority opinions upholding the communities. Stanley v. Coler, 190 U.S. 437 (1903); Siebert v. Lewis, 122 U.S. 284 (1887); Ralls County v. United States, 105 U.S. 733 (1881). He did join one of Miller's many dissents when the Court sustained the claims of the bondholders. Calhoun County v. Galbraith, 99 U.S. 214 (1878).

[81] Brenham v. German American Bank, 144 U.S. 173 (1892).

[82] *Id.* at 197.

[83] City of Evansville v. Dennett, 161 U.S. 435, 446 (1896); Citizens' Savings and Loan v. Perry County, 156 U.S. 689, 712 (1895); Gunnison County v. E. H. Rollins & Sons, 173 U.S. 255, 275 (1899).

already unwarranted extensions of *Tyson*, and were based squarely
upon the Court's mistaken reading of that decision. When Harlan
based holdings on both *Tyson* and *Gelpke*, he added to the existing
confusion. Two of these cases involved bondholders who had purchased securities knowing that their invalidity had already been
determined by the state courts. They unctuously repaired to the
federal courts and claimed their rights had been violated.[84] Harlan
did not fail these "innocents." The Court, he assured them, would
apply the law as the Court determined it to have been at the time
the referenda were held. For it was then that the rights (he did not
say whose) had accrued and might later be claimed by the purchasers despite their awareness when they purchased the bonds that
state courts would not honor such rights.[85] One of the cases came
from Michigan where Judge Cooley's court, unlike those in other
states, refused to capitulate and re-establish the validity of the
bonds.[86] Harlan put it bluntly enough. The plaintiff admittedly
knew of the latest rulings. "It [was] to be presumed," however,
that he was "also" aware that similar holdings had been overturned
by the Supreme Court.[87] Destroying this expectation amounted to
a judicial violation of the Contract Clause, and since federal rights
were thus jeopardized, Harlan was not obligated to follow Judge
Cooley's lead.

In these cases Harlan's employment of *Tyson/Gelpke* is so gar-
bled that it is impossible to determine the grounds for the decisions.
In a later case,[88] he attempted to follow the *Gelpke* Contract Clause
doctrine, was uncertain of the fit, and rather lamely summoned
Tyson. The facts were these: The Illinois Supreme Court upheld
legislation which retroactively legalized tax levies voted upon to
issue school bonds. Subsequently the Court ruled that the state constitution forbade similar legislation that legalized the issuance of
railroad bonds. Harlan said that the earlier cases "seemed" to "rest
on the principle" that the state constitution did permit such statutes.
While the two situations were not strictly "analogous," it was quite

---

[84] Thompson v. Perrine, 106 U.S. 589 (1883), also involved an element of collusion.
The bonds were transferred in order to create diversity jurisdiction. Taylor v. Ypsilanti,
105 U.S. 60 (1883): see FAIRMAN, note 59 *supra*, at 122, n. 13.

[85] Thompson v. Perrine, 106 U.S. 589, 591 (1883).

[86] WENDELL, note 42 *supra*, at 157–59.

[87] Taylor v. Ypsilanti, 105 U.S. 60, 70 (1883).

[88] Anderson v. Santa Ana, 116 U.S. 356 (1886).

possible that the Court, by these reversals (if, indeed, that is what they were) had violated the Contract Clause. But, in case the Court was mistaken, and since contract rights were claimed, the Court would make an independent determination as to what was the law of Illinois when the "rights of the parties . . . accrued."[89]

All Harlan, and usually the majority, required in these cases was that some manner of enabling legislation had at some time or another been on the statute books.[90] If so, the bondholders would get all, or some, of their money back. It was not an especially attractive chapter in the Court's history. The image projected was of hard-hearted judges determined to extract their pound of flesh, willing to wield any instruments to do the job.[91] But whatever the inequities, both for resident bondholders and the duped and insolvent communities, whatever the sloppiness of the judicial reasoning and the misuse of precedent, it can be argued that the decisions were perhaps functional during a critical period in the development of American industrial capitalism.[92] The bond cases, which had once crowded the docket and aroused high political passions,[93] were soon forgotten. But the crazy-quilt of constitutional and legal doctrine which they introduced was not.

III. The Doctrines of the Bond Cases Extended

Tyson, by itself, encouraging forum-shopping and spawning uncertainty in "those rules of law which [should] guide people in their everyday affairs"[94] was bad enough, and Harlan did his part in applying the doctrine.[95] These might be called "pure" *Tyson* cases. But I will not dwell on the "pure" *Tyson* cases except to

---

[89] *Id.* at 361, 366.

[90] In City of Evansville v. Dennett, 161 U.S. 435 (1896), Harlan said that it was not incumbent on purchasers to inquire into the circumstances attendant upon the issuance and sale of the bonds. It was to be presumed that the town or county had complied with all relevant statutory and constitutional requirements and that local officials had acted legally and properly. See also Knox v. Aspinall, 21 How. 539 (1859).

[91] Judge Dillon wrote that the Court turned a "face of flint" toward the communities. Dillon, The Law of Municipal Corporations 7 (1876).

[92] 2 Warren, note 18 *supra*, at 531.

[93] Westin, note 38 *supra*.

[94] Hart & Wechsler, The Federal Courts and the Federal System 616 (1953).

[95] Oates v. National Bank, 100 U.S. 239 (1880); Railroad Co. v. National Bank, 102 U.S. 14 (1880).

hazard a guess as to what might have been Harlan's position in *Baltimore & Ohio R. R. Co. v. Baugh.*[96]

In that case the Court refused to follow the state common law of torts which had modified the fellow-servant doctrine. Applying that ancient doctrine in unadulterated form the Court reversed a state court decision awarding damages to an injured railway worker. Usually, at this time, these negligence cases went this way, with the Court, over the protests of Harlan, Field, Fuller, and sometimes White, following state court rulings that favored the employer.[97] In *Baugh,* Field announced that he had changed his mind about the *Tyson* construction of § 34, and entered the dissent which provided, in part, the basis for Brandeis's *Erie* opinion.[98] Harlan, who was serving on the Bering Sea Tribunal at the time, had a reasonably pro-employee record in labor cases and on numerous occasions indicated his solicitude and compassion for the workingman.[99] While he would have been unable to join Field's denunciation of *Tyson* and all its fruits, he would also have been unable to join in this particular exercise of independent judgment and, surely, would have dissented separately.

The first example of *Tyson*-cum-*Gelpke* that was not a municipal bond case was *Burgess v. Seligman.*[100] On the surface it looked

---

[96] 149 U.S. 368 (1893).

[97] Central R.R. v. Keegan, 160 U.S. 259 (1895); Northern Pac. R.R. v. Hambley, 154 U.S. 349 (1894); Northern Pac. R.R. v. Dixon, 194 U.S. 338 (1904). See KING, MELVILLE WESTON FULLER 183–84 (Phoenix ed. 1967); SWISHER, STEPHEN FIELD: CRAFTSMAN OF THE LAW 428–29 (Phoenix ed. 1963).

[98] Field maintained that the *Tyson* ruling was unconstitutional. 149 U.S. at 399, 401.

[99] Robertson v. Baldwin, 165 U.S. 275 (1897). Harlan, holding fast to the "liberty of contract" doctrine, nevertheless, dissented separately in Lochner v. New York, 198 U.S. 45, 65 (1908), on the ground that the hazards of the bakers' trade warranted legislative interference with their freedom of contract. He concurred in Holden v. Hardy, 169 U.S. 366 (1898), and in Muller v. Oregon, 208 U.S. 412 (1908). He delivered the opinion in Atkin v. Kansas, 191 U.S. 207 (1903), sustaining, with obvious reluctance, an eight-hour day for laborers engaged in public work. The work was healthy, but the Court, he said, could not deny a state the right to regulate the hours of labor of its own employees. He also joined Moody's dissent in the *First Employer's Liability Case,* Howard v. Illinois, 207 U.S. 463 (1908).

On the other hand, he concurred in *In re* Debs, 158 U.S. 564 (1895); *The Danbury Hatters' Case,* Loewe v. Lawlor, 208 U.S. 274 (1908), and delivered the opinion in Adair v. United States, 208 U.S. 161 (1908). His approval of the union movement would, thus, seem to have been somewhat less than enthusiastic.

[100] 107 U.S. 20 (1883).

like an unadorned *Tyson* problem, but close examination illustrates to what extent *Gelpke* had become the silent partner of *Tyson*. The decision reversed a state court and followed a federal circuit court ruling concerning the statutory liability of stockholders. Bradley said that in cases "balanced with doubt" the Court would, in the interests of "comity," "lean toward" agreement with state court construction of state constitutions and statutes.[101] (Story had said that the Court would show this deference even to common-law rulings.) When, however, "contracts and transactions" had ᵎbeen "entered into" and "rights" had "accrued" under certain assumptions about state law, the federal courts, as long as state courts had not construed said law, were free to exercise independent judgment, for "the very object of giving to the national courts jurisdiction to administer the laws of the states in controversies between citizens of different states was to institute independent tribunals which would be unaffected by local views."[102]

The reasoning is elusive. Bradley did not claim that the out-of-state stockholders had been, or might be, treated differently from resident stockholders. He claimed that he had followed *Tyson*, which of course, he had not. *Greene v. Neal* was ignored. What happened is that *Gelpke* provided precedent for following the first of two conflicting constructions of the same law when the second interfered with rights sustained under the first. But the allegation of judicial impairment of federal rights had justified this in *Gelpke* and the other bond cases. No federal question was raised in *Burgess*. How could it have been? But it was "present" nonetheless because of the similarity with *Gelpke* and because rights had been at one time judicially affirmed. Consequently, the distinction between legislative contracts within the meaning of the Constitution and ordinary contracts and commercial transactions was significantly blurred. Had the state court acted before the federal court, the Supreme Court presumably would have had to follow the former. But the crucial point was that precedent had been established for the Court to disregard state court construction of positive state law even in the absence of federal question.

This precedent might never have been pushed to its limit had the Court not at that time been engaged in a long battle with Virginia over that state's ingenious efforts to scale down public debts

---

[101] *Id.* at 33–34.   [102] *Ibid.*

incurred by Reconstruction and Redeemer legislatures.[103] The Court was finally able to invalidate statutes which, while not amounting to outright repudiation, made it prohibitively time-consuming and expensive for bondholders to present their coupons and collect interest due.[104] But the Virginia judiciary, battle-wise from its many struggles against its national counterpart, was not easily brought to surrender.

This is what happened in *McCullough v. Virginia*.[105] McCullough, a Virginia citizen, managed to establish the validity of his coupons and submitted them, in accordance with provisions of a statute sustained by the Court as payment for taxes.[106] The Virginia Court of Appeals agreed with the arguments of state officials that the coupons were unacceptable because the original funding act, under which the debt was incurred, was repugnant to the state constitution. It was the first ruling on the funding act, and the court was careful not to refer to any of the subsequent "coupon crusher" acts, so that in all strictness it could not be claimed that effect had been given to legislation which violated the federal Constitution by impairing a contract made by a prior legislative act.[107] It seemed air-tight. *Gelpke* was not applicable. Nor was *Tyson* in the sense that it had been employed in either the Ohio bank cases or in *Burgess*. But the Virginia Court of Appeals had reckoned without the *Tyson/Gelpke/Burgess* muddle, as well as the Court's determination to protect the market in public securities.

Brewer started out in the usual manner of the *Tyson*-based holdings. The Court as a "general rule" accepted state court construction of positive state law.[108] But then *Gelpke* crept in. Allegations of the impairment of contractual obligations compelled the Court to exercise independent judgment. While there was not, to be sure,

---

[103] See 2 WARREN, note 18 *supra*, at 663–67; WOODWARD, THE ORIGINS OF THE NEW SOUTH, LOUISIANA 86–100 (1951); cases cited in note 36 *supra*.

[104] Virginia Coupon Cases, 114 U.S. 270 (1885); Royall v. Virginia, 116 U.S. 572 (1886).

[105] 172 U.S. 102 (1899).

[106] Antoni v. Greenhow, 107 U.S. 769 (1882) (Harlan, J., dissenting).

[107] In Hartman v. Greenhow, 102 U.S. 672 (1881), a statute that drastically scaled down the state debt was held unconstitutional and the state was ordered to make good on the bonds. It was after that that the state enacted the effectively annoying "coupon crusher" acts.

[108] 172 U.S. at 109.

a direct question of legislative impairment of contract, and while the Virginia court had not discussed the repudiating legislation, its judgment did, as a matter of fact, give effect to these subsequent statutes. He seemed to be saying that the implied interpretation of the later acts impaired rights secured by the first. In short, legislation which the Court considered finally and safely buried was alive and well once again. Thanks to its own precedent, however, the Court could not rule that this judicial sleight-of-hand constituted a violation of the Contract Clause. The situation was not analogous to the Ohio bank cases in which the federal question had been properly presented. So *Gelpke* had to depart, having made its mark, as unobtrusively as it had entered. Only *Tyson* remained; but how to use it here? Again, the Ohio bank cases were of no help. *Tyson*, in those nondiversity cases, had been employed to ascertain if legislative withdrawal of a legislative grant amounted to an impairment of contractual obligations. While the Virginia legislature had made a contract with McCullough, it had not been responsible for rendering his coupons worthless. The Virginia Court of Appeals had done that by invalidating the authorizing statute. What Brewer settled on was to exercise his independent judgment. "[W]e are not limited to a mere consideration of the language used in the opinion, but may examine and determine what is the real effect of the decision."[109] And this effect was to make worthless "bonds, amounting to many millions of dollars" which had "for a quarter of a century" circulated in "the markets of the world."[110] That would never do. The funding act was, therefore, valid and so were McCullough's coupons.

The Court was undoubtedly correct in refusing to permit the state finally to wriggle away free, but in forestalling this latest and most brazen attempt of Virginia to circumvent the prohibitions of the Contract Clause and the clear mandates of the Court, the Court, as the dissenting Peckham tried to explain, had sunk even deeper into the *Tyson/Gelpke* morass. Picking his way patiently, Peckham pointed out that the precedent upon which the majority had so confidently relied had "nothing to do with this case."[111] In cases coming to the Court on writs of error, the Court had indeed concluded, state courts to the contrary, that contracts within the meaning of the Constitution existed, but it then found legislative impair-

---

[109] *Id*. at 117.   [110] *Id*. at 108.   [111] *Id*. at 129.

ment. However, lacking legislation "to which any effect has been given by the state court, this Court cannot review the decisions of state tribunals even though that decision makes worthless a contract which it had previously held valid."[112]

Peckham was kind and did not reconstruct the whole chain of causality. What the Court had done was to apply the precedent of cases where jurisdiction obtained because of diversity (the municipal bond cases) to a case where jurisdiction was claimed on the Contract Clause as a federal question. And then, of course, there was *Burgess*, permitting independent determination in the face of state court construction of positive state law and in the absence of a federal question. A Court determined to become a "mecca to which all dissatisfied suitors in state courts [might] turn"[113] would scarcely concede that "prior decision is not the foundation of jurisdiction."[114]

Peckham had no objections to the *Tyson* doctrine per se, but only to its misapplication, and it would be a few more years before Holmes would join his efforts to disentangle *Tyson* from its progeny. But the extent to which *Tyson* had become dependent upon *Gelpke* was not fully grasped, even by Peckham, as witnessed by his concurrence in Harlan's opinion in *Great Southern Fire Proof Hotel Co. v. Jones*,[115] a decision which, for the first time, reversed a state court ruling that violated the state constitution when no federal question was present.

The dispute was over an enforcement of a lien for labor and materials furnished for hotel construction. The hotel company, resident plaintiff, claimed that the statute under which it was sued was repugnant to the Ohio constitution, and the state Supreme Court had so ruled before the suit was initiated. Judge Lurton,[116] on the federal circuit court, disagreed. Harlan, following Lurton's reasoning, pointed out that the Ohio court ruling had come after the rights of the parties had accrued. It will be recalled that in *Burgess* it was asserted that rights had accrued, but the crucial point was that they had been judicially affirmed and since the defendants had entered into the agreement upon presumption of the statute's validity, the federal courts might determine for themselves if the law

---

[112] *Id.* at 130.

[113] *Ibid.*

[114] *Id.* at 132.

[115] 193 U.S. 532 (1903).

[116] Lurton was to become a Supreme Court Justice in 1909.

met the state's constitutional requirements. But *Great Southern Hotel* concerned only a private contract. Harlan ignored this. Furthermore, he utilized *Burgess* only by contorting the facts of that case. *Burgess,* concerned with one statute and two rulings of different jurisdictions, was twisted to mean that the federal courts might pick and choose among rulings dealing with the same subject matter from a variety of jurisdictions. Citing a number of decisions from other state courts, he announced the Court's agreement with the majority of them. "The great weight of authority in this country as to the meaning and scope of constitutional provisions substantially like this found in the constitution of Ohio . . . is against the conclusion reached by the learned state court."[117] This, surely, carried Story's hopes for legal uniformity beyond his fondest (or wildest) expectations.

What all this seemed to mean was that nonresident parties to a business agreement might expect the federal courts to reaffirm their understanding of state law, as long as that law had not been judicially construed at the time the agreement was made. Put another way: As long as nonresidents were not forewarned that their investments were insecure, the federal courts could, if they so wished, guarantee those investments. In the most extreme form: In diversity cases, the terms of a contract entered into in good faith may be enforced, state law notwithstanding, in the federal courts. *Great Southern Hotel* implied, and could not help implying, given its *Gelpke* background, that the Court might view any sort of an agreement as constitutionally guaranteed. The suspicion was confirmed in *Muhlker v. New York & Harlem R. R.*[118]

IV. Some Matters of Real Estate Law: Holmes v. Harlan

Muhlker came, as did *McCullough,* from a state court and, like *McCullough,* found the Court scratching around for a basis for ruling on the merits when it should have dismissed. The plaintiffs appealed a New York court holding that property owners were not deprived of easements of light and air by a statute ordering the elevation of a street railroad. Earlier state rulings issued prior to the passage of the statute upheld the owners' rights to the easement as stipulated in agreements with the city. The Court faced a dilemma:

---

[117] 193 U.S. at 550.   [118] 197 U.S. 544 (1905).

Had the legislature, which had not granted the easement, impaired the contract? Could the state court, in this nondiversity case, have impaired contract rights? The answer, in both cases, would certainly have to be no.[119] Moreover, the question was one of local real estate law, declared in *Tyson* and reaffirmed in *Burgess*, to be beyond the purview of the federal courts.

The difficulties were circumvented by two means. McKenna, while refusing to "discuss the power and limitations of the courts of New York to declare rules of property," held that "such power cannot be exercised to take away rights which have been acquired by contract."[120] Did this construction of the statute amount to an impairment of a contract? It did. For "we determine for ourselves the existence and extent of such contracts,"[121] and the Constitution forbids the states to impair the obligations of contract. This, unfortunately, still left the awkward question of who had done what to whom. And so the Court then triumphantly concluded that the plaintiffs had been deprived of property without due process of law.[122] This designation of the easement as property (or a contract, or whatever it was considered to be) might have indicated that the majority was uneasy with the Contract Clause basis of the ruling, or that the newly appointed Holmes, beginning the long advocacy

---

[119] "It would seem . . . that the time at which to estimate the obligation is when the allegedly impairing legislation is enacted. The Supreme Court appears, however, to have emphasized the date of the agreement. See . . . Muhlker v. Harlem R.R." Hart & Wechsler, note 94 *supra*, at 465–67.

[120] 197 U.S. at 571.

[121] *Ibid.*

[122] For a discussion of *Muhlker, McCullough,* and *Great Southern Hotel,* see Dodd, *Impairment of the Obligation of Contract by State Judicial Decisions,* 4 Ill. L. Rev. 155, 327, 332 (1909). The cases "seem to warrant the statement that the Supreme Court will, in practically every case, be able to find a statute to serve as a 'lay figure' in order to justify its taking jurisdiction over state courts where contract rights are impaired by reversal or modification of rules of law previously established by such courts. This rule may be easily extended to state cases passing on the first time and holding unconstitutional laws acted upon as valid, and under which contract rights had arisen before they were declared invalid; and in such a manner was the rule in *Geipke v. Dubuque* extended to cover such cases as *Great Southern Hotel v. Jones.*" The problem raised by *Gelpke, Great Southern Hotel,* and *Muhlker,* Dodd wrote, is that while the state rulings hold for the future, they do not affect the rights that have accrued in the past. He suggested that the difficulties could be resolved by not applying the Contract Clause in diversity cases and relying completely on *Tyson.* Insofar as cases would come from the state courts, the Court could employ the Fourteenth Amendment's Due Process Clause, which applied to both judicial and legislative acts.

leading to *Erie,* had made his mark. For he was joined not only by Peckham, as would be expected, but by two members of the *Mc-Cullough* majority, Chief Justice Fuller and Justice White.

It is in particular Holmes's dissection of the Court's use of *Tyson/Gelpke* that one turns to with almost a sense of relief. The easement was nothing more than a right *in rem,* "called a contract merely to bring it within the Contract Clause of the Constitution."[123]

> It seems to me a considerable extension of the power to determine for ourselves what the contract is, which we have assumed when it is alleged that the obligation of a contract has been impaired, to say that we will make the same independent determination when it is alleged that property is taken without due compensation. But it seems to me that it does not help the argument.[124]

The connection between the statute and the so-called contract was, he pointed out, remote, and was made only to justify federal question jurisdiction.[125] (Had Peckham's *McCullough* dissent struck home?) The case was, for all intents and purposes, one at common law, and what, he wanted to know, did the Constitution have to do with it? For all that had happened was that the New York court had distinguished, since circumstances had changed, its latest from its earlier rulings. It had not reversed them. But plaintiffs had nonetheless asked the Court "to extend to the present case the principle of *Gelpke* v. *Dubuque. . . .* That seems to me a great, unwarranted, and undesirable extension of a doctrine which it took this Court a good while to explain."[126]

Tyson/Gelpke had now evolved to this point: The Court would make independent determinations in nondiversity cases to ascertain if state court construction of state law impaired contract rights. If so, then the Court might find that the state, either through its legislature or its courts, had taken property without due process of law. The Court had taken a long step toward getting into the business of creating a federal common law of real estate, applying its collective wisdom to such matters as the locations of "pillars" and other "structures"[127] on the sidewalks of New York. All was in readiness, precedent perched crazily upon precariously teetering

---

[123] 197 U.S. at 575.

[124] *Ibid.*

[125] See Dodd, note 122 *supra.*

[126] 197 U.S. at 573.

[127] *Id.* at 572.

precedent, for "old Harlan" to "roll off the cases"[128] in *Kuhn v. Fairmont Coal Co.*[129]

The litigation pertained to a simple question of local real estate law, uncomplicated by additional factors such as the construction of a will or the common law of negligence—factors which, in the past, had involved the Court peripherally in matters of local land law.[130] It was a diversity case, and no federal question was raised.

What happened was that Kuhn, an Ohio citizen, sold the mining rights in some West Virginia property he owned to a mining company. The grantee, as was customary, erected pillars to provide surface support. He then sold the mining rights to the Fairmont Coal Company which removed the pillars while engaged in the mining operations. The surface eventually, and predictably, cracked and the land lost its natural water supply as a result. In January 1906, Kuhn brought suit in the federal circuit court. In the meantime, Griffin, a West Virginia citizen, brought a similar suit in the state courts. In March 1906, the highest state court held that owners of surface land could not collect for damages unless the deed of conveyance stipulated that subsurface supports be employed. The federal court followed this holding and ruled against Kuhn. Kuhn then took his grievances to the Circuit Court of Appeals which, indicating that no statute, decision, or local custom governing the question had existed until the *Griffin* case, certified to the Supreme Court to inquire if it was bound by the *Griffin* decision.[131]

Harlan held that an owner of surface land was entitled to proper support of his property. The ruling was based, as was his ruling in *Great Southern Hotel*, on *Burgess*. In order to get around the problem of local real estate law he cited instances when the Court had held that contracts "having more or less connection with land" had been brought under the rubric of "general law."[132]

It was a spurious use of precedent. The whole point of *Burgess* (according to Bradley's opinion) was that out-of-state litigants not be subject to the possibilities of bias in state courts. If this meant anything, it should have placed Kuhn in the same unfortunate posi-

---

[128] 1 Holmes-Pollock Letters 157–58 (Howe ed., 1942).

[129] 215 U.S. 349 (1910).

[130] See cases cited in note 55 *supra*.

[131] For a discussion of this case, see Wendell, note 42 *supra*, at 132–34.

[132] 215 U.S. at 361.

tion as Griffin. The other rulings cited were inapplicable, for it was not land at all, but other matters, which the Court declared to be part of federal common law. Sweeping all this aside, Harlan plunged ahead to list four rules "no longer to be questioned":[133]

> 1. When administering state laws and determining rights accruing under those laws, the jurisdiction of the federal courts is an independent one, not subordinate to, but coordinate and concurrent with, the jurisdiction of state courts. 2. Where, *before the rights of the parties* accrued, certain rules relating to real estate have been so established by state decisions as to become rules of property and action in the state, those rules are accepted by the federal court as authoritative declarations of the law of the state. 3. *But where the law of the state has not been thus settled*, it is not only the right, but the duty of the federal court to exercise its own judgment, as it always does when the case before it depends upon doctrines of commercial law and general jurisprudence. 4. So, when contracts and transactions are entered into and rights have accrued under a particular state of local decision, or where there has been no decision by the state court on the particular question involved, then the federal courts properly claim the right to give effect to their own judgment as to what is the law of the state applicable to the case, even where a different view has been expressed by the state court after the rights of the parties had accrued.

Rule 1 overlooked Story's interpretation of § 34 by making no mention of the obligation of the federal courts to follow state court construction of positive state law—understandably, perhaps, since federal courts so often did do so. Rule 2 referred to *Tyson/Burgess* with the added qualification, implied by neither Story nor Bradley, that federal court acceptance of state court rulings on real estate depended upon the existence of a body of *settled* common law on the subject. Rule 3 referred to *Tyson*, minus Story's exceptions, and to *Gelpke* in the sense that the case involved unsettled law (state court reversals on the same subject matter). *Burgess* and *Great Southern Hotel* also have bearing. In *Burgess* the law was unsettled to the extent that a federal court beat a state court to the draw. In *Great Southern Hotel* the law was unsettled because it had yet to be construed by a state court. Rule 4 referred to the post-*Gelpke* bond cases, to *Burgess*, to *Great Southern Hotel*, and indirectly, to

---

[133] *Id.* at 360. (Emphasis in original.)

McCullough without which *Great Southern Hotel* would have been impossible. And underlying the entire rationale of rules 2 and 4 was *Muhlker* in which the Court for the first time directly made an independent judgment concerning real estate law.

Holmes, joined by White and McKenna, dissented. Peckham clearly considered this to be a pure *Tyson* case. White had dissented in *Muhlker*. It would seem that McKenna, who had delivered the *Muhlker* opinion, found the lack of a federal question persuasive. Holmes remarked that there was considerable precedent to support the decision, unsurprising considering the *Tyson-Gelpke* jumble. *Tyson*, he said, rested upon the fiction that judges do not make law. *Gelpke* destroyed that fiction by ruling, in effect, that courts, no more than legislatures, may impair contract rights:[134]

> The cases of the class to which I refer have stood not on the ground that this Court agreed with the first decision, but on the ground that the state decision made the law for the state, and therefore, should only be given a prospective operation when contracts had been entered into under the law as earlier declared.

Unless there was a question of a contract "smack[ing] of a constitutional right"[135] *Tyson* could not be used to disregard a state court ruling simply because some imagined rights had accrued prior to the state ruling:[136]

> I know of no authority in this Court to say that in general state decisions shall make law only for the future. Judicial decisions have had retrospective operation for near a thousand years.

Holmes suggested that what Harlan had done was to take bits and pieces of *Tyson, Gelpke, Burgess, McCullough, Great Southern Hotel*, and *Muhlker* to come up with the proposition explicitly denied by Story and Bradley, that the independent judgment of the federal courts extends to matters of real estate law:[137]

> Whether *Swift* v. *Tyson* can be reconciled with *Gelpke* v. *Dubuque*, I do not care to inquire. I assume both cases to repre-

---

[134] *Id.* at 371. "The many decisions upon the authority of *Swift* v. *Tyson* declare that the decisions of the courts of justice do not make law, whereas the cases that follow *Gelpke* v. *Dubuque* as confidently assert the contrary." Rand, note 60 *supra*, at 350–51.

[135] 215 U.S. at 372.   [136] *Ibid.*   [137] *Ibid.*

sent settled doctrines, whether reconcilable or not. But the
moment you leave those principles which it is desirable to
make uniform throughout the United States, and which the
decisions of the Court tend to make uniform, obviously it is
most undesirable for the courts of the United States to appear
as injecting an occasional arbitrary exception to a rule that
in every other case prevails. The rule in *Gelpke* v. *Dubuque*
gives no help when the contract or grant in question has not
been made on the faith of a previous declaration of law.

Harlan's failure to address himself to the logical difficulties indicated by Holmes has been admitted by even a supporter of the decision.[138] And, as a matter of fact, while Holmes did point out that the
Griffin ruling would have to have had a retroactive effect, he either
overlooked, or mercifully ignored perhaps, the contradictions contained in rule 4. Harlan said there that federal courts might exercise
independent judgment when there had been no relevant ruling from
a state court and when there had been a decision "after the rights of
the parties . . . accrued."[139] The rule is, thus, quite meaningless. The
state court either has or has not made a decision. The West Virginia
court had. As long as it had, the Supreme Court's "authority [was]
at an end."[140] To take the opposite position would be to maintain that
state court rulings are to be discarded by the federal courts unless
those rulings are advantageous to out-of-state litigants. Whatever
Harlan had in mind, it was nothing as preposterous as that.

In any case, within the context of Harlan's opinion, precedent
not logic supplied the necessary authority. All he had to do was to
list the instances in which the Court had for some reason or another
made independent determinations. That one case might not be
analogous to another, that nowhere had the principles of one case
been extracted and applied to another, that the steps leading from
Tyson to *Kuhn* were neither orderly nor plausible, did not matter.
Sixty-eight years of precedent rumbled like a "steam roller"[141] over
Holmes's protests that the *Griffin* decision was as much state law as
a legislative enactment and that "the source" of the common law
was to be found in state courts:[142]

---

[138] Schofield, *Swift v. Tyson: Uniformity of Judge-Made State Law in State and Federal Courts*, 4 ILL. L. REV., 533, 535 (1910).

[139] 215 U.S. at 360.   [141] Schofield, note 138 *supra*.

[140] *Id.* at 372.   [142] 215 U.S. at 372.

It is said that we must exercise our independent judgment—but as to what? Surely as to the law of the states. Whence does that law issue? Certainly not from us. . . . The law of a state does not become something outside of the state court and independent of it by being called the common law.

And there it ended. Holmes had delivered two of his four mighty blows against *Tyson*.[143] Harlan died the next year. It would be another eighteen years before the *Kentucky Taxicab Case*[144] would bring home the full folly of *Tyson* and its accumulated and unmanageable baggage. And without reiterating the dreary and well-known facts of that case, it can be maintained that the results would have been impossible had not *Tyson* reached such proportions. For while a federal question was not raised there, it was "present" simply because the plaintiffs would be prevented by state common law from carrying out the terms of a contract. Some loose dicta about "liberty of contract[ing]"[145] suggest that the Court considered itself duty-bound to constrain states, whatever their policies, to permit the formation of any sort of contract. *Tyson/Gelpke* had not only gone a long way, it had gone as far as it could go.

V. CONCLUSIONS

What, then, is the lesson to be learned from Harlan's long adherence to and active espousal of the doctrine of *Swift v. Tyson?* The question, to be answered equitably, should be preceded by another. Was Harlan's position in these cases at all defensible?

Within the context of his jurisprudence, it was. There is evidence to support the contention that Harlan viewed the diversity jurisdiction (as well as the Contract Clause and the Due Process and Equal Protection Clauses of the Fourteenth Amendment) as adjuncts to the Commerce Clause.[146] He had a horror of the possibilities of economic balkanization and reached into a grab-bag of

---

[143] The opinions in Southern Pacific Co. v. Jensen, 244 U.S. 205 (1917), and Black & White Taxi Co. v. Brown & Yellow Taxi Co., 276 U.S. 518 (1928), were the other half of the quartet.

[144] 276 U.S. 518 (1928).

[145] *Id.* at 528.

[146] For a discussion of the relationship between interstate commerce and diversity jurisdiction, see Friendly, *The Historic Basis of the Diversity Jurisdiction*, 41 HARV. L. REV. 483, 495–97 (1928); Frank, *Historical Bases of the Federal Judicial System*, 13 L. & CONT. PROBS. 2, 22–28 (1948).

constitutional and/or legal doctrine for any weapon to combat state interference with enterprises which he deemed of national import.[147] The municipal bond cases provided all the classical ingredients for such cases: out-of-state bondholders, the financing of a nationwide transportation and communications system, legislatures and judiciaries hostile to railroad and creditor interests, threats to future investments in public utility securities. The cases represented national problems calling for national solutions. Judicial intervention, unsatisfactory as it, perforce, had to be, could be regarded as the only available response to the scheme of Congress. On this basis the decisions made some sense.[148]

The difficulty was that *Tyson* and the bond cases, dealing as they did with negotiable instruments, were projected into other areas of the common law, areas which, by no stretch of the imagination, had any effect whatsoever upon commerce among the states.[149] On the other hand, some of Harlan's opinions in such cases were fundamentally fair and wise, even if not meet for federal rather than state disposition. The fellow-servant rule was not only an anomaly in an industrial age, but to apply it was to perpetuate a savage form of exploitation. The *Fairmont Coal* decision was bad law, but not a bad principle of public policy, and one which mining states might have done well to put into practice.[150] Now it may be too late.

Thus, a case can be made that Harlan, in terms of his policy preferences and the imperatives of his times was right—as he so often was. But there is a critical difference between immediate and long-term "rightness." One test is that the latter is solidly grounded in constitutional and legal doctrine. Immediate rightness, as the

---

[147] See Smyth v. Ames, 169 U.S. 466 (1898); Roberts v. New York, 171 U.S. 658 (1898); Hooper v. California, 155 U.S. 648 (1895); Security Mutual Life Ins. Co. v. Prewitt, 202 U.S. 246 (1906).

[148] Congressmen from midwestern states tried, without success, to prohibit suits brought against municipalities that had pledged credit. See 7 CONG. REC. 4835 (1878); Westin, note 38 *supra*, at 7. Could this be interpreted to mean that Congress acquiesced in the Court's exercise of power?

[149] Examples are to be found in HOLT, CONCURRENT JURISDICTION OF THE FEDERAL AND STATE COURTS 159–88 (1888).

[150] In *Southern Pacific Co. v. Jensen*, Pitney spoke to the proposition that *Tyson* represented "a conclusion upon considerations of right and justice generally applicable." 244 U.S. at 249.

cases discussed illustrate, is self-defeating unless the following minimal conditions have been met: The decision provides working principles derived from and applicable to similar cases. The boundaries of the ruling are mapped out with reasonable precision. The opinion of the Court is clearly written and its mandates unmistakable. Harlan's *Tyson/Gelpke* decisions certainly do not pass muster, and thus despite his laudable efforts to promote and protect interstate commerce, to frustrate sectionalism and parochialism, his position is quite unacceptable.

To return to the first question: It is clear that as far as Harlan's use of *Tyson/Gelpke* is concerned, the ends not only did not justify the means, but the means eventually threatened the very end sought. The more uniformity and certainty the Court attempted to impose, the greater the chaos which emerged.[151] The more aspects of the common law it embraced, the more it lost sight of Story's reading of § 34. The more precedent it created, the more it painted itself into a corner.

There may have seemed, at the time, to be good reasons for each separate ruling, just as there may seem to be good reasons today for the creation and application of federal common law.[152] But the immediate good, the proximate benefits of so doing must be subject to a long-range view. Is the federal interest so pervasive? Is state policy so incompatible with the federal interests?[153] Federalism and a dual court system call for the utmost in tact and forebearance from the highest court. When state laws are not followed in diversity cases the reasons must be so clear that "he who should run could read,"[154] and so principled that any objections to results would be matched

---

[151] HOLT, note 149 *supra;* Friendly, note 2 *supra,* at 178.

[152] Judge Friendly makes the distinction between the pre-*Erie* "spurious uniformity" and the post-*Erie* "specialized common law." Friendly, note 2 *supra,* at 178.

[153] For an attempt to define the "zones" in which federal common law may be made, see Hill, *The Law-Making Power of the Federal Courts: Constitutional Preemption,* 67 COLUM. L. REV. 1024 (1967). The zone approach is criticized in Note, *The Federal Common Law,* 82 HARV. L. REV. 1512 (1969). For the proposition calling for remand to Congress in case of unclear congressional directives, see Bickel & Wellington, *Legislative Purpose and the Judicial Process, the Lincoln Mills Case,* 71 HARV. L. REV. 1 (1957). See also Note, *The Competence of Federal Courts to Formulate Rules of Decision,* 77 HARV. L. REV. 1084 (1964).

[154] Judge Gibson, in Eakin v. Raub, 12 Sargent & Rawle 330, 352 (Pa. 1825).

by respect for the arguments presented and the restraint exercised
by the courts. For ninety-six years the federal courts not only rode
rough-shod over the delicate federal arrangements but failed to give
good reasons for so doing. The result was, at worst, a perversion,
and at best, a caricature, of the judicial process. It should not happen again.

ALLISON DUNHAM

DUE PROCESS AND COMMERCIAL LAW

I. JUDICIAL REVOLUTION?

It is a long time since Sir Henry Maine recorded the movement of Anglo-American law from one based on the concept of status toward one based on the notion of contract.[1] It may well be that in the social service states that now exist in the Anglo-American world, the movement described by Maine has been reversed. But the distinction between status and contract continues to exist. And so, too, therefore, does the question whether a given legal problem should be characterized as one of status, determined by the state's prescription for the rights of a class within the society.

In 1970 in this *Review*, Professor Robert O'Neil suggested that there was a "general presumption that one who is constitutionally entitled to be heard at all should be heard before the change in status occurs."[2] He was talking here about the power of the state to remove a welfare recipient from the rolls of its beneficiaries. A relationship between the state and the individual, not between two individuals, was the subject of his concern. This may well be considered a question of status. Nevertheless, language like Professor O'Neil's has been used to argue that where there is a contract arrangement between individuals relating to their respective interests in property, the same rule should be observed. There has been a spate of litigation about the "due process" requirements of notice and op-

---

Allison Dunham is Arnold and Freda Shure Professor of Law, The University of Chicago.

[1] MAINE, ANCIENT LAW 163–65 (1861).

[2] O'Neil, *Of Justice Delayed and Justice Denied: The Welfare Prior Hearing Cases*, 1970 SUPREME COURT REVIEW 161, 169.

portunity to be heard in which the courts are asked to behave as though the actions of individuals are inhibited in the same way as are the actions of the state in dealing with its welfare clients.

It is true that our society in general and our legal institutions in particular are going through a period of reexamination. Received learning about even the oldest and simplest of legal concepts is being questioned and often found wanting. This reassessment can be and often is highly desirable, whether it occurs in the legislature or in the courts. The legislature, framing general rules as it does, need not rationalize its conclusions as expressed in its enactments. Courts, however, are engaged in the resolution of particular controversies between particular individuals. Unless they afford reasons for their conclusions, there is no guide for the resolution of a subsequent similar dispute between other parties.

It is my intention here to explore the implications of some recent propositions about the constitutional right to a hearing before adverse action in order to determine whether Professor O'Neil's presumption should be equally applicable to private contractual relationships. The context of the discussion will be that of private law rather than public law, of contract rather than status.

On the question of the obligation of one party to a contract to give notice to another before changing the relationship between them, the most useful starting point, perhaps, is Mr. Justice Jackson's statement in *Mullane v. Central Hanover Bank & Trust Co.*:[3]

> Many controversies have raged about the cryptic and abstract words of the Due Process Clause but there can be no doubt that at a minimum they require that deprivation of life, liberty or property *by adjudication* be preceded by notice and opportunity for hearing appropriate to the nature of the case.

At about the same time, Mr. Justice Frankfurter announced that the essence of due process required "the right to be heard before being condemned to suffer grievous loss of any kind."[4]

Do such statements support Professor O'Neil's presumption in a contract setting? Certainly *Mullane*, on its facts, does not. That case arose out of some doubts about the validity of a system whereby a trustee managing several small accounts for the benefit of others could put the trust funds in a common pool. The legislature author-

---

[3] 339 U.S. 306, 313 (1950). (Emphasis added.)

[4] Joint Anti-Fascist Refugee Committee v. McGrath, 341 U.S. 123, 168 (1951).

ized this fiduciary behavior on condition that specified records of the common trust fund be maintained and that the trustee could— and sometimes must—seek judicial authorization for its behavior.[5] In the event of judicial approval of the trustee actions, the statute, following general principles of res judicata, provided that the trustee be immune from further challenge as to the validity of the actions. The approval of trustee accounts by the court, under the statute, was to be determined in an adversary judicial proceeding after notice to all interested parties. The statute provided that notice could be by newspaper publication, even as to beneficiaries whose locations were known to the trustee.

The Supreme Court, speaking through Mr. Justice Jackson, held that for purposes of the judicial proceeding newspaper publication was not sufficient notice to satisfy the Due Process Clause. Since more adequate notice could be afforded to those who had an interest, a party who received only an inferior form of notice like newspaper publication would not be foreclosed from a later attack on the judgment approving the trust account.

It is important to notice what the *Mullane* decision did not reach. It was not a case involving the power of the trustee to act without prior judicial approval. Under ordinary trust law, a trustee may make investment decisions, pay charges, allocate between interest and principal, and pay out to beneficiaries what the trustee determined to be due them. Ordinary trust law provides that after the trustee has acted, a beneficiary may institute judicial proceedings challenging the validity of the trustee's actions. Where, however, the trustee is seeking the protection of a judicial judgment to shield him against claims by the beneficiaries, the adjudicatory standards of fairness of notice and opportunity to be heard must be observed or the Due Process Clause will be violated. The case did not involve a legislative attempt or contractual agreement to provide that the determination of the trustee is final and conclusive as to all matters.[6]

In a real sense, *Sniadach v. Family Finance Corporation*,[7] in the 1968 Term, and *Fuentes v. Shevin*,[8] in the 1971 Term, involved the problem of immunity from challenge and finality of determination rather than a question of the propriety of taking action before no-

---

[5] New York Banking Law § 100-c *et seq.*

[6] See 2 Scott, Trusts §§ 201 *et seq.*, 220 (2d ed. 1956).

[7] 395 U.S. 337 (1969).   [8] 407 U.S. 67 (1972).

tice and hearing. *Sniadach* involved garnishment of wages before judgment. The Wisconsin statute under examination there provided, as did many other such statutes, that prior to a creditor's action for judgment for the amount of an unpaid debt, the creditor could obtain an order from the judicial system directing the debtor's employer (or bank) to pay the debtor's wages (or money on deposit) to the creditor. This order was obtainable without a prior judicial determination that the debtor-employee was in default or even in debt to the creditor.

Fuentes was concerned with seizure of a debtor's property—a stove—by a court officer. Under the Florida replevin statute,[9] which was not untypical in this regard, a person claiming that he has a right to possession of a chattel being detained by another can obtain an order directing the sheriff to take possession of the claimed property and give it to the claimant, on condition that the claimant provide an affidavit setting forth the basis for his claim and a bond to protect the alleged debtor from any loss resulting from an invalid claim.

In both *Sniadach* and *Fuentes*, there had been a credit transaction pursuant to which the creditor had supplied the property to the debtor with the debtor's agreement that on the occasion of some event specified in the contract, usually "on default of payment," the creditor would be entitled to receive a portion of the debtor's wages or possession or repossession of the chattel. The reason that the creditor did not go directly to the employer or bank or repossess the chattel directly rather than go to court first was to afford to the employer or the bank or the repossessing agent authorization for their actions, thereby protecting them from suit by the debtor for wrongful action. If the third party acted pursuant to official order, such liability would ordinarily not arise.

Neither *Sniadach* nor *Fuentes* held that the creditor could not resort to direct action, but only that if the creditor wanted the judicial order to assist him in his collection processes, the debtor must first be afforded notice and an opportunity to be heard on the question whether the judicial order should be issued.

Swarb v. Lennox[10] and *D. M. Overmyer Co. v. Frick Co.*[11] were

---

[9] Fla. Stat. Ann. § 78.08 (1971–72 supp.).

[10] 405 U.S. 191 (1972).   [11] 405 U.S. 174 (1972).

also decided during the 1971 Term. They dealt with similar issues of notice and opportunity to be heard, this time under "confession of judgment" laws. It has been common practice for a debtor to sign a note in which he agrees to pay the amount of the debt and further agrees that the creditor or an agent may, in a lawsuit commenced by the creditor, confess judgment for the amount which the creditor claims that the debtor owes. The creditor or his agent is authorized to "confess" judgment, either "at any time" or "on default." In *Overmyer*, the debtor was a large commercial corporation. In *Swarb*, the debtors concerned were individual consumers purchasing property "on time." Whereas in *Overmyer* the Court found an arm's-length transaction which barred the debtor from complaining about its agreement to "confession of judgment," it was made clear that the consumer transactions in *Swarb* were of a different nature.

The factual difference between a confession of judgment, on the one hand, and garnishment and replevin before judgment, on the other, is important. Unlike garnishment and replevin, the entry of a confession judgment does not itself terminate the debtor's possession and enjoyment. A judgment only empowers a judgment creditor later to obtain enforcement orders, including in appropriate cases garnishment and replevin. (Garnishment, it should be noted, is not available in Pennsylvania where the *Swarb* case originated.) From the moment it is entered, a confession judgment constitutes a lien on all property of the debtor within the jurisdiction, both that which the debtor then owned or that subsequently acquired. The debtor does not lose ownership because of the lien. The creditor must take appropriate statutory steps to "foreclose" the lien by having the property seized and sold to satisfy the debt. Thus, a confessed judgment is, in a sense, a substitute for a clause in a debt instrument in which the debtor assigns as security "all of the property I now own and all that acquired by me before the debt is paid"; it is a substitute for an "after-acquired property clause" in the agreement itself.

The difference between the utilization of the agreement to establish the lien and the utilization of the judgment to establish the lien lies essentially in the relative ease of recording the judgment. And there may be a difference as to the interests of third parties. Basically, however, both systems are designed to compel the debtor to make his peace with his creditor before he sells or otherwise disposes of his property. And many loan companies use the confession-of-judgment note as a means of getting what is in effect a "second mortgage," without going through the technicalities and costs that such a mortgage would require.

In the confession of judgment cases, the Court seems to have made the due process issue one of "unconscionability." It could have said—but it did not—that confession-of-judgment notes are invalid because they are entered without any notice or opportunity to be heard. (And, indeed, some emphasis was placed on the power to reopen the judgments when they were entered by default.) Instead, the Court's emphasis was on the nature of the transaction and the equality of bargaining power of the parties concerned.

All the cases described are alike in one important factor. They were concerned with relationships which are founded on consensual agreements. The beneficiary contracted for the common trust fund, either when he set up the trust or when he accepted the beneficial enjoyment of the gift. The wage earner contracted for the creditor's right to seize his wages in payment of his debt, either by expressly assigning a portion of his wages or by agreeing that the creditor might collect in any way recognized by the law of the jurisdiction. The consumer, when he borrowed money on a cognovit note, contracted for the entry of judgment against him on the occurrence of specified conditions. The consumer, when he purchased a stove, contracted for the creditor's repossession "on default." Did the Court mean, in invalidating the enforcement of some of these contractual arrangements, that it is a denial of due process of law to provide in a contract that one of the parties may make a unilateral decision invoking his remedies without first giving the other party an opportunity to be heard on the rightness of that decision? Hardly. But that would be the logical result of applying the O'Neil status standard to private contractual arrangements. The magnitude of such a change in our legal system would be hard to overstate. There is probably no executory contract in existence which does not have implicit or explicit provisions by which one party can unilaterally affect the interests of the other in the subject matter of the contract without prior resort to adjudication on notice and hearing. To underscore the magnitude of the problem, I propose to examine several areas of commercial law, one established by common-law rules, the others controlled by provisions of the Commercial Code.

II. Concurrent Conditions and the Commercial Code

This ancient idea of "concurrent conditions" in bilateral contracts empowers one promisor to decide, without giving the other party a hearing, that he will not perform his promise because the other party is in default.[12] In the classic bargain and sale, for example, where the seller agrees to sell a described object and to deliver it at a specified time and the buyer agrees to pay a specified price at the same time and place, if the seller asserts that the buyer's tender of the price in marks or rubles or pounds is not performance, the seller may refuse to make delivery or tender his own performance. After the seller refuses to convey, his decision will stand unless the buyer initiates a proceeding to obtain a judicial overruling of the seller's claim that the buyer was in default. Until now—and even now, I submit—the seller has not been required, either as a matter of contract law or of constitutional law, to have an adjudication of the correctness of his position before he refuses to convey. In such a situation there obviously is notice of the refusal just as there is notice to the welfare recipient of the termination of welfare payments. The buyer is aware that he has not received that which the seller promised to deliver to him. The question is the right to be heard in advance of the seller's action based on his conclusion that the buyer is in default. The importance of this idea of self-determination cannot be underestimated. Recent political and legal writings concerning landlord and tenant law, for example, argue that covenants in leases ought to be made concurrent or dependent rather than independent as received law said they were,[13] so that a tenant can refuse to pay rent until the landlord performs his bargain, such as the promise or duty to obey the housing code. Tenants are beginning to win this argument[14] in case law and proposed statutory form.[15] Is it the correct reading of the cases discussed here that this newly won right of tenants is illusory because due process requires that the landlord be given the right to be heard in an adjudication before suffering the grievous loss of rent?

---

[12] See 6 WILLISTON, CONTRACTS §§ 887–89 (3d ed, Jaeger ed. 1957); A.L.I., RESTATEMENT OF CONTRACTS § 274 (1932).

[13] See Comments to § 1.404, UNIFORM RESIDENTIAL LANDLORD AND TENANT ACT.

[14] See Saunders v. First National Realty Corp., 428 F.2d 1071 (D.C. Cir. 1970).

[15] See UNIFORM RESIDENTIAL LANDLORD AND TENANT ACT. But see Lindsey v. Normet, 405 U.S. 56 (1972).

The importance of the Uniform Commercial Code (UCC) derives from the fact that for a period of twenty-five years (1940–65) legal, business, and lawmaking organs considered the resolution of problems therein presented. Where the legislature approved a system providing that the opportunity to be heard should come after the determination of one contracting party and must come, if at all, on the initiative of the opposing party, its decision came as a result of balancing competing interests. The question was thoroughly considered and proponents and opponents of positions given an opportunity to be heard in the legislative forum.

Even a cursory look at the Uniform Commercial Code will reveal a number of instances where terms of a contract are construed to empower the contracting party to make a legal decision unilaterally (*e.g.,* "the other party has *defaulted*") and to take appropriate action before the other party has an opportunity to be heard as to the correctness of the legal conclusion of the first party. A closer look at the default provisions will indicate how often the draftsmen and the legislators concluded that one party can decide there is a default, without prior court approval, and can thereupon proceed to liquidate his debt or to take other appropriate legal action before the other party is heard as to the correctness of the position asserted. That, of course, does not mean that the other party is left without remedy. It means only that if he wants to be heard he must make a timely complaint to an official adjudicating agency (a court) for that determination. Only a few of these provisions need be discussed here. Three categories have been selected:

1. Provisions, such as an acceleration or default clause, empowering the actor to demand immediate payment of a debt or to demand additional collateral.
2. Provisions empowering one party to retain or seize possession and control on the basis of his own unilateral decision.
3. Provisions providing for liquidation or winding up of a matter on the basis of the assertion of one party that there has been a default—*i.e.,* provisions for "foreclosure" or termination of the other's interest without a judicial proceeding and thereby without an opportunity to be heard before the initial decision is made.

A little analysis will indicate that category 1 is related to confession of judgment; category 2 is related to replevin and to payment of money such as wages to a creditor before judgment; category 3 involves categories 1 and 2 and the much broader question of the consent to foreclose without lawsuit.

A. ACCELERATION CLAUSE

U.C.C. Article 1, § 1-208, provides that a term of a contract allowing one party to accelerate payment or performance or to demand additional collateral "at will" means that the party has that power "only if he in good faith believes that the prospect of payment or performance is impaired." This was a controversial section and continues to be controversial in various specialized areas such as landlord and tenant law (*e.g.*, "tenant cannot assign without the consent of the landlord") and consumer credit (whenever the creditor deems himself insecure he may demand the entire sum as due and payable). Three positions were asserted: (1) "At will" means in the irresponsible discretion of the actor, without judicial check; (2) "at will" requires the actor to act in good faith, *i.e.*, responsibly to the extent of honesty; (3) "at will" requires the actor to be responsible to the fullest extent—to observe reasonable commercial standards.

The first position denies the other party any opportunity to have a hearing on the propriety of the actor's decision. Finality is obtained once the party to the contract asserts his position. Assuming that state or federal governmental action is involved, the first position could be said to be a denial of fundamental due process because it means, in reality, that the person aggrieved by the actor's decision has no opportunity ever to obtain an official or adjudicatory determination of the propriety of the actor's conduct. The tide has been running against this position whether it is found to be unconscionable, void as against public policy, or a denial of due process. Almost without exception the overwhelming judicial and legislative conclusion is that there is an exception to this finality "where fraud is involved." The Wunderlich Act[16] provides that the decision of the contract officer is "final and conclusive unless the same is fraudulent or capricious or arbitrary or so grossly erroneous as necessarily to imply bad faith or is not supported by substantial evidence." Both the U.C.C. and the Wunderlich Act entitle the non-actor to a hearing on the propriety of the conduct of the actor. Neither of them provides that before the actor can

---

[16] 41 U.S.C. §§ 321–22 (1965).

assert his position there must be an adjudication. Thus, if the contract officer refuses to certify sufficient completion for a payment to be made, the assertion results in nonpayment and the intended receiver of the payment must initiate a proceeding to obtain his hearing. Put another way, the contract officer's decision is not final until after the time for a hearing has expired but it becomes final without a hearing unless the party aggrieved by the decision seeks a judicial hearing.

The second and third positions do not involve a right to be heard. Both recognize that there are some matters on which the aggrieved party is entitled to be heard, but place the burden on him to initiate proceedings to have the hearing. Do either of these positions violate the constitutional teaching of *Goldberg v. Kelly*[17] and *Wheeler v. Montgomery*[18] involving a governmental decision not to continue to make welfare payments? This question will be dealt with later. It should be noted here that this problem may arise in a whole series of different contexts: *e.g.*, a tenant withholding rent from a poor pensioner because he believes his pensioner-landlord has violated a term of a lease; a laborer refusing to pay union dues or payments to various union welfare schemes because he believes the union has violated its obligation to him; a consumer refusing to make an instalment payment because he believes the conditional seller failed to perform his part of the contract.

It should also be noted that U.C.C. § 1-208, when it involves the right to demand additional collateral "at will," gets very close to the confession of judgment cases. It is true that under § 1-208 a demand for additional collateral does not automatically produce a lien on the debtor's property, the way a confession of judgment and its docketing does. Normally, the creditor who wants additional collateral from an objecting debtor must initiate some kind of adjudicatory proceeding to impress a lien on the debtor's "additional" collateral and in that proceeding the debtor gets his opportunity to be heard. But if that is true, it is only because the rule of substantive law does not operate automatically to impress the collateral with a lien. U.C.C. § 9-204 does attach a lien automatically on acquisition except in the case of consumer goods. Where it does attach automatically on the basis of a general description ("this debt is secured by all of my office files whenever acquired"), there is

---

[17] 397 U.S. 254 (1970).   [18] 397 U.S. 280 (1970).

very little difference between empowering a creditor to confess judgment and asserting in advance that the creditor has a lien immediately on acquisition. If there is a difference for the question of due process, it must arise on some other principle.

B. KEEPING OR TAKING POSSESSION

In several articles of the U.C.C. there are provisions empowering the creditor to retain or retake possession before his right to do so has been finally determined. U.C.C. §§ 2-702 and 2-705, in the article on sales, empower the seller to refuse to deliver goods for which the buyer has contracted "when the seller discovers the buyer to be insolvent;" and, when the goods are neither in his possession nor that of the buyer (*e.g.*, when with a carrier or other bailee), the seller "may stop delivery" when he discovers the buyer to be insolvent or, in certain cases when "the buyer repudiates or fails to make a payment due before delivery." U.C.C. § 3-121, in those states adopting alternative A, provides that where a maker signs an instrument "payable at a bank," he has empowered the holder of the instrument to demand payment from the bank as if the instrument were a draft.

Article 8, on investment securities, in § 8-315, empowers any person "against whom the transfer of a security is wrongful" to "reclaim possession" from anyone except a bona fide purchaser. While the section expressly authorizes reclamation by legal action, it is silent as to whether reclamation can legally occur without judicial process (if there is a factual situation where this could occur without breach of the peace).

Article 9, concerned with security interests in many kinds of personal property, deals with the creditor obtaining control and possession. On default by the debtor, a creditor may, under § 9-502, require the obligor of an account assigned to the creditor as security for a debt to make payment to him rather than the debtor. For tangible chattels it is provided that the creditor on default has "a right to take possession" and under § 9-503, he "may proceed without judicial process if this can be done without breach of the peace."

In all of these cases under U.C.C. Articles 2, 3, 8, and 9 the creditor, in the first instance, determines that he is entitled to possession or control. Thereafter there is a difference both in fact and analysis between the case where possession is recovered from a third party and where possession is recovered from the debtor. In the third-party situation, the creditor must persuade the third party to give him possession. If he does so, he acquires the property without any opportunity for the debtor to challenge the propriety of his claim. Where the debtor is in possession, a different question is presented. Any person, other than a court official, who obtains possession from the debtor is responsible to the debtor for both the validity of the creditor's claim and the damage caused by the manner of repossessing. Again, except for the court official, any proceeding against the debtor or third party for possession gives the debtor the opportunity to be heard. Thus, the narrow question in *Fuentes* was whether it was a denial of due process to vary the obligation as to manner of repossession depending on whether the third party was a government official (a sheriff or court officer) or some other person. It may be argued that the denial of due process arises from the state's lending the immunity of its officials to a creditor simply on an affidavit of the creditor, as a substitute for the creditor taking full responsibility for the manner of repossession. If this is an essential fact, then *Fuentes* does not control repossession by the creditor through his own agents who remain responsible for the manner of repossession. In the stoppage in transit situation under § 2-705, where the creditor persuades the bailee to surrender possession to him, where the creditor obtains official help of a ministerial variety as in *Fuentes*, and where the creditor obtains repossession himself, the debtor is in the same position to assert any defenses he may have against the creditor's assertion of a default. The debtor must initiate a lawsuit. The only difference arises when the state immunizes the creditor from damage from the manner of repossession, by permitting use of its own officials. This clearly is enough of a difference to justify a difference in legislative policy. Is it a sufficient difference in terms of constitutional due process requirements? I shall return to this question.

It should also be noted that Article 9 empowers a person to assign as security for a debt various accounts and claims which he may have, including his right to wages. Credit unions, particularly those organized on employer lines (XYC Co. Employees Federal Credit Union), have for years loaned money to employees and have taken assignments of the employees' wages. Sometimes the assignment takes the form of an immediate assignment of a specified amount so that the employer pays directly to the creditor out of the employee's wages, the monthly instalment due on the instalment loan, like withholding for taxes. In the other form, the assignment is intended to operate only "in case of default." In this form the creditor notifies the employer that he has obtained an assignment of wages as security for a debt in event of default. On default the employer is then notified to pay out of the wages the amount of the unpaid debt. Under § 9-318(4), a clause in an agreement between the obligor (employer) and obligee (employee), attempting to prohibit an assignment of the obligee's right to receive payment, is ineffective. Thus, the employee is empowered, absent some statute peculiarly applicable to wages, to assign all or part of his wages. Suppose that an employee assigns his wages as in the credit union illustration above and thereafter a dispute arises between him and the credit union as to the amount due. The employee thereupon notifies the employer to stop withholding from his wages as previously directed. What does the employer now do? He has to draw a legal conclusion as to whether the assignment is revocable or as to whether the asserted claim of the employee is correct. In either case, if the employee is wrong, the employer is liable to the credit union for failing to honor the assignment. In either case, the creditor makes this determination without giving the credit union any required opportunity to be heard.

If the assignment is in the second form and the creditor notifies the employer to start paying him, the employer has a similar problem. He pays the creditor wrongfully if there is no default. In this case he makes his determination without any required opportunity for the employee to assert his defenses. If the employer decides to honor the request of the credit union, the employee must then proceed to court to secure an official determination of the correctness of the creditor's claim. This situation is similar to the *Sniadach* situation, with one exception. If the employer honors the creditor's request, he does so at his peril. If he honors the request of the court in garnishment before judgment, he is discharged of his wage obligation even though subsequent litigation determines that the payment ordered by the court was erroneous. Does the due process question as suggested above in replevin reduce itself to use of official processes to immunize a person from erroneous judgments? That looks like *Mullane*.

C. POWER OF SALE

The third type of self-determination provision in the U.C.C. is the most important policy innovation of the U.C.C., and it is vital both to the business community and to debtors as a class. It is a rare case where the person claiming breach of a contract will find that the property from which he hopes to realize his losses are in the possession and control of a third party. Most often the object will be either in the creditor's possession and control (*e.g.*, on pledge), or in the possession and control of the other contracting party. In connection with contracts to sell, the historic common-law resolution was by an adjudication of the claim of monetary damage or, in unusual cases, specific reparation. In either of these remedies, the adjudicatory process was initiated by the aggrieved party and the other had wide latitude in asserting defenses. In any event there was court supervision and final determination of the various claims of the disputants. For secured transactions the required procedures on default have vacillated. Judicial foreclosure, both to cut off the defaulter's interest in the collateral and to hold a formal judicial sale, occupies the middle period in time. First, on the theory that the debtor has conveyed title to the creditor, default was regarded as destroying the debtor's right to title; so it was the debtor who sought judicial determination that his right to title had not been forfeited by the creditor's earlier decision. Then through equity and statute, the process came to be one for a judicial determination of the right to forfeit the debtor's interest. During this period it was the creditor who initiated a court proceeding to cut off the debtor's "equity of redemption" and the ultimate form of the court order provided that a default had occurred and that "unless the debtor cured his default within a time specified in the decree, the property was to be sold at a judicial sale and the proceeds applied in satisfaction of expenses of sale and debt." This process unlike the earlier one, compelled the creditor to give the debtor an opportunity to be heard before he took any action. Even before the advent of the U.C.C., procedures were developing whereby the creditor declared a default and undertook to sell the collateral for the account of the debtor. Under this procedure, the creditor was regarded as having a power of sale which could be exercised "on default," and when the creditor undertook to exercise his power, a debtor who wanted to be heard had to initiate a proceeding which had the effect of restraining the sale until the court had certified that the creditor was entitled to sell.

The U.C.C. adopted a uniform policy preferring, in all cases, realization or sale by the seller or creditor over any judicially supervised procedure. This type of remedy is found in §§ 2-706 and 2-

703. Where the buyer "wrongfully rejects or revokes acceptance of goods" then the seller "may resell the goods," and where the sale is made "in good faith and in a commercially reasonable manner," the seller may recover the difference between the resale price and the contract price. Resale included a private as well as a public sale, but the seller had to give the buyer notice of the intended sale. The effect of this process was that a buyer who denied that he was in breach either had to prevent the sale from being held by a court proceeding initiated by him or to allow the sale and assert that the seller's subsequent lawsuit for money damages was not proper because, if there was no default, the seller was selling for his own account and not for that of the buyer. The buyer was thus entitled to an opportunity to be heard, but he had to claim the opportunity by initiating an appropriate judicial proceeding or defending in one ultimately brought by the seller. This became the procedure adopted in the U.C.C. So, too, a warehouseman or carrier may assert a lien for unpaid storage or carriage charges under §§ 7-210 and 7-308 by conducting a public or private sale after giving a statutory notice to various claimants. And perhaps most important, in Article 9, on secured transactions, the secured creditor may sell the collateral after default at a similar public or private sale. In each of these cases the Code provides that the sale gave the purchaser at the sale a title free of the rights of all other claimants "even though the secured party fails to comply" with the statutory requirements for conducting the sale. As a substitute for a continuing right in the property, in the case of a wrongful sale, the person whose interest was sold may proceed to restrain the sale or, if it has already occurred, proceed against the seller for damages. Thus, the debtor who challenges the creditor's assertion that the debtor was in default is put to the burden of seeking an adjudication of this claim and of restraining the sale pending exercise of his right to be heard. If the collateral is an account receivable, the creditor after default could collect the account directly and apply the proceeds to the debt, subject to the debtor's assertion, in a proceeding commenced by him, that he is not in default or that the collection process was not commercially reasonable.

The key question, therefore, is whether the recent line of cases referred to at the beginning of this article mean that it is a denial of due process if a hearing is not required or offered the debtor before the creditor makes any of the necessary determinations.

Stated simply, is it the teaching of these cases that something approaching "judicial foreclosure" is a constitutional requirement of due process?

It would be an easy answer for the bulk of transactions today to dismiss the problem by asserting that even with the teaching of *Shelley v. Kraemer*,[19] no state action is involved. The creditor or seller or warehouseman is asserting a right which his private agreement gives him, and his sale, without benefit of court action, is not sufficient state action to bring the Fourteenth Amendment into play. At most the state recognizes only the private arrangement. Even if this were acceptable as an answer, it will only partially dispose of the problem. There is a rapidly expanding governmental participation in commercial transactions. The national government, for example, is involved through the Federal Housing Administration, the Veterans Administration, the Federal Land Bank, the Small Business Administration, and a host of other programs in credit transactions and even in selling goods and serving as a warehouseman. Even the states are extensively involved in loan and sales programs. These programs are likely to expand in number and volume, if the recent trends are any indication. Do we mean that if the Federal Housing Administration or the Illinois Housing Development Authority (IHDA) is the creditor in a real estate mortgage and if the applicable law authorizes the described power of sale procedure, FHA and IHDA are constitutionally prohibited from using it but the Workingman's Savings and Loan Association and the Workingman's Personal Loan or Sales Finance Company is privileged to use this procedure? What readings of the cases are possible?

Private persons who make decisions are, in our legal system, responsible for their decisions; after they act they will be accountable for the consequences of those acts. Government officials who make the same decision in their official capacity are less responsible for the consequences of those acts. This is particularly true of officials acting within the judicial system. A judge is least responsible and officials who carry out judgments, decrees, and other instructions of the judge have reduced responsibility. Even private individuals who act pursuant to court orders have less responsibility than if they perform the same act without a court order. If the court order does not impose a duty to act but only an authorization, the act result-

---

[19] 334 U.S. 1 (1948).

ing from the authorization has more legitimacy than the same act performed without benefit of court authorization. Thus, if a trustee makes an investment decision to sell or buy a capital asset for his trust, a higher degree of responsibility is placed on him than if he has asked for and obtained a court authorization to make the same decision. In part this difference in responsibility results from an assumption that the relevant facts have been fully considered by the court and the appropriate policy and other matters brought to its attention and carefully weighed.

One possible rationale of the cases is that if the private actor seeks the advantages of diminished responsibility resulting from action pursuant to court authority, the process of law requires that the diminished responsibility be available to him only after the person who bears the consequences of the act has had notice and an opportunity to be heard. This could explain why a trustee must give notice and opportunity to be heard on a trust account before it acquires conclusiveness, but need not give notice and opportunity to be heard in advance of decision when the trustee makes an accounting or investment subject to later challenge by the beneficiary. It may explain why a creditor and his "agent" must give notice and opportunity to be heard prior to action when he seeks a court authorization or direction that the agent carry out the creditor's wishes by using money belonging to the debtor and in the agent's control to pay the obligation to the creditor, but need not give similar notice and opportunity to be heard when he persuades or induces the custodian of money to apply it directly in payment of the debt (*e.g.*, pursuant to an earlier assignment made by the debtor). It could also explain why a person claiming a right to take possession of property in the hands of another must give notice and an opportunity to be heard on the rightfulness of his claim to possession when he seeks court authorization of his proposed seizure via the sheriff in a replevin action, but need not give notice and an opportunity to be heard in advance of decision when he or his agent seek to repossess without benefit of court authorization.

Under this rationale the denial of due process arises from an attempt by legislation or otherwise to give the major elements of adjudicatory legitimacy to an act that does not result from a process with the significant trappings of the adjudicatory process. Where the actor is willing to take the risk of responsibility for his acts, postponing hearing and even notice until the person suffering the consequences of the act raises the question of legitimacy does not deny due process.

But how does the Court's approval of confession of judgments (in some cases) prior to an opportunity to determine the rightfulness of the judgment, and the Court's disapproval of termination of welfare payments without prior opportunity to be heard square with this principle? Similarly, the cases requiring state universities and perhaps others to have a prior adjudication of the validity of an expulsion of a student or a termination of employment of a faculty member do not square with this rationale.[20] And what about the state or federal internal revenue service "ordering" the employer to withhold a sum of money for taxes from a wage earner before it has been adjudicated that a tax is due? The answer is that this principle cannot serve as a rationale for all the current disputes about notice and hearing in advance of decision. We must under this principle resort to consideration of other factors such as the purpose of the legislation involved. For example, providing sustenance for the welfare recipient and collecting the public revenue may call for different procedural requirements. We must also resort to a balancing act regarding the *de minimis* consequences when the actor's decision is "passive" rather than a disruption of possession, as in the lien resulting from a confession of judgment.

Action interfering with the continuing or periodic enjoyment of an object of property or of a status previously acquired has historically been a special concern of the legal system. The amount of force which can be used to retake possession of property has been limited. Remedies have been invented and existing ones made speedy to induce resort to judicial process rather than recovery of possession by some form of self-help. The same solicitous attitude toward continuing enjoyment is evident where no possession in the physical sense is involved. Both legislation and judge-made doctrines have protected wages and periodic receipts (*e.g.*, spendthrift trust) from interference. When a person has "temporarily" allowed another to use his property, summary remedies have been devised quickly to restore the property to him (forcible entry and detainer). These remedies are not available in many areas to buyers, grantees, or other "new" claimants to the right to permanent possession and enjoyment.

---

[20] See Perry v. Sinderman, 408 U.S. 593 (1972); Board of Regents v. Roth, 408 U.S. 564 (1972).

A second possible rationale of the cases is that due process requires a prior adjudication after notice and hearing when the decision, or at least its effect, is to terminate an existing possession and continuous enjoyment. This rationale permits explanation of the cases requiring prior notice and opportunity to be heard in the partial termination of a right to wages (garnishment before judgment); termination of the enjoyment of a stove (replevin cases); and the termination of welfare payment cases. It permits us to distinguish the confession of judgment cases (where held valid). It would also permit us to explain why a seller may, without notice and hearing, refuse to deliver a new possession to a buyer whom he alleges to be in default; why a promissor in a bilateral contract, particularly the government, may refuse to make payment in the isolated contract case when the contract officer believes the other party to be in default. It would also permit justification for permitting a creditor to exercise a power of sale without prior judicial approval of the creditor's assertion of a default. But consistency with this rationale would require a conclusion that repossession of collateral (be it a car or a truck of a large trucking company) without benefit of judicial process, withholding of periodic rent payments on the tenant's assertion that the lessor has defaulted on his obligations, refusal to pay the eighth instalment of a contract for a delivery of goods in ten instalments, a banker's lien on a bank account, a repairman's possessory lien on an automobile temporarily in his possession, an assignment of rents, wages, or other rights to receive payment where the assignment is to become effective "on default" or some other condition, and a host of other situations would be a denial of due process insofar as the rule permitted public or private persons to act on the basis of his assertion of a legal right without opportunity for the opposing party to be heard.

A third possible rule derived from the cases considered is that any conduct which seeks and has the effect of terminating the interest of another, or creating an interest in the actor, cannot be made without a prior opportunity to be heard on the matter. This would mean that sale foreclosure procedure applicable in all states for personal property under the U.C.C. and in about one-half the states in real estate mortgage foreclosure would be unconstitutional and that the only constitutionally valid process would be judicial foreclosure and a court-supervised or court-conducted sale. This implication of the recent line of cases seems almost unthinkable because of its impact on the ability of consumers and industry to obtain cheap and easy credit and because it would be such a stark reversal of the trend of the past twenty-five years.

Finally, the current spate of cases may be raising to constitutional status a doctrine of unconscionability. Under this principle it would be a denial of due process to affect any interest without giving the person who suffers the consequences of the decision a right to assert the invalidity of the action because of its unfairness, in the circumstances, to him. This approach has a deceptive simplicity. It might explain why a confession of judgment is constitutional for a corporate debtor or an individual whose debt is larger than $10,000 but not for an individual whose debt is small in amount. It might explain why wages below a poverty level could not be garnisheed before judgment or assigned "on default" but larger sums and sums arising in transactions between "merchants" could be assigned or garnished before judgment. It could explain why the replevin statute as written could be applied to replevy a large piece of construction equipment but not the family stove. Moreover, it would appear to direct the court's attention to the "essential fairness" of the whole situation in the particular circumstances, a version of due process which is congenial to many. It would explain most of the existing cases and it would be based on some of the language in them about the catastrophic effect of the loss of welfare payments, hourly wages, and consumer goods.

Its major difficulty results from the role of the national court within a federal system in which the bulk of the legal relationships are a matter of state law, at least until Congress has spoken. In effect this approach would repeal *Erie v. Tompkins*[21] and reinstate *Swift v. Tyson*[22] with a vengeance by elevating the newly created (or revived) "federal contract law" to the status of constitutional law.

Moreover, as the state courts have found in attempting to apply the doctrine of unconscionability as a matter of nonconstitutional law, there are no true guides. Without such guides the doctrine lends itself to decision on the basis of personal predilection or prejudice—*e.g.*, all blacks or Spanish speaking people are "overreached" on contracts, individual farmers are overreached in contracts with creditors, "wage earners" means persons of low incomes, who are more needy than any landlord to whom they pay rent or any seller,

---

[21] 304 U.S. 64 (1938).   [22] 16 Pet. 1 (1842).

including even the blue collar worker from whom a wage earner–
debtor has purchased the property subject to a purchase money
security interest.

At the moment the Court does not seem to have enunciated any
principle which it can apply in any rational way on the question
of "hearing" prior to decision, where the private decision results
from rights created by contractual relations. Perhaps the Burger
Court can yet point the way.

JULIUS G. GETMAN

THE EMERGING CONSTITUTIONAL
PRINCIPLE OF SEXUAL EQUALITY

I. The Court Changes Position

Sexual equality, a matter for joking only a few years ago, seems today on the verge of being incorporated into the Constitution as a basic right. Courts, once committed to the doctrine that the sexes are inherently unequal, seem now eager to recant. The Supreme Court too has revised its former approach to sex discrimination, although without apparent enthusiasm and without formal announcement of a change of policy.

In *Reed v. Reed*,[1] the Court invalidated an Idaho statute which gave a preference to the man whenever two persons, a man and a woman equally entitled by degree of relationship to the deceased, filed letters seeking appointment as administrator of an estate. In *Stanley v. Illinois*,[2] the Court held that denial to an unwed father of a hearing on his fitness before removing a child from his custody

---

Julius G. Getman is Professor of Law, Indiana University.

AUTHOR'S NOTE: I wish to thank students who participated in the course entitled "Law and Social Change: The Status of Women" which was held in the winter quarter, 1972, at The University of Chicago. Many of the ideas contained herein were first brought to my attention by them. I received excellent research assistance from Barry Roseman, a third-year law student at The University of Chicago, and from Terry Miller Mumford, a third-year law student at Indiana University, who also served as an able editor, critic, and commentator. I also wish to thank Professor Owen Fiss of The University of Chicago, who read an early draft under trying circumstances and made excellent suggestions. My colleague Alan Schwartz also made useful criticisms.

[1] 404 U.S. 71 (1971). [2] 405 U.S. 645 (1972).

violated the Equal Protection Clause when unwed mothers in similar circumstances were entitled to a hearing.

Neither in *Reed* nor in *Stanley* did the Court repudiate its earlier decisions which had uniformly recognized the constitutionality of government action that differentiated between the sexes. Perhaps the most significant authority in support of sex discrimination was *Muller v. Oregon*,[3] in which the Court affirmed the right of the Oregon legislature to set minimum hours for women even though similar legislation regulating men's hours was earlier held unconstitutional. The opinion was heavily influenced by the famous brief filed by Louis D. Brandeis which sought to demonstrate that women, because of physiological differences, were less capable of physical labor and were in greater need of protection against burdensome job requirements than men. The *Muller* case established the legitimacy of state efforts "to afford special protection to women." In subsequent cases the Court showed considerable ingenuity in ascribing to the state legitimate or protective reasons for sex discrimination.

The brief for the appellant in *Reed* strongly urged the Court either to declare sex a suspect classification or otherwise to elaborate on the approach it would take in future cases.[4] The Court declined to do so. It justified its decision on the traditional grounds that the sex of the competing applicants did not bear "a rational relationship to a state objective that is sought to be advanced by the operation" of the statutes in question.[5] The Court did not stress the importance of sexual equality as a constitutional goal. It also failed to explain why the legislative weighing of interests was improper.[6]

Despite the cautious nature of the opinions and the lack of elabo-

---

[3] 208 U.S. 412 (1908).

[4] Appellant was represented by Ruth Bader Ginsburg, Pauli Murray, Dorothy Kenyon, Melvin L. Wulf, and Allen R. Deer. Thirty-nine pages of argument were devoted to urging the Court to declare sex a suspect classification. This section of the brief contained an excellent summary of the various ways in which the law has traditionally discriminated against women. Only six pages were devoted to arguing that the classification did not bear a reasonable relationship to a legitimate legislative purpose.

[5] 404 U.S. at 76.

[6] The decision by the Idaho court did not discuss possible reasons for choosing men over women in such cases. 93 Idaho 511 (1970). The *Stanley* case was argued in terms of rationality of the state's differentiating between unwed fathers and other parents. The Court simply announced that "denying such a hearing to Stanley and those like him while granting it to other Illinois parents is inescapably contrary to the Equal Protection Clause." 405 U.S. at 658.

ration on the limits of sexual classification, the decisions in *Reed* and *Stanley* mark a significant change in the Court's approach to sex discrimination.

1. The Court in *Reed* did not attempt to supply a rationale to justify the sexual discrimination. In earlier cases the Supreme Court either did so or simply assumed legislative competence to determine areas unsuitable for women. Thus, in *Goesaert v. Cleary*,[7] the Court upheld a statute forbidding women from being licensed as bartenders. Even though women were permitted to serve as waitresses in places in which liquor was served, the Court concluded that the legislation was aimed at reducing moral and social problems which might result from women working as bartenders.[8] Had the Court in *Reed* utilized a similar approach, it might have justified the statute on the grounds that men are more experienced at managing financial affairs than women; or the statute's provision preferring men might have been treated as equivalent to the legislature choosing among classes of relatives.

2. The Court stated in *Reed* and indicated in *Stanley* that the administrative gains involved in eliminating a hearing could not be accomplished at the cost of giving one sex preference over the other.

The Idaho Supreme Court had upheld the statute on the grounds that it was a legitimate way to eliminate the administrative burden which would be placed on the probate court if hearings were required in such cases. The Supreme Court, in rejecting this justification, stated:[9]

> Clearly the objective of reducing the workload on probate courts by eliminating one class of contests is not without some legitimacy. The crucial question, however, is whether §15-314 advances that objective in a manner consistent with the command of the Equal Protection Clause. We hold that it does not. To give a mandatory preference to members of either sex over members of the other, merely to accomplish the elimination of hearings on the merits, is to make the very kind of arbitrary legislative choice forbidden by the Equal Protection Clause of the Fourteenth Amendment.

The priority given to the rule of sexual equality over ease of administrative convenience is in marked contrast with earlier cases.

---

[7] 335 U.S. 464 (1948).

[8] The appellant contended that the motive was preserving jobs for male bartenders. The Court refused to "give ear to the suggestion" that such an "unchivalrous desire" was the real purpose. *Id.* at 467.

[9] 404 U.S. at 76.

In *Hoyt v. Florida*[10] the Court upheld a system of jury selection by which women were excluded from the rolls unless they specifically asked to serve while men were relieved only if they claimed a specific exemption. The Court rejected the argument that it was improper for the state to assume without a hearing that all women had competing responsibilities which made jury service a hardship:[11] We "cannot regard it as irrational for a state legislature to [assume] that it would not be administratively feasible to decide in each individual instance whether family responsibilities of a prospective female juror were serious enough to warrant an exemption." And in the cases in which it upheld the exclusion of women from certain occupations or limited their hours of work, the Court did not suggest a hearing to determine whether individual women were in fact capable of doing the prohibited work or working longer hours.[12]

3. Perhaps most significantly, the Court in both *Reed* and *Stanley* rejected the contention that the sex discrimination involved could be justified by the state's interest in regulating family relationships. The Court in *Reed* stated that "whatever the state's interest in 'avoiding intrafamily controversy,' it could not achieve this end by differentiating 'solely on the basis of sex.' "[13] The Court in *Stanley* rejected the argument that differentiating between unwed fathers and other parents was a part of "a comprehensive legislative plan which affects all children in need of protection from abuse, neglect or abandonment."[14]

The regulation of family relationships has traditionally been recognized as a significant state interest justifying differentiation between classes of persons. Thus, in *Labine v. Vincent*[15] it was held that the state could deny inheritance rights to illegitimate children as an incident of its "power to make rules, to establish, protect, and strengthen family life."[16] The cases which have permitted the state to exclude women from full participation in our society have ulti-

---

[10] 368 U.S. 57 (1961).   [11] *Id.* at 63.

[12] Muller v. Oregon, 208 U.S. at 422; Radice v. New York, 264 U.S. 292 (1924).

[13] 404 U.S. at 77.

[14] See Brief for the State at p. 11. The decision in *Stanley* is less significant than that in *Reed*. Four Justices joined the majority opinion in *Stanley*, two dissented, and Douglas, J., concurred separately.

[15] 401 U.S. 532 (1971).   [16] *Id.* at 538.

mately rested on this basis. In *Bradwell v. State*,[17] Justice Bradley, concurring, explained that the state could exclude women from the practice of law on the grounds that "it is within the province of the legislature to ordain what offices, positions and callings shall be filled and discharged by men" in order to preserve "the family organization, which is founded in the divine ordinance, as well as in the nature of things."[18] As recently as 1961 the Court justified the automatic exemption from jury service for women using similar reasoning if somewhat less florid language:[19]

> Despite the enlightened emancipation of women from the restrictions and protections of bygone years and their entry into many parts of community life formerly considered to be reserved to men, woman is still regarded as the center of home and family life. We cannot say that it is constitutionally impermissible for a State, acting in pursuit of the general welfare, to conclude that a woman should be relieved from the civic duty of jury service unless she herself determines that such service is consistent with her own special responsibilities.

The Court in *Reed* did not hold that the regulation of family relations may never justify treating the sexes differently. Nevertheless, the summary rejection of this traditional basis for sexual discrimination in a case where the interest being vindicated was not very significant suggests that the Court has fundamentally altered the balance between sexual equality and state regulation of family relations. The *Stanley* case is further indication of the Court's shift. Not only did the majority reject the argument that the state could distinguish between unwed mothers and fathers to protect the welfare of illegitimate children, but perhaps for the first time in American jurisprudence, it was unwilling to indulge the presumption of the unique nature of mother's love. This assumption was repeatedly invoked in the brief for the state. It was accepted by Chief Justice Burger, who was prepared to uphold the state system on the grounds that it merely reflected an observable difference between the sexes:[20]

---

[17] 16 Wall. 130 (1872). See also *In re* Lockwood, 154 U.S. 116 (1894). Both were overruled, *sub silentio*. Konigsberg v. State Bar, 353 U.S. 252 (1957); Schware v. Board of Bar Examiners, 353 U.S. 232 (1957).

[18] 16 Wall. at 142, 141.   [19] 368 U.S. at 61–62.

[20] 405 U.S. at 665–66. It is curious that the Chief Justice who wrote the Court's opinion in *Reed* dissented in *Stanley*. He was prepared to accept the constitutionality of Illinois's conclusion that women make better parents (at least when the parents are unwed) but was not willing to accept the constitutional validity of Idaho's assumption

I believe that a state is fully justified in concluding, on the basis of common human experience, that the biological role of the mother in carrying and nursing an infant creates stronger bonds between her and the child than the bonds resulting from the male's often casual encounter. This view is reinforced by the observable fact that most unwed mothers exhibit a concern for their offspring either permanently or at least until they are safely placed for adoption, while unwed fathers rarely burden either the mother or the child with their attentions or loyalties. Centuries of human experience buttress this view of the realities of human conditions and suggest that unwed mothers of illegitimate children are generally more dependable protectors of their children than are unwed fathers.

The decisions in *Reed* and *Stanley* demonstrate that the Court can significantly alter the constitutional importance of sexual equality without formally changing the standard of review under the Fourteenth Amendment. The traditional tests under the Fourteenth Amendment have always left considerable discretion to the Court through the technique of defining the statute's purpose. If the purpose is described narrowly in terms of the immediate ends which a statute seeks to achieve, then distinctions which serve peripheral or secondary goals may be held improper. Thus, the statute in *Reed* was described as a way to resolve disputes about administration. Differentiation between the sexes was neither necessary nor directly related to the purpose. It also could have been characterized as seeking to resolve disputes without disturbing interfamily harmony.

While the *Reed* opinion does not suggest what type of justification would be adequate to support sexual discrimination, it together with *Stanley* suggests that the factors to be considered are the importance of the state interest being served by the discrimination and the possibility of achieving the objective by other means. These are the same factors which would be considered were the Court to announce that sex is a suspect classification. Recent cases suggest a general policy of stricter judicial scrutiny of state classifications in equal protection cases. In *Weber v. Aetna Casualty Co.*,[21] Mr. Justice Powell, writing for the majority, stated that the balance to be struck in determining how closely to examine state action is, "What

---

that men are better or more desirable administrators. His seemingly contradictory opinions would indicate that the state's power to distinguish between the sexes is inevitably affected by whether the Justices think particular distinctions reflect actual differences between men and women.

[21] 406 U.S. 164 (1972).

legitimate state interest does the classification promote? What fundamental personal rights might the classification endanger?"[22] Following this approach the Court invalidated Louisiana's workmen's compensation law which denied equal recovery to illegitimate and legitimate children. The Court recognized the state interest in regulating family relationships but closely examined how that regulation was to be accomplished. The Court required a "significant relationship" between the purpose and the means. The dissent called this standard a hybrid of the rational relationship and strict scrutiny standards.[23]

In *Eisenstadt v. Baird*,[24] the Court used the same formulation that it used in *Reed* to invalidate a Massachusetts law making it a felony to distribute contraceptives. Not only was the Court unwilling to supply the necessary justification, it rejected the purposes proposed by the state (protection of health, public morals, and family relationships) as too broad or too attenuated. The Court was clearly looking for more than a possible rational basis to justify state action, though not stating that it was using anything stricter. It is not clear, however, that this general trend will continue because there is a dispute within the Court about the extent to which the Equal Protection Clause should be used to review the reasonableness of legislation. Justices Rehnquist, Blackmun, and Burger all dissented in one or more of the cases applying the Fourteenth Amendment to invalidate state legislation.[25]

The change in the standard of review in *Reed* and *Stanley* was made so indirectly, however, that the *Reed* opinion has given rise to conflicting interpretations in the lower courts.[26] This conflict and the increase in the amount of litigation concerning women

---

[22] *Id.* at 173.   [23] *Id.* at 181.   [24] 405 U.S. 438 (1972).

[25] Stanley v. Illinois, 405 U.S. 645 (1972); Eisenstadt v. Baird, 405 U.S. 438 (1972); Peters v. Kiff, 407 U.S. 493 (1972); Dunn v. Blumstein, 405 U.S. 330 (1972).

[26] Thus, in Schattman v. Texas Employment Commission, 4 FEP Cases 353 (CA 5th, 1972), in upholding a policy of forced maternity leave, the court cited *Reed* for the proposition that "in applying the Equal Protection Clause the Supreme Court has consistently recognized that the Fourteenth Amendment does not deny the States the power to treat different classes of persons in different ways. The clause does prohibit the States from placing people in different classes 'on the basis of criteria wholly unrelated to the objective of the statute.'" *Id.* at 359. On the other hand, in LaFleur v. Board of Education, 4 FEP Cases 1070 (CA 6th, 1972), the court in rejecting a forced maternity leave program cited *Reed* for the proposition "there is a marked trend of cases to invalidate regulations based on sex classification unless supported by a valid state interest." *Id.* at 1073. In Green v. Board of Regents, 335 F. Supp. 249 (1971), the court stated, "The Supreme

make it inevitable that the Court will have an opportunity to reconsider the application of the Fourteenth Amendment to sex discrimination. The general political and social commitment to equal rights for women is too great to retreat from *Reed* and *Stanley* and return to the Court's casual acceptance of the state's ability to "draw sharp lines" between the sexes.[27] The inclusion of sex discrimination in Title VII of the 1964 Civil Rights Act has made a significant impact on employment practices and concepts. It has in recent years been vigorously pursued by the EEOC and has led to similar provisions in many state laws.[28] A variety of administrative and legal techniques have recently been developed for the purpose of eliminating sex discrimination.[29] The Equal Rights Amendment has passed both houses of Congress, and the platforms of both major parties contain pledges to achieve legal equality between the sexes. Thus, distinction based on the concept of separate spheres has become much less consistent with the general fabric of our legal system.[30] It seems

---

Court of the United States has recently made it quite clear that discrimination . . . on the basis of sex is not to be tolerated." *Id.* at 250.

[27] Forbush v. Wallace, 341 F. Supp. 217 (M.D. Ala. 1971), *aff'd*, 405 U.S. 970 (1972), does not mark a retreat from the Supreme Court's position in *Reed* and *Stanley*. In *Forbush*, the lower court held that Alabama's common law requiring women to assume their husband's surname on marrying does not violate the Equal Protection Clause. The lower court opinion was based in part, however, on the fact that no real injury was involved because it was easy for the woman to change her name. Moreover, the Supreme Court's affirmance of a case such as this one on its appellate docket, without hearing or opinion as here, is considered equivalent to a mere denial of certiorari. See Serrano v. Priest, 5 Cal.3d 584, 615–18, and especially note 34 (1971).

[28] Forty states currently ban sex discrimination in employment.

[29] See, in general, *Developments in the Law—Employment Discrimination and Title VII of the Civil Rights Act of 1964*, 84 HARV. L. REV. 1109, 1166–94, 1242–1303 (1971) (hereinafter cited as *Developments—Title VII*); BLUMROSEN, BLACK EMPLOYMENT AND THE LAW 408–16 (1971). An area ripe for testing is the state action implication in tax benefits to private schools and associations that discriminate in admissions. Tax-exempt status may not be granted, and tax-deductible contributions may not be made to schools or other associations that discriminate on racial grounds. Green v. Connally, 330 F. Supp. 1150 (D.D.C.), *aff'd sub nom.* Coit v. Green, 404 U.S. 997 (1971); McGlotten v. Connally, 338 F. Supp. 448 (D.D.C. 1972); Pitts v. Wisconsin Department of Revenue, 333 F. Supp. 662 (E.D. Wisc. 1971). See recent action of NLRB General Counsel on the unions' duty of fair representation in sex discrimination. 80 BNA LABOR REPORTER 65 (1972).

[30] This is not to say that the concept of sexual equality has been generally accepted. It is still widely assumed that certain types of work are for one sex or the other, that men's and women's personalities are unalterably different, and that certain types of behavior which are suitable for men or boys are unsuitable for women or girls. See Brown, Emerson, Falk & Freedman, *The Equal Rights Amendment: A Constitutional Basis for*

likely that *Reed* and *Stanley* are the forerunners of a policy of strict review in cases involving discrimination on the basis of sex.

The change in policy should be made explicit. The simplest method for declaring legal equality between the sexes to be an important constitutional principle is to hold that sex is a suspect classification under the Fourteenth Amendment. Such a declaration would acknowledge that sexual classification has historically been used as a technique for depriving women of opportunities available to men. It would also be implicit acceptance of the analogy between sexual and racial discrimination which has been urged so forcefully by proponents of women's rights.[31]

Despite the historic significance involved in these determinations, the precise ways in which existing law would be changed are unclear. Under the suspect classification analysis, it is still necessary in particular cases to determine whether a compelling state interest justifies the use of sexual classification. The Court would have to consider the extent to which the classification is based on what it considers to be legitimate differences between the sexes, the importance of the state interest being served, and whether the goal could be achieved in ways which do not involve sexual classification. The doctrine of suspect classification does not supply answers in particular cases to the questions raised by these considerations.[32] Announcement that sex is to be treated as a suspect classification would be understood as rejecting traditional justifications for sex discrimination and as notice that the national commitment to sexual equality will be given great weight in future cases. The interest in achieving sexual equality, however, does not always militate against the use of sexual classification. Indeed, in certain cases the promotion of sexual equality may be the compelling state interest which permits the use

---

Equal Rights for Women, 80 YALE L.J. 871, 882 nn.29, 30 (1971). What has been accepted, however, is the principle that the law should not be used to prevent women from full participation in national life.

[31] See, *e.g.*, Murray, *The Negro Woman's Stake in the Equal Rights Amendment*, 6 HARV. CIV. RTS.—CIV. LIB. L. REV. 253, 257 (1971); Sail'er Inn v. Kirby, 95 Cal. Rep. 329 (1971).

[32] Indeed, had the suspect classification formulation been used when such cases as *Muller v. Oregon*, and *Goesaert v. Cleary*, were considered, they might well have been decided the same way. *Muller*, which involved the constitutionality of legislation regulating hours of work for women, could have been justified by the compelling state interest in protecting women from the perils of overwork, and *Goesaert* by the state's interest in regulating the sale of liquor to prevent social harm to women.

of sexual classification. The Court must still address itself to the difficult question of elaborating the legal implications of sexual equality and of weighing the importance of various types of justification for sexual classification.

The application of the suspect classification doctrine to sex may be made unnecessary by passage of the Equal Rights Amendment, which provides: "Equality of rights under the law shall not be denied or abridged by the United States or by any state on account of sex." The Amendment also authorizes the Congress and the states to enforce the Amendment by appropriate enforcement legislation. Although it has been suggested that the Equal Rights Amendment would prohibit almost any classification based on sex, this is not necessarily so. Indeed, it can be read as specifically authorizing such sexual classification for the purpose of promoting equality. Thus, under the Equal Rights Amendment, as under the doctrine of suspect classification, the Court will have to decide the extent to which programs employing sexual classifications are consistent with the elusive concept of sexual equality. In the rest of this paper I will discuss the interests which the Court should consider in answering questions likely to arise after passage of the Equal Rights Amendment or application of the suspect classification doctrine to sex. The discussion is focused primarily in the area of education.

II. Affirmative Action Programs

Fair employment practices laws, including Title VII, were originally aimed at preventing conscious discrimination by providing remedies in specific cases.[33] This approach, however, did not make a significant impact on hiring or promotional practices. Employers changed avowedly discriminatory policies without substantially changing the composition of their work force. Standards frequently used and seemingly objective turned out to have discriminatory impact.[34] It has proved difficult to establish whether neutral

---

[33] See generally *Developments—Title VII*, 1113–19, 1123–26; Blumrosen, *The Duty of Fair Recruitment under the Civil Rights Act of 1964*, 22 Rutgers L. Rev. 465, 465–66, 509–27 (1968); H.R. Rep. No. 570, 88th Cong., 1st Sess. (1963). See also Sovern, Legal Restraints on Racial Discrimination in Employment (1966).

[34] Griggs v. Duke Power, Co., 401 U.S. 424 (1971); Quarles v. Philip Morris, Inc., 279 F. Supp. 505 (E.D. Va. 1968); Gould, *Seniority and the Black Worker: Reflections on Quarles and Its Implications*, 47 Texas L. Rev. 1039 (1969).

standards are in fact being applied in a discriminatory fashion. Techniques for evasion are many. Nondiscriminatory policies which may have been adopted in good faith can be subverted by those taking part in the hiring process.[35] Only a small fraction of violations were ever called to the attention of the agencies, and even then the process was slow and the result uncertain. The EEOC and the courts responded by permitting the use of racial statistics as a way of establishing a violation of the Act and of treating cases as class actions.[36] It became possible to prove discrimination by showing that the existing work force did not contain qualified women or blacks and that existing recruitment and promotion techniques were not serving to redress the balance.

Affirmative action programs began as a way of overcoming the limitations involved in case-by-case adjudication. They began as voluntary programs with little or no enforcement machinery. Government contractors simply pledged themselves to seek out qualified minority group members. The Philadelphia Plan combined the concept of affirmative action with the use of racial statistics. The program, adopted by the Office of Federal Contract Compliance in the Philadelphia area, required construction contractors to establish a program which recruited qualified minority group workers in order to obtain or continue working under a government contract.[37] The Department of Labor announced the percentage of minority group employees which it expected would be hired by a specified date if nondiscriminatory hiring policies were used. While the plan also provided that no qualified worker was to be denied a job because of race, failure to hire the proscribed percentage was deemed a prima facie evidence of discriminatory hiring, which could lead to loss of contracts unless adequately explained. The plan was hailed by some because it promised results.[38] It was attacked by others as involving the use of quotas and therefore illegal.[39] Its legality was, however, upheld in the Court of Appeals on the grounds that it did

---

[35] Penn v. Stumpf, 308 F. Supp. 1238 (N.D. Cal. 1970); see also Brown *et al.*, note 30 *supra*, at 899, n.51, for cases and sources.

[36] Fiss, *A Theory of Fair Employment Laws*, 38 U. Chi. L. Rev. 235 (1971).

[37] Jones, *The Bugaboo of Employment Quotas*, 1970 Wisc. L. Rev. 341; for revised guidelines, see 401 F.E.P. 25, 255, 262 (1972).

[38] Jones, note 37 supra, at 347, 364–73, 398–403.

[39] The Comptroller General took this position. *Id.* at 358–61, 394–98.

not involve a fixed hiring quota.[40] Similar plans have since been adopted in other areas.

The widespread use of affirmative action programs in higher education developed after a finding by HEW (which had responsibility for eliminating discrimination by government contractors in education) that the University of Michigan had been guilty of sex discrimination. The university was threatened with loss of government contracts. Since such contracts are now crucial to the economic well-being of colleges and universities, and since the Michigan hiring policies did not seem very different from those employed by most other major institutions, the finding created serious concern among academic administrators throughout the country. Under pressure from HEW, which has since established guidelines for affirmative action programs,[41] and from women's groups, many universities have now adopted affirmative action programs dealing with the recruitment and hiring and promotion of women. Although there are considerable variations among the programs, generally they involve the commitment to an effort to recruit or hire a stated percentage of women and to equalize salaries of men and women. All these programs require that those making significant decisions consider the sex of those receiving benefits.

There has been very little discussion of the constitutionality of benign quotas and compensatory programs for women under either the Equal Rights Amendment or the suspect classification doctrine. The landmark article interpreting the Equal Rights Amendment by Brown, Emerson, Falk, and Freedman takes the position that under the Fourteenth Amendment, such programs could be justified by "compelling [state] reasons," but that under the Equal Rights Amendment, "the guarantee of equal rights for women may not be qualified in the manner that 'suspect classification' or 'fundamental interest' doctrines allow."[42]

---

[40] Contractors Association of Eastern Pennsylvania v. Secretary of Labor, 442 F.2d 159 (CA 3d, 1971).

[41] 29 C.F.R. § 1604, Guidelines; Institute of Continuing Legal Education, *Women's Work Has Just Begun: Legal Problems of Employing Women in Universities*, Ann Arbor (1972).

[42] Brown *et al.*, note 30 *supra*, at 904. The Senate Judiciary Committee's Majority Report on the Equal Rights Amendment, 14 March 1972, stated that although that Amendment would not permit separate-but-equal schools, it would also "not require quotas for men and women, nor would it require that schools accurately reflect the sex distribution in the population." P. 17.

The compelling reason used to justify affirmative action programs is that they promote sexual equality. A similar justification
has been implicitly accepted in some cases of affirmative action
aimed at eliminating racial disparities.[43] As noted above, however,
this argument can be made with equal force under the Equal Rights
Amendment. The purpose of the Equal Rights Amendment is to
remove barriers preventing women from full participation in national life. Affirmative action programs are consistent with this goal.
On the other hand, affirmative action programs may be challenged
under either the Fourteenth Amendment or the Equal Rights
Amendment on the ground that they involve singling out women
for favored treatment. It has been argued that any system which
grants benefits on the basis of group affiliation is inconsistent with
the principle of evaluation based on individual merit, traditionally
considered to be central to the concept of equal treatment.[44]

Judicial authority and public sentiment are both profoundly divided on the question whether equality permits recognition of
group affiliation.[45] It is unnecessary for the Court in resolving this
question to reject either the principle of individual merit or the
concept of compensatory affirmative action. Affirmative action pro-

---

[43] Balaban v. Rubin, 14 N.Y.2d 192 (1964). The New York Court of Appeals approved
a school board plan to rezone a junior high school. In addition to the usual factors, the
board considered improving racial balance in drawing the boundaries. The plan was
challenged under a law that said that a child could not be denied admittance to a school
on the basis of race. The court approved the plan on the basis that these laws were intended to protect blacks and other minority groups. See also Fiss, *Racial Imbalance in the
Public Schools: The Constitutional Concepts*, 78 HARV. L. REV. 564 (1965).

[44] See Kaplan, *Equal Justice in an Unequal World: Equality for the Negro—The Problem
of Special Treatment*, 61 Nw. U.L. REV. 363 (1966); Seabury, *HEW and the Universities*,
53 COMMENTARY 38 (1972).

[45] See *Quotas: The Sleeper Issue of 1972*, NEWSWEEK 36–37 (18 September, 1972). In
DeFunis v. Odegaard, No. 741727, Wash. King County Super. Ct. (Washington, Sept.
22, 1971), the court ordered the admission to law school of the plaintiff because his
academic credentials seemed superior to minority applicants who were admitted. In
Carter v. Gallagher, 452 F.2d 315 (CA 8th, 1971), the court upheld a plan for remedying
past discrimination, which required that one out of every three hired must be a minority
group member until twenty were hired.

The Democratic party at its 1972 national convention insisted that each delegation
contain minimum percentages of women and minority group members. The Republicans
specifically rejected such an approach and insisted that a system of quotas is discriminatory and, in fact, contrary to the basic principle of individual merit. Good statements of
opposing considerations are to be found in the exchange of letters between Professors
Gould and Glazer in the *New York Times* on 2 March 1972, 11 April 1972, and 20
April 1972.

grams differ in the extent to which they depart from a standard of individual merit and in their potential for furthering equality. Each should be evaluated separately considering several factors.

1. How likely is it that objective or nonbiased standards will be used if the affirmative action program is invalidated? Much of the criticism of compensatory hiring and promotional programs in universities is based on the assumption that the current system selects the ablest teachers and scholars available and rewards them according to merit without regard to race, religion, sex, or other extraneous considerations. Thus, Professor Paul Seabury of the University of California, a severe critic of affirmative action programs, recently wrote in *Commentary*:[46]

> Fifteen years ago, David Riesman in his *Constraint and Variety in American Education* pointed to certain qualities which distinctively characterized avant-garde institutions of higher learning in this country. The world of scholarship, he said "is democratic rather than aristocratic in tone, and scholars are made, not born." . . . Paradoxically this democratization of the university (with its stress not on status but upon excellence in performance) had not begun in rank-and-file small colleges of the nation, which were exemplars of America's ethnic, religious, and cultural diversity. Rather it had come out of those innovating institutions which, in quest of excellence, either abandoned or transcended much of their discriminatory sociological parochialism. . . . The egalitarianism of excellence, a democracy of performance, was an ethos consummated by the avant-garde.
>
> . . . by the 1950's the great American universities attained an authentic cosmopolitanism of scholarship matched by no other university system in the world. And the outward reach of American higher education toward the best the world of scholarship could offer generated an inward magnetism, attracting to itself the most qualified students who could be found to study with these newly renowned faculties.
>
> This system of recruitment also left a myriad of American sociological categories statistically underrepresented in the highest precincts of American higher education. Today, with respect to race and ethnicity, blacks, Irish, Italians, Greeks, Poles, and all other Slavic groups (including Slovaks, Slovenes, Serbs, Czechs, and Croatians) are underrepresented. On faculties, at least, women are underrepresented. Important religious categories are underrepresented.

---

[46] Seabury, note 44 *supra*, at 40.

Despite Professor Seabury's eloquence, the picture which he paints of university hiring and selection processes is unduly flattering. Subtle but real discrimination has traditionally been a part of the process of faculty appointment even at leading universities.[47] For example, the factor of personal recommendation, which is crucial to the hiring process, has built into it an unconscious sex bias. Certain students call themselves to the attention of their professors as likely prospects for future teaching positions. They appear to be seriously committed to scholarship and to possess the necessary mental abilities. For the most part they are skillful at argument, verbally aggressive, what we like to call tough-minded, and willing to challenge the professor openly in class discussion. Whatever their characteristics, women students are less likely than men to be seen as serious scholars by their teachers. Moreover, verbal aggressiveness and tough-mindedness have been discouraged in young girls and, when demonstrated by women, verbal aggressiveness and tough-mindedness often seem less praiseworthy, even offensive.[48]

The same considerations will affect the impression which a woman applicant makes in an interview. Many men unconsciously desire or expect submissive behavior from women in a discussion. Many women are accustomed to complying.[49] If they do, they may be thought to lack the toughness necessary for a good teacher or scholar. If the expected behavior is not forthcoming, the man may feel uncomfortable, possibly even threatened, and conclude that the woman would not be a desirable colleague.[50]

2. To what extent are the people benefited by the affirmative action program likely to be the same ones disadvantaged by previous policies? *E.g.*, a program to give special financial assistance or

---

[47] The statistics are set forth and the dynamics pointed out in Murray, *Economic and Educational Inequality Based on Sex: An Overview*, 5 VALPO. L. REV. 237, 258–68 (1972); Indiana University AAUP Committee on the Status of Women, *Study of Women: Study of the Status of Women Faculty at Indiana University, Bloomington Campus* (1971).

[48] Cavanagh, *A Little Dearer Than His Horse: Legal Stereotypes and the Feminine Personality*, 6 HARV. CIV. RIGHTS—CIV. LIB. L. REV. 260 (1971); Romer & Secor, *The Time Is Here For Women's Liberation*, 397 ANNALS 129 (1971); Horner, *Women's Will to Fail*, PSYCHOLOGY TODAY (November 1969).

[49] Cavanagh, note 48 *supra*, at 274.

[50] Even the evaluation of publications will in many disciplines contain an element of sex bias. For an interesting description of the way sexual expectations may affect critical reaction to published work, see Ozick, *We Are the Crazy Lady and Other Feisty Feminist Fables*, Ms., p. 40 (Spring 1971).

hiring preference to older married women with children would have a special claim to validity. In the recent past it was especially difficult for married women to obtain a desirable teaching position or admission to a graduate school. Some admissions committees felt that a professional education would be wasted on married women. It was often assumed that job offers would be declined or that positions accepted would be given up eventually to serve family needs. If a woman had children, all of these concerns were increased, and maternity policies in many institutions were so framed as to create severe conflict between motherhood and professional interests.

It is impossible to reconstruct the ways in which these policies affected individual women because the impact was felt at so many levels. Some women were denied education or employment because of these policies. Some did not apply or even consider certain careers because of their awareness of the policies or because of their own acceptance of the underlying value judgment that a woman's primary obligation was to her family.[51]

3. Is the program in an area in which achieving equality will serve significant social interests or in which existing inequalities have special costs? The Supreme Court has noted that methods of selection which keep women off juries deprive the deliberative process of qualities which women bring to bear. The classic statement was made by Mr. Justice Douglas in *Ballard v. United States:*[52]

> The truth is that the two sexes are not fungible; a community made up exclusively of one is different from a community composed of both; the subtle interplay of influence one on the other is among the imponderables. To insulate the courtroom from either may not in a given case make an iota of difference. Yet a flavor, a distinct quality is lost if either is excluded.

Most institutions will function better if they can avail themselves more fully of the diverse experiences of different groups.[53] In addition, the inclusion of either sex in an area previously reserved to the

---

[51] Cavanagh, note 48 *supra*, at 272.

[52] 329 U.S. 187, 193–94 (1946). The Supreme Court adopted this approach in Peters v. Kiff, 407 U.S. 493 (1972), holding that a white man was deprived of due process of law because blacks had been systematically excluded from the jury that convicted him. "When any large and identifiable segment of the community is excluded from jury service, the effect is to remove from the jury room qualities of human nature and varieties of human experience, the range of which is unknown and perhaps unknowable." *Id*. at 503.

[53] MEAD, MALE AND FEMALE: A STUDY OF THE SEXES IN A CHANGING WORLD 357 (1968).

other serves an educational function. When women assume positions formerly held by men, it educates women to the fact that a wider range of choice is now available, and it causes men to re-evaluate their conception of women. No easy method exists to identify those areas in which the benefits of inclusion are greatest. Some of the applicable considerations can be recognized.

a) Equality is particularly important for institutions such as education, the legal profession, and the arts which play a major role in shaping the standards and goals of the society.

b) Equality is also necessary in those positions which involve stating or effectuating public policy. This includes legislative, judicial, and high-level administrative positions.

c) The availability of different models is most crucial in areas of high prestige and in occupations which have traditionally been thought of as requiring attributes associated with one sex or the other. This would include the military and police, athletics, and grade school teaching.

4. Does the program require rejecting qualified people on the basis of sex? A requirement that the next person hired for a department must be a woman might mean that a highly qualified man will not even be considered. Such an approach is much more inconsistent with the idea of judging individuals on their own merits than a flexible program of percentages, which forces those in charge of hiring to make special efforts to locate qualified women or minorities. The latter is only marginally, if at all, inconsistent with the concept of individual merit. Of course to be effective any program requires an enforcement mechanism. Where flexible targets are involved, however, those doing the selecting are given an opportunity to demonstrate that failure to meet the target was not the result of lack of sincere or reasonable effort.

5. Is there a significant existing imbalance in the work force or student population? Such an imbalance would suggest past discrimination against women or that women have been discouraged from entering the field. In such cases affirmative action programs may be necessary to make known that opportunities do exist or that it is acceptable for women to enter the field.

III. PREGNANCY

The policies which an institution adopts concerning pregnancy and childbirth will significantly affect employment opportunities for women. Neither the Equal Rights Amendment nor the suspect classification doctrine provides the standards to be applied in evaluating the validity of programs applicable to pregnancy. Because pregnancy is unique to one sex, considerations of equality are necessarily interwoven with questions concerning the reasonableness of the program.[54] Determining the meaning of equality requires a decision as to the appropriate standard for comparison. Reasonableness requires attention both to the legitimate needs of the institution and to the principle of equality of economic opportunity. Different considerations apply and different institutional policies are arguably pertinent depending upon the nature of the regulation applied and whether it is being applied to pregnancy, delivery, or the post-delivery period.

A. MATERNITY LEAVE

The easiest issue involves the common policy of requiring a pregnant woman to take leave after a certain number of months

---

[54] In Miller v. Industrial Commission, 480 P.2d 565 (Col. 1971), the Supreme Court of Colorado rejected the argument that singling out pregnancy for special treatment under the employment insurance law was a form of sex discrimination: "[T]he act treats men and women workers the same for purposes of eligibility and qualification for unemployment benefits, . . . It is only where the woman worker has become pregnant that she is treated differently, placed in a separate classification from other men and women workers. Such a classification founded on the special consideration of pregnancy cannot be said to be unreasonable and therefore unconstitutional. . . . Such a classification is not based upon sex alone . . . which classification then might be subject to a valid criticism of unreasonableness." Id. at 568.

The court distinguished between categories based on sex and categories based on sex in combination with some other attribute. This distinction (the so-called "sex plus" doctrine) has been rejected in Title VII cases. Cohen v. Chesterfield, 4 FEP CASES 1237 (CA 4th, 1972). Both the EEOC and the courts have taken the position that when all or substantially all of the people in a class singled out for special treatment are of one sex, sex discrimination exists.

Guideline 1604.3 provides that it is "not . . . relevant that the rule is not directed against all females . . . for so long as sex is a factor in the application of the rule, such application involves discrimination based on sex."

As the Seventh Circuit stated in rejecting the contention that distinctions not phrased in terms of sex do not constitute sex discrimination for purposes of Title VII, "The effect of the statute is not to be diluted because discrimination adversely affects only a portion of the protected class. Discrimination is not to be tolerated under the guise of physical properties possessed by one sex." Sprogis v. United Air Lines, Inc., 444 F.2d 1194 (7th Cir. 1971) aff'g 308 F. Supp. 959 (N.D. Ill. 1970). In Phillips v. Martin Marietta Corporation, 400 U.S. 542 (1971), the Supreme Court, without discussion, rejected the argument that categories based on sex plus some other factor cannot constitute discrimination for the purposes of Title VII. There is little reason to suppose it will adopt a different standard in construing the Fourteenth Amendment or the Equal Rights Amendment.

of pregnancy. Such regulations have been challenged in a number of recent cases by women teachers who wished to remain on the job.[55] In each case the pregnant woman has introduced medical evidence to support her contention that she was not physically disabled in any way from performing her duties. The institution has typically responded with evidence indicating that pregnant women in general require assistance or that the rule eliminates administrative problems which would be involved in making individual determinations of disability. In one case a school system suggested that pregnant teachers had been subject in the past to some minor harassment by pupils.[56] The institution did not challenge medical testimony indicating that the woman was medically capable of performing her duties.

In some cases such rules have been affirmed without recognition of the fact that sex discrimination was involved. Thus, in *Cerra v. East Stroudsburg Area School District*,[57] the court upheld the constitutionality of a rule requiring the resignation of schoolteachers after the fifth month of pregnancy. The court did not address itself to the wisdom of the regulation nor did it consider whether the regulation was discriminatory. It merely referred to testimony by the Secretary of Education that the regulation "was a reasonable one" and within the Board's authority. Most recent cases, however, have recognized that the question is not solely whether the regulation serves a legitimate purpose but also whether pregnant women are being denied benefits available to men who have no greater claim to them. In holding a forced maternity leave policy to be invalid under the Fourteenth Amendment, the Sixth Circuit recently stated:[58]

> Male teachers are not subject to pregnancy but they are subject to many types of illnesses and disabilities. This record indicates clearly that pregnant women teachers have been singled out for unconstitutionally unequal restrictions upon their employment.

---

[55] See Cohen v. Chesterfield County School Board, 4 FEP CASES 1237 (CA 4th, 1972); LaFleur v. Board of Education, 4 FEP CASES 1070 (CA 6th 1972); Schattman v. Texas Employment Commission, 4 FEP CASES 353 (CA 5th, 1972); William v. San Francisco Unified School District, 340 F. Supp. 438 (N.D. Cal. 1972). Bravo v. Board of Education, 4 FEP CASES 995 (N.D. Ill. 1972).

[56] See LaFleur v. Cleveland Board of Education, 326 F. Supp. 1208 (N.D. Ohio 1971), *reversed*, 4 FEP CASES 107 (CA 6th, 1972).

[57] 285 A.2d 206 (Pa. Comm. Ct. 1971).

[58] LaFleur v. Board, note 55 *supra*, at 1073.

The application of such rules to women capable of working is inconsistent with the Court's decision in *Reed v. Reed*. The major thrust of the *Reed* decision is that administrative convenience does not justify treating women as a class and thereby ignoring the specific claims of individual women. Under a strict standard of review, pregnant women should not be treated as a class and healthy pregnant women should not be treated differently from healthy men. Moreover, equality cannot be obtained if the negative reactions of others are grounds for continuing to disfavor the group previously discriminated against.[59]

Even under a more lenient standard, such regulations are probably invalid. Where teachers are concerned, the institution's interest in preventing mishaps is offset by the desirability of maintaining continuity in the educational experience of the pupils. Moreover, forced maternity leave programs have a significant impact upon the employment situation of the women affected by them. Where substantial periods of leave are involved, a teacher may be forced to miss two semesters. In addition to the financial sacrifice, the woman's professional development is halted. She does not accrue benefits during this period, and she may not be able to return to the precise position which she was forced to give up even if she is entitled to return to work. Thus, as the Court of Appeals for the Fourth Circuit recently stated:[60]

> We need not concern ourselves with the applicable test to discriminate validity on the basis of sex . . . because under either we think the regulation denies equal protection. The record is literally devoid of any reason medical or administrative why a pregnant teacher must accept an enforced leave by the end of the fifth month of pregnancy if she and her doctor conclude that she can perform her duties beyond that date.

There are many possible issues concerning pregnancy and childbirth which pose more complicated questions. Some of these are discussed below. The preliminary discussion assumes that these

---

[59] Buchanan v. Warley, 245 U.S. 60 (1917); Diaz v. Pan American World Airways, Inc., 442 F.2d 385, 389 (CA 5th, 1971).

[60] Cohen v. Chesterfield County School Board, note 54 *supra*, at 1239. One way in which pregnancy-related leave might be treated differently from other forms of temporary disability is in requiring advance notice of the employee's decision to stop work at a certain point in the pregnancy if she does not desire to work as long as is medically possible.

issues will be treated as constitutional questions. It would in general be more desirable to handle these problems under currently applicable statutes.

B. THE RIGHT TO RETURN TO WORK

In some cases so much time off will either be required or voluntarily sought that under established sick leave or disability standards the woman would not be automatically entitled to return to work. In such cases pregnant women would not be treated differently from employees in comparable leave situations. Moreover, such policies serve legitimate institutional interests in continuity of employment. A rational argument can be made, however, to support special constitutional protection for pregnant women.[61]

Childbirth has a unique social value not possessed by other human behavior. A great percentage of women become pregnant at an early and crucial state of their professional development. If women are forced to choose between motherhood and career, the goal of economic equality cannot be achieved. Even if those terminated returned to the work force, denial of the right to return to the job held before pregnancy would prevent them from developing seniority rights for promotion and accruing fringe benefits. The Court might compromise by holding that a constitutional right to return to work after pregnancy exists, limited to the time of medical disability.[62]

C. THE RIGHT TO HEALTH BENEFITS

Normally illness and disability are compensated by health insurance and paid sick leave which is accrued by seniority. With respect to insurance benefits, current programs might exclude medical ex-

---

[61] Comment, *Love's Labor's Lost: New Conceptions of Maternity Leave*, 7 HARV. CIV. RIGHTS—CIV. LIB. L. REV. 260, 268 (1972); *Developments—Title VII*, at 1170.

[62] If a woman takes off more time than is medically necessary, she would be treated as are other people who take leave for personal reasons. Such a rule would be extremely difficult to operate effectively. Fine questions about the meaning of medical necessity would inevitably arise, and there would be little guidance available to school administrators in deciding the category in which a particular employee fell. Moreover, such a rule would fail to recognize the important psychological need which may exist for a family to adjust to a new life. It would be administratively simpler and more responsive to the interests involved for the Court to require that in addition to the woman's being able to take off the time medically required, either parent should be permitted leave for a reasonable time after birth without risking his or her job.

penses connected with childbirth on the theory that pregnancy is a voluntarily acquired condition. In addition, most policies do not provide benefits for conditions which predate the time of hire or else have a one-year waiting period for maternity benefits. The denial of insurance benefits on the grounds that pregnancy is voluntary should not be permitted.[63] Pregnancy is unlike other voluntary disability requiring medical care because it is socially useful. On the other hand, the requirement of a waiting period makes sense as a way of preventing women from seeking a job primarily as the means of financing the cost of delivery of their children. In this case, the reasons for the general policy apply to pregnancy as well.

D. UNWED MATERNITY

Some schools treat unwed maternity as grounds for expulsion or other sanctions.[64] Such policies are obviously discriminatory unless they are made applicable to unwed fathers as well. Even where such rules are theoretically applicable to both men and women, often only the mother will be affected because only she will be identified. Since it is difficult to defend such rules in terms of legitimate institutional concerns, their validity should not be upheld unless it can be shown that in practice they are applied to both men and women.[65]

E. PREGNANCY AND AFFIRMATIVE ACTION

An institution seeking to increase the number of its women employees or students might permit pregnant women to work part time or carry a reduced course load and provide special insurance benefits or leave with pay.

It is arguable that such programs deny equal protection of the laws to men. The argument should be rejected. As the discussion above indicates, the concept of equality cannot be applied with precision in cases involving questions of pregnancy. Moreover,

---

[63] *Id*. at 283 *et seq*.

[64] Some schools penalize students who become mothers by keeping them from extracurricular activities. In such cases the program would be discriminatory unless a similar program was in existence for men students who became unwed fathers. Recent cases have held that unwed mothers may not be barred from high school. Ordway v. Hargraves, 323 F. Supp. 1155 (D. Mass. 1971); Shull v. Columbus Municipal School District, 338 F. Supp. 1376 (N.D. Miss. 1972).

[65] Doe v. Osteopathic Hospital, 333 F. Supp. 1357 (D. Kans. 1971); Dec. No. 71-562, 1 CCH EMPL. PRAC. GUIDE ¶6184 (EEOC) (4 December 1970).

even with special benefits, there will be some educational or professional costs involved for the woman and for her family. The most that any economically and politically feasible affirmative action program could do is minimize the cost.

Sexual equality would, however, require that any program of leave after the birth of a child apart from that required for delivery should be available to men and to women equally.[66] It should be for the parents to decide which of them will take leave to care for the child. Limiting such leaves to women would mean that the professional careers of women but not of men would be interrupted if the parents decide that a newborn child should have close parental attention during infancy.

F. THE AVOIDANCE OF CONSTITUTIONAL DETERMINATION

Constitutional litigation does not seem the best way to resolve the conflicting interests of educational institutions and pregnant women. The delicate interest-balancing engaged in above is highly theoretical and based in part on conjecture. The practical and financial implications involved in many of the positions argued for cannot be understood until they are tried. It is important that the law change as practical experience reveals problems and issues not now clearly perceived. Currently, either Title VII, Executive Order 11,246 as amended by 11,375, or the Equal Educational Opportunities Act, and state law cover all the questions raised. The agencies which enforce these statutes and regulations are in a position to develop rules and guidelines as experience shows them to be necessary and feasible. Accordingly, it would make sense for the courts to deal with these questions to the extent possible as matters of statutory construction. The courts should give great weight to administrative determination so as not to foreclose questions under the statute prematurely. The Constitution should be invoked only where statutes do not provide a remedy.

IV. CONCLUSION

The principle of sexual equality does not require that sex always be treated as an invalid consideration.[67] Indeed, in certain cir-

---

[66] Danielson v. Board of Higher Education, 4 FEP CASES 885 (S.D. N.Y. 1972).

[67] Athletic programs are another area in which equality may require recognition of sex. There are currently far more male students than females involved in sports. Certain

cumstances achieving equality requires specific awareness of sex. The next decade will involve the courts in the difficult task of enunciating the circumstances under which recognition of sex can coexist with the Equal Rights Amendment or with the concept of sexual equality embodied in the Fourteenth Amendment. Sure answers are likely to be as elusive here as they have proved to be in race cases.

---

sports such as football, basketball, and baseball are almost entirely masculine enterprises. These are the top priority sports involving the greatest expenditure of money and the active interest of other students and the outside community. Participation by girls is limited to being cheerleaders, pompom girls, or drum majorettes, all of which are subordinate positions emphasizing attractiveness rather than athletic skills.

Some progress can be made by opening up existing programs to women. However, the removal of formal barriers is likely to have only a limited effect. Current differences between the sexes make it unlikely than many women would enter into existing athletic programs, and most would be at a competitive disadvantage. Affirmative action is necessary if women are to participate equally in athletics. This would require in most schools establishing or substantially strengthening women's athletic programs and focusing on areas not currently emphasized in women's intra- or extramural athletics. The measure of equality for athletic programs should be the number of women participating, the amount of money spent by the system, and the availability of resources. These, rather than technical eligibility under existing programs or whether male and female programs concentrate on the same areas, should determine whether a school system is complying with the Fourteenth Amendment or the Equal Rights Amendment.

PHILIP B. KURLAND

1971 TERM: THE YEAR OF THE
STEWART-WHITE COURT

In its third year, the Burger Court continued in a condition of flux. Each of the two previous Terms had seen the appointment of one new Supreme Court Justice. In the 1971 Term, after the President presented a list of possible appointees, with a preference for two whom even the American Bar Association found unpalatable, he nominated Lewis Powell and William Rehnquist. Both were confirmed by the Senate with relative ease, Powell without any real opposition whatsoever and Rehnquist after some spirited hearings. If many took exceptions to the points of view that the new Justices had previously adopted toward issues likely to come before the Court, none questioned their superior intellectual capacities. As successors to Justices Black and Harlan, the new Justices faced the challenge of filling the places of two of the strongest Justices of recent years. Whether those challenges will be met is a matter for the future to answer. After but one Term, or rather a part of one Term, for the new Justices were not participants in about half the cases decided during the Term, it looks as though Mr. Justice Powell has cast himself in the role of heir to the Frankfurter-Harlan mantle, while Mr. Justice Rehnquist gives the appearance of playing the part for the right wing of the Court that Mr. Justice Douglas has so long played for the left wing.

Philip B. Kurland is Professor of Law, The University of Chicago.

NOTE: To help establish the reader's bias against bias, it is appropriate to note that the author was of counsel to amici curiae in Gravel v. United States, 408 U.S. 606 (1972); Healy v. James, 408 U.S. 169 (1972); and counsel to the appellants in Bradley v. City of Richmond, 462 F.2d 1058 (CA 4th, 1972).

Despite the differences already evident between the two new Nixon appointees, it is quite clear that the freshmen jurists have shifted the balance of the Court considerably. For where Black and Harlan tended to find themselves in the middle grouping with Justices Stewart and White, Powell and Rehnquist are more usually to be found in association with the Chief Justice and Mr. Justice Blackmun. With Justices Douglas, Brennan, and Marshall continuing to cluster closely, the votes if not the opinions of Justices Stewart and White have been dominant in the judgments of the 1971 Term.

I. CONFIGURATIONS

As usual, the statistical—perhaps arithmetical would be a more accurate adjective—data tend to support the conclusions reached by the Court watchers without the need for them.

First, it should be noted that the Court engaged in its busiest session since the passage of the 1925 Judiciary Act, suggesting once again that the Justices are pressed beyond their capacities by the business imposed on them. The Chief Justice has created a commission to investigate and suggest remedies for the problems deriving from this overwork. It is to be hoped that recommendations to Congress will soon be forthcoming.[1]

In addition to their other overwhelming burdens, the Justices issued 146 majority and plurality opinions, 67 concurring opinions, and 129 dissenting opinions. Table 1 shows the distribution among the Justices. The relationships of the Justices in these opinions are demonstrated by table 2, which may be compared with those in the earlier articles in this *Review* on the first two Terms of the Burger Court.[2]

Table 2 reveals the groupings, not only in terms of results but in terms of affinity of one Justice for another's form of expression. The Chief Justice expressed the views of Justices Blackmun, Powell, and Rehnquist in every one of his opinions. Burger reciprocated this expression of confidence in the opinions of Rehnquist and, while never in dissent from the opinions of the other two members of his

---

[1] For one earlier suggestion for appropriate relief, see Kurland, *The Court Should Decide Less and Explain More*, N.Y. TIMES MAGAZINE 34 (9 June 1968).

[2] See Kurland, *Enter the Burger Court: The Constitutional Business of the Supreme Court, O.T. 1969*, 1970 SUPREME COURT REVIEW 1, 4; Kurland, *1970 Term: Notes on the Emergence of the Burger Court*, 1971 SUPREME COURT REVIEW 265, 270.

team, concurred specially with regard to Blackmun in 8 percent of the latter's opinions, and with reference to 17 percent of Powell's opinions. The proximity of views of Blackmun and Rehnquist was of a similar magnitude. Neither of the other two groupings on the Court shows such mutuality, although Stewart accepted Marshall's opinions 100 percent of the time and White did the same for Rehnquist.

Measured by the totality of judgments rendered during the 1971 Term, the Court's results were in accord with the positions of Powell in 94.4 percent of the cases in which he participated, with

TABLE 1

Opinions	Majority Plurality	Concurring	Dissenting
Burger............	12	15	10
Douglas..........	13	14	44
Brennan..........	17	2	19
Stewart...........	18	6	7
White............	19	11	6
Marshall.........	15	3	23
Blackmun........	12	8	11
Powell...........	12	4	2
Rehnquist........	11	4	7
Per curiam........	17	...	...
Totals........	146	67	129

those of White in 91.8 percent of the cases, with those of Stewart in 90.2 percent. The others trailed behind as follows: Rehnquist 84.4 percent, Blackmun 84 percent, Burger 82.9 percent, Marshall 75.3 percent, Brennan 72 percent, and Douglas 56.8 percent. If we regard Justices Douglas, Brennan, and Marshall as the true heirs of the Warren Court philosophy, it can readily be seen that the Court is certainly no longer dominated by that jurisprudence.

More revealing than the totality of cases are those in which the Court was closely divided over results. Here the ordering of the Justices according to their agreement with the conclusions reached places White at the head of the list with 82.1 percent, followed by Stewart with 78.7 percent, Powell with 71.8 percent, Rehnquist with 71.1 percent, Burger with 70.1 percent, Blackmun with 65.1 percent, Marshall with 50.7 percent, Brennan with 39.1 percent, and Douglas with 38.8 percent. Once again the movement away from the trinity's views is easily seen. Shown, too, however, is dominance

TABLE 2

Votes of / Opinions by	Burger	Douglas	Brennan	Stewart	White	Marshall	Blackmun	Powell	Rehnquist
Burger		A77 C0 D23	A41 C18 D41	A39 C28 D33	A79 C0 D21	A74 C0 D26	A92 C0 D8	A83 C17 D0	A100 C0 D0
Douglas	A33 C8 D58		A65 C0 D35	A50 C11 D39	A26 C16 D58	A53 C7 D40	A25 C8 D67	A50 C17 D33	A27 C9 D64
Brennan	A42 C16 D42	A62 C15 D23		A61 C0 D39	A58 C5 D37	A73 C7 D20	A58 C17 D25	A50 C8 D42	A36 C0 D64
Stewart	A42 C16 D42	A69 C31 D0	A77 C6 D17		A78 C0 D22	A100 C0 D0	A75 C0 D25	A92 C0 D8	A73 C0 D27
White	A92 C0 D8	A77 C0 D23	A94 C6 D0	A61 C11 D28		A86 C7 D7	A67 C33 D7	A67 C16 D17	A100 C0 D0
Marshall	A67 C0 D33	A92 C0 D8	A88 C0 D12	A78 C0 D22	A68 C0 D32		A50 C17 D33	A58 C0 D42	A36 C0 D64
Blackmun	A100 C0 D0	A85 C0 D15	A56 C19 D25	A39 C22 D39	A73 C11 D16	A50 C28 D22		A83 C0 D17	A91 C0 D9
Powell	A100 C0 D0	A60 C20 D20	A44 C0 D56	A0 C50 D50	A80 C0 D20	A86 C14 D0	A67 C0 D33		A80 C10 D10
Rehnquist	A100 C0 D0	A60 C20 D20	A64 C0 D36	A67 C0 D33	A80 C0 D20	A71 C15 D14	A100 C0 D0	A67 C11 D12	

A: joins in opinion without separate statement; C: concurs specially; D: dissents in whole or in part.

The table is expressed in percentages. By reading across one can see how each Justice in the left-hand column reacted to the opinions of the Justices listed at the top. By reading down, one can determine how the opinions of each Justice were received by the others.

of the middle pair, drawing most often on the Nixon quartet for their needed support. Of the two wings, the most likely conservative to aid the middle is Powell, the most likely liberal is Marshall. Blackmun seems to represent the most rigid position on the one hand, as Douglas does on the other. The minority trio contributed more than 60 percent of the dissenting votes. Douglas alone cast more than four times as many dissents as Stewart and more than five times as many as White.

The pairings in the closely divided cases again reveal the same patterns, as table 3 shows.[3]

The data then is clear that the Minnesota Twins have expanded into the Nixon quartet, while the Warren Court trio remains a minority of three. The new plurality has come essentially at the expense of the middle. None the less, Stewart and White, somewhat more closely paired than in the previous Term, have come to dominate the Court because theirs are the crucial votes that neither bloc can anticipate. The Burger-Blackmun-Powell-Rehnquist grouping occurred in 70.6 percent of the closely divided cases in which they all sat. The Douglas-Brennan-Marshall bloc were together in 64.1 percent. Only once in all these cases was a majority made up without either White or Stewart. The trio secured the support of Stewart and White, both of whom they needed for a majority, in 22 percent of the cases. The quartet more frequently secured the acquiescence of White or Stewart, only one or the other of which was necessary. In 47 percent of these cases in which the quartet was joined together, they were joined by White, and in 29 percent of the cases by Stewart.

So long as the personnel of the Court remains unchanged, the precarious balance weighted toward the right wing but controlled by Stewart and White will continue, and so presumably will their dominance. They reveal, themselves, no clear ideological preferences, although it is clear that White's bent is toward the Burger team and Stewart's toward the other side. It is yet possible that defections can come from either extreme, with Powell and Marshall moving more frequently to join their two senior brethren in the establishment of a vital and strong center. Indeed, Powell, alone with his Harlanesque attitudes, may very well cause the Court to be more evenly split into three equal parts.

---

[3] Compare the table in Kurland, *1970 Term: Notes on the Emergence of the Burger Court*, 1971 SUPREME COURT REVIEW 265, at 269.

TABLE 3

AGREEMENT BETWEEN JUSTICES ON RESULTS IN SHARPLY DIVIDED CASES

(Percent)

	Burger	Douglas	Brennan	Stewart	White	Marshall	Blackmun	Powell	Rehnquist
Burger.........		04.2	10.9	50.0	64.2	20.9	87.9	84.6	94.7
Douglas.........	04.2		81.3	51.5	32.8	76.1	09.1	17.9	13.2
Brennan.........	10.9	81.3		47.6	42.7	70.3	12.7	19.4	10.5
Stewart.........	50.0	51.5	47.6		65.1	66.7	61.5	55.5	47.4
White.........	64.2	32.8	42.2	65.1		41.8	66.7	56.4	57.6
Marshall.........	20.9	76.1	70.3	66.7	41.8		21.2	15.4	07.9
Blackmun.........	87.9	09.1	12.7	61.5	66.7	21.2		76.3	67.6
Powell.........	84.6	17.9	19.4	55.3	56.4	15.4	76.3		88.6
Rehnquist.........	94.7	13.2	10.5	47.4	57.6	07.9	67.6	88.6	

But these numbers like all numbers, are abstractions. The 1971
Term, like all Supreme Court Terms, was concerned with cases
of complicated facts and complex issues not necessarily reducible to
the simplicity of numbers.

II. RACE RELATIONS

In the 1971 Term as in earlier years, race relations were
among the more important issues that called for resolution by the
Court. That the issues deriving from the consistent confrontation
of the black and white races in this country will continue to call
for judicial resolution seems patent. That the Court's attitude is
changing from one of commitment to give black litigants what they
want to one perhaps more consonant with the concept of the equality of the races is also apparent. The easier questions precluding
adverse governmental discrimination have been answered. The new
ones tend to present the question how much must the present generation compensate blacks for the deprivations they have suffered in
the past. There are, indeed, two sets of questions likely to arise here:
(1) To what extent can Congress discriminate in favor of this or
any other minority? (2) To what extent does the Constitution itself
compel such "reverse discrimination"? And yet some of the old
questions—What is or is not state action? for example; Can a state
gerrymander school districts to prevent or destroy the creation of
a unitary school system? is another—continue to arise.

A. STATE ACTION

The impossible question of state action was raised once more in
Moose Lodge No. 107 v. Irvis.[4] The Warren Court had struggled
with the concept without being able to reduce it to a principle.[5]
Seeking to bring more and more activity that had not in the past
been regarded as state action under the umbrella of the Fourteenth
Amendment prohibitions, the Court was effectively reduced to ad
hoc resolutions, thereby binding neither themselves nor their successors. Thus, in *Burton v. Wilmington Parking Authority,*[6] the
Court announced a large number of facts, stirred them together,
and concluded that the mixture amounted to state action. The Court

---

[4] 407 U.S. 163 (1972).

[5] See the cases referred to in Black, *"State Action," Equal Protection, and California's
Proposition 14*, 81 HARV. L. REV. 69 (1967).

[6] 365 U.S. 715 (1961).

in *Moose Lodge No. 107* stirred a similar mixture, but a majority concluded that there was no state action which warranted relief.

K. Leroy Irvis is an important Pennsylvania state legislator who was refused service at a Harrisburg Moose Lodge because he was black. He sought an injunction against the continuance of the Lodge's liquor license. It was his claim that the Lodge was engaged in state action because it was licensed to serve liquor by the Pennsylvania Liquor Authority, which exercised a large amount of control over private club activities, including a command that each licensed private club must abide by its own by-laws, thereby giving the club's exclusionary policy state sanction.

Speaking for six members of the Court, Mr. Justice Rehnquist reversed the decision of the three-judge district court which had granted the requested relief to the plaintiff. Admittedly the exclusionary policy was a result of the constitution and by-laws of the Moose national organization. Admittedly the refusal of service was solely because of plaintiff's race. Admittedly the bar was licensed and extensively regulated by the state. The relief sought was simply the withdrawal of the liquor license until the Lodge surrendered its discriminatory policies:[7]

> The Court has never held, of course, that discrimination by an otherwise private entity would be violative of the Equal Protection Clause if the private entity receives any sort of benefit or service at all from the State, or if it is subject to state regulation in any degree whatever. Since state-furnished services include such necessities of life as electricity, water, and police and fire protection, such a holding would utterly emasculate the distinction between private as distinguished from State conduct set forth in the *Civil Rights Cases* [109 U.S. 3 (1883)] and adhered to in subsequent decisions. Our holdings indicate that where the impetus for the discrimination is private, the State must have "significantly involved itself with invidious discriminations," *Reitman* v. *Mulkey*, 387 U.S. 369, 380 (1967), in order for the discriminatory action to fall within the ambit of the constitutional prohibition.

---

[7] 407 U.S. at 173. The question of statutory command is different from that of constitutional compulsion. Earlier in the Term the Court had affirmed a federal trial court decision that schools that discriminated on the basis of race were not entitled to exemption from taxation afforded in the Internal Revenue Code. *Coit v. Green*, 404 U.S. 997 (1971). The implications for religious schools, which by their nature are discriminatory, are potentially important.

The Court then distinguished *Wilmington Parking Authority* on its facts and found no reasonable relationship to the first restaurant sit-in cases. "With the exception hereafter noted, the Pennsylvania Liquor Control Board plays absolutely no part in establishing or enforcing the membership or guest policies of the club which it licenses to serve liquor."[8] The exception was the requirement that a licensed private club adhere to its own by-laws. The Court granted relief to the plaintiff restricted to this provision:[9]

> Appellee was entitled to a decree enjoining the enforcement of § 113.09 . . . insofar as that regulation requires compliance by Moose Lodge with provisions of its constitution and by-laws containing racially discriminatory provisions. He was entitled to no more.

The Court made it clear that the result was applicable only to true private clubs. "There can be no doubt that the label 'private club' can be and has been used to evade both regulations of state and local liquor authorities, and statutes requiring places of public accommodation to serve all persons without regard to race, color, religion, or national origin. This Court in *Daniel* v. *Paul*, 395 U.S. 298 (1969), had occasion to address this issue in connection with the application of Title II of the Civil Rights Act of 1964."[10] That was not the problem addressed here, however, because Moose Lodge No. 107 "is a private club in the ordinary meaning of that term. It is a local chapter of a national fraternal organization having well-defined requirements for membership. It conducts all of its activities in a building that is owned by it. It is not publicly funded. Only members and guests are permitted in any lodge of the order; one may become a guest only by invitation of a member or upon invitation of the house committee."[11]

Mr. Justice Douglas would have reached a different conclusion. He conceded that a private club is not in the public domain. "And the fact that a private club gets some kind of a permit from the State or municipality does not make it *ipso facto* a public enterprise or undertaking, any more than the grant to a householder of a permit to operate an incinerator puts the householder in the public domain. We must, therefore, examine whether there are special

---

[8] 407 U.S. at 175.

[9] *Id*. at 179.

[10] *Id*. at 177–78.

[11] *Id*. at 171.

circumstances involved in the Pennsylvania scheme which differentiate the liquor license possessed by Moose Lodge from the incinerator permit."[12] Not surprisingly he found such a distinction.

The number of licenses for the sale of liquor is limited. The Harrisburg quota is full. This "restricts the ability of blacks to obtain liquor, for liquor is commercially available *only* at private clubs for a significant portion of each week."[13] New nondiscriminatory clubs cannot get licenses because of the full quota. "Thus, the State of Pennsylvania is putting the weight of its liquor license, concededly a valued and important adjunct to a private club, behind racial discrimination."[14] *Q.E.D.* And so, householders with licensed incinerators had better be wary after all.

Mr. Justice Brennan reached the same conclusion but not by the same route. He would have relied on his own separate opinion in *Adickes v. Kress & Co.*,[15] which incidentally received the support of no other member of the Court, for the proposition that the licensing scheme here was sufficiently pervasive to make the discriminatory action the action of the state. Mr. Justice Marshall joined both dissenting opinions.

No doubt that there is some validity in the dissenting position if it is taken to assert that the Court as earlier constituted, perhaps even as of last Term, would have reached a different conclusion. But there is nothing in the proposition that prior decisions compel the result that they would reach. The decisions on state action remained unprincipled, except to the extent that it be regarded as a principle to expand the concept even if rational justification is not forthcoming. It is obvious that the new Court is not going to be so latitudinarian in its reading of the Fourteenth Amendment's strictures. But it can take this stand even while paying full obligation to *stare decisis*. It can do so, too, in recognition that the conclusion is closer to the original understanding, whatever weight that should be given in constitutional adjudication.

Once more the Burger Court seems to have marked the end of a long road created and traveled by the Warren Court.

B. JURY SELECTION

The Court also rationalized the judgments of earlier Courts that held that improper exclusion of Negroes from jury service was the

---

[12] *Id*. at 180.
[13] *Id*. at 182.
[14] *Id*. at 183.
[15] 398 U.S. 144, 190–91 (1970).

basis for reversal of convictions of Negroes. Mr. Justice Marshall could muster only three votes for his opinion in *Peters v. Kiff*[16] and so announced the judgment but not the opinion of the Court.

Joined by Justices Douglas and Stewart, Mr. Justice Marshall noted the early cases on the subject, dating back to the Reconstruction period,[17] and agreed that the Equal Protection Clause and the Reconstruction statute were held to protect Negro defendants in criminal cases. There was nothing in the past that read against a broader protection. Indeed, there were some indications that a fair trial meant a jury properly selected. Marshall went on:[18]

> If it were possible to say with confidence that the risk of bias resulting from the arbitrary action involved here is confined to cases involving Negro defendants, then perhaps the right to challenge the tribunal on that ground could be similarly confined. The case of the white defendant might then be thought to present a species of harmless error.
>
> But the exclusion from jury service of a substantial and identifiable class of citizens has a potential impact that is too subtle and too pervasive to admit of confinement to particular issues or particular cases. . . . [T]he opportunity to appeal to race prejudice is latent in a vast range of issues, cutting across the entire fabric of our society.
>
> Moreover, we are unwilling to make the assumption that the exclusion of Negroes has relevance only for issues involving race. When any large and identifiable segment of the community is excluded from jury service, the effect is to remove from the jury room qualities of human nature and varieties of human experience, the range of which is unknown and perhaps unknowable. It is not necessary to assume that the excluded group will consistently vote as a class in order to conclude, as we do, that their exclusion deprives the jury of a perspective on human events that may have unsuspected importance.

It is clear why the concurring Justices joined only in the judgment. Mr. Justice White, writing for Justices Brennan and Powell as well, rested his conclusion on the statute that forbade discrimination by race in jury selection. Harking back to *Fay v. New York*,[19] he was apparently willing to take the ruling no further

---

[16] 407 U.S. 493 (1972).

[17] Strauder v. West Virginia, 100 U.S. 303 (1879); Virginia v. Rives, 100 U.S. 313 (1879); *Ex parte* Virginia, 100 U.S. 339 (1879). The earlier cases are collected in Note, *The Defendant's Challenge to a Racial Criterion in Jury Selection*, 74 YALE L.J. 919 (1965).

[18] 407 U.S. at 503–04.   [19] 332 U.S. 261, 282–83 (1947).

than the invalidity of exclusion of blacks, whereas the Marshall opinion certainly had wider portent.

The minority, whose spokesman was the Chief Justice, was unwilling to accept the fact that any prejudice could be shown by the defendant "without the benefit of tentative, fragmentary or any other kind of empirical data indicating that all-white juries tend to be prejudiced against white defendants in nonracial criminal proceedings."[20] For Burger, Blackmun, and Rehnquist, "The question of jury bias or prejudice is totally factual in nature. . . . The constitutional and statutory prohibition against such conduct is extraneous to the due process question, for it in no way renders the possibility of prejudice less remote or less speculative."[21]

The fact is, of course, that there is an absence of empirical data in the earlier cases to demonstrate that all-white juries are in any way prejudiced against blacks, or all male juries prejudiced against women.[22] Whether such factual data exists or not, it has not heretofore been the sine qua non for reversal of convictions. That the Chief Justice and his colleagues do not take kindly to the institution of the jury has been evident since *Williams v. Florida*[23] and was demonstrated again this Term in *Johnson v. Louisiana*.[24] For them apparently neither a cross-section of the community nor a twelve-man jury nor a unanimous verdict is an essential ingredient of constitutional trial by jury. Which leaves the question what are the essential ingredients of a constitutional jury?

It must be recognized that the opinions here make no inroad on the requirement that the exclusion must be systematic and purposeful and not merely accidental. In this regard note might be taken of the dissent of Mr. Justice Douglas, joined by Mr. Justice Marshall, from the denial of certiorari in *Donaldson v. California*.[25] There a black defendant took exception to the composition of the jury on the ground that blacks and Chicanos had been systematically and purposefully excluded by the utilization of intelligence tests as jury qualifiers. The evidence was clear that the rate of failure among blacks and Chicanos—measured by geographic areas—was about four times that of whites. The dissenters, unpersuasively so far as their brethren were concerned, asserted that this was proof

---

[20] 407 U.S. at 510.   [21] *Id*. at 511.

[22] See Ballard v. United States, 329 U.S. 187, 193–94 (1946).

[23] 399 U.S. 78 (1970).   [24] 406 U.S. 356 (1972).   [25] 404 U.S. 968 (1971).

that the tests were "culturally biased." Mr. Justice Brennan expressed separately his view that certiorari should be granted but refrained from joining the dissenting opinion which went to the merits. Perhaps the more unusual aspect of the case to be noted is that three votes to grant certiorari, on a seven-man Court, were not sufficient to gain a hearing for the case.

Not to be ignored is the restoration by Mr. Justice Marshall in *Peters* of part of *Hurtado v. California*[26] to the pantheon of viable precedents. Mr. Justice Marshall announced that "the Fifth Amendment right to a grand jury dues not apply in a state prosecution."[27]

C. SCHOOL SEGREGATION

Three school segregation cases were also resolved by the Court during the 1971 Term. In *Wright v. City of Emporia*,[28] the city of Emporia, which had theretofore had its schools within the countywide school system, removed its schools from the county system, with the consequence that the desegregation of the county school system was adversely affected. Five members of the Court, through Mr. Justice Stewart, held that the dismantling of the school district violated the constitutional command for desegregation. The Court noted:[29]

> Both before and after it became a city, Emporia educated its children in the county schools. Only when it became clear—15 years after our decision in *Brown* v. *Board of Education*, 347 U.S. 483—that segregation in the county system was finally to be abolished, did Emporia attempt to take its children out of the county system. . . . The effect of Emporia's proposal was to erect new boundary lines for the purpose of school attendance in a district where no such lines had previously existed, and where a dual school system had long flourished. Under the principles of *Green* [*v. County School Board*, 391 U.S. 430 (1968)] and *Monroe* [*v. Board of Commissioners*, 391 U.S. 450 (1968)], such a proposal must be judged according to whether it hinders or furthers the process of school desegregation. If the proposal would impede the dismantling of the dual system, then a district court, in the exercise of its remedial discretion, may enjoin it from being carried out.

The Court rejected the "dominant purpose" test that it found to be the basis for the lower court's judgment. A combination of

---

[26] 110 U.S. 516 (1884).

[27] 407 U.S. at 496.

[28] 407 U.S. 451 (1972). See Note, *supra*, at 181.

[29] 407 U.S. at 459–60.

three factors was the basis for the ban on Emporia's secession from the county school system. First, the newly devised school attendance zones would change a system that was 34 percent white and 66 percent Negro into one that was 48 percent white and 52 percent Negro in Emporia and 28 percent white and 72 percent Negro in the county. The result would be a further flight of whites from the county schools and a return of whites to the city schools from the private academies to which they had retreated. The Court made it clear, however, that it was not holding that "this disparity in racial composition of the two systems would be a sufficient reason, standing alone, to enjoin the creation of the separate school district."[30]

The second factor was that the Emporia facilities were of a superior quality to those in the remainder of the county system. The third factor was the "timing of Emporia's action."[31]

> While Emporia had long had the right under state law to establish a separate school system, its decision to do so came only upon the basis of—and, as the city officials conceded, in reaction to—a court order that prevented the county system from maintaining any longer the segregated system that had lingered for 15 years after *Brown I*.

The Court concluded by rejecting other legitimate factors, such as local control and improved educational quality, as overbalancing the factors already mentioned. It reiterated its position that "our holding today does not rest upon a conclusion that the disparity in racial balance between the city and county schools resulting from separate systems would, absent other considerations, be unacceptable."[32]

> Once the unitary system has been established and accepted, it may be that Emporia, if it still desires to do so, may establish an independent system without such an adverse effect upon the students remaining in the county, or it may be able to work out a more satisfactory arrangement with the county for joint operation of the existing system. We hold only that a new school district may not be created where its effect would be to impede the process of dismantling a dual system.

Despite the repeated protestations of the majority that racial balance was not the determining factor in the conclusion it reached, the dissent written by the Chief Justice and joined by Justices

---

[30] *Id.* at 464.   [31] *Id.* at 465.   [32] *Id.* at 470.

Blackmun, Powell, and Rehnquist centered its attack on the use of racial balance as a factor. Relying on the Court's pronouncement in *Swann v. Charlotte-Mecklenburg*,[33] the dissenters asserted what the majority did not seem to deny:[34]

> It is quite true that the racial ratios of the two school sys-
> tems would differ, but the elimination of such disparities is not
> the mission of desegregation. . . . It can no more be said that
> racial balance is the norm to be sought, than it can be said that
> mere racial imbalance was the condition requiring a judicial
> remedy.

The dissent rejected the factors utilized by the majority to distinguish the case from "mere" balancing. It found that the threat of white flight was negligible, not willing to accept the proposition that the threat was any greater when the majority was 72 percent black than when it was 66 percent black. It said there were no findings of fact to support the superiority of the city schools over the county schools. And it rejected any inference of psychological impact on the blacks that would result from the change.

The dissent sounded a new note when it challenged the proposition that the matter of relief here rested within the proper discretion of the trial court:[35]

> A local school board plan that will eliminate dual schools, stop
> discrimination and improve the quality of education ought not
> to be cast aside because a judge can evolve some other plan that
> accomplishes the same result, or what he considers a preferable
> result, with a two percent, four percent or six percent differ-
> ence in racial composition. Such an approach gives controlling
> weight to sociological theories, not constitutional doctrine.

The dissent also took note of the importance of local government units, not to be trifled with by federal district courts because they prefer different governmental units:[36]

> The discretion of a district court is further limited where,
> as here, it deals with totally separate political entities. This is
> a very different case from one where a school board proposes
> attendance zones within a single school district or even one
> where a school district is newly formed within a county unit.
>
> . . . .
>
> Although the rights and powers of a bona fide political en-
> tity may not be used as a cloak for evasive action, neither can

---

[33] 402 U.S. 1 (1971).   [35] *Id.* at 477.
[34] 407 U.S. at 473.   [36] *Id.* at 478–79.

those powers be nullified by judicial intervention to achieve a unitary system in a particular way. When a plan devised by local authorities crosses the threshold of achieving actual desegregation, it is not for the district courts to overstep local prerogatives and insist on some other alternative. Judicial power ends when a dual school system has ceased to exist.

The dissent finally took issue with what seems to have been the ultimate factor in the majority conclusion despite its rejection of it. The question was why did Emporia suddenly seek to opt out of the county system. The majority thought spurious the protestations of desire for an improved educational system. The minority thought those factors relevant and controlling. The majority thought the choice was made in response to the duty of the county to desegregate its schools through the creation of a unitary system. The minority conceded that the District Court's desegregation plan had some effect in this direction, but the City did not act out "of any desire to manipulate the racial balance of its schools."[37]

The Court's conclusion was buttressed in *United States v. Scotland Neck City Board of Education*.[38] There, too, an attempt was made to remove a city school from a countywide system in which it had functioned. The same majority of the Court, led by Mr. Justice Stewart, reiterated its position "that any attempt by state or local officials to carve out a new school district from an existing district that is in the process of dismantling a dual school system 'must be judged according to whether it hinders or furthers the process of school desegregation.' "[39] It concluded that the creation of a city district and a county district would result in a white city school system and a black county system. The result followed *a fortiori* from *Emporia*, but this time the "white flight" argument, used on the other side, was held irrelevant, suggesting its lack of substantial weight in the *Emporia* case as well.

In *Scotland Neck*, the dissenters in *Emporia* turned into concurring votes. The reasons were that here "the operation of a separate school system . . . would preclude meaningful desegregation in the southeastern portion of Halifax county."[40] Second, Scotland Neck,

---

[37] The result of *Emporia* is to place the burden on those who would redistrict school boundaries in the face of a desegregation order to show that no deleterious effect on desegregation would occur. However often "motive" was rejected as relevant, it would seem to have been dispositive.

[38] 407 U.S. 484 (1972).   [39] *Id.* at 489.   [40] *Id.* at 491.

unlike Emporia, was a newly created governmental unit for purposes of school operations. Third, the clear motivation for the action was to create a predominantly white school system.

The third case of school desegregation came not from the South but from the North and involved not the secession of a school district but the conglomeration of several. The Court, in *Spencer v. Kugler*,[41] affirmed without opinion the decision of a three-judge federal court in New Jersey that refused to redraw school district lines that coincided with political subdivisions in order to effectuate a "better racial mix." Mr. Justice Douglas entered a spirited dissent in behalf of the power of a federal court to engage in the creation of metropolitan planning districts. His argument was that the demographic distribution of blacks and whites was the result of "state action." That proposition the district court found unacceptable as, apparently, did eight of the brethren. Whether the distinction between *Spencer* and the other two cases rested on the proposition that housing patterns resulting in school segregation were not the result of state action or on the proposition that gerrymandering of school districts is different from adherence to local government units of long standing or both, *Spencer* fell on one side of the line and the Fourth Circuit cases on the other.

D. STATUTORY CONSTRUCTION

In two other race-related cases, the Court was unanimous in its judgments. In *Love v. Pullman Co.*,[42] the Court rejected the technical construction of Title VII of the Civil Rights Act of 1964 that would have created an artificial barrier to relief. There a written charge had been filed with the EEOC, which had appropriately referred the matter to the state commission. The state commission terminated its own jurisdiction without affording relief. Thereupon the EEOC, without further written charge by the complainant, had filed a complaint on behalf of the complainant. The argument that

---

[41] 404 U.S. 1027 (1972). The Court also affirmed a trial court judgment that Virginia could not elevate one of its predominantly white two-year colleges to a four-year college in a community in which a predominantly black four-year college already was operating and the result would be the continuance or creation of dual school systems, albeit at the college level. *Board of Visitors v. Norris*, 404 U.S. 907 (1972). Again there are broad implications for the continued maintenance of black colleges and universities. And it is far from clear that the Constitution should be construed to inhibit the state support of such schools.

[42] 404 U.S. 522 (1972).

the statute required a second written charge by the complainant before the EEOC could proceed was rejected. Again it was Mr. Justice Stewart who wrote for the Court:[43]

> We see no reason why further action by the aggrieved party should be required. The procedure complies with the purpose both of § 706(b), to give state agencies a prior opportunity to consider discrimination complaints, and of § 706(d), to ensure expedition in the filing and handling of those complaints. The respondent makes no showing of prejudice to its interests. To require a second "filing" by the aggrieved party after termination of state proceedings would serve no purpose other than the creation of an additional procedural technicality. Such technicalities are particularly inappropriate in a statutory scheme in which laymen, unassisted by trained lawyers, initiate the process.

The other case did not directly involve a race issue, but only the construction of a civil rights act, § 1983 of Title 42. The Court, in *Mitchum v. Foster*,[44] again through the voice of Mr. Justice Stewart, held that the civil rights provision was a specific statutory exemption from the anti-injunction statute, 28 U.S.C. § 2283, that bars a federal court from enjoining state court proceedings. Conceding that "principles of equity, comity, and federalism . . . must restrain a federal court when asked to enjoin a state proceeding,"[45] the Court held that Congress had not totally removed federal judicial power to issue such an injunction.

Justices Powell and Rehnquist did not participate in either of the statutory construction cases. In the latter the Chief Justice and Justices White and Blackmun concurred, emphasizing that the acknowledgment of power in the federal trial courts did not itself justify its use.

III. The Electoral Process

It will be recalled that the man who lost his sight by jumping into the bramble bush regained it by jumping out again. The Court, on the other hand, has never emerged from the political thicket. It is, however, acting somewhat more gingerly than when it began this exercise. And, in at least one instance has refused to go deeper into the morass.

There was no lack of causes célèbres for the 1971 Court. But,

---

[43] *Id.* at 526–27.   [44] 407 U.S. 225 (1972).   [45] *Id.* at 243.

there being no rest for the wicked or the weary, as the case may be, the Court, after closing its busiest Term in history, was called into special session to confront a question of immediacy with reference to the composition of the ill-fated Democratic Convention.[46]

A. O'BRIEN V. BROWN

Theoretically, the decision in *O'Brien v. Brown*[47] did not decide any question but the propriety of the stay of judgment of the Court of Appeals for the District of Columbia, not even the question whether the issues presented were beyond the competence of the judiciary. In fact, it was a decision that kept the federal courts from still one more expression of their omnicompetence if not omniscience.

The issue arose when the credentials committee of the Democratic National Convention ruled that 151 delegates committed to Senator McGovern should not be seated because the California law providing for a winner-take-all primary was inconsistent with the spirit of the new "democratic processes" by which the delegates to the convention were to be chosen. The same committee ruled that 59 uncommitted delegates elected according to Illinois law should not be seated because their election violated the quota system of the convention. In their place were to be seated 59 delegates committed to McGovern who conformed to the quota system, even though they were self-selected rather than elected. Both sets of originally elected delegates went to court to compel their seating in accordance with the laws of the states in which they were elected. The trial court denied relief to both sets of plaintiffs on the ground that the issues presented were not justiciable ones. The Court of Appeals for the District of Columbia voted for McGovern by sustaining the California claim and rejecting the Illinois claim. Certiorari was sought from the Supreme Court on July 6. The decision was made not to pass on the petition, but rather to stay the order of the Court of Appeals. The vote was seven to two, with Justices Douglas and Marshall in dissent, and Mr. Justice Brennan, the other member of the trinity, concurring specially.

The majority per curiam opinion's rationale was short: "The Court concludes that it cannot in this limited time [before the con-

---

[46] The convention case is not included in the statistics for the 1971 Term that are set out in Part I hereof.

[47] 92 S. Ct. 2718 (1972).

vention on July 10] give to these issues the consideration warranted for final decision on the merits; we therefore take no action on the petition for certiorari at this time."[48] This, it will be recalled, was the position unsuccessfully asserted by the Chief Justice and Justices Harlan and Blackmun in the *Pentagon Papers* case of the previous Term.[49]

Nevertheless, on the question of the stay, the majority did indicate its doubts about the validity of the court of appeals decision:[50]

> It has been understood since our national political parties first came into being as voluntary associations of individuals that the convention itself is the proper forum for determining intra-party disputes as to which delegates shall be seated. Thus, the cases involve claims of the power of the federal judiciary to review actions heretofore thought to lie in the control of political parties. Highly important questions are presented concerning justiciability, whether the action of the Credentials Committee is state action, and if so the reach of the Due Process Clause in this unique context. Vital rights of association guaranteed by the Constitution are also involved. While the Court is unwilling to undertake final resolution of the important constitutional question presented without full briefing and argument and adequate opportunity for deliberation, we entertain grave doubts as to the action taken by the Court of Appeals.

The Court obviously recognized that a stay would be likely to moot the question, with the same result as a holding of nonjusticiability. Moreover, such a judgment will prevent the questions or questions like them from ever being reviewed by the Court, so long as the decisions of the credentials committees are made so close to convention time or at the convention itself, as was the earlier practice. Nevertheless, the Court may not have eluded the problem as successfully as it thought. An Illinois state court had enjoined the self-selected quota delegates from participating in the convention, an order which was disobeyed and which, therefore, subjected these delegates to a contempt citation. Whether the Illinois court will press its claim is not clear. If it does, a contempt sentence may well provide a suitable case for decision of the issues on the merits. And, then, too, the Republican Convention of 1972 adopted rules for

---

[48] *Id.* at 2719.

[49] New York Times Co. v. United States, 403 U.S. 713 (1971).

[50] 92 S. Ct. at 2720.

selection of delegates for the 1976 convention, affording time and opportunity for those challenging these rules to seek a judicial resolution.

The major dissent was written by Mr. Justice Marshall, who argued, with some cogency, that the stay should not be granted because the subject was justiciable, as demonstrated by the earlier party primary cases among others.[51] An interesting constitutional question is thus raised. If the convention and the primary elections of delegates are governmental action as direct primaries are, does the quota system adopted by the Democratic Convention comport with the requirements of the Equal Protection or Guarantee Clause? Is a corporate state compatible with the command for a republican form of government?

The minority position would have accepted the Court of Appeals decision. And, indeed, the Democratic Convention reached the same result. But the majority view seems to be a step away from participation in the election processes rather than adherence to the more recent views about the minimal character of "political questions." In any event, it would seem that if this kind of brouhaha is to be successfully avoided in the future, relief will best be provided by the enactment of a national statute regulating the processes for delegate selection for the national conventions. Clearly the authority exists.[52] Certainly, too, such a statute could eliminate the problems of justiciability. It might also more effectively preserve the constitutional rights of the people to a voice in the selection of their presidential nominees, free from the dictates of the new kinds of party bosses as well as the old ones.

The reticence shown by the majority in *O'Brien* could not be said to be typical of the Court's work during the 1971 Term that preceded that decision. It dealt with many political issues, sometimes on the basis of national legislation but often without it.

B. REAPPORTIONMENT

As with school desegregation so with reapportionment. The Court's broad general guidelines have proved inadequate to prevent a persistent demand on the Court for elucidation of its position in terms of particular cases. The simplistic "one man, one vote" slogan

---

[51] See, *e.g.*, Nixon v. Herndon, 273 U.S. 536 (1927); United States v. Classic, 313 U.S. 299 (1941); *cf.* Ray v. Blair, 343 U.S. 214 (1952).

[52] See Oregon v. Mitchell, 400 U.S. 112 (1970).

may not be so simple after all. Little note may be taken of the reapportionment cases of the 1971 Term because they were all disposed of by memorandum orders. Not unimportant decisions lurk in these interstices of the United States Reports, as some of the extensive minority opinions filed in these cases attest.

The Court by per curiam order reversed the trial court's reapportionment plan in *Sixty-seventh Minnesota State Senate v. Beens.*[53] The federal court had rejected the legislative plan that called for sixty-seven legislative districts, reduced the number of such districts to thirty-five, the number of senators by 50 percent, and the number of representatives by 25 percent. The Court held that this reduction of districts and representatives was beyond the power of the trial court:[54]

> We know of no federal constitutional principle or requirement that authorizes a federal reapportioning court to go as far as the District Court did and, thus, to bypass the State's formal judgment as to the proper size of legislative bodies. No case decided by this Court has gone that far and we have found no district court decision that has employed such radical surgery in reapportionment. There are cases where judicial reapportionment has effectuated minor changes in a legislature's size. Nearly all those cases reflect an increase or decrease of only a few seats and most appear to have been justified by a state constitutional demand, agreement of the parties, the observance of geographical boundaries, or mathematical convenience. . . . We repeat what was said recently in another legislative apportionment case: "The remedial powers of an equity court must be adequate to the task, but they are not unlimited." *Whitcomb* v. *Chavis,* 403 U.S. 124, 161 (1971).

Strangely, only Mr. Justice Stewart was in dissent. So long as the Court itself adhered to the rigidities of its reapportionment formula, he would leave such matters within the discretion of the trial courts:[55]

> I have disagreed with the Court's Procrustean view of the Fourteenth Amendment's substantive requirement of "one man, one vote." But until and unless those established requirements are modified, the federal courts are going to be faced with hard remedial problems such as those presented in this case. Difficult problems produce solutions that are difficult to review, even after full briefing and oral argument. I cannot believe that summary action here is either wise or appropriate.

---

[53] 406 U.S. 187 (1972).   [54] *Id.* at 198–99.   [55] *Id.* at 203–04.

And, indeed, the discretion of the trial court was the basis for sustaining a judicially created Missouri reapportionment plan rejecting one that the state legislature had proposed.[56]

Two challenges to the Illinois reapportionment were rejected by the high court. The Independent Voters of Illinois objected to the validity of a state law that provided for a commission representing the two major parties to draw up a reapportionment plan where the legislature was incapable of doing so itself. The district court upheld the Illinois plan and was sustained by the Supreme Court.[57] The plan itself, which has a deviation of 1.37 between the largest and smallest districts, was approved by the trial court, although by a divided partisan judicial vote, and that decision, too, was affirmed by the Supreme Court.[58]

The Connecticut legislature's reapportionment plan was also a matter of controversy that reached the high court for decision. An appeal from the district court judgment holding unconstitutional the state legislature's reapportionment plan was taken to the Supreme Court. The trial court denied a stay of its order; Mr. Justice Marshall referred the application for a stay to the Court, which granted the stay, over the dissent of Mr. Justice Stewart without opinion and Mr. Justice Douglas with an opinion.[59] The latter asserted with reason that the only possible basis for the stay could be the error of the judgment below. He, therefore, in a not unusual solo opinion, attempted to justify the lower court decision.

Mr. Justice Douglas had no doubts that *Kirkpatrick v. Preisler*[60] establishing requirements for congressional apportionment was also applicable to state legislative apportionments. And he found that the disparities between the demands of *Kirkpatrick v. Preisler* and those of the Connecticut plan to be unjustified. According to the Justice, the justifications for the Connecticut plan included a desire to achieve "a partisan balancing of strength in each house" as well as the retention of incumbents. He responded:[61]

> This Court has never decided whether political gerrymandering or "'fair political balance" is per se unconstitutional, irre-

---

[56] Danforth v. Preisler, 407 U.S. 901 (1972).

[57] Independent Voters of Illinois v. Lewis, 406 U.S. 913 (1972).

[58] Grivetti v. Illinois State Electoral Board, 406 U.S. 913 (1972).

[59] Gaffney v. Cummings, 407 U.S. 902 (1972).

[60] 394 U.S. 526 (1969).   [61] 407 U.S. at 906.

spective of population variances. . . . But we have said, in no
uncertain terms, that gerrymandering is not a justification
where population variances do result.

Nor could there be adequate ground for the state plan because of
the desire to preserve town lines, since the state plan itself cut across
town lines. The third reason was equally unappealing to him, for he
found that the reduction by the trial court of the Connecticut lower
house from 151 to 144 members to be different in kind from that
which was forbidden by the Court in the Minnesota case.[62]

The Court itself was obviously less certain of the applicability
of *Kirkpatrick v. Preisler* to state reapportionment. In *Connor v.
Williams*,[63] the Court unanimously held that elections conducted
under an unconstitutional reapportionment plan need not be invalidated or new elections ordered. The Mississippi legislative apportionment had been upset by the district court because of a disparity of 26 percent between the largest and smallest senatorial
districts. The trial court's own plan, under which the elections were
held, had a disparity of 19.7 percent in house districts and 18.9
percent in senate districts. While the Court reiterated its preference
for single-member districts, it announced a desire to await review
of the case until all proceedings in the lower courts were completed.
"If we are to consider the applicability of *Preisler* and *Wells*[64] to
state legislative districts, it would be preferable to have before us a
final judgment with respect to the entire state."[65] The Court also
indicated that perhaps the state legislature might be able to fashion
a reapportionment plan of its own in the interim.[66] That *Preisler*
and *Wells* might not be applicable to state legislative apportionments will come as a surprise to more aficionados of the *Baker v.
Carr*[67] progeny than Mr. Justice Douglas. There are, indeed, new
shadows on this Warren Court doctrine which may well be in the
process of change as indicated in the 1970 Term by *Gordon v.
Lance*,[68] *Whitcomb v. Chavis*,[69] and *Abate v. Mundt*.[70]

The problem of gerrymandering was again presented in *Ferrell v.
Hall*,[71] where it was contended that the reapportionment plan that
divided Tulsa, which has a majority black population, among three

[62] See text *supra*, at note 53.

[63] 404 U.S. 549 (1972).

[64] Wells v. Rockefeller, 394 U.S. 542 (1969).

[65] 406 U.S. at 551–52.

[66] *Id*. at n.4.

[67] 369 U.S. 186 (1962).

[68] 403 U.S. 1 (1971).

[69] 403 U.S. 124 (1971).

[70] 403 U.S. 182 (1971).

[71] 406 U.S. 939 (1972).

districts going outside city lines, none of which had a majority black population, was invalid. Here was the converse of the New York case, in which it was alleged that blacks were concentrated in one district instead of being dispersed among several.[72] The judgment in both cases was the same. Neither afforded a sound objection to the reapportionment plan. So, too, the Court dismissed for want of a substantial federal question an attack on a countywide election for all five members of a school board when, it was contended, district elections within the county should have been held.[73] Indeed, the appointment rather than election of a vocational school board, even though it had the right to impose taxes, violated neither the one man–one vote rule nor yet the Declaration of Independence.[74]

The Court disposed of the review of the Louisiana reapportionment by bouncing the ball back to the court of appeals. The Court held in *Taylor v. McKeithen*[75] that the failure of the Fifth Circuit to write an opinion in reversing the trial court's judgment in a case involving racial gerrymandering as well as the one man–one vote concept, and the inadequacy of the record to inform the Supreme Court of the issues, required that certiorari be granted, the judgment of the Fifth Circuit vacated, and the case remanded to the lower appellate court. Mr. Justice Blackmun concurred in the Court's action, but Mr. Justice Rehnquist wrote a dissenting opinion in which he was joined by the Chief Justice and Mr. Justice Powell, pointing out that the Fifth Circuit was already inundated with business and should not be asked to write opinions in cases in which, so far as the dissenters were concerned, "the issues in the case [were] well developed in the record."[76]

No conclusions can be drawn from the decisions reached in this area except that there is a conflict in the Court over the future of the reapportionment doctrines which must, therefore, be considered subject to change without much notice.

C. RESIDENCE AND ALLEGIANCE

No more certain acknowledgment of the rootlessness and peripatetic nature of American society could have been made by the

---

[72] Wright v. Rockefeller, 376 U.S. 52 (1964).

[73] Spellerberg v. Adams, 404 U.S. 803 (1972).

[74] Village of West Milwaukee v. Area Board of Vocational Education, 404 U.S. 981 (1972).

[75] 407 U.S. 191 (1972).				[76] *Id.* at 195.

Court than its ruling in *Dunn v. Blumstein*[77] that a period of residence as a qualification for voting was invalid. Only the Chief Justice, among the seven Justices participating, dissented from the conclusion. The judgment was based on the invocation of two slogans as though they were reasons: "the right to travel" was one and the "lack of a compelling state interest to overcome a suspect classification" was the other. "A compelling state interest" like "a suspect classification" and "the right to travel" remain subjective determinations dependent on the personal proclivities of each of the Justices.

Tennessee law had required that a person be resident for one year in the state and for three months in the county before being qualified to vote. James Blumstein arrived in Tennessee on 12 June 1970, sought unsuccessfully to register to vote on 1 July, and filed suit a few days later to compel the state to register him as a qualified voter. A three-judge court granted the relief he sought, holding the state statute unconstitutional because it interfered with the right to vote and because it created a suspect classification that discriminated against those who had recently been in interstate travel.

The Court announced that there was no issue about the *bona fides* of Blumstein's residence, *i.e.*, he "had no intention of leaving Nashville"[78] so that his domicile was established there. The important decision came in the form of putting the burden of proof of the validity of the statute on the state. The notion of *communitas*—or at least of a community smaller than the nation—was antiquated. The Court's earlier decisions in *Pope v. Williams*[79] and *Drueding v. Devlin*,[80] upholding Maryland residence requirements were found to be obsolete, essentially because seven years had passed since the latter decision was reached.

The Court also pointed out that Congress had dispensed with durational residential requirements for presidential and vice-presidential elections. This was adduced as evidence that "durational residence requirements and more restrictive registration practices do 'not bear a reasonable relationship to any compelling state interest in the conduct of presidential elections.' "[81] That Congress specified only presidential elections cannot be taken as *inclusio unius*. Instead it must be taken to mean that if a person ought not to be deprived

---

[77] 405 U.S. 330 (1972).

[78] *Id.* at 334, n.4.

[79] 193 U.S. 621 (1904).

[80] 380 U.S. 125 (1965).

[81] 405 U.S. at 344.

of his vote for president by moving from one state to another, neither should he lose his vote for local or congressional candidates,
although in the former case the choice remains essentially the same
wherever the voter is located within the country while in the second the slate is necessarily totally different.

The law cannot be justified as a means of evading fraud, because
Tennessee like other states has a registration procedure to avoid
that possibility. Moreover, if the three-month period is adequate
for local residence within the county, there is no function to be
served by the longer period of one year for residence in the state.
Longevity of residence, the Court said, adds nothing to the proof
of *bona fides*.

A desire for "knowledgeable voters" cannot support the durational requirement, for the duration does not go to the *bona
fides* of residence. Nor does it assure that the voter has a common
interest with other voters. New voters are just as likely to be intelligent voters as old voters. Besides the screen is too small: it excludes
not only those whom the state wants to exclude but others as well.
Moreover, Tennessee has never measured knowledge or competence
of its long-term residents and provides for absentee ballots for those
who are out of the state.

Excluding voters as it does, and putting a barrier in the way of
interstate travel because of the people who will not change their
residence if it disqualifies them from voting, the statute necessarily
falls afoul of both the Equal Protection Clause and whatever provision of the Constitution it is that guarantees the right to travel. It
will be interesting to see how the Court will react to a suit by a
domiciled non-citizen for a right to exercise his franchise. The opinion's reasoning would support the constitutional obligation of the
state to afford such a foreigner the right to vote, especially if the
right to travel does not derive from the Privileges or Immunities
Clause whose protection is restricted to citizens.

Mr. Justice Blackmun's concurring opinion is of interest. He
wanted to make it clear that there was, in his mind, no uniform
minimum requirement for all states, such as the thirty days provided
by national law for presidential elections. More interesting is the
fact, as he points out, that the decision is inconsistent with all precedents. *Carrington v. Rash*,[82] on which the Court relied, as well as
McDonald v. Board of Election Commissioners,[83] had rejected the

---

[82] 380 U.S. 89 (1965).   [83] 394 U.S. 802 (1969).

test of "compelling state interest" adopted by the Court here. The mystery then is why did Mr. Justice Blackmun join the majority judgment?

The Chief Justice in his dissent pointed out that the demand by the Court for a "compelling state interest" was not a reason but a conclusion; "no state law has ever satisfied this seemingly insurmountable standard, and I doubt one ever will, for it demands nothing less than perfection."[84]

The Tennessee statute was not, despite Mr. Justice Blackmun's view, the only one that bit the dust last Term. Those of Alabama, Indiana, Massachusetts, Minnesota, North Carolina, Vermont, and Virginia met the same fate,[85] while the coups de grace to the Arizona, District of Columbia, Illinois, and Mississippi statutes were left to the district courts to deliver.[86]

As the Court was at pains to point out in *Blumstein*, however, the elimination of the durational residence requirement was not a ban on a *bona fide* residence requirement. The latter was not at issue in the *Blumstein* case. To underline the distinction, the Court affirmed a lower court ruling that a class action could not be filed on behalf of college students to establish their rights to vote as residents of their college community.[87] The lower court had, apparently properly, ruled that the *bona fides* of domicile is an individual matter. More strangely, the Court dismissed for want of a substantial federal question an appeal from a decision sustaining the requirement of eleven months' enrollment in a party to qualify for a place on its primary ballot.[88] It may be that candidates must be more "knowledgeable" than voters about what goes on in their communities, or perhaps only more clearly loyal to their party. The latter would seem to be the dominant proposition in light of the Court's decision in *Lippitt v. Cipilone*[89] sustaining the validity of an Ohio statute which provided that "no person shall be a candidate for nomination or election at a

---

[84] 405 U.S. at 363–64.

[85] Amos v. Hadnott, 405 U.S. 1035 (1972); Whitcomb v. Affeldt, 405 U.S. 1034 (1972); Caniffe v. Burg, 405 U.S. 1034 (1972); Donovan v. Keppel, 405 U.S. 1034 (1972); Cody v. Andrews, 405 U.S. 1034 (1972); Davis v. Kohn, 405 U.S. 1034 (1972); Virginia State Board of Elections v. Bufford, 405 U.S. 1035 (1972).

[86] Cocanower v. Marston, 405 U.S. 1036 (1972); Lester v. Board of Elections, 405 U.S. 1036 (1972); Fitzpatrick v. Board of Election Comm'rs of Chicago, 405 U.S. 1036 (1972); Ferguson v. Williams, 405 U.S. 1036 (1972).

[87] Manard v. Miller, 405 U.S. 982 (1972).

[88] Jordan v. Meisser, 405 U.S. 907 (1972).   [89] 404 U.S. 1032 (1972).

party primary if he voted as a member of a different political party at any primary election within the next preceding four calendar years."[90] Mr. Justice Douglas dissented and pointed to the careers of "Teddy Roosevelt, Strom Thurmond, Wayne Morse, John Lindsay, George Wallace, and a host of others"[91]—Winston Churchill was certainly the most famous of such turncoats—whose careers would have been blighted by such a statute. The ad hominem argument made no more impression here than did Douglas's lack of a compelling state interest proposition. He dissented alone.

The Court, in *Socialist Labor Party v. Gilligan*,[92] refused to reach the question whether loyalty to the country was required in addition to loyalty to a party. The Ohio law requires that a party seeking to qualify for a place on the ballot file an affidavit "stating in substance that the party is not engaged in an attempt to overthrow the government by force or violence, is not associated with a group making such an attempt, and does not carry on a program of sedition or treason as defined by the criminal law."[93] The Socialist Labor Party, although it had met the requirement in the past, sought a declaratory judgment that such requirement was invalid. Speaking through Mr. Justice Rehnquist, the Court held that there was an absence of factual data in the complaint on which to base a judgment: there was no indication in the pleadings or elsewhere of what injuries the party would allegedly suffer if the requirement were to be imposed.

Clearly this was a return to the Brandeis-Frankfurter notions about the necessity for a real rather than an abstract case before the Court would indulge in the decision of constitutional issues.[94] The triumvirate was in dissent. Speaking through Mr. Justice Douglas, they found the statute unconstitutional on its face and would, therefore, in keeping with a large number of Warren Court cases that Douglas cited, have rendered a judgment to that effect without any demonstration of threatened harm to the party seeking the declaration. The decision here is reflective of the attitude displayed in *Younger v. Harris*,[95] in the preceding Term, substantially cut-

---

[90] Ohio Rev. Code § 3513.191 (Page ed. 1960).   [92] 406 U.S. 583 (1972).

[91] 404 U.S. at 1034.   [93] *Id.* at 585.

[94] See, *e.g.*, Kurland, Mr. Justice Frankfurter and the Constitution chs. 2 & 3 (1971).

[95] 401 U.S. 37 (1971). See Kurland, *1970 Term: Notes on the Emergence of the Burger Court*, 1971 Supreme Court Review 265, 293–97.

ting back on the availability of federal courts to enjoin state court proceedings because of their alleged "chilling effects" on First Amendment rights. The trend away from free and easy access to the federal courts for abstract declarations of constitutional invalidity was thus confirmed.[96]

D. FUNDING ELECTIONS

For better or for worse, but not for good, money is a vital ingredient in the campaign processes. And the need for money increases by geometric progression as the office sought moves up the scale from local government representative to President of the United States. The essential problem addressed by Congress is how to remove the possibility of the purchase of influence by campaign contributions while leaving the citizen free to express his political preferences with his cash as well as with his voice and his vote.[97] Various congressional efforts to meet the problem have failed of accomplishment. One of those was the subject of review in *Pipefitters Union v. United States.*[98] But a majority of the Court, including the three Justices who dissented in *Socialist Labor Party v. Gilligan,* managed to avoid the constitutional problem by adroit construction of the statute.

The statute in question made it illegal "for any corporation whatever, or any labor organization to make a contribution or expenditure in connection with any election at which Presidential and Vice Presidential electors or a Senator or Representative" is to be elected or nominated."[99] The defendants were charged with conspiring to create and maintain a fund to which systematic payments from union members' wages would be made, the moneys to be used for the election activities forbidden to unions by the statute. The defendants were also charged with giving the fund an appearance of separate entity from the Union in order to conceal the violation of 18 U.S.C. § 610. The facts proved that the fund was separate from the Union treasury and control only in that the accounts were

---

[96] See also Kirk v. McMeen, 405 U.S. 949 (1972), aff'g application of *Younger v. Harris;* Koehler v. Ogilvie, 405 U.S. 906 (1972), aff'g abstention by federal court; Non-Resident Taxpayers Ass'n v. Philadelphia, 406 U.S. 951 (1972), and Northern Nat. Gas Co. v. Wilson, 403 U.S. 949 (1942), aff'g application of Tax Injunction Act.

[97] See Casper, *Williams v. Rhodes and Public Financing of Political Parties under the American and German Constitutions,* 1969 SUPREME COURT REVIEW 271.

[98] 407 U.S. 385 (1972).   [99] 18 U.S.C. § 610.

segregated, the funds were used only for election purposes, and the money was secured from the membership under authorization cards that recited that the contributions were "voluntary." The jury found the defendants guilty. Among other defenses, the union and its officers asserted that the statute, in limiting the political activities of unions and union members, was unconstitutional.

Between the time of the oral argument in the Supreme Court and its decision, the Federal Election Campaign Act of 1971 became law.[100] But the Court held that this amendment of 18 U.S.C. § 610 merely codified existing law. It went on to reverse the conviction, but not on constitutional grounds. It was conceded, Mr. Justice Brennan noted, that a truly separate campaign organization financed by truly voluntary contributions was not banned by the statute. The Court read the statute to mean:[101]

> that such a fund must be separate from the sponsoring union only in the sense that there must be a strict segregation of its monies from union dues and assessments. We hold, too, that although solicitation by union officials is permissible, such solicitation must be conducted under circumstances plainly indicating that donations are for a political purpose and that those solicited may decline to contribute without loss of job, union membership, or any other reprisal within the union's institutional power.

It followed, according to the Court, that the judgments must be reversed because the trial court's jury "instructions . . . clearly permitted the jury to convict without finding that donations to the Pipefitters fund had been actual or effective dues or assessments. This was plain error."[102]

Mr. Justice Powell dissented. He saw the majority as straining the legislative history to read out of the statute what Congress had put into it, a desire to insulate elections from the pressures of money tainted by the power of unions and corporations to secure the funds much in the manner that old-time political bosses secured "voluntary" contributions from patronage employees:[103]

> The opinion of the Court provides a blueprint for compliance with § 610 . . . which will be welcomed by every corporation and union which wishes to take advantage of a heretofore unrecognized opportunity to influence elections in this country.

---

[100] 86 Stat. 20 (1971).

[101] 407 U.S. at 414.

[102] *Id.* at 442.

[103] *Id.* at 448–49.

It may be that the unions, by virtue of a system of collecting "political contributions" simultaneously with the collection of dues and regularizing such collections to the point where they are indistinguishable from dues, will be the primary beneficiaries. But the corporations are more numerous than the unions. They have millions of stockholders and hundreds of thousands of nonunion employees. Both unions and corporations have large financial resources. Today's interpretation of § 610 will enable a more direct and extensive political employment of these resources by both unions and corporations.

Only the Chief Justice joined in the Powell dissent. Mr. Justice Blackmun had disqualified himself and Mr. Justice Rehnquist joined the remnants of the Warren Court to make up the six-man majority. It is clear that the intention of Congress was distorted. But it was distorted in order to avoid an extraordinarily sticky constitutional question. Whether the same result would have been forthcoming if the test had involved a corporation's check-off of its employees, union and nonunion, under similar authorization cards is doubtful. As it is, unions and corporations are now licensed to tax for political campaign funds although it is far from clear that Congress itself has that authority.

Indeed, states may not impose on primary candidates filing fees sufficient to meet the costs of the primary election. In *Bullock v. Carter*,[104] a unanimous seven-man Court, speaking through the Chief Justice, held that a $1,424 assessment for the primary election of a county commissioner nominee, and a $6,300 assessment for a county judge candidate, and a $1,000 assessment for a General Land Office candidate violated the Equal Protection Clause. The answer was implicit in the question as phrased by the Court: "whether a state law that prevents potential candidates for public office from seeking the nomination of their party due to their inability to pay a portion of the cost of conducting the primary election is state action that unlawfully discriminates against the candidates so excluded or the voters who wish to support them."[105]

Unlike *Harper v. Virginia Board of Education*,[106] where the Court held that a $1.50 poll tax was invalid as discriminating against the poor, the Court here recognized that modest filing fees are not invalid. But, said the Chief Justice, falling into the trap which he so frequently accused others of setting:[107]

---

[104] 405 U.S. 134 (1972).

[105] *Id.* at 141.

[106] 383 U.S. 663 (1966).

[107] 405 U.S. at 144.

Because the Texas filing-fee scheme has a real and appreciable impact on the exercise of the franchise, and because this impact is related to the resources of the voters supporting a particular candidate, we conclude, as in *Harper*, that the laws must be "closely scrutinized" and found reasonably necessary to the accomplishment of legitimate state objectives in order to pass constitutional muster.

Thus, the Court now has three tests for equal protection issues. The classification by a state legislature will ordinarily be indulged if there is any reasonable basis for it. On the other hand, it will almost never be indulged where the classification may adversely affect "a fundamental interest" and the state cannot show "a compelling state interest."[108] And, now, as with the second category, the burden of sustaining the statute is placed on the state to demonstrate that the statute under attack is "reasonably necessary to the accomplishment of legitimate state objectives." This category may include those situations in which the less well-off fare differently from the well-off in meeting the requirements of the law.

There was no question in the Court's mind that the primary elections constituted "state action." And, the question framed as it was, there was little question that the state could not meet the burden imposed on it. The cost of financing the elections was not adequate excuse, nor was this a proper meanse of limiting the number of candidates on the ballot. The imposition was not mitigated by the fact that a candidate could get his name on the ballot at the election—not the primary—without paying such costs, both because some primaries were dispositive of the election and the right to party endorsement could not be secured by this means:[109]

Since the State has failed to establish the requisite justification for this filing-fee system, we hold that it results in a denial of equal protection of the laws. It must be emphasized that nothing herein is intended to cast doubt on the validity of reasonable candidate filing fees or licensing fees in other contexts. By requiring candidates to shoulder the costs of conducting primary elections through filing fees and by providing no reasonable alternative means of access to the ballot, the State of Texas has erected a system that utilizes the criterion of ability to pay as a condition to being on the ballot, thus excluding some candidates otherwise qualified and denying an

---

[108] See the dissent of the Chief Justice in the *Blumstein* case, 405 U.S. at 363–64.

[109] 405 U.S. at 149.

undetermined number of voters the opportunity to vote for candidates of their choice. These salient features of the Texas system are critical to our determination of constitutional validity.

Of course, any filing fee will draw a line between those with the ability to pay it and those who cannot. If reasonableness is not measurable by the cost of the election to the taxpayers, it can only be of such a magnitude as to pay some lesser costs, but which ones is not clear. The reasonableness of filing fees thus becomes one more area in which the judgment of the courts will be substituted for that of the legislatures.[110]

Nor does the *Bullock* opinion apparently extend to other aspects of the electoral process. In *Carey v. Elrod*,[111] where the question was whether the state could assess the costs of a recount on the party demanding it, the Court dismissed the appeal for want of a substantial federal question.

That the states may regulate recounts, even in senatorial contests, was established in *Roudebush v. Hartke*.[112] Mr. Justice Stewart, on behalf of five of the seven participating Justices, held that:[113]

> It is true that a State's verification of the accuracy of election results pursuant to Art. I, § 4, powers is not totally separable from the Senate's power to judge elections and returns. But a recount can be said to "usurp" the Senate's function only if it frustrates the Senate's ability to make an independent final judgment. A recount does not prevent the Senate from independently evaluating the election any more than the initial count does. The Senate is free to accept or reject the apparent winner in either count, and, if it chooses, to conduct its own recount.

The patent hyperbole in the last sentence was qualified by a footnote:[114]

> The Senate's power to judge the qualifications of its members is limited to the qualifications expressly set forth in the Constitution. *Powell v. McCormack*, 395 U.S. 486. One of those qualifications is that a Senator be elected by the people of his state. U.S. Const., Amend. XVII.

---

[110] The Court continued to strike down as invalid elections requiring property ownership as a qualification for voting. See Police Jury of Parish of Vermilion v. Hebert, 404 U.S. 807 (1971).

[111] 408 U.S. 901 (1972).

[112] 405 U.S. 15 (1972).

[113] *Id.* at 25–26.

[114] *Id.* at 26, n.23.

Justices Douglas and Brennan, however, suggested that the Senate and the Senate alone had jurisdiction to determine whether the state should be allowed to conduct the recount. The limited role of the courts, according to them, was "to protect the Senate's choice, not to make the choice for or on behalf of the Senate,"[115] on the questions how, when, and whether a recount should take place. The tenderness toward senatorial prerogatives is both touching and heartening, if not persuasive.

IV. The First Amendment

Claims arising under the First Amendment continued to be one of the larger elements of the Supreme Court's business during the 1971 Term. Again, the cases reveal a process of shifting from the Warren Court's broad readings of protection in the free speech area toward a more traditional and less elastic interpretation. While, again, there is no indication of an intention to throw over the earlier decisions, there is clear indication of refusal to take further steps down the same road.

A. THE RELIGION CLAUSES

When the Court, in *Wisconsin v. Yoder*,[116] decided that the Amish were constitutionally exempt from the compulsory school attendance laws, the most surprising element of the case was not the result but the rationalization. Surprising, too, was the apparent unanimity of the Court. Of the seven Justices who participated,[117] only Mr. Justice Douglas wrote a dissenting opinion and that was concerned with an issue that was not really the subject of the litigation.

The state of Wisconsin, unlike Pennsylvania and Indiana, had refused to fudge the question by treating post–grammar school work on Amish farms with three hours a week of classroom study as the equivalent of high school work, although many American universities have come around to granting college degrees for equally mundane efforts. And so the respondents in the *Yoder* case were fined $5 each for failing to send their respective fourteen- and fifteen-year-old children to high school after graduation from grammar school.

---

[115] *Id.* at 33.   [116] 406 U.S. 205 (1972).

[117] Justices Powell and Rehnquist did not participate in the case.

The conflict between the Amish faith and high school education was summarized by the Chief Justice in his opinion for the Court:[118]

> Amish . . . object to the high school and higher education generally because the values it teaches are in marked variance with Amish values and the Amish way of life; they view secondary school education as an impermissible exposure of their children to a "worldly" influence in conflict with their beliefs. The high school tends to emphasize intellectual and scientific accomplishments, self-distinction, competitiveness, worldly success, and social life with other students. Amish society emphasizes informal learning-through-doing, a life of "goodness," rather than a life of intellect, wisdom, rather than technical knowledge, community welfare, rather than competition, and separation, rather than integration with contemporary worldly society.

Obviously, these values in our increasingly urbanized society with all the evils that surround it made a deep appeal not merely as a permissible way of life but as the more desirable one, only, however, if the motivating force is religion. It was here that the Court drew some lines that are difficult to accept.

It will be remembered that after the Supreme Court had first held that religious beliefs did not exempt children of Jehovah's Witnesses from compulsory flag-salute ceremonies,[119] the Court reversed itself.[120] But when it did rule that the interest of the state in compelling flag-salute ceremonies was not sufficient to overcome the conscientious objections to participating in such patriotic ceremonies, the exemption was not rested on the Religion Clauses of the First Amendment, but on that Amendment's more general application. In short, in *Barnette*, when the Court established the freedom of religious objectors to be exempted from the ceremony, it also established the exemption of all whose conscientious objections—whether religiously based or not—led them to the same conclusion. Not so with the Court in *Yoder*:[121]

> A way of life, however virtuous and admirable, may not be interposed as a barrier to reasonable state regulation of education if it is based on purely secular considerations; to have the protection of the Religion Clauses, the claims must be rooted in religious belief. Although a determination of what is

---

[118] 406 U.S. at 210–11.

[119] Minersville School Dist. v. Gobitis, 310 U.S. 586 (1940).

[120] Board of Education v. Barnette, 319 U.S. 624 (1943).

[121] 406 U.S. at 215–16.

a "religious" belief or practice entitled to constitutional protection may present a most delicate question, the very concept of ordered liberty precludes allowing every person to make his own standards on matters of conduct in which society as a whole has important interests. Thus, if the Amish asserted their claims because of their subjective evaluation and rejection of the contemporary secular values accepted by the majority, much as Thoreau rejected the social values of his time . . . , their claim would not rest on a religious basis. Thoreau's choice was philosophical and personal rather than religious, and such belief does not rise to the demands of the Religion Clause.

Thus, not only were nonreligious objections to the defects that the Amish found in the school systems of the nation inadequate to protect the children of parents whose beliefs were just as conscientious but grounded in merely "philosophical" or "personal" values but the Court would also reject similar claims by other religious groups to whom, as the Court would judge, the abstention from post–grammar school education was not "central" to their beliefs:[122]

> It cannot be overemphasized that we are not dealing with a way of life and mode of education by a group claiming to have recently discovered some "progressive" or more enlightened process for rearing children for modern life.
> Aided by a history of three centuries as an identifiable religious sect and a long history as a successful and self-sufficient segment of American society, the Amish in this case have convincingly demonstrated the sincerity of their religious beliefs, the interrelationship of belief with their mode of life, the vital role which belief and daily conduct play in the continued survival of the Old Order Amish communities and their religious organization, and the hazards presented by the State's enforcement of a statute generally valid as to others. Beyond this, they have carried the even more difficult burden of demonstrating the adequacy of their alternative mode of continuing informal vocational education in terms of precisely those overall interests that the State advances in support of its program of compulsory high school education. In light of this convincing showing, one which probably few other religious groups or sects could make, and weighing the minimal difference between what the State would require and what the Amish already accept, it was incumbent on the State to show with more particularity how its admittedly strong interest in compulsory education would be adversely affected by granting an exemption to the Amish.

---

[122] *Id.* at 235–36.

Certainly such a conclusion raised questions whether the special dispensation for the Amish violated the establishment provisions of the Religion Clauses. Here we were told, we must trust the judgment of the Court to make practical adaptations:[123]

> The Court must not ignore the danger that an exception from a general obligation of citizenship on religious grounds may run afoul of the Establishment Clause, but that danger cannot be allowed to prevent any exception no matter how vital it may be to the values promoted by the right of free exercise. By preserving doctrinal flexibility and recognizing the need for a sensible and realistic application of the Religion Clauses "we have been able to chart a course that preserved the autonomy and freedom of religious bodies while avoiding any semblance of established religion. This is a 'tight rope' and one we have successfully travelled." *Walz* v. *Tax Commission*, [397 U.S.] at 672.

The opinion is thus in keeping with the pro–organized religion tendencies heretofore revealed in the first two Terms of the Burger Court. Tax exemptions for churches on the ground of their "unique" contributions to the pluralism of American society as in *Walz*, like this judgment, are not out of keeping with the growing populistic expressions of the American people. But the opinion also contains seeds for further growth of privilege to the religious, at least that portion of the religious who are "successful and self-sufficient segment[s] of American society." Whether it means that fundamentalist Mormons may practice polygamy without harassment or whether it means that conscientious exemption may once again be limited to adherents of established churches are questions raised but not necessarily answered by the majority opinion. The latter is a more likely consequence than the former. *Yoder* certainly gives the appearance of having chosen Stone's dissent in *Gobitis* over the more cogent majority opinion in *Barnette* as its model. The consequences may be unfortunate.

Mr. Justice Douglas's dissent went to the proposition that Amish children rather than their parents should ultimately determine whether they want exemption from higher schooling. Mr. Justice Stewart's concurrence, in which he was joined by Mr. Justice Brennan, appropriately pointed out that the question that concerned Douglas was not an element in the decision that the majority

---

[123] *Id.* at 220–21.

reached. Brennan's own concurrence rested on the fact that the Amish were not claiming total exemption from compulsory education but only from what he regarded as the peripherally justified demands for attendance after grammar school graduation.

Of Catholic parents who cannot afford private school education but who conscientiously object to the godless education of the public schools, the opinions say nothing and offer no light. "Take therefore no thought for the morrow: for the morrow shall take thought for the things of itself. Sufficient unto the day is the evil thereof."

But, if Amish are excused from the obligations of "higher education," Quakers are not exempt from a requirement of a loyalty oath for government jobs. Just how the cases are to be distinguished, the Court did not say, for it disposed of the latter question by a memorandum order.[124]

Another troublesome church-state problem was avoided when the Court vacated the judgment in *Diffenderfer v. Central Baptist Church of Miami, Florida*[125] as moot. The question sought to be raised there was whether a state could, within the confines of the Religion Clauses, grant tax-exempt status to church-owned properties that were also used for commercial purposes. Before the Supreme Court could answer the question, the state law was changed so that the exemption will be made to depend on the degree of use for church as distinguished from commercial purposes. Reading the complaint as essentially seeking relief *in futuro*, the Court vacated as moot the judgment below in favor of the church. Mr. Justice Douglas would have invoked the Florida certification process so that the Florida court would advise of the effect a declaration of unconstitutionality would have. He was alone in this position.

B. FIRST AMENDMENT ON THE CAMPUS

In two cases during the 1971 Term, the Court was called upon to determine whether a right to tenure was improperly denied in such a way as to violate the teacher's First Amendment rights. Both cases were concerned with state universities. Presumably the private

---

[124] Biklen v. Board of Education, 406 U.S. 951 (1972). Mr. Justice Douglas dissented, as he did when the Court affirmed Arizona's refusal to grant a corporate charter to the "Peyote Church." Native American Church v. Arizona Corp. Comm., 405 U.S. 901 (1972). In the latter case he was joined by Justices Stewart and Rehnquist.

[125] 404 U.S. 412 (1972).

universities that survive the other pressures of our times will be at least as insulated from their teachers' demands for tenure as were the public institutions in these cases.

Perry v. Sinderman[126] involved a professor at a two-year college who had had his one-year nontenure contracts renewed on three successive occasions. During the period of his last renewal, he had become president of the Texas Junior College Teachers Association and on several occasions he had abandoned his classes to testify before the Texas legislature in that capacity. He also came into conflict with the Regents of the school by advocating conversion to a four-year college, a change that the Regents opposed. The Regents then refused him renewal of his contract. They gave him no reason for nonrenewal but did issue a press release setting forth allegations of his insubordination. He then brought suit in the federal court to secure an order compelling his rehiring on the ground that the failure to do so was because of his public criticism of Regents' policies and therefore in violation of his First Amendment rights.

The college involved did not have a tenure system—all contracts were term contracts. But this was held irrelevant to the free speech problem presented. There was an absence of opportunity to prove that his denial of reemployment was because of his criticism of the Regents, and so the case was remanded for proof on that question. The applicable rule was set out by the Court, in an opinion by Mr. Justice Stewart:[127]

> For at least a quarter century, this Court has made clear that even though a person has no "right" to a valuable governmental benefit and even though the government may deny him the benefit for any number of reasons, there are some reasons on which the government may not act. It may not deny a benefit to a person on a basis that infringes his constitutionally protected interests—especially, his interest in freedom of speech. For if the government could deny a benefit to a person because of his constitutionally protected speech or associations, his exercise of those freedoms would in effect be penalized and inhibited. . . . Such interference with constitutional rights is impermissible.

On the other question in the case, whether Sinderman was entitled to a hearing before determination that his contract would not be

---

[126] 408 U.S. 593 (1972).   [127] *Id.* at 597.

renewed, the Court followed *Roth*,[128] decided at the same time. "As in *Roth*, the mere showing that he was not rehired in one particular job, without more, did not amount to showing a loss of liberty. Nor did it amount to a showing of loss of property."[129] Therefore, the mere failure to rehire could be accomplished without a hearing. But there might be facts that would give rise to a right to a hearing and the teacher here seems to have adequately alleged them:[130]

> A teacher, like the respondent, who has held his position for a number of years, might be able to show from the circumstances of this service—and from other relevant facts—that he has a legitimate claim of entitlement to job tenure. Just as this Court has found there to be a "common law of a particular industry or of a particular plant" that may supplement a collective-bargaining agreement, . . . so there may be an unwritten "common law" in a particular university that certain employees shall have the equivalent of tenure. This is particularly likely in a college or university . . . that has no explicit tenure system even for senior members of its faculty, but that nonetheless may have created such a system in practice.

The lesson of the case for the universities is that if they have no tenure system, they should write legislation that would negative the possibilities of a "common law" creating such a right even in the fact of unwritten policy to the contrary. For, as the Court noted, this is a contract question not a constitutional question.

Mr. Chief Justice Burger's concurring opinion and the dissenting positions of Justices Douglas, Brennan, and Marshall, were those taken by them in *Board of Regents v. Roth*. There, too, the opinion for the Court was written by Mr. Justice Stewart. The university there was the University of Wisconsin, which did have a tenure policy, providing that those faculty members on tenure contracts could not be fired except for failure to meet the standards of "efficiency and good behavior":[131]

> There are no statutory or administrative standards defining eligibility for reemployment. State law thus clearly leaves the decision whether to rehire a nontenured teacher for another year to the unfettered discretion of University officials.

Roth, like Sinderman, asserted two reasons for the invalidity of his dismissal. First, that it resulted from his statements critical of the

---

[128] Board of Regents v. Roth, 408 U.S. 564 (1972).   [130] *Id.* at 602.

[129] 407 U.S. at 599.   [131] *Id.* at 566–67.

university's administration. This, he contended, denied him his rights of free speech. Second, he had not been given notice and an opportunity to be heard on the nonrenewal of his contract. The free speech question was aborted because of the state of the record: the trial court had stayed proceedings on this issue and taken no evidence. The Court did note, however: "Whatever may be a teacher's right of free speech, the interest in holding a teaching job at a state university, simpliciter, is not itself a free speech interest."[132] In *Sinderman,* the Court clarified this point by saying:[133]

> The Court of Appeals suggested that the respondent might have a due process right to some kind of hearing simply if he *asserts* to college officials that their decision was based on his constitutionally protected conduct. . . . We have rejected this approach in *Board of Regents v. Roth,* 408 U.S. at 575, n. 14.

The failure to rehire was not in itself a denial of any liberty. It "imposed on him [no] stigma or other disability that foreclosed his freedom to take advantage of other employment opportunities."[134] Had it done so this would have been a "different case."

There was no right to a hearing on the ground that Roth had been deprived of property without due process of law, because he had no property of which he could be deprived. He had no more than a contract right, which specifically terminated at the end of his contract term. "In these circumstances, the respondent surely had an abstract concern in being rehired, but he did not have a *property* interest sufficient to require the University authorities to give him a hearing when they declined to renew his contract of employment ."[135]

The Chief Justice's opinion, relating both to *Roth* and *Sinderman,* sought merely to underline the proposition that the issue is one of state contract law and only if the state law gives a right to reemployment is there any Fourteenth Amendment issue for the Supreme Court to review. "If relevant state contract law is unclear, a federal court should, in my view, abstain from deciding whether he is constitutionally entitled to a prior hearing, and the teacher should be left to resort to state courts on the questions arising under state law."[136]

---

[132] *Id.* at 575, n. 14.

[133] *Id.* at 599, n.5. (Emphasis in original.)   [135] *Id.* at 578. (Emphasis in original.)

[134] *Id.* at 573.   [136] *Id.* at 604.

Mr. Justice Douglas, conceding that "[t]here may not be a constitutional right to continued employment in private schools and colleges," thought the law different with regard to public institutions. He would decide the cases differently because:[137]

> If this nonrenewal implicated the First Amendment, then Roth was deprived of his constitutional rights because his employment was conditioned on a surrender of First Amendment rights; and apart from the First Amendment he was denied due process when he received no notice and hearing of the adverse action contemplated against him. Without a statement of the reasons for the discharge and an opportunity to rebut those reasons—both of which were refused by petitioners—there is no means short of a lawsuit to safeguard the right not to be discharged for the exercise of First Amendment guarantees.

Mr. Justice Marshall would go much further. For him, a teaching contract was a property right, even before it is first made and certainly when the question of renewal arises:[138]

> In my view, every citizen who applies for a government job is entitled to it unless the government can establish some reason for denying the employment. This is the "property" right that I believe is protected by the Fourteenth Amendment and that cannot be denied "without due process of law." And it is also liberty—liberty to work—which is the "very essence of the personal freedom and opportunity" secured by the Fourteenth Amendment.

Whether the adoption of such a theory would result in a large number of lawyers making application for each Supreme Court vacancy, general counsel's job, etc., we shall probably never know. Certainly there would be many instances in which the Government, having the burden under the rule, could not show that the rejection of an applicant in favor of the person employed could be justified by reason other than personal prejudice. But perhaps the Justice is referring only to that kind of government personnel, like university professors, who are regarded as fungibles.

In any event, for the time being, public university employment is subject to contract limitations, so long as there is no showing that the limitations constitute unconstitutional conditions. It is doubtful whether a general rule requiring publication of reasons and hearings on nonrenewal would be a blessing or a curse to the employee.

---

[137] *Id.* at 585.   [138] *Id.* at 588–89.

Published reasons for nonretention by one university are not likely to enhance the chances for employment at another.

If a faculty member at a public university is not entitled to a hearing on the question of denial of reemployment, there is a different rule for accreditation of a student organization. In *Healy v. James*,[139] the Court said that denial of campus accreditation to a college SDS chapter placed the burden on the college to establish reasons for denial lest First Amendment rights of free expression or association be invaded. Because the record was not adequate to reveal whether the denial was attributable to the organization's proclivities toward violence or disagreement by the administration with the "philosophy" of SDS, the case had to go back to trial for explication. Exclusion for violent tendencies would be justified; disagreement with revolutionary philosophy would not.

Chief Justice Burger, while joining Mr. Justice Powell's opinion for the Court, made clear his reading of it:[140]

> I read the basis of the remand as recognizing that student organizations seeking the privilege of official campus recognition must be willing to abide by valid rules of the institution applicable to all such organizations. This is a reasonable condition insofar as it calls for the disavowal of resort to force, disruption and interference with the rights of others.

Since, in fact, the record shows a direct refusal of the applicants to disavow resort to violence, it is a somewhat dubious reading.

Mr. Justice Douglas satisfied himself with a concurring opinion that was a diatribe against the status quo on the American college campus and a paean in favor of ferment. A sample should suffice:[141]

> Many inside and out of faculty circles realize that one of the main problems of faculty members is their own re-education or re-orientation. Some have narrow specialities that are hardly relevant to modern times. History has passed others by, leaving them interesting relics of a bygone day. More often than not they represent those who withered under the pressure of McCarthyism or other forces of conformity and represent but a timid replica of those who once brought distinction to the ideal of academic freedom.

What Mr. Justice Douglas, like the SDS, has done is to mark well the distinction between McCarthyism of the right and McCarthyism

---

[139] 408 U.S. 169 (1972). See Note at p. 181, *supra*.

[140] *Id*. at 195.   [141] *Id*. at 196–97.

of the left. For him, it is only the first that must be regarded as reprehensible.

Mr. Justice Rehnquist also wrote a concurring opinion and, like the Chief Justice, may have read into the majority opinion what he would like to have seen there rather than what it actually contained. For him:[142]

> The government as employer or school administrator may impose upon employees and students reasonable regulations that would be impermissible if imposed by the government upon all citizens. And there can be a constitutional distinction between the infliction of criminal punishment, on the one hand, and the imposition of milder administrative or disciplinary sanctions, on the other, even though the same First Amendment interest is implicated by each.

To find this implicit in the Powell opinion is, indeed, to ascribe to it a subtlety that others may find difficult to discover.

C. THE LEWD, THE NUDE, AND THE SCURRILOUS

For the most part, the Court made little new law in a field that has plagued it for many years. The problem with any doctrine in the area of obscenity is that none has been discovered that will cover all the desired results. At the same time, the Court is obviously not in the position of acting as Lord Chamberlain for each publication and public showing to which local communities might take exception. But once again, there is clear indication that the new Justices will not take kindly to some of the old cases, and some changes are likely to be seen. Meanwhile the issues have been dealt with by evasion or memoranda orders that fail to bring fully to light the divisions within the Court.

In *Rabe v. Washington*,[143] the petitioner had been convicted of showing, at an outdoor theater, a picture "containing sexually frank scenes but no instances of sexual consummation [were] explicitly portrayed."[144] Evidence revealed that the film was viewable from the roadway and through the fence and was in fact witnessed by minors watching from that vantage point. The Court held that the conviction had to be upset because it was conceded that the film would not be obscene if shown to a viewing audience consisting solely of consenting adults. The paying audience fell into that cate-

---

[142] *Id.* at 203.   [143] 405 U.S. 313 (1972).   [144] *Id.* at 313–14.

gory. "The statute . . . is impermissibly vague as applied to petitioner because of its failure to give him fair notice that criminal liability is dependent upon the place where the film is shown."[145] The suggestion here followed that in *Cohen v. California*,[146] a statute specifically banning the place of showing films otherwise viewable by adult audiences could well make the activity indulged by the petitioner here properly subject to punishment.

The Chief Justice and Mr. Justice Rehnquist concurred in the result reached by the per curiam opinion, but clearly showed their attitudes toward such displays:[147]

> Public displays of explicit materials such as are described in this record are not significantly different from any noxious public nuisance traditionally within the power of the States to regulate and prohibit, and, in my view, involve no significant countervailing First Amendment considerations. That this record shows an offensive nuisance that could properly be prohibited, I have no doubt, but the state statute and charge did not give the notice constitutionally required.

The condonation of this film as not improper for consenting adult audiences cannot be taken to mean what some commentators have alleged, that no conviction for obscenity can rest on the presentation or sale of materials to consenting adults. In *Strasbourg v. California*,[148] the Court dismissed for want of a substantial federal question an appeal from an obscenity conviction for the sale of materials to a willing adult buyer.

The "vague for voidness" doctrine was again trotted out in *Gooding v. Wilson*,[149] this time over the dissents of the Chief Justice and Mr. Justice Blackmun. The five-man majority spoke through Mr. Justice Brennan.

Gooding held invalid a conviction under the Georgia Code that made it illegal for: "Any person who shall, without provocation, use to or of another, and in his presence . . . opprobrious words or abusive language, tending to cause a breach of the peace."[150] The defendant had been one of several persons who sought to block the entrance to an induction station so that the inductees could not enter. When the police attempted to remove them, after they had

---

[145] *Id.* at 315–16.   [146] 403 U.S. 15, 19 (1971).   [147] *Id.* at 317.

[148] 404 U.S. 804 (1971). Mr. Justice Douglas would have noted probable jurisdiction.

[149] 405 U.S. 518 (1972).   [150] Quoted *id.* at 519 n.1.

refused requests to leave, a scuffle resulted. The defendant "committed assault and battery on . . . two police officers."[151] The defendant, at that time, said to one of the police officers: "White son of a bitch, I'll kill you." "You son of a bitch, I'll choke you to death." To the other: "You son of a bitch, if you ever put your hands on me again, I'll cut you all to pieces."[152]

Concerned rather about the possible applications of the Georgia statute to other situations than about the words actually used, the Court found the statute void because it threatened punishment for speech other than that form of "fighting words" that was held punishable in *Chaplinsky v. New Hampshire*.[153] It was not that the actual words used did not qualify, but that more innocent words in more innocent circumstances would also fall afoul of a condemnation of "opprobrious words or abusive language:[154] "Unlike the construction of the New Hampshire statute by the New Hampshire Supreme Court, the Georgia appellate courts have not construed [the statute in question here] 'so as to avoid all constitutional difficulties.' *United States v. Thirty-seven Photographs*, 402 U.S., at 369."

It may well be that the majority wants to say that no words, however offensive, are punishable. And clearly that is the view of at least some members of the majority. But to do so in this indirect manner is to invite more problems than the issue is worth. Certainly both dissenting opinions are more convincing than that offered by the majority. The Chief Justice concluded his by saying:[155]

> The Court makes a mechanical and, I suggest, insensitive application of the overbreadth doctrine today. As Mr. Justice Blackmun correctly points out, it is difficult to imagine how a State could enact a statute more clearly and narrowly aimed at regulating the type of conduct that the unanimous holding of *Chaplinsky* tells us may be regulated. It is regrettable that one consequence of this holding may be to mislead some citizens to believe that fighting words of this kind may be uttered free of any legal sanctions.

But this may well be the only proper lesson to be derived from the decision. Unless, of course, it were to be recognized that the object of the vituperation—police officers—no less than the words and the

---

[151] *Id*. at 519.

[152] Quoted *id*. at 521 n.1.

[153] 315 U.S. 568 (1942).

[154] 405 U.S. at 528.

[155] *Id*. at 534.

circumstances are what really led the Court to its conclusion. Certainly, it may be that these officials are not considered properly to take offense at such language. "Off the pigs" and its various equivalents may now be regarded as proper common parlance. But if that is the meaning of the Constitution, the Court should say so.

Justices Powell and Rehnquist did not participate in the *Gooding* case, but their views, consistent with those of the Chief Justice and Mr. Justice Blackmun were revealed when the Court reversed three other convictions under similar statutes on the basis of *Gooding* and *Cohen v. California*.[156] Here the four dissenting Justices were not so concerned with the preservation of the *Chaplinsky* fighting words doctrine as with a broader reading of that case.

Mr. Justice Powell concurred specially in *Lewis v. City of New Orleans*[157] on the ground that policemen are required to have thicker skins than ordinary mortals:

> Here a police officer, while in the performance of his duty, was called "g-- d--- m----- f------" police.
> If these words had been addressed by one citizen to another face to face and in a hostile manner, I would have no doubt that they would be "fighting words." But the situation may be different where such words are addressed to a police officer trained to exercise a higher degree of restraint than the average citizen.

He was, therefore, willing to remand the case for consideration in light of *Chaplinsky*, but he found no basis for a ruling of statutory overbreadth. And in *Brown v. Oklahoma*,[158] disposed of in the same manner as *Lewis* by the Court, he was prepared to accede even to the overbreadth proposition. But he joined the Chief Justice and Justices Blackmun and Rehnquist in dissent in *Rosenfeld v. New Jersey*.[159] In his opinion in *Rosenfeld*, he adopted the position voiced by Judge McGowan for the Court of Appeals for the District of Columbia. In so doing, he would not restrict *Chaplinsky* to a "fighting words" doctrine:[160]

> Perhaps appellant's language did not constitute "fighting words" within the meaning of *Chaplinsky*. While most of those attending the school board meeting were undoubtedly outraged and offended, the good taste and restraint of such an

---

[156] 403 U.S. 15 (1971).

[157] 408 U.S. 913 (1972).

[158] 408 U.S. 914 (1972).

[159] 408 U.S. 901 (1972).

[160] *Id.* at 905.

audience may have made it unlikely that physical violence would result. Moreover, the offensive words were not directed at a specific individual. But the exception to First Amendment protection recognized in *Chaplinsky* is not limited to words whose mere utterance entails a high probability of an outbreak of physical violence. It also extends to the willful use of scurrilous language calculated to offend the sensibilities of an unwilling audience.

Powell was joined in this opinion by the Chief Justice and Mr. Justice Blackmun.

The Chief Justice wrote an opinion, dissenting in all three of these cases in which he was joined by Justices Blackmun and Rehnquist. Mr. Justice Rehnquist also wrote a dissenting opinion in all three cases. It is apparent that both the overbreadth doctrine and the *Chaplinsky* rule will remain in their current state of vitality only so long as the Court's personnel does not change.

Other opinions of an earlier day fared somewhat better. In two cases the Court reversed on the basis of *Redrup v. New York*,[161] with only three Justices dissenting: Burger, White, and Blackmun.[162] The reference to *Redrup* as the basis for reversal, however, does suggest the continued absence of agreement among the Justices as to what the proper standard for measuring obscenity may be. That there continue to be actions, if not words, that are punishable was suggested by the dismissal for want of a substantial federal question of a Florida case upholding conviction of a nude "dancer."[163]

Two other obscenity problems were avoided by the Court in the 1971 Term. In *Hicks v. Grove Press, Inc.*,[164] the Court, in accordance with its decision of last Term in *Perez v. Ledesma*,[165] vacated the action of the lower federal court enjoining the state court obscenity proceedings. And, in *Monger v. Florida*,[166] over the vigor-

---

[161] 386 U.S. 767 (1967). *Redrup* decided that whatever standard for measuring obscenity might be proper, the materials in question did not violate the standard.

[162] Hartstein v. Missouri, 404 U.S. 988 (1971); Wiener v. California, 404 U.S. 988 (1971).

[163] Hoffman v. Carson, 404 U.S. 981 (1971). Mr. Justice Douglas would have noted probable jurisdiction.

[164] 404 U.S. 806 (1971). Mr. Justice Douglas excused himself in accordance with his scrupulous abstention from cases involving publishers who have had the privilege of publishing his own writings.

[165] 401 U.S. 82 (1971).   [166] 405 U.S. 958 (1972).

ous dissent of Mr. Justice Douglas, who made out a most plausible case, the Court denied certiorari because the state court had refused to review an obscenity conviction on somewhat dubious procedural grounds, dubious at least in the light of *Henry v. Mississippi*[167] on which the dissenting Justices relied. The Douglas opinion was joined by Justices Brennan and Stewart.

The Court used the memorandum order procedure to dispose of other censorship outside the obscenity area. It affirmed two cases upholding the validity of the Public Health Smoking Act that banned "electronic" media advertising of cigarettes, while leaving such advertising in other media free from restraint.[168] And it allowed a stop-order against the delivery of mail to a business organization engaged in fraudulent practices.[169] In each of the three cases, Mr. Justice Douglas disagreed with the disposition and was joined by Mr. Justice Brennan in the cigarette-advertising cases. The denial of certiorari in a case raising the question of propriety of censorship of prison mail also evoked a strong dissent from Mr. Justice Douglas joined by Mr. Justice Brennan: "Under our regime the right to use the mail free of censorship is basic whether the censor be a federal official working for the post office or a federal official working for the Department of Justice. The problem is squarely raised here, free from all problems of prison security."[170] The problem was exacerbated, however, by the fact that the inmate's letter was used against him at his trial.

Censorship in a "service state" is certainly a serious problem. It is, perhaps, unfortunate that the emphasis on obscenity has tended to push out of sight issues more fundamental to the right to speak and write free of government surveillance.

D. MILITARY SURVEILLANCE OF CIVILIANS

The Supreme Court, in a five-to-four decision, over the vehement and cogent objections of Senator Sam J. Ervin, Jr., held that problems of military surveillance of civilians fell outside the ken of the Court but within the jurisdiction of the legislature. In *Laird v.*

---

[167] 379 U.S. 443 (1965). See Sandalow, *Henry v. Mississippi and the Adequate State Ground: Proposals for a Revised Doctrine*, 1965 SUPREME COURT REVIEW 187.

[168] Capital Broadcasting Co. v. Acting Attorney General, 405 U.S. 1000 (1972); National Association of Broadcasters v. Acting Attorney General, 405 U.S. 1000 (1972).

[169] Lynch v. Blount, 404 U.S. 1007 (1972).

[170] Polk v. United States, 404 U.S. 1053 (1972).

Tatum,[171] a group of individuals, none of whom asserted that they had suffered measurable harm, sought to enjoin the army from continuing a system of surveillance of civilian activities. There was no doubt that the army had engaged in such actions, purportedly as part of its function of maintaining the peace pursuant to 10 U.S.C. § 331 and the constitutional authority of the President to use the troops to quell insurrections and other domestic violence. There was some question about the breadth and depth of these activities. As most charitably described by the Chief Justice, the army information consisted primarily of information gathered from the news media and by personal observation at open meetings. Only 6 percent of the military intelligence operation, consisting of one thousand persons, was devoted to these tasks. But since neither the legislature nor the courts had been able fully to determine the extent of the military intelligence operation, this must be taken to be the least that the military had done in this area.

The five-man majority included the Chief Justice and Justices White, Blackmun, Powell, and Rehnquist. They concluded that the plaintiffs were in no position to seek judicial relief. The Chief Justice wrote:[172]

> The decisions in these cases[173] fully recognize that governmental action may be subject to constitutional challenge even though it has only an indirect effect on the exercise of First Amendment rights. At the same time, however, these decisions have in no way eroded the "established principle that to entitle a private individual to invoke the judicial power to determine the validity of executive or legislative action he must show that he has sustained or is immediately in danger of sustaining a direct injury as a result of that action. . . ." *Ex parte Levitt*, 302 U.S. 633, 634 (1937). . . . The respondents do not meet this test; their claim simply stated, is that they disagree with the judgments made by the Executive Branch with respect to the type and amount of information the Army needs and that the very existence of the Army's data gathering system produces a constitutionally impermissible chilling effect upon the exercise of their First Amendment rights. That alleged "chilling" effect may perhaps be seen as arising from respondents' very perception of the system as inappropriate to

---

[171] 408 U.S. 1 (1972).   [172] *Id.* at 12–14.

[173] The cases referred to by the Chief Justice here were: Baird v. State Bar of Arizona, 401 U.S. 1 (1971); Keyishian v. Board of Regents, 385 U.S. 589 (1967); Lamont v. Postmaster General, 381 U.S. 301 (1965); Baggett v. Bullitt, 377 U.S. 360 (1964).

the Army's role under our form of government, or as arising from respondents' beliefs that it is inherently dangerous for the military to be concerned with activities in the civilian sector, or as arising from respondents' less generalized yet speculative apprehensiveness that the Army may at some future date misuse the information in some way that would cause direct harm to respondents. Allegations of a subjective "chill" are not an adequate substitute for a claim of specific present harm or a threat of specific future harm; "the federal courts established pursuant to Article III of the Constitution do not render advisory opinions." *United Public Workers* v. *Mitchell*, 330 U.S. 75, 89 (1947).

In short, all shudders are not caused by chills. But what the majority refused to accept was the proposition that the surveillance was injury itself, whether the information secured was "misused" or not.

Perhaps with a Court less willing to invade the province of the legislature in other matters, the bow to legislative authority would sound more sincere. But the bow was gracefully made:[174]

Carried to its logical end, this approach [i.e., the Court of Appeals willingness to review the decisions of the Secretary of the Army in this matter] would have the federal courts as virtually continuing monitors of the wisdom and soundness of Executive action; such a role is appropriate for the Congress acting through its committees and the "power of the purse"; it is not the role of the judiciary, absent actual or immediately threatened injury resulting from unlawful governmental action.

The door was thus left open for one "directly affected" by military activities to invoke the protection of the judiciary. This the Chief Justice made doubly clear:[175]

Indeed, when presented with claims of judicially cognizable injury resulting from military intrusion into the civilian sector, federal courts are fully empowered to consider claims of those asserting such injury; there is nothing in our Nation's history or in this Court's decided cases, including our holding today, that can properly be seen as giving any indication that actual or threatened injury by reason of unlawful activities of the military would go unnoticed or unremedied.

The essence of the majority position is that a person who has been subjected to military surveillance is not, *ipso facto*, harmed by such

---

[174] 408 U.S. at 15.　　　　　　　　　　[175] *Id.* at 15–16.

scrutiny. Perhaps the record should have contained a copy of George Orwell's *1984* or even William Shirer's *The Rise and Fall of the Third Reich*. It is to be hoped, however, that the judicial refusal to review the disposition and action of American troops abroad, once again concurred in by the Supreme Court at the 1971 Term,[176] will not be considered a precedent for a refusal to review the domestic disposition and activities of the armed forces vis-à-vis the citizens of this country.

Mr. Justice Douglas's dissenting opinion was joined by Mr. Justice Marshall. On the merits, it was clear to them that there was neither statutory nor constitutional authority for the behavior of the military. Douglas repeated the proposition of *Ex parte Milligan*[177] that "civil liberty" and "martial law" are "irreconcilable."[178] He concluded this portion of his opinion thus:[179]

> The act of turning the military loose on civilians even if sanctioned by an Act of Congress, which it has not been, would raise serious and profound constitutional questions. Standing as it does only on brute power and Pentagon policy, it must be repudiated as a usurpation dangerous to the civil liberties on which free men are dependent. For, as Senator Sam Ervin has said, "this claim of an inherent executive branch power of investigation and surveillance on the basis of people's beliefs and attitudes may be more of a threat to our internal security than any enemies beyond our borders." Ervin, Privacy and Government Investigations, 1971 U. Ill. L.F. 137, 153.

On the question of respondents' standing to maintain the action, Douglas was equally clear about the required results:[180]

> One need not wait to sue until he loses his job or until his reputation is defamed. To withhold standing to sue until that time arrives would in practical effect immunize from judicial scrutiny all surveillance activities regardless of their misuse and their deterrent effect.

Mr. Justice Brennan, joined by Justices Stewart and Marshall, made the point of standing somewhat differently. Quoting from the Court of Appeals opinion, they maintained that the plaintiffs had in fact already been subjected to harm and the threat of harm because "most if not all of the [respondents] and/or organizations

---

[176] DaCosta v. Laird, 405 U.S. 979 (1972).

[177] 4 Wall. 2, 124 (1866).

[178] 408 U.S. at 17.

[179] *Id*. at 24.

[180] *Id*. at 26.

of which they are members have been the subject of Army surveillance reports and their names have appeared in the Army records.
Since this is precisely the injury of which [respondents] complain,
they have standing to seek redress for that alleged injury in court
and will provide the necessary adverse interest that is required by
the standing doctrine."[181] In the light of the vast expansion by the
Court of those qualified to bring suits in other areas of national
law,[182] the dissenting position seems unassailable as a matter of reason if not as a matter of Supreme Court judgment.

E. WHERE OR WHEN

Much of the Supreme Court's free speech doctrine has been concerned not so much with what could or could not be said but rather
with where or when the right to speak free of interference obtained.
The 1971 Term saw a large number of these cases. It is hard to say
that there was any doctrinal consistency as distinguished from ad
hoc judgment. Sometimes the Court was sharply divided, at others
strange unanimity prevailed.

Early in the Term the Court evaded the problem of the right of
a university board of regents to restrict distribution of newspapers
and to limit the solicitation of funds for political purposes. In *Board
of Regents v. New Left Education Project*,[183] the Court vacated
the judgment of a three-judge court holding invalid university
regulations for some colleges within the University of Texas system "governing the campus distribution of certain kinds of literature and the solicitation of dues from members of political organizations."[184] The regulations, ruled the Court, were not of statewide
applicability and, therefore, did not warrant the invocation of a
three-judge court to test their validity. Since the three-judge court
was improperly convened, its judgment was not reviewable directly
by the Supreme Court. Mr. Justice White's opinion secured the concurrence of six of the seven participating Justices. Mr. Justice Douglas dissented. His point was that the university system regulated by
the board's rules, seventeen different campuses throughout the state,

---

[181] *Id.* at 39.

[182] See Data Processing Service v. Camp, 397 U.S. 150 (1970); Barlow v. Collins,
397 U.S. 159 (1970); Arnold Tours v. Camp, 400 U.S. 45 (1970); Bivens v. Six Unknown Narcotics Agents, 403 U.S. 388 (1971).

[183] 404 U.S. 541 (1972).   [184] *Id.* at 542.

did in fact make the regulation one of statewide application. His reliance on precedent seemed well placed,[185] unless the Court was in fact pulling in its horns and giving a narrower reading to the jurisdictional statute than it has in the past. But the majority asserted that the earlier cases were compatible with its decision in the Texas case. Certainly there is much to be said for abolishing the requirement of three-judge courts with direct appeals to the Supreme Court as placing an undue burden on both the trial court system and the Supreme Court. But retrenchment should not take place on an ad hoc basis, for the resulting confusion is likely to add to the burdens of the system rather than provide relief from them.

Municipal regulations banning picketing near public schools were held invalid in two cases. In the first of them, *Police Dept. of City of Chicago v. Mosley*,[186] the ordinance banned picketing within 150 feet of any school, except peaceful picketing relating to a labor dispute in which the school was involved. The opinion for the Court was delivered by Mr. Justice Marshall, but not on broad free speech grounds: "We hold that the ordinance is unconstitutional because it makes an impermissible distinction between labor picketing and other peaceful picketing."[187] The ordinance thus fell afoul the Equal Protection Clause rather than the First Amendment. The Court made clear that it was not compelling the city to license all picketing near public schools: "We have continually recognized that reasonable 'time, place and manner' regulations of picketing may be necessary to further significant governmental interests."[188] Indeed, a state may differentiate among potential users of the public forum. But if it does so, it must be prepared to show that the "discriminations among picketers [was] tailored to serve a substantial governmental interest."[189] Here the Court could see no such governmental interest in distinguishing between peaceful labor picketing and peaceful picketing of other kinds: "Far from being tailored to a substantial governmental interest, the discrimination among picketers is based on the content of their expression. Therefore, under the Equal Protection Clause, it may not stand."[190]

---

[185] Alabama State Teachers Ass'n v. Alabama Public School Authority, 393 U.S. 400 (1969); McLaurin v. Oklahoma State Regents, 339 U.S. 637 (1950); Board of Visitors v. Norris, 404 U.S. 907 (1971).

[186] 408 U.S. 92 (1972).

[187] *Id.* at 94.

[188] *Id.* at 98.

[189] *Id.* at 99.

[190] *Id.* at 102.

The Court conceded the power of the City to draft a more specific statute discriminating against the narrow evils it sought to
abate. It is not quite clear why the discrimination should be treated
as one based on subject matter rather than geographic considerations that make the proximity of labor picketing of a different kind
than picketing not relating to the place of employment. Equally
puzzling is why the result should not have been the invalidation of
the exception to the ordinance rather than the general proposition,
and why, in any event, the City should not be given the choice of
uniformity of regulation rather than uniformity of nonregulation.
Nevertheless, the Court was unanimous in result. Justices Blackmun
and Rehnquist joined only in the judgment and the Chief Justice
concurred specially, stating reservations to some of the broad First
Amendment language contained in the Marshall opinion.

Insofar as the Rockford ordinance in question in *Grayned v.
City of Rockford*,[191] presented the same problem of banning all
picketing except labor picketing, the Court reached the same result.
But that portion of the regulation which prohibited the willful
"making of any noise or diversion which disturbs or tends to disturb the peace or good order of" school sessions or classes was held
valid and a conviction of student demonstrators was upheld. The
ordinance was not void for vagueness, although the question was
"close." Nor, if there was a difference in the two standards, was it
"overbroad":[192]

> Rockford punishes only conduct which disrupts or is about to
> disrupt normal school activities. That decision is made, as it
> should be, on an individual basis, given the particular fact situ-
> ation. Peaceful picketing which does not interfere with the
> ordinary functioning of the school is permitted. And the ordi-
> nance gives no license to punish anyone because of what he is
> saying.
>   We recognize that the ordinance prohibits some picketing
> which is neither violent nor physically obstructive. Noisy
> demonstrations which disrupt or are incompatible with normal
> school activities are obviously within the ordinance's reach.
> Such expressive conduct may be constitutionally protected at
> other places or other times ... but next to a school while
> classes are in session, it may be prohibited.

Mr. Justice Blackmun, who refused to join the opinion in the
Chicago case, here joined the opinion with regard to the Rockford

---

[191] 408 U.S. 104 (1972).   [192] *Id.* at 119–20.

anti-picketing ordinance, but concurred only in the result as to the noise ordinance. Mr. Justice Douglas dissented, but only from the affirmation of the anti-noise ordinance. It is not clear whether this was on the ground that the facts failed to show that the "appellant was noisy or boisterous or rowdy" or because the demonstration was by black students directed to "an issue dealing with race." But, in either event, it would seem that he took exception to the application of the ordinance rather than its general validity. As a result of this decision, Rockford may well have established an ordinance that will be widely imitated, with potential application to "busing protesters" no less than to student demonstrators, at least if the resulting ordinances are applied in an even-handed manner.

The comparative unanimity of the Court on the issues of "where or when" in the Rockford and Chicago cases was lost in the other cases of the Term presenting the same kinds of question. In *Lloyd v. Tanner*,[193] the question was, as Mr. Justice Powell writing for the Court put it, the one "reserved by the Court in *Amalgamated Food Employees Union Local 590* v. *Logan Valley Plaza Inc.*,[194] . . . as to the right of a privately owned shopping center to prohibit the distribution of handbills on its property when the handbilling is unrelated to the shopping center's operation."[195] Five Justices of the Court held that the ban was valid. They did not distinguish the *Chicago* picketing case, which also drew the line between different kinds of publication based on subject matter, but accentuated the nonpublic nature of the property on which the handbilling would take place. The case was not like *Logan Valley*, nor yet like *Marsh v. Alabama*[196] because those cases involved places somehow dedicated to public use, whereas here the owners clearly delineated the property as nonpublic and the subject matter of the handbills did not relate to the activities of the shopping center.

Mr. Justice Marshall, writing for himself and Justices Douglas, Brennan, and Stewart, thought that the distinction of *Logan Valley* was tenuous both with regard to the question whether the area was "dedicated to the public use" and that of the relevance of the handbilling—concerned with protest against the Vietnam war—to the activities of the shopping center. On the first question, the minority opinion is quite persuasive, but not on the second. With regard to

---

[193] 407 U.S. 551 (1972).

[194] 391 U.S. 308 (1968).

[195] 407 U.S. at 552.

[196] 326 U.S. 501 (1946).

the latter, however, the Court's position in the *Chicago* case would have better supported the dissenting position.

The reading given the *Logan Valley* case in *Lloyd v. Tanner* had immediate consequences in *Central Hardware Co. v. N.L.R.B.*,[197] where the opinion was again written by Mr. Justice Powell, but with only Justices Douglas, Brennan, and Marshall in dissent this time. The petitioner was the owner of two hardware stores with their own parking lots; neither of the stores was located in a shopping center. The Retail Clerks' Union sought to organize petitioner's employees and were ordered off the parking lots when they solicited membership there. The NLRB held this an unfair labor practice. The Board distinguished *N.L.R.B. v. Babcock & Wilcox Co.*[198] which had ruled that refusal of use of the employer's facilities for soliciting was an unfair labor practice "when the inaccessibility of employees made ineffective the reasonable attempts by nonemployees to communicate with them through the usual channels."[199] The Board held that the rule was mitigated by the *Logan Valley* case which gave the solicitors a First Amendment right to use the property for soliciting purposes. This was an erroneous reading of *Logan Valley* according to the Court:[200]

> Before an owner of private property can be subjected to the commands of the First and Fourteenth Amendments the privately owned property must assume to some significant degree the functional attributes of public property devoted to public use. The First and Fourteenth Amendments are limitations on state action, not on action by the owner of private property used only for private purposes. The only fact relied upon for the argument that Central's parking lots have acquired the characteristics of a public municipal facility is that they are "open to the public." Such an argument could be made with respect to almost every retail and service establishment in the country regardless of size or location.

The Court did not decide whether the *Babcock & Wilcox* case authorized a finding of unfair labor practice here. That was an issue concerned with the propriety of the trial examiner's findings, a matter for the competence of the Court of Appeals. The dissenting opinion by Mr. Justice Marshall conceded that this was an NLRA

---

[197] 407 U.S. 539 (1972).   [199] *Id.* at 112.

[198] 351 U.S. 105 (1956).   [200] 407 U.S. at 547.

issue and not one governed by *Logan Valley*. He and the dissenting Justices, in an untypical pose, asserted that the majority should never have dealt with the constitutional issue at all.

In spite of the dissent, the *Central Hardware* case may well mark a watershed in constitutional law. The new reading of private property, both there and in *Lloyd v. Tanner*, with the resulting limitation of the scope of state action, clearly indicates a new direction away from the elasticity and expansiveness of the state action doctrine. Such a position, if applied to racial controversies, for example, will call an end to the constitutional commands to individuals to conform to the standards that the Fourteenth Amendment has imposed on governments. It will result in a return to the legislature of control over discriminatory behavior of individuals. The dissenters were right in thinking this opinion on the constitutional issue to be a threat to a broad area of Warren Court doctrine.

The doctrine of right to use a public forum was not abolished certainly, as *Flower v. United States* [201] revealed. There a civilian who had been distributing antiwar literature on a military base had been arrested upon returning to the base after being ordered off it. In a per curiam reversal of the conviction, the Court said that so long as the military compound was open to the public for all other legal purposes, it would be treated in the same way as the streets of any municipality. "The base commandant can no more order petitioner off of this public street because he was distributing leaflets than could the city police order any leafleteer [*sic*] off of any public street."[202]

Mr. Justice Blackmun would have awaited decision until after argument on the merits. Mr. Justice Rehnquist dissented in an opinion joined by the Chief Justice. They were of the view that there were adequate reasons why a military base should be treated, for this purpose, as different from the ordinary streets of an ordinary municipality. Moreover, there was an argument to be made that the issue was not properly raised in this proceeding. "While full argument in this case on the merits might persuade me that the Court's result was required by the Constitution, its present opinion certainly has not done so."[203]

---

[201] 407 U.S. 197 (1972).

[202] *Id*. at 198.   [203] *Id*. at 202.

F. OATHS AND LOYALTY

It was only a short time ago that the question was put whether the loyalty oath had been outlawed by the Supreme Court.[204] Apparently reports of its demise were premature. In *Cole v. Richardson*[205] a sharply divided Court sustained the validity of a Massachusetts statute requiring public employees to swear to "uphold and defend" the Constitution of the United States and Massachusetts and to "oppose the overthrow of the government of the United States of America or of this Commonwealth by force, violence or by any illegal or unconstitutional method."[206]

The trial court ruled the "uphold and defend" clause valid,[207] but thought the opposition to overthrow clause unduly vague and, therefore, a violation of the First Amendment. The Supreme Court's opinion by the Chief Justice reviewed the oath cases at length and rejected the argument that the second part of the oath lacked adequate definiteness:[208]

> The purpose of the oath is clear on its face. We cannot presume that the Massachusetts Legislature intended by its use of such general terms as "uphold," "defend," and "oppose" to impose obligations of specific, positive action on oath takers. Any such construction would raise serious questions whether the oath was so vague as to amount to a denial of due process.

The difficulty with oath requirements, of course, are not with the threat of action against the swearer for perjury, but that, as Mr. Justice Harlan had earlier pointed out, the oath is no more than an amenity. Given this recognition of the facts, ought the meaninglessness of the oath to qualify it for survival? The Court said yes. The dissenters said no. The issue will come back to the Court, perhaps in a context where the oathtaker is prosecuted for its violation. At that time, it will likely receive a less sympathetic judicial audience than when the only matter at stake is the squeamishness of the would-be public employee.[209]

---

[204] See Israel, *Elfbrandt v. Russell: The Demise of the Oath?* 1966 SUPREME COURT REVIEW 193.

[205] 405 U.S. 676 (1972).   [206] *Id.* at 677–78.

[207] This position rested on Knight v. Board of Regents, 390 U.S. 36 (1968).

[208] 405 U.S. at 684–85.

[209] In Willis v. State Board of Control, 405 U.S. 950 (1972), the Court dismissed for want of a substantial federal question a decision upholding an oath requirement on public

G. PRIVILEGES OF THE PRESS

Until quite recently it had not been thought that newspaper reporters were constitutionally privileged to refuse to reveal the sources of their information to a properly constituted judicial tribunal. But the question whether the First Amendment did indeed confer such a privilege divided the Court five to four in three cases decided under the title *Branzburg v. Hayes*.[210] Mr. Justice White, writing for the Court, opened with a delusively simple proposition, which he explained and qualified at some length: "The issue in these cases is whether requiring newsmen to appear and testify before State or federal grand juries abridges the freedom of speech and press guaranteed by the First Amendment. We held that it does not."[211]

The primary problem with the cases is that they were disposed of in a judicial atmosphere of abstraction. Facts were at a discount, imaginary evils were conjured up by both sides of the case and offered as the basis for judgment by the Court. One might suspect— and the suspicion could be allayed only by a legislative kind of investigation not available to the Court[212]—that it really would make little difference whether the privilege sought was afforded or denied. In the first event, it is unlikely that the criminal investigatory processes would be seriously curtailed; in the second, it is equally unlikely that many, if any, sources of news would be dried up. The Court, because it is a court, had to resolve contentions on behalf of idealized concepts of grand juries on the one hand and the press on the other. It was this shortage of hard facts that most warranted the refusal of the Court to create a privilege that had not even been thought to emanate from the First Amendment until 1958 and had not been found by any judge to be implicit in that Amendment until recent months.

---

employees even where alien employees were exempted from it. And in Rogoff v. Anderson, 404 U.S. 805 (1971), the Court similarly disposed of an oath requirement that a public employee forswear the right to strike as a condition of employment. The latter ruling was made over the objection of Justices Stewart and Marshall.

[210] 407 U.S. 665 (1972).   [211] *Id.* at 667.

[212] Such an investigation might seek facts—not opinions, for of those there are a superabundance—as to what actual evils had resulted from the nonexistence of the privilege to date; whether recent times have exacerbated a heretofore moribund problem because of government behavior toward the press; what differences are in fact to be found between those American jurisdictions that do afford the privilege here sought and those that have not acceded to the demand for privilege. Painting halos or horns on the heads of the press on the one hand or the grand jury on the other reveals naught.

Neither the claim of privilege nor its rejection was as absolute as the original statement of the question would suggest. The claim was, as Mr. Justice White set it forth,[213]

> that the reporter should not be forced either to appear or to testify before a grand jury or at trial until and unless sufficient grounds are shown for believing that the reporter possesses information relevant to a crime the grand jury is investigating, that the information the reporter has is unavailable from other sources, and that the need for the information is sufficiently compelling to override the claimed invasion of First Amendment interests occasioned by the disclosure.

Certainly, as the majority recognized, such a rule would be difficult if not impossible of administration. But that was not of the essence of the majority's objection. For the majority, the press has obligations as well as rights, duties as well as privileges. Newspapers have always been subject to conforming to the same laws that are applied to others, by way of the NLRA, the FLSA, the antitrust laws, and nondiscriminatory taxes, as examples. Nor are newspapers free to publish with impunity what they publish with malice. They do have special privileges and the Court has been foremost among the protectors of those privileges.

The great weight of decisional authority is and always has been that the privilege asserted in these cases does not exist. Some states have created such privileges, not from a reading of the First Amendment, but by the passage of statutes, just as most confidential communication privileges are the offspring of legislative rather than judicial creation. Nor was there any evidence other than surmise that there would be a significant limitation on news sources if the privilege were not created. Certainly a long history with the absence of such a privilege affords no such evidence.

To indulge such a privilege verges on making a virtue out of a crime, for since the beginning of our legal history misprision of a felony has been a federal offense as well as one at common law. Nor is there any showing that grand juries have subjected the press to harassment. Certainly when and if that should happen the protection of the courts would be available to the press.

In any event, Congress is free to create such a privilege if it wishes to do so, as are the state legislatures and courts, so far as their own

---

[213] 408 U.S. at 680.

proceedings are concerned. A statutory privilege would have the virtue of being more flexible, both in its standards and in its less permanent nature.

> Fair and effective law enforcement aimed at providing security for the person and property of the individual is a fundamental function of government, and the grand jury plays an important, constitutionally mandated role in this process. On the records now before us, we perceive no basis for holding that the public interest in law enforcement and in ensuring effective grand jury proceedings is insufficient to override the consequential, but uncertain, burden on news gathering which is said to result from insisting that reporters, like other citizens, respond to relevant questions put to them in the course of a valid grand jury investigation or criminal trial.[214]

There was also a passage that those interested in the Pentagon papers and other current events will be certain to mark:[215]

> It would be frivolous to assert—and no one does in these cases— that the First Amendment, in the interest of securing news or otherwise, confers a license on either the reporter or his news sources to violate otherwise valid criminal laws. Although stealing documents or private wiretapping could provide newsworthy information, neither reporter nor source is immune from conviction for such conduct, whatever the impact on the flow of news. Neither is immune, on First Amendment grounds, from testifying against the other, before the grand jury or at a criminal trial.

But those consequences that were regarded as merely speculative by the majority were assumed as certainties by the dissenters. In any event, it was not for Mr. Justice Stewart, who wrote an opinion joined by Justices Brennan and Marshall, a matter of proof but of "common sense" or intuition:[216]

> The impairment of the flow of news cannot, of course, be proven with scientific precision, as the Court seems to demand. Obviously, not every news-gathering relationship requires confidentiality. And it is difficult to pinpoint precisely how many relationships do require a promise or understanding of nondisclosure. But we have never before demanded that the First Amendment rights rest on elaborate empirical studies demonstrating beyond any conceivable doubt that deterrent effects exist; we have never before required proof of the exact

---

[214] *Id.* at 690–91.   [215] *Id.* at 691.   [216] *Id.* at 733.

number of people potentially affected by governmental action, who would actually be dissuaded from engaging in First Amendment activity.

Certainly he is right in this proposition. But no one even now called for "scientific precision" or "elaborate empirical studies demonstrating beyond any conceivable doubt that deterrent effects exist." All that was asked for was some evidence to support the proposition. Hyperbole doesn't answer the demand. Nor does the proposition that other constitutional precepts rest on equally flimsy factual bases. It is no doubt true that there is little or no evidence to support the proposition that the exclusionary rule has in fact deterred the misbehavior of police or even that the fourfold benediction of *Miranda*[217] has had any of the desirable effects that were anticipated by its promulgation.[218]

The question remains after Mr. Justice Stewart is through: how is it that the fundamental rights of the First Amendment which have always prevailed and which would bar the denial of the privilege have never before in our history been seen to establish such a privilege. If there have been no changes in doctrine and no facts on which to base a change in doctrine, on what does the minority rely to afford this innovation? The answer remains, too, "common sense"; the common sense of the minority rather than the common sense of the majority.

The problem is also that even the minority did not contend for an absolute privilege, which would be the logical consequence of the principles of "common sense":[219]

> I would hold that the government must (1) show that there is reasonable cause to believe that the newsman has information which is clearly relevant to a specific probable violation of the law; (2) demonstrate that the information sought cannot be

---

[217] Miranda v. Arizona, 384 U.S. 436 (1966).

[218] Stewart is less than persuasive in his proposal that unprovable values are to be preferred to facts. The argument runs thus: "Empirical studies, after all, can only provide facts. It is the duty of courts to give legal significance to facts; and it is the special duty of this Court to understand the constitutional significance of facts. We must often proceed in a state of less than perfect knowledge, either because the facts are murky or the methodology used in obtaining the facts is open to question. It is then that we must look to the Constitution for the values that inform our presumptions. And the importance to our society of the full flow of information to the public has buttressed this Court's historic presumption in favor of First Amendment values." 408 U.S. at 736, n.19. The argument calls for no further comment.

[219] 408 U.S. at 743.

obtained by alternative means less destructive of First Amendment rights; and (3) demonstrate a compelling and overriding interest in the information.

Of course, it would be under these circumstances that common sense would tell us that the importance of confidentiality of the news source would be at its apogee. If he did not have the information relevant to the crime being investigated, there is nothing to keep confidential. If the data were otherwise available, confidentiality is empty. If punishment of criminals is not a compelling and overriding interest in all cases, it is not a compelling and overriding interest in any, unless the demand be that only where the national security is at stake could such an interest be shown.

Mr. Justice Douglas's dissent seems more persuasive, at least if the inferences are properly drawn. We have arrived at a stage, he seems to suggest, where the threat of government to individual liberty approaches the critical stage between freedom and totalitarianism. One of the primary forces of restraint on government misbehavior is a free and independent press. The danger of abuse of the press by the government through the power to subpoena reporters is not a past danger but a present and future one. The failure to take this power from the government leaves it with a weapon that threatens the independence of the press. This we can no longer afford: [220]

> The intrusion of government into this domain is symptomatic of the disease of this society. As the years pass the power of government becomes more and more pervasive. It is a power to suffocate both people and causes. Those in power, whatever their politics, want only to perpetuate it. Now that the fences of the law and the tradition that has protected the press are broken down, the people are the victims. The First Amendment, as I read it, was designed precisely to prevent that tragedy.

Even though labeled by Mr. Justice Stewart as "an enigmatic concurring opinion," Mr. Justice Powell's reading of the majority opinion is of no small significance, since his was the casting vote, the vote that made the judgment possible: [221]

---

[220] *Id.* at 724–25. Again, Mr. Justice Douglas's arguments would sound more persuasive in these cases concerned with such basic issues, if he did not treat others as if they were of the same importance. See, *e.g.*, his dissent from the denial of certiorari in a case concerned with the power to regulate the length of a student's hair. Olff v. East Side Union High School, 404 U.S. 1042 (1972).

[221] 408 U.S. at 709–10.

The Court does not hold that newsmen, subpoenaed to testify before a grand jury, are without constitutional rights with respect to the gathering of news or in safeguarding their sources. Certainly, we do not hold, as suggested in the dissenting opinion, that state and federal authorities are free to "annex" the news media as "an investigative arm of government." . . .

. . . the Court states that no harassment of newsmen will be tolerated. If a newsman believes that the grand jury investigation is not being conducted in good faith he is not without remedy. Indeed, if the newsman is called upon to give information bearing only a remote and tenuous relationship to the subject of the investigation, or if he has some other reason to believe that the testimony implicates confidential source relationships without a legitimate need of law enforcement, he will have access to the Court on a motion to quash and an appropriate protective order may be entered.

Exactly what is enigmatic about the opinion does not appear on its face.

The *Branzburg* case is of interest in terms of the personal dynamics at work on the Court. It represents one of the few cases that split the center asunder. And the two center Justices were the spokesmen for the contending positions. More, Mr. Justice Powell, the potential third member of the center felt it necessary, perhaps because of the rhetoric of both majority and minority opinions to state the essence of the judgment for which he voted.

The issue of a newsman's privilege is not foreclosed by the opinion. It is once more in the lap of Congress which, if it did nothing about it in the waning days of the Ninety-second Congress, will certainly find the question before it when it reconvenes. For it is championed by Senator Ervin, chairman of both the Committee on Government Operations and the Subcommittee on Constitutional Rights, and by members of the House Government Operations Committee, all concerned to protect the press against the Leviathan of the executive branch. A statute more readily amendable to meet changing circumstances may prove, in the end, a better device than the constitutional one so ardently pleaded for by the dissenting members of the Court.

The rule of *New York Times I*[222] also came to issue, if not so forcefully, during the 1971 Term. Mr. Justice Douglas pleaded, at

---

[222] New York Times Co. v. Sullivan, 376 U.S. 254 (1964).

length if in vain, for the extension of the rule against liability except
for malice to commercial reports of the kind for which Dun & Bradstreet are most noted.[223] His voice was raised in exception to a denial of certiorari. And the Court found no substantial federal question in a case sustaining the power of the state to afford itself even
greater immunity than the *New York Times Case* offered by asserting its immunity to suit in a libel action.[224]

H. DISSEMINATION OF BIRTH CONTROL INFORMATION AND DEVICES

Appellant delivered a lecture on birth control to a group of students at Boston University and, at its conclusion, he gave a female
member of the audience a package of vaginal foam. His objective
was to be arrested so that he could test the constitutionality of
Massachusetts legislation that prohibited the dissemination of information about birth control devices and the distribution of birth control devices except under specified circumstances. He was arrested
and convicted in the Massachusetts court for the delivery of both
the information and the foam. The Supreme Judicial Court held
that the delivery of the information was protected by the First
Amendment but that the conviction for the delivery of the vaginal
foam was valid. Habeas corpus in the federal courts followed and
the First Circuit Court of Appeals ordered appellant's release. For
some mysterious reason, the Court granted the State's petition for
certiorari.

In an opinion delivered by Mr. Justice Brennan, the Court asserted that it was hard put to understand the purpose of the Massachusetts legislation.[225] Its purpose could not be the deterrence of
fornication, although at least one Massachusetts court thought so,
because there were too many statutory exceptions to the ban on distribution, and its five-year penalty could not be reconciled with the
ninety-day penalty on fornication. Its purpose could not be public
health, for it would be both discriminatory in distinguishing between married and unmarried recipients and overbroad because certainly not all contraceptive devices could be considered dangerous
to health. Moreover, there were ample state and federal regulations
protecting against the dissemination of unhealthful contraceptives.

---

[223] Dun & Bradstreet v. C. D. Grove, 404 U.S. 878 (1971).

[224] Carolyne v. Youngstown State University, 404 U.S. 1007 (1972).

[225] Eisenstadt v. Baird, 405 U.S. 438 (1972).

Finally, if its purpose was to prevent contraception, it would have the unusual objective of allowing the prevention of birth for married couples but not for unmarried couples. The Court could not believe that it was intended to aid in the creation of bastards, no matter what rights the Court had recently given persons of this class.

Certainly, as the Court knew as well as anyone, the intention of the statute was to discourage sexual intercourse among the unmarried. But this it did rather clumsily, since it did not proscribe access to contraceptives that also served the function of preventing the spread of venereal disease. In any event, the Court said, the statute, in distinguishing between the married and unmarried violated the Equal Protection Clause. "If under *Griswold* the distribution of contraceptives to married persons cannot be prohibited, a ban on distribution to unmarried persons would be equally impermissible."[226] Apparently, *Griswold* was not, after all, concerned with the privacy of the marital bedroom as that opinion had suggested. It takes two to couple, said the Court in *Baird*, whether married or unmarried. The privacy constitutionally protected is that of each individual, whether married or unmarried.

The importance of the decision then lies in the revelation that the Court was as cognizant as everyone else that the rationale of *Griswold* was not dependent on the privacy of the marital relationship but rather on the privilege to engage in sexual intercourse with reasonable certainty of avoiding the possible consequences of pregnancy. If, as Chief Justice Burger said in his solo dissent, this smacks of substantive due process, it will not deter the Court from its conclusion, so long as it doesn't impose such a label on its result.

Mr. Justice Douglas's separate concurring opinion asserted that handing out the vaginal foam was all part of the lecture process and as protected by the First Amendment as the lecture itself. There was no showing, he said, that, if not for the arrest of the respondent, the beneficiary of his generosity would not have returned it to him after examining it.

Justices White and Blackmun concurred only in the result, on the ground that the record was barren of evidence of the recipient's marital status. If she were in fact married, there could have been no violation of the statute. Mr. Justice White, at least, was not prepared to find the statute unconstitutional on its face. "Had Baird

---

[226] *Id.* at 453.

distributed a supply of the so-called 'pill,' I would sustain his conviction under this statute."[227]

Since Justices Powell and Rehnquist did not participate; the Chief Justice dissented; and Justices White and Blackmun contemplated circumstances under which the Massachusetts statute could be validly applied, the sheriff of Middlesex County need not give up all hope that he may still punish the distribution of at least some contraceptives to unmarried persons. Certainly that is a worthy pursuit for such a historic office. If he can no longer ban books, he may still inhibit the effectuation of the lessons those books contain.

I. THE RIGHT TO HEAR HERE

Kleindienst v. Mandel[228] presented the question whether the exclusion of an alien, an exclusion to which, the cases make abundantly clear, the alien himself cannot successfully object, can be overcome by those who want to see, hear, and talk to the alien in this country. The alien had been excluded allegedly because on an earlier visit he had violated the condition of his visa. The Solicitor General's office apparently sought to establish the principle that such an exclusion, no matter who the complainants, was a matter for executive discretion or that the reason for exclusion stated on the record was valid and conclusive. It is not clear that as a pragmatic matter there is any real distinction between the two positions. But certainly the Court, speaking through Mr. Justice Blackmun, thought that there was:[229]

> In summary, plenary congressional power to make policies and rules for exclusion of aliens has long been firmly established. In the case of an alien excludable under § 212(a)(28), Congress has delegated conditional exercise of this power to the Executive. We hold that when the Executive exercises this power negatively on the basis of a facially legitimate and bona fide reason, the courts will neither look behind the exercise of that discretion, nor test it by balancing its justification against the First Amendment interests of those who seek personal communication with the applicant. What First Amendment or other grounds may be available for attacking exercise of discretion for which no justification whatsoever is advanced is a question we neither address or decide in this case.

---

[227] *Id.* at 463.

[228] 407 U.S. 753 (1972).   [229] *Id.* at 769–70.

Mr. Justice Douglas dissented without the need to reach the constitutional question, although it was clear that he would decide that question contrary to the majority opinion as well. For him, however, it was sufficient that Congress could not have intended to vest this discretion of exclusion except on grounds of "national security, importation of drugs, and the like."[230]

Like Mr. Justice Douglas, the other dissenting Justices, Marshall and Brennan, thought that the exclusion, no matter what was on the record, was because of the ideological—Marxist—beliefs of the alien. It was not, they were sure, that his behavior during an earlier visit was improper. Even if admission to the country could be denied to him, the Department of Justice could not deny those who wished to hear him in this country their rights to do so.

The right to listen, unlike the right not to listen or the right to speak or the right to read, is still young. The fact that it was recognized as one of some consequence by all segments of the Court can give a measure of satisfaction even to those discouraged by the result in the case. What satisfaction the Government may take is somewhat more dubious. Mandel is certainly likely to make more converts by reason of his exclusion and his propaganda based on it, as the dissent asserted, than he could have made by his personal appearance.

V. Equal Protection of Mothers, Fathers, and Children

The Court entered the maelstrom created by the demand for sexual equality without awaiting the passage of the Equal Rights Amendment, to which the more knowledgeable and more "chauvinistic male pigs" look forward with eagerness. Early in the 1971 Term, the unanimous Court, speaking through the Chief Justice, ruled that the state of Idaho could not arbitrarily prefer males over females, both having the same relationship to the deceased, in the appointment of an administrator for a decedent's estate.[231]

The case had all the trappings of concocted piece of litigation or a grudge fight. The deceased was a young adopted child whose parents had separated before his death. The estate had an aggregate value of less than $1,000. Both mother and father applied for appointment as administrator. The Idaho court awarded the administration to the father pursuant to § 15-314 of the Idaho Code which

---

[230] *Id.* at 774.   [231] Reed v. Reed, 404 U.S. 71 (1971).

provided that of "several persons claiming and equally entitled to administer males must be preferred to females, and relatives of the whole blood to those of the half blood." And so the case was on its way to the Supreme Court of the United States, although the statute in question was amended early in 1971 to eliminate this mandatory preference for males:[232]

> The Equal Protection Clause . . . does . . . deny to States the power to legislate that different treatment be accorded to persons placed by a statute in different classes on the basis of criteria wholly unrelated to the objective of that statute. . . . The question presented by this case, then, is whether a difference in sex . . . bears a rational relationship to a state objective that is sought to be advanced by the operation of [the Idaho statutes].

Since the only objective of the legislation providing for this arbitrary choice was to eliminate controversies that would otherwise require court resolution in the event of a conflict over letters of administration, the answer to the Court's question was no:[233]

> To give a mandatory preference to members of either sex over members of the other, merely to accomplish the elimination of hearings on the merits, is to make the very kind of arbitrary legislative choice forbidden by the Equal Protection Clause of the Fourteenth Amendment; and whatever may be said as to the positive values of avoiding intrafamily controversy, the choice in this context may not lawfully be mandated solely on the basis of sex.

Strangely, the women's rights movement was not satisfied with winning the case. The Court had failed to say that classifications by sex were inherently invalid. The Court did not even suggest that such classifications were to be treated as suspect, as are racial classifications. But then, what more than this demand for a rational basis for sexual classification could be expected from a Court whose membership hardly reflected the division of the American population between men and women.

Indeed, the Court turned around after declaring that women were equal to men as administrators of intestate estates and held that unmarried men were equal to unmarried women as proper custodians for their illegitimate children, this time over the dissent of the Chief

---

[232] *Id.* at 75–76.   [233] *Id.* at 76–77.

Justice, who was joined by Mr. Justice Blackmun.[234] In *Stanley v. Illinois*,[235] the Court ruled invalid Illinois statutes that provided for children of unwed parents automatically to become wards of the state on the death of the mother. Guardianship is denied to no other parents, married, divorced, or unwed mothers, except after a hearing and showing that the parent is unfit to assume the responsibility. Only in the case of an unwed father does the state assume the unfitness of the parent without proof. The Court held that the Illinois scheme violated both the Due Process and the Equal Protection Clauses of the Fourteenth Amendment:

> The State's interest in caring for Stanley's children is *de minimis* if Stanley is shown to be a fit father. It insists on presuming rather than proving Stanley's unfitness solely because it is more convenient to presume than to prove. Under the Due Process Clause that advantage is insufficient to justify refusing a father a hearing when the issue at stake is the dismemberment of the family.[236] . . . Stanley's claim in the state courts and here is that failure to afford him a hearing on his parental qualifications while extending it to other parents denied him equal protection of the laws. We have concluded that all Illinois parents are constitutionally entitled to a hearing on their fitness before their children are removed from their custody. It follows that denying such a hearing to Stanley and those like him while granting it to other Illinois parents is inescapably contrary to the Equal Protection Clause.[237]

Mr. Justice Douglas joined Mr. Justice White's majority opinion on the Due Process but not the Equal Protection Clause ground.

The Chief Justice, in dissent, rejected the due process argument because the issue was not raised in the state courts. On the equal protection argument, he would reach an opposite conclusion. The distinctive treatment afforded unwed mothers was based on "common human experience":[238]

> I believe that a State is fully justified in concluding, on the basis of common human experience, that the biological role of the mother in carrying and nursing an infant creates stronger bonds between her and the child than the bonds resulting from the male's often casual encounter. This view is reinforced by the observable fact that most unwed mothers exhibit a concern for their offspring either permanently or at

---

[234] Justices Powell and Rehnquist were nonparticipants in both cases.

[235] 405 U.S. 645 (1972).

[236] *Id.* at 657–58.

[237] *Id.* at 658.

[238] *Id.* at 665–66.

least until they are safely placed for adoption, while unwed
fathers rarely burden either the mother or the child with their
attentions or loyalties. Centuries of human experience buttress
this view of the realities of human conditions and suggest that
unwed mothers of illegitimate children are generally more dependable protectors of their children than are unwed fathers.

It is dubious that what was clearly intended to be complimentary
to the female sex will be received with enthusiasm by the ardent
supporters of the equality of the sexes before the law, although even
they will have to concede the existence of different biological functions in the creation of viable human life.

The Court declined the opportunities further to explore the question of different legal status for men and women. In *Forbush v.
Wallace*,[239] it affirmed without opinion a judgment upholding a
state law that required a married woman to use her husband's surname in applying for a driver's license. And, in *Pacheco v. Pacheco*,[240] the Court found no substantial federal question in the
state law that barred alimony to adulterous wives. Mr. Justice
Douglas would have chosen to hear argument before deciding the
case as the Court did.

Adultery and illegitimate children were the features of still another decision. In earlier terms, the Court had decided first, that a
Louisiana statute that denied an illegitimate child recovery for
wrongful death of its mother when legitimate children could secure
such relief was invalid as a denial of equal protection of the laws;[241]
second, that a Louisiana statute that provided for intestate succession but did not equate legitimate and illegitimate children was not
a violation of the Equal Protection Clause.[242] Last Term, the question was whether a Louisiana statute that preferred legitimate over
illegitimate children in distributions under its workmen's compensation laws fell afoul of the Equal Protection Clause.[243] The Court,
through Mr. Justice Powell, chose the wrongful death precedent
rather than the intestate succession precedent and ruled the Louisiana statute to be unconstitutionally discriminatory. The distinction
between the two cases was paper thin: the deceased had the power
to make a will and thus avoid the consequences of adverse discrimi-

---

[239] 405 U.S. 970 (1972).   [240] 404 U.S. 804 (1971).

[241] Levy v. Louisiana, 391 U.S. 68 (1968).

[242] Labine v. Vincent, 401 U.S. 532 (1971).

[243] Weber v. Aetna Casualty & Surety Co., 406 U.S. 164 (1972).

nation against illegitimate inheritances. Mr. Justice Powell's compassionate conclusion was: [244]

> The status of illegitimacy has expressed through the ages society's condemnation of irresponsible liaisons beyond the bonds of marriage. But visiting this condemnation on the head of an infant is illogical and unjust. Moreover, imposing disabilities on the illegitimate child is contrary to the basic concept of our system that legal burdens should bear some relationship to individual responsibility or wrongdoing. Obviously, no child is responsible for his birth and penalizing the illegitimate child is an ineffectual—as well as an unjust—way of deterring the parent. Courts are powerless to prevent the social opprobrium suffered by these hapless children, but the Equal Protection Clause does enable us to strike down discriminatory laws relating to the status of birth where—as in this case—the classification is justified by no legitimate state interest, compelling or otherwise.

Labine, the intermediate Louisiana case would seem, after this, to have been headed for either overruling or isolation as *sui generis*, were it not for the affirmance by an equally divided Court, with Mr. Justice Powell not participating, in *Willis v. Prudential Insurance Co.*,[245] where the question was whether illegitimate children qualified as beneficiaries under the Serviceman's Insurance Act.

Weber afforded Mr. Justice Rehnquist, in his solo dissent, an opportunity quickly to reveal his attitude toward judicial review of state legislation under the Fourteenth Amendment. It is undoubtedly a statement that he will find it difficult to abide by in all cases. But it is certainly a ringing statement of a position that he will surely assert, at least from time to time, in the future: [246]

> While the Court's opinion today is by no means a sharp departure from the precedents on which it relies, it is an extraordinary departure from what I conceive to be the intent of the framers of the Fourteenth Amendment and the import of the traditional presumption of constitutionality accorded to legislative enactments. Nowhere in the text of the Constitution, or in its plain implications, is there any guide for determining what is a "legitimate" state interest, or what is a "fundamental personal right." The traditional police power of the States has been deemed to embrace any measure thought to further the well-being of the State in question, subject only to the specific prohibitions contained in the Federal Consti-

---

[244] *Id.* at 175–76.   [245] 405 U.S. 318 (1972).   [246] 406 U.S. at 181–82, 185.

tution. That Constitution of course contains numerous guarantees of individual liberty, which I would have no trouble
describing as "fundamental personal liberties," but the right of
illegitimate children to sue in state court to recover workmen's compensation benefits is not among them.

The relationship of the "legitimate" state interest and "fundamental personal right" analysis to the constitutional guarantee of equal protection of the law is approximately the same
as that of "freedom of contract" to the constitutional guarantee that no person shall be deprived of life, liberty, or property without due process of law. It is an invitation for judicial
exegesis over and above the commands of the Constitution,
in which values that cannot possibly have their source in that
instrument are invoked to either validate or condemn the
countless laws enacted by the various States. . . .

All legislation involves classification and line drawing of
one kind or another. When this Court expands the traditional
"reasonable basis" standard for judgment under the Equal Protection Clause into a search for "legitimate" state interests
that the legislation may "promote," and "for fundamental
personal rights" that it might "endanger," it is doing nothing
less than passing policy judgments upon the acts of every state
legislature in the country.

The *Weber* case may not be of great intrinsic importance. But
it revealed, as no other case during the Term, the vastly different
judicial temperaments that were brought to the Supreme Court by
the simultaneous appointments of Justices Powell and Rehnquist.
In Rehnquist, the President clearly secured the "strict construction-
ist" he has always talked about; in Powell, he has a successor to the
Holmes-Cardozo-Frankfurter traditions, which he has also talked
about, on the erroneous assumption that the two were the same.
The similarities and differences between the two new Justices
should make for interesting Court-watching in the Terms to come.

VI. WELFARE

The transmogrification of welfare from a concept of charity
to one of constitutional right received a strong push in *Shapiro v.
Thompson*[247] and *Goldberg v. Kelly*,[248] the first concerned with

---

[247] 394 U.S. 618 (1969). See Rosenheim, *Shapiro v. Thompson: "The Beggars Are
Coming to Town,"* 1969 SUPREME COURT REVIEW 303.

[248] 397 U.S. 254 (1970). See O'Neil, *Of Justice Delayed and Justice Denied: The Welfare
Prior Hearing Cases,* 1970 SUPREME COURT REVIEW 161.

the substantive right to payments and the second with the proper remedies to assure the substantive rights. The movement might have had a setback in the 1970 Term in *Wyman v. James*.[249] But the direction is clear and the Burger Court opinions suggest that if there will be no rush forward neither will there be any substantial turning back. A large part of its business in the 1971 Term was taken up with defining the "new property" that is a natural consequence of the modern service state. The issue gave rise to much controversy among the Justices as might be expected at the frontiers of the law.

Early in the Term there was a surprisingly unanimous decision that an Illinois statute and regulations denying AFDC assistance to families with dependent children who were attending colleges or universities, while allowing such aid to families with children of the same ages attending high school or vocational school, violated the Supremacy Clause of the Constitution, *i.e.*, they were inconsistent with the Social Security Act.[250] The lurking Equal Protection Clause problem helped the Court to reach its statutory conclusion.

Mr. Justice Brennan wrote the Court's opinion. It was a candid reading of the legislative history of the Social Security Act's relevant provisions. It concluded:[251]

> In sum, when application of AFDC was extended to a new age group—in 1939 to 16–17-year-olds and in 1964 to 18–20-year-olds—Congress took care to make explicit that the decision whether to participate was left to the individual States. However, when application of AFDC within the age group was enlarged—in 1956 to all 16–17-year-olds and in 1965 to 18–20-year-olds attending college or university—the evidence, if not as clear, is that financial support of AFDC programs for the age group was to continue only in States that conformed their eligibility requirements to the new federal standards. Any doubt must be resolved in favor of this construction to avoid the necessity for passing upon the equal protection issue. . . . [W]e think there is a serious question whether the Illinois classification can withstand the strictures of the Equal Protection Clause. . . . We doubt the rationality of the classification as a means of furthering the goal of aiding needy

---

[249] 400 U.S. 309 (1971).

[250] Townsend v. Swank, 404 U.S. 282 (1971). See also Digesauldo v. Shea, 404 U.S. 1008 (1972); Carpenter v. Sterrett, 405 U.S. 971 (1972).

[251] 404 U.S. at 290–91.

children to become employable and self-sufficient; we are not
told what basis in practical experience supports the propo-
sitioñ that children with a vocational training are more readily
employable than children with a college education.

The Chief Justice concurred, somewhat reluctantly, in the result,
emphasizing that the federal power extended only to control of the
funds it would afford the states. He would make it clear that "Congress has used the 'power of the purse' to force the States to adhere
to its wishes to a certain extent, but adherence to the provisions of
Title IV is in no way mandatory upon the States under the Supremacy Clause."[252] His proposition was that there is no constitutional right to AFDC funds except where the state succumbs to the
fiscal blandishments of the national government.

A challenge to the validity of § 224 of the Social Security Act
because of inequality of treatment was beaten back in a four-to-
three decision in *Richardson v. Belcher*.[253] The Social Security Act
provides that a reduction in Social Security benefits shall be made
when the recipient is also receiving payments under a workman's
compensation law but it does not reduce those payments when the
recipient is getting payments from private insurance, tort claim
awards, or various other government programs. The classification,
it was argued, was an invalid denial of equal protection of the laws.
Not so, said Mr. Justice Stewart, for himself, the Chief Justice,
and Justices White and Blackmun.[254]

> We agree that a statutory discrimination between two like
> classes cannot be rationalized by assigning them different
> labels, but neither can two unlike classes be made indistin-
> guishable by attaching to them a common label. The original
> purpose of state workmen's compensation laws was to satisfy
> a need inadequately met by private insurance or tort claim
> awards. Congress could rationally conclude that this need
> should continue to be met primarily by the States, and that
> a federal program that began to duplicate the efforts of the
> States might lead to a gradual weakening or atrophy of the
> state programs.

Stewart went on to say that it wasn't for the Court to decide that
other kinds of payments should also be treated as offsets to Social
Security payments, although it is clear that the dissenters did not

[252] *Id.* at 292.
[253] 404 U.S. 78 (1971). See also Bartley v. Richardson, 404 U.S. 980 (1971).
[254] 404 U.S. at 83–84.

expect that equality would be accomplished by reducing the level of all payments wherever additional government payments were made but only by eliminating the offset in the workmen's compensation category.

The dissent by Mr. Justice Douglas pointed out that there were a variety of public payment programs that were not the basis for reduction of Social Security payments and he saw no way of distinguishing them. Mr. Justice Marshall's more extensive dissent, joined by Mr. Justice Brennan, was a plea for a more rigid requirement of equality in nonbusiness cases: [255]

> Judges should not ignore what everyone knows namely that legislation regulating business cannot be equated with legislation dealing with destitute, disabled, or elderly individuals. Thus, in assessing the lawfulness of the special disadvantages suffered here by workmen's compensation beneficiaries, the Court should consider the individual interests at stake. Federal disability payments, even when supplemented by other forms of disability compensation, provide families of disabled persons with the basic means for getting by. I would require more than a mere "rational basis" to justify a discrimination that deprives disabled persons of such support in their time of need.

While suggesting that he need not reach the question whether the Social Security benefits were vested property rights that could not be reduced,[256] he clearly hinted that he would be prepared to support that result.

The reliance of the Court on *Dandridge v. Williams*[257] in *Richardson v. Belcher* was repeated in *Jefferson v. Hackney*[258] in which the Court divided five to four because the dissenting trio found Mr. Justice Stewart in their camp, at least in part. *Dandridge* had been written by Mr. Justice Stewart, sustaining a Maryland rule that AFDC payments would not be increased beyond a fixed ceiling despite a larger number of children in the family. As Mr. Justice Rehnquist, writing for the Court in *Jefferson*, said, *Dandridge* had ruled that in "the area of economics and social welfare, a State does not violate the Equal Protection Clause merely because the classifications made by its laws are imperfect."[259]

---

[255] *Id.* at 90–91.   [256] *Id.* at 96, n.10.   [257] 397 U.S. 471 (1970).

[258] 406 U.S. 535 (1972). See also Goodwin v. Wyman, 406 U.S. 964 (1972).

[259] 397 U.S. at 485, quoted 406 U.S. at 546.

The problem in *Jefferson* derived from the fact that the Texas constitution places a limit on the amount that the state can spend in welfare grants. In order to meet that limit, the state computes the monetary needs for which persons are eligible under each assistance program and then awards a percentage of that amount to those within each category. The challenge derived from the fact that the percentage awarded in the AFDC category was lower than that in other aid categories, *i.e.*, Old Age Assistance, Aid to the Blind, and Aid for Permanently and Totally Disabled. This disparity, said the complainants, violated both the Social Security Act and the Equal Protection Clause. The latter claim was rested in part on the argument that a higher proportion of AFDC beneficiaries are blacks and Mexican-Americans than in the other categories.

The argument directed to inconsistency with the Social Security Act was framed more in terms of the act's purposes than its language. This Rehnquist rejected. The act, he said,[260]

> does not, however, enact by implication a generalized federal criterion to which States must adhere in their computation of standards of need, income, and benefits. Such an interpretation would be an intrusion into an area in which Congress has given the States broad discretion, and we cannot accept appellants' invitation to change this long-standing statutory scheme simply for policy consideration reasons of which we are not the arbiter.

He found no greater cogency in the argument that the State was prohibited by the Equal Protection Clause from paying only 75 percent of need to AFDC recipients, while paying 100 percent to the aged, and 95 percent to the disabled and to the blind:[261]

> So long as its judgments are rational and not invidious, the legislature's efforts to tackle the problems of the poor and the needy are not subject to a constitutional straitjacket. The very complexity of the problems suggests that there will be more than one constitutionally permissible method of solving them.

Nor did the allegations that the disfavored category contained a higher proportion of discrete minorities call for a different result. "The acceptance of appellants' constitutional theory would render suspect each difference in treatment among the grant classes, however lacking in racial motivation and however otherwise rational

---

[260] 406 U.S. at 545.   [261] *Id.* at 546–47.

the treatment might be."[262] He concluded his opinion with a long quotation from *Dandridge* to the effect that the Court was not subscribing to the wisdom of the state's election, but only recognizing that the discretion belonged to the state legislature and not the national judiciary.

Mr. Justice Stewart was convinced by the *Dandridge* argument, but joined the dissenters as to the requirements of the Social Security Act which, he thought, negated this power of the state to distinguish among the categories in this manner.

Mr. Justice Douglas's dissent suggested that the discrimination was a racial one because 87 percent of the recipients of AFDC awards were blacks and Chicanos. The Social Security statute, in any event, required a treatment by the states that did not "raise equal protection questions."[263]

Mr. Justice Marshall found that, although the national legislation permitted the state to accept federal funds in only some rather than all of the categories, if it should so choose, it was precluded by that law from discriminating among them. He suggested that the burden of proving that this discrimination was not racial should have rested on the state, and that, as he had said in *Belcher*, the ordinary standards of rational classification were not appropriate here. But because of the clear mandate of the statute—clear to him at least—that constitutional issue need not be reached.

The Court was not always so unreceptive to constitutional claims to receipt of categorical assistance. Thus, the Court affirmed a judgment that a state could not condition AFDC payments on parents' cooperation in collecting support from responsible parties.[264] Nor could a state cut off AFDC payments because the mother refused to claim support from the absent father.[265] And the same result was reached where the father was unemployed through his own fault: AFDC payments could not be withdrawn.[266] And assistance payments could not be denied to an alien on grounds of noncitizenship consistently with the Equal Protection Clause.[267]

The requirement of a six-month time lapse between the exit of

---

[262] *Id*. at 548.   [263] *Id*. at 557.

[264] Juras v. Meyers, 404 U.S. 803 (1971).

[265] Carleson v. Taylor, 404 U.S. 980 (1971).

[266] Dickens v. Ernesto, 407 U.S. 917 (1972).

[267] State Dept. of Health v. Zarate, 407 U.S. 918 (1972).

the father and the availability of AFDC funds was held to present a substantial federal question.[268] And the exclusion from AFDC benefits of children whose father was absent in the military service was held invalid under the Supremacy Clause.[269]

On the other hand, it is apparently constitutionally permissible to reduce AFDC payments to children whose father is receiving unemployment compensation, even where children of a mother receiving such payments would be entitled to full AFDC benefits.[270] Mr. Justice Douglas also objected to summary affirmance in cases that classified enrollees in a training program as "employed";[271] that required owners of real and personal property to pledge that property as security as a condition of receiving assistance;[272] that limited eligibility for Medicaid to those who were receiving categorical assistance.[273]

If these distinctions were not constitutionally invalid, neither were they compelled. The Equal Protection Clause challenge to AFDC payments to beneficiaries whose income exceeded that of the qualification limit presented no substantial federal question.[274]

Shapiro v. Thompson also showed continued vitality. In *Pease v. Hansen*,[275] the Court made it clear that the ban on residence requirements was not restricted to funds supplied by the federal government but applied as well to fully state-financed welfare programs. The Chief Justice would have preferred to have a full hearing on the question rather than summary disposition. Attempts to set up residence requirements that would get around the *Shapiro v. Thompson* rule were quickly and summarily rejected.[276] On the other hand, the Court also summarily affirmed the constitutionality of a state law that required welfare beneficiaries to be removed

---

[268] Carter v. Stanton, 405 U.S. 669 (1972); see also Metcalfe v. Swank, 406 U.S. 914 (1972).

[269] Carleson v. Remillard, 406 U.S. 598 (1972).

[270] Burr v. Smith, 404 U.S. 1027 (1972). Mr. Justice Douglas objected to summary affirmance and would have called for argument on the question.

[271] Cloud v. Deitz, 405 U.S. 906 (1972).

[272] Charleston v. Wohlgemuth, 405 U.S. 970 (1972).

[273] Fullington v. Shea, 404 U.S. 963 (1971).

[274] County of Alameda v. California Welfare Rights Organization, 406 U.S. 913 (1972).

[275] 404 U.S. 70 (1971).

[276] Dunn v. Rivera, 404 U.S. 1054 (1972); Wyman v. Lopez, 404 U.S. 1055 (1972).

from their place of residence to their place of "legal settlement," by finding the absence of a substantial federal question.[277]

The scope of *Goldberg v. Kelly* was less well defined. In *Richardson v. Wright*[278] a challenge to the validity of the HEW procedures for termination of disability payments was avoided by the Court because in the interim new regulations had been promulgated. Mr. Justice Douglas took exception to the order of remand. He also joined the opinion of Mr. Justice Brennan, as did Mr. Justice Marshall, which prescribed what they thought to be the appropriate constitutional rule. Nothing less than an evidentiary hearing with opportunity to introduce evidence must be afforded a recipient of disability funds before they can be cut off. The alleged $16,000,000 annual cost estimated for such hearings was regarded by the three dissenters as both inflated and irrelevant.

The same three Justices also dissented from the affirmance of a judgment that validated suspension of unemployment insurance payments without evidentiary hearings where the recipient had a right of allocution.[279] And two of them, Justices Douglas and Brennan, took exception to the ruling that the absence of judicial review procedures in cases of denial of aid presented no substantial federal question.[280]

Certainly the poor will always be with us. The Supreme Court is institutionally incompetent to design programs for relief of the afflicted. It can only assure that the measures commanded by Congress are afforded by the states, that discrimination among the needy not be arbitrary or invidious, that processes are available to assure the needy that they are not improperly denied those rights which the legislatures have afforded them. We are still some way from the constitutionalization of the "new property" rights or from the establishment of a presumption of a right to equal economic conditions for all. The new Justices are certainly proving less friendly to such ideas than are most of those of longer tenure.

VII. Criminal Procedure

The largest category of constitutional questions presented to the Court was, again in the 1971 Term, in the area of criminal

---

[277] Reitz v. Town of Vanden Broek, 406 U.S. 902 (1972).

[278] 405 U.S. 208 (1972).

[279] Torres v. New York State Dept. of Labor, 405 U.S. 949 (1972).

[280] Kirkwood v. Winstead, 404 U.S. 963 (1971).

procedure. Despite the vast concern demonstrated in the past, and because of it, the Court was busily engaged in applying and often limiting earlier holdings and in clarifying the ambiguities that earlier decisions had created. So far as the Supreme Court is concerned, it would seem that criminals, like the poor, will always be with us, perhaps because the two elements of our society are, though not identical, certainly not disparate.

A. SEARCH AND SEIZURE

A part of the problem faced by the Court in the area of criminal procedure is certainly attributable to the fact that no matter how lucid the governing rules may be, the application of those rules to the numberless variations of fact will continue to create huge amounts of appellate judicial business. Certainly the law of the Fourth Amendment has provided more than its share of work for the Court simply because different judges read the same record as giving rise to different inferences.

In *Colonnade Catering Corp. v. United States*,[281] the Court had ruled that federal officers need not have a warrant to inspect the premises of a licensed dealer in alcoholic beverages, but that they were not authorized to effect the inspection by forcible entry. A similar federal statute authorizes federal inspection of federally licensed gun dealers. In *United States v. Biswell*,[282] such a warrant-less search was attacked as invalid, despite the statutory authorization and in the face of the fact that the entry made was peaceful and with the acquiescence of the shopkeeper. In an opinion by Mr. Justice White for seven members of the Court, the Court rejected the attack:[283]

> We have little difficulty in concluding that where, as here, regulatory inspections further urgent federal interest and the possibilities of abuse and the threat to privacy are not of impressive dimensions, the inspections may proceed without a warrant where specifically authorized by statute. The seizure of respondent's sawed-off rifles was not unreasonable under the Fourth Amendment.

Mr. Justice Blackmun concurred in the result because, had he been a member of the Court, he would have dissented from the

---

[281] 397 U.S. 72 (1970).

[282] 406 U.S. 311 (1972). See also Corsetti v. Dept. of Alcoholic Beverage Control, 404 U.S. 997 (1971).

[283] 406 U.S. at 317.

ruling of invalidity in the *Colonnade* case. And Mr. Justice Douglas dissented, because all warrantless entries, whether peaceful or not, should be recognized as "forcible entries" within the *Colonnade* rule. Certainly Mr. Justice Douglas has come a long way since he wrote his opinion in *Davis v. United States.*[284]

The more typical factually difficult problem was to be seen in *Adams v. Williams.*[285] There, on the basis of an informer's tip, a policeman on patrol duty in a "high-crime area" tapped on a car window and requested the occupant to open the door. The occupant rolled down the window instead and the policeman reached in and removed a loaded revolver from the waistband of the occupant. After arresting the defendant for unlawful possession of the revolver, the policeman, with the help of additional officers whom he had summoned, searched the defendant and the car and discovered quantities of heroin on the defendant's person and a machete and a second revolver in the car. Defendant was convicted of illegal possession of weapons and illegal possession of heroin. He sought habeas corpus on the ground that the conviction was tainted by the use of the evidence illegally seized.

In an opinion by Mr. Justice Rehnquist, the Court held that the policeman had a right to effect a "stop and frisk" in accordance with the Court's position in *Terry v. Ohio.*[286] The cause for the stop need not be the police officer's personal observation. He was entitled to investigate on the basis of the informer's tip:[287]

> Informant's tips, like all other clues and evidence coming to a policeman on the scene, may vary greatly in their value and reliability. One simple rule will not cover every situation. Some tips, completely lacking in indicia of reliability, would either warrant no police response or require further investigation before a forcible stop of a suspect would be authorized.

Rehnquist conceded that under earlier authorities the information given by the tipster here would not have justified an arrest or a search warrant.[288] But it was enough to justify a stop and once the stop had been made and the gun was obvious to the officer, the seizure was justified and so, in turn, was the arrest and the subsequent search.

---

[284] 328 U.S. 582 (1946).   [286] 392 U.S. 1 (1968).

[285] 407 U.S. 143 (1972).   [287] 407 U.S. at 147.

[288] Spinelli v. United States, 393 U.S. 410 (1969); Aguilar v. Texas, 378 U.S. 108 (1964).

Mr. Justice Douglas objected. The tip alleged a narcotics offense. The carrying of a gun, concealed or otherwise, is not illegal in Connecticut unless it is not licensed. The arrest could not have properly been made for illegal possession of the weapon on the evidence that the officer had. He then attacked the failure to enact meaningful gun-control laws and offered the gratuitous opinion: "There is no reason why all pistols should not be barred to everyone except the police."[289] But he would prefer "to water down the Second rather than the Fourth Amendment."[290] In any event, he thought that the rule of *Terry* ought not to be extended to "possessory offenses." Mr. Justice Brennan's dissent also took exception to the extension of the *Terry* doctrine.

Mr. Justice Marshall's opinion essentially said that he was wrong and Mr. Justice Douglas was right when the latter dissented from *Terry*. Mr. Justice Douglas joined in this opinion.

The *Biswell* and *Adams* cases cannot be taken simply as a movement by the Court toward licensing police interference with individual privacy. In *United States v. United States District Court*,[291] the question arose whether the President, through the Attorney General, was allowed to undertake "electronic surveillance" of individuals in "national security" cases without the judicial equivalent of a search warrant. The answer given by Mr. Justice Powell for six members of the Court was a resounding negative. The problem was posed thus:[292]

> As the Fourth Amendment is not absolute in its terms, our task is to examine and balance the basic values at stake in this case: the duty of Government to protect the domestic security, and the potential danger posed by unreasonable surveillance to individual privacy and free expression. If the legitimate need of Government to safeguard domestic security requires the use of electronic surveillance, the question is whether the needs of citizens for privacy and free expression may not be better protected by requiring a warrant before such surveillance is undertaken. We must also ask whether a warrant requirement would unduly frustrate the efforts of Government to protect itself from acts of subversion and overthrow directed against it.

On balance, the Court concluded that neither the President's responsibilities in the area of national security, nor the need for

---

[289] 407 U.S. at 150.

[290] *Id.* at 151.

[291] 407 U.S. 152 (1972).

[292] *Id.* at 153.

secrecy, nor the alleged "subtleties" of the problems suffice to remove the constitutional requirement for judicial approbation in advance.

Nevertheless, the Court was concerned to point out that there might be different standards applied in "security" cases from those required in criminal investigations cases. And the opinion, it was noted, said nothing about the power to exercise surveillance with regard to the activities of foreign powers or their agents. Congressional discretion in this area was conceded to have an important place.

There were no dissents. The Chief Justice concurred in the result without opinion. Mr. Justice Rehnquist, appropriately, recused himself. Mr. Justice Douglas wrote a concurring opinion, although he joined the opinion of the Court. His was largely an attack on the witch-hunting proclivities of the government as best illustrated by the McCarthy era, the Palmer raids, and the period of the alien and sedition laws. Although not speaking in the language of George Orwell, the Justice concluded, "we have as much or more to fear from the erosion of our sense of privacy and independence by the omnipresent electronic ear of the Government as we do from the likelihood that fomenters of domestic upheaval will modify our form of governing."[293] Mr. Justice White felt it unnecessary to reach the constitutional question. For him, it was clear that Congress had specified the conditions for electronic surveillance, that these conditions were applicable to the factual situation presented, that there had been no compliance with the statute, and so the Government must fail.

The ardent support given the citizen against civilian surveillance is in sharp contrast to the refusal of the Court to afford protection against military surveillance in *Laird v. Tatum*.[294] So, too, was Mr. Justice Rehnquist's attitude toward nonparticipation.

If a judge's authorization was required for the justification of electronic surveillance, a magistrate's clerk's was all that was needed to issue an arrest warrant. The language in *Shadwick v. Tampa*,[295] a unanimous opinion by Mr. Justice Powell, did not attempt to distinguish arrest warrants from search warrants, in finding that a clerk was sufficiently qualified as a "judicial officer" to allow the local community to entrust him with the issuance of warrants. Whether

---

[293] *Id.* at 154.   [294] See text *supra*, at notes 171–82.   [295] 407 U.S. 345 (1972).

this really reflects the automatism so dominant in the issuance of arrest warrants even by fully qualified judges, the clerk looked to the Court as much like a person capable of impartial and neutral behavior as was required by the Constitution. There was no need to "determine whether a State may lodge warrant authority in some one entirely outside the sphere of the judicial branch."[296] Nevertheless, there is no doubt from the tenor of the opinion in *Shadwick* as well as that in the security surveillance case that whoever may be given the warrant authority, it could not be an agent of the branch of the government seeking the warrant.

There were other straws in the wind. In one case in which the four-man majority vacated a judgment in light of *Coolidge v. New Hampshire*,[297] three Justices, the Chief Justice, and Justices White and Blackmun, indicated their continuing dissent from that case's authority.[298] *Coolidge*'s viability is therefore clearly dependent on the dispositions of the two new Justices, who did not participate either in *Coolidge* or in the memorandum disposition on the basis of *Coolidge*. And the Court over the objection of Mr. Justice Douglas refused review to a decision limiting the potential use of *Bivens v. Six Unknown Narcotics Agents*,[299] by holding that a decision of admissibility in the criminal proceeding precluded attack by way of suit for damages for violation of the Fourth Amendment.[300] Nor is *Katz v. United States*[301] to be an excuse to ban information secured by listening to telephone conversations. The Court refused review, again over the dissent of Mr. Justice Douglas, joined this time by Mr. Justice Brennan, to a decision allowing the evidence to be admitted where the phone call was initiated and recorded by the police.[302] Mr. Justice Douglas dissented again when the Court denied certiorari, expressing his view that the Omnibus Crime Act authority for wiretapping was unconstitutional.[303]

A decision validating an implied consent statute, which authorized the securing of blood and urine from a driver charged with

---

[296] *Id.* at 346.

[297] 403 U.S. 443 (1971).

[298] Harless v. Turner, 404 U.S. 932 (1971).

[299] 403 U.S. 388 (1971).

[300] Lauchli v. United States, 405 U.S. 965 (1972).

[301] 389 U.S. 347 (1967). See Kitch, *Katz v. United States: The Limits of the Fourth Amendment*, 1968 SUPREME COURT REVIEW 133.

[302] Williamson v. United States, 405 U.S. 1026 (1972).

[303] Cox v. United States, 406 U.S. 934 (1972).

operating a vehicle while intoxicated, was found by the Court to present no substantial federal question.[304] Mr. Justice Douglas dissented, as he did against the denial of certiorari in one of those cases that presented hard factual issues as to the adequacy of probable cause for arrest and search in a dope smuggling situation.[305]

The probabilities seem to be that Mr. Justice Powell will be more receptive to Fourth Amendment arguments than Mr. Justice Rehnquist, leaving the Court in a precarious balance toward maintaining the protections heretofore provided by that constitutional provision. This is an area where the unity of the Nixon group will be confined to three of its members, balancing the three Warren Court survivors, leaving the decisions largely in the hands of Stewart, White, and Powell.

B. DOUBLE JEOPARDY

In *Colten v. Kentucky*,[306] defendant was convicted of violating the disorderly conduct statute of Kentucky. The Kentucky procedure provided for trial in such cases first in an inferior court and then, if a conviction resulted, an opportunity for a second *de novo* trial before a court of general criminal jurisdiction. At the first trial, defendant was convicted and fined $10; at the second, he was convicted and fined $50. He contended first that the arrest was in violation of his First Amendment rights. The Court, through Mr. Justice White, labeled this claim frivolous, but Mr. Justice Douglas dissented on this ground. Defendant's second claim was that the statute was unconstitutionally vague or overbroad. No member of the Court accepted this argument. The third issue offered was that the "two-tier" system was inherently invalid insofar as it made possible a higher penalty after the second conviction than the first.

The majority distinguished *North Carolina v. Pearce*,[307] because here the second conviction was not by the same court and there was no evidence to support the proposition that the higher penalty was vindictive. As in *Pearce*, the Court rejected the proposition that a higher penalty on the second trial per se violated the Double

---

[304] Brown v. Colorado, 404 U.S. 1007 (1972).

[305] Hull v. United States, 404 U.S. 893 (1971). He also concurred separately in the remand of a case to determine whether defendants had standing to assert the Fourth Amendment issue. Combs v. United States, 408 U.S. 224 (1972).

[306] 407 U.S. 104 (1972). *Cf.* North Carolina v. Rice, 404 U.S. 244 (1971).

[307] 395 U.S. 711 (1969).

Jeopardy Clause. For Mr. Justice Marshall, the "two-tier" system was inherently defective because "a defendant has good reason to fear that his case will not be well received by a second court after he rejects a disposition as favorable as the sentence originally imposed in this case."[308] It was Marshall's contention, apparently, that such a system has to be constructed so that the defendant has a chance for reduced sentence on second conviction but never a chance for an enhanced sentence. No other member of the Court joined him in this proposition.

Duncan v. Tennessee[309] presented a Double Jeopardy Clause problem that the Court avoided by dismissing a petition for certiorari after briefing and argument on the ground that the issues in the case were so entwined with state procedural laws as to make a decision on the constitutional question inappropriate. This did not, however, deter three Justices from dissenting on the merits in a lengthy opinion, written by Mr. Justice Brennan and joined by Justices Douglas and Marshall. The defendant had been brought to trial on a charge of armed robbery with a deadly weapon, the weapon specified in the indictment as a pistol. After the jury was impaneled, the first government witness testified that the defendant's weapon was a rifle and the prosecutor conceded that the indictment had used the word "pistol." Because of this variance, the State itself moved for a directed verdict of acquittal, which was granted, and brought in a new indictment for the same crime but describing the weapon as a ".22 rifle." The trial court held that if, under state law, the variance between pistol and rifle was sufficient to require a directed verdict, the same difference made it appropriate to treat the new indictment as being one for a different crime. The dissent obviously made out a most plausible case that, whatever the deficiencies of the Tennessee procedures, the defendant had been improperly brought to trial a second time for the same crime for which he was acquitted the first time. The six-man majority paid no attention to the argument. But they didn't say why.

C. RIGHT TO COUNSEL

The right to counsel cases reached their logical conclusion in *Argersinger v. Hamlin*,[310] where the Court ruled, in an opinion by Mr. Justice Douglas, that in the absence of a knowing and intelli-

---

[308] 407 U.S. at 126–27.   [309] 405 U.S. 127 (1972).   [310] 407 U.S. 25 (1972).

gent waiver, the right to counsel extended to all criminal cases whether they involved charges of felonies, misdemeanors, or petty offenses. Douglas conceded that "[w]hile there is historical support for limiting the 'deep commitment' to trial by jury to 'serious criminal cases,' there is no such support for a similar limitation on the right to assistance of counsel."[311]

The Court reasoned:[312]

> The requirement of counsel may well be necessary for a fair trial even in a petty offense prosecution. We are by no means convinced that legal and constitutional questions involved in a case that actually leads to imprisonment even for a brief period are any less complex than when a person can be sent off for six months or more.

It is clear that the operative words here are "actually leads to imprisonment" rather than the tests in other areas where the mere possibility of imprisonment gives right to the constitutional protection. Late in his opinion, the Justice concluded that "no person may be imprisoned for any offense, whether classified as petty, misdemeanor, or felony, unless he was represented by counsel at his trial."[313] As to the obvious question whether this includes traffic offenses, the Court's words were: "The fact that traffic charges technically fall within the category of 'criminal prosecutions' does not necessarily mean that many of them will be brought into the class where imprisonment actually occurs."[314] This does not mean that where there is a chance for imprisonment, but in fact no imprisonment imposed, the right to counsel does not exist. "We need not consider the requirements of the Sixth Amendment as regards the right to counsel where loss of liberty is not involved, however, for here, petitioner was in fact sentenced to jail."[315] Certainly a court cannot avoid the right to counsel by nonimprisonment of a convicted defendant in felony and major misdemeanor cases.

The opinion by Mr. Justice Powell, joined by Mr. Justice Rehnquist, concurred in the result of the case, but would make the rule more flexible: "I would hold that the right to counsel in petty offense cases is not absolute but is one to be determined by the trial courts exercising a judicial discretion on a case-by-case basis."[316]

---

[311] *Id.* at 30.

[312] *Id.* at 33.

[313] *Id.* at 37.

[314] *Id.* at 38.

[315] *Id.* at 37.

[316] *Id.* at 63.

Their concern was that an absolute rule would burden the courts intolerably, not only in regard to the number of lawyers who would have to be available, but in the extension of the trial processes in courts already unable to keep up with their dockets. To this, Mr. Justice Brennan's concurring opinion, joined by Justices Douglas and Stewart, suggested that law students as well as lawyers should be adequate to meet the requirements of some of this burden. And the Chief Justice's concurrence emitted a note of cautious optimism: "The holding of the Court today may well add large new burdens on a profession already overtaxed, but the dynamics of the profession have a way of rising to the burdens placed on it."[317]

Certainly the Court has created one more argument for a careful reconsideration by legislatures of the overuse of the criminal law as a means of governmental regulation when alternative sanctions—or the abolition of sanctions in some cases—would make the criminal law both more rational and more readily enforceable.

Even so sweeping a ruling as *Argersinger*, however, is not sufficient to eliminate the host of problems that derive from the right-to-counsel rule, as the other opinions in the area during the 1971 Term so clearly demonstrate,[318] not only because of their nature, but because in none of them were the Justices able to coalesce sufficiently to offer an opinion for the Court.

The Court once again faced the question of retrospective application of one of its new right-to-counsel rules. Right to counsel at trial, on appeal, and at some forms of arraignment have all been made retroactive in their application. The question in *Adams v. Illinois*[319] was whether the decision in *Coleman v. Alabama*,[320] extending the right to counsel to preliminary hearings was also to be a requirement that had to have been met before the decision in *Coleman* on 22 June 1970 or only thereafter. The Court's judgment was that the rule should not be made retroactive. In an opinion, joined only by Justices Stewart and White, Mr. Justice Brennan expressed the view that the deficiency was not clearly one that destroyed the credibility of the trial as was the case with the other right-to-counsel cases. He was, therefore, not prepared to pay the price of

---

[317] *Id.* at 44.

[318] There was agreement on the right to counsel to prepare petitions for certiorari to the Supreme Court. See Doherty v. United States, 404 U.S. 28 (1971); Schreiner v. United States, 404 U.S. 67 (1971).

[319] 405 U.S. 278 (1972).   [320] 399 U.S. 1 (1970).

relitigation of a large number of cases where the requirement had not been met.

The Chief Justice and Mr. Justice Blackmun, in separate concurring opinions, announced their continued disagreement with the rule of *Coleman* and, therefore, agreed only that so long as it remained unchanged it should have only prospective effect. Mr. Justice Douglas's dissent, in which he was joined by Mr. Justice Marshall, would have brought about a fully retrospective result since the taint on the cases where counsel were not present at the preliminary hearing was as deep as in the other right-to-counsel cases and the jurisdictions not anticipating the result in *Coleman* had only themselves to blame.

The problem addressed in *Loper v. Beto*[321] was whether impeachment by prior conviction could properly be rested on convictions which were secured when the defendant had been without counsel. A plurality of the Court, in an opinion by Justice Stewart, joined by Justices Douglas, Brennan, and Marshall, held that the convictions resulting when defendant lacked counsel were not usable against him in this fashion. The Court had already held that the use of convictions in cases where the right to counsel had not been afforded was improper where the earlier convictions were used to show a basis for punishment as a recidivist.[322] And earlier in the 1971 Term, the Court had affirmed the proposition that where the earlier invalid convictions were utilized by the trial court to impose a higher sentence, the sentence should be upset in order to be reconsidered without taking into account the invalid conviction.[323] The logical conclusion of these cases, combined with the retroactive applicability of *Gideon v. Wainwright*,[324] according to the four Justices, required the overruling of the conviction.

Mr. Justice White's solo concurrence would have required remand to the lower court to determine whether in fact there was an absence of counsel in the earlier cases; whether there had been a proper waiver, if counsel was not present; and, finally, whether the use of the prior convictions, even if they had been obtained in violation of the *Gideon* rule, constituted harmless error. These

---

[321] 405 U.S. 473 (1972).

[322] Burgett v. Texas, 389 U.S. 109 (1967).

[323] United States v. Tucker, 404 U.S. 443 (1972).

[324] 372 U.S. 335 (1963); Linkletter v. Walker, 381 U.S. 618 (1965).

questions he would leave for answer by those with access to the factual data necessary to make the determination.

The Nixon appointees were all in dissent and it took three opinions to express their views. The Chief Justice thought that the retroactivity argument was being carried to a point of absurdity. The conviction challenged by the habeas corpus petition in *Loper* was a decision of 1947, prior to *Gideon,* and of necessity the convictions relied on for impeachment were even earlier, entered in 1931, 1932, 1935, and 1940:[325]

> When we held that *Gideon* is retroactive, we meant that *Gideon* applies to an uncounseled felony conviction obtained in the past and renders *that conviction* invalid for all *future* purposes, *i.e.,* it renders unlawful the continuation into the future of the convicted person's incarceration unless a new trial is had. *Gideon* does not, however, render such a conviction retroactively invalid for all purposes to which it may have already been put *in the past.* The Court, in giving such an enlarged effect to *Gideon,* plows new ground, disregarding the implications that will surely follow from the broadening of scope it now gives to the doctrine of retroactivity. For there must be many convictions that will be senselessly rendered vulnerable to attack by today's holding.

He distinguished *Burgett* essentially on the ground that the Court was dealing with a post-*Gideon* time so that the introduction of the conviction in a case without counsel was known to the trial court to be a use of an invalid conviction. Here the trial court could not possibly have known that some years after his admission of the evidence, *Gideon* would make such evidence improper. Mr. Justice Powell joined the Chief Justice. Mr. Justice Blackmun suggested that the practicalities of the affair gave the edge to the dissenting opinions.

Mr. Justice Rehnquist's opinion was joined by all the dissenting Justices. He would have dismissed the writ as improvidently granted on the ground that there was not sufficient evidence that the earlier convictions used for impeachment purposes were in fact cases in which the defendant had been without counsel. Getting to the merits, however, he would have affirmed the judgment below.

The question presented in *Kirby v. Illinois*[326] was whether defendant had been denied the right of counsel at the time of his

---

[325] 405 U.S. at 491. (Emphasis in original.)   [326] 406 U.S. 682 (1972).

identification by his victim. While petitioner was under arrest, there was found in his possession identification items bearing the name of "Shard." Shortly thereafter the police learned of a robbery of Shard, who was brought to the lockup and identified the defendant as one of those who had robbed him. At the time of the identification, the defendant was not advised of his right to counsel nor did he request or receive legal assistance. The contention was that the defendant had thereby been deprived of his right to counsel as prescribed in the line-up cases[327] and the evidence secured should have been excluded from the trial. Once again the Court was badly split in disposing of the question.

Writing for four members of the Court, Mr. Justice Stewart ruled that the per se exclusionary requirement of *Wade* and *Gilbert* would not be applied to proceedings before a prosecution is inaugurated:[328]

> What has been said is not to suggest that there may not be occasions during the course of a criminal investigation when the police do abuse identification procedures. Such abuses are not beyond the reach of the Constitution. As the Court pointed out in *Wade* itself, it is always necessary to "scrutinize *any* pretrial confrontation. . . ." 388 U.S., at 277. The Due Process Clause of the Fifth and Fourteenth Amendments forbids a lineup that is unnecessarily suggestive and conducive to irreparable mistaken identification. *Stovall* v. *Denno*, 388 U.S. 293; *Foster* v. *California*, 394 U.S. 440. When a person has not been formally charged with a criminal offense, *Stovall* strikes the appropriate constitutional balance between the right of a suspect to be protected from prejudicial procedures and the interest of society in the prompt and purposeful investigation of an unsolved crime.

The Stewart opinion announcing only the judgment of the Court was joined by Justices Blackmun and Rehnquist and the Chief Justice,

The Chief Justice noted his concurrence specially. And Mr. Justice Powell's special concurrence was short: "As I would not extend the *Wade-Gilbert per se* exclusionary rule, I concur in the result

---

[327] United States v. Wade, 388 U.S. 218 (1967); Gilbert v. California, 388 U.S. 263 (1967). One is reminded that Justices Douglas and Brennan unsuccessfully sought to secure reconsideration of the limitation on Miranda v. Arizona, 384 U.S. 436 (1966), by Harris v. New York, 401 U.S. 222 (1971). See Riddell v. Rhay, 404 U.S. 974 (1971).

[328] 406 U.S. at 690–91.

reached by the Court." If *Wade* is not done in by congressional legislation—a question still avoided by the Court—it certainly will be a narrowly confined rule for the future.

Mr. Justice Brennan's dissent for himself and Justices Douglas and Marshall contended that the rationale behind *Wade* and *Gilbert* was equally applicable to the present case. And Mr. Justice White separately asserted that the decision here should have been controlled by *Wade* and *Gilbert*. Certainly the line between the cases seems to be an arbitrary one. But then the per se exclusionary rule of *Wade* and *Gilbert* is also an arbitrary one. A decision not to extend it only avoided the question whether it should be continued. That question will certainly come back to the Court as the lower courts seek to determine whether cases fall on the one side or the other of the line between the *Kirby* case and its predecessors.

On the right to counsel for trial, the Court remains firmly committed to *Gideon*. The cases on the periphery will probably suffer more and more distinctions until some of them, at least, are distinguished to death.

D. COMMITMENT, BAIL, AND SPEEDY TRIAL

The detention of the criminally accused prior to the time that they have been proved guilty of the crime charged is certainly one of the major problems faced by the administrators of criminal justice today. It is likely to be a growing rather than a declining difficulty. Society has claims for protection from those threatening them harm, especially physical harm. But the individual accused has—and must have—the right most precious to a free society, the right not to be deprived of his liberty until by due process of law he has been found to have committed that act against society that warrants loss of his freedom.

1. *Commitment without trial.* The question in *Jackson v. Indiana*[329] was whether the state had the power under the circumstances to detain the defendant, incompetent to stand trial, so long as he remained in that condition which, on the best prognosis, would be forever. The Court, in a unanimous opinion, disposed not only of the case before it but sought to afford a declaratory opinion that would resolve a large number of other cases. Strangely, perhaps, this essay into unnecessarily broad dicta was ventured on behalf of the Court by Mr. Justice Blackmun.

---

[329] 406 U.S. 715 (1972).

The Court ruled in the case of the Indiana accused who was party to this case that he had been deprived of the equal protection of the laws because the requirements for commitment applied to him—and applicable to all accused of crime—were different from, laxer than, the requirements for similar commitment of those not accused of crime. This was sufficient to dispose of the case. But the Court went on to examine the situation under federal law and the laws of the states in general. It then issued a ruling that the Indiana law and all others of similar ilk would be considered to fall afoul the Due Process Clauses if they were to permit indefinite commitment without adequate proof that it was necessary to bring about improvement in the defendant's condition, that the defendant could not function in society at large, that the defendant was a danger to others, or that the defendant was a danger to himself. It was not abundantly clear what the proper standards of proof of these circumstances would be. But in the absence of cogent evidence and the opportunity to present such evidence, a commitment without hope of release was invalid.

One must acknowledge the very real threat to individual freedom that derives from lax standards for commitment of the incompetent, both those accused of crime and those simply accused of incompetence because of mental deficiency or mental illness. One need not hypothecate the political uses of such relaxed criteria. One need only recognize that commitment to an institution, whatever the reason, involves such destruction of the human personality as to require extraordinary justification. That is the essential reason behind so many of the safeguards that the Court has sought to impose on the processes of criminal adjudication. They are certainly not less required when the defendant is not himself in a condition to present the best case against his loss of freedom.

Jackson represents the second important step to assure no undue incarceration of the incompetent. *Baxstrom v. Herold*[330] was the first. It is to be expected that there will be little controversy within the Court in moving further toward equality of standards between the criminally accused and the criminally convicted, on the one hand, and those for whom commitment is sought without the criminal law being involved, on the other. And, as the gratuitous second portion of the *Jackson* opinion suggests, a legally justifiable ration-

---

[330] 383 U.S. 107 (1966).

alization of the processes for commitment of the incompetent is surely a goal to which the Court aspires.

It is not yet clear what the means will be. In *Oswald v. Gesicki*,[331] the Court affirmed a judgment that the New York Youthful Offenders Act was void for vagueness in authorizing incarceration of those found to be "morally depraved," a term of no more certainty, but not less certain either, than some of the statutory standards for commitment of alleged incompetents. On the other hand, in *Haynes v. New York*,[332] over the objection of only Mr. Justice Brennan, the Court found no substantial federal question in a directed verdict of narcotic addiction, certainly as fraught with danger as those matters which the Court seems to have taken under its protective wing.

2. *Bail. Schilb v. Kuebel*[333] was concerned with the validity of the reformed Illinois bail system. The question raised was one of equal protection of the laws. Under the Illinois system there are effectively three categories of accused but released persons. One group is released on their own recognizance; the second posts security in full; the third puts up security of 10 percent of the bail fixed. If the accused is found innocent or for other reason bail requirements are ended, the person in the third category gets back only 90 percent of the deposit, while the person in the second category receives a return of 100 percent of his deposit. On behalf of the third class, plaintiff brought suit alleging the invalidity of the Illinois statute on equal protection grounds. He also asserted that the result of retention of 1 percent of the bail fixed was to exact punishment from an innocent man in violation of the Due Process Clause.

Although everyone agreed that the new Illinois system was a vast improvement over what had taken place before, especially with reference to the 10 percent deposit class who theretofore would have had to deposit 10 percent with a bail bondsman, none of which would have been returnable, the Court divided four to three over the results.

The majority, speaking through Mr. Justice Blackmun, found that the classification was valid, in part on historical grounds, in part on cost grounds. The due process question was more difficult

---

[331] 406 U.S. 913 (1972).

[332] 404 U.S. 804 (1971).   [333] 404 U.S. 357 (1971).

of answer, but this was taken care of by a label that marked this as an expense properly chargeable to those who chose to invoke the 10 percent deposit rather than the 100 percent security with consequent additional expenses to the state. A prosecutorial cost cannot be imposed on an exonerated defendant, but an administrative fee can.

Mr. Justice Marshall, though joining with the majority that included the Chief Justice and Mr. Justice White, epitomized the pragmatic approach: "Members of this class now pay 1% instead of 10%. In the evolving struggle for bail reform I cannot find the present Illinois move toward that objective to be unconstitutional."[334]

Mr. Justice Douglas decided that the Due Process Clause had been violated by reason of the cost imposed on an innocent defendant. He invoked but did not rely upon *Giaccio v. Pennsylvania*,[335] which bore the same relationship to this case as the peaks of the Rockies to the hills of Indiana. There the Court found invalid a statute that allowed the jury to determine that an acquitted defendant should pay the costs of a criminal trial. But the invalidity was predicated on the vagueness of the standard under which the juries were given discretion to act. If Douglas's argument from precedent is not persuasive, however, the adequacy of distinguishing some costs from others simply by affixing a label is at least as doubtful. Douglas rejected the equal protection argument that the other dissenters accepted: this was a discrimination in favor of the rich against the poor. Douglas would need, and the other dissenters should have needed, more evidence to make out the case of discrimination. It certainly would be ironical to strike down the Illinois bail reform act, especially if the state would revert to the bail practices that obtained before its passage. And this, apparently, was the lesson that Mr. Justice Marshall was teaching here.

---

[334] *Id.* at 373.

[335] 382 U.S. 399 (1966). In James v. Strange, 407 U.S. 128 (1972), the Court also forbade a line to be drawn between criminal defendants and others. A statute taxing convicted indigent defendants for the cost of provided counsel was held invalid because it did not afford the same exemptions to these debtors as to other nonconvict indigents. The Court, without dissent, however, found no substantial federal question in rejection of the challenge to a statute assessing treatment costs but not incarceration costs on convicted juvenile delinquents. Dundon v. Jesmer, 404 U.S. 953 (1971). On the other hand, these cannot be considered a retreat from Boddie v. Connecticut, 401 U.S. 371 (1971), holding that court costs could not be made the predicate for bringing a lawsuit where plaintiffs were impoverished. The case was reaffirmed in Lloyd v. Third Judicial District, 404 U.S. 1035 (1972).

3. *Speedy trial.* For many, the central source of difficulty in the effective administration of the criminal law derives from the extensive time between the commitment of the crime and the time of the trial. It is not merely—or even usually—the defendant who suffers injustice during or because of this interval. Society, too, has paid a heavy toll. The Court under its new Chief Justice seemed anxious to address itself to the Sixth Amendment mandate for speedy trial.[336] The two central issues in this area were presented last Term, but the Court was not prepared to be bold.

In *United States v. Marion,*[337] the complaint was essentially that three years elapsed between the time of the alleged crime and the bringing of an indictment. Although the statute of limitations had not run, the contention was that the undue delay violated the speedy trial provision of the Sixth Amendment. Not so said the Court, in an opinion by Mr. Justice White:[338]

> Invocation of the speedy trial provision . . . need not await indictment, information, or other formal charge. But we decline to extend the reach of the amendment to the period prior to arrest. Until this event occurs, a citizen suffers no restraint on his liberty and is not the subject of public accusation: his situation does not compare with that of a defendant who has been arrested and held to answer. Passage of time, whether before or after arrest, may impair memories, cause evidence to be lost, deprive the defendant of witnesses, and otherwise interfere with his ability to defend himself. But this possibility of prejudice at trial is not itself sufficient reason to wrench the Sixth Amendment from its proper context. Possible prejudice is inherent in any delay, however short; it may also weaken the Government's case.

Essentially, the Court suggested, the problem was one for legislative provisions establishing the time within which suit may be brought. But if there were prejudice demonstrated, the result might be otherwise. The defendants did not carry that burden in this case:[339]

> No prejudice to the conduct of the defense is alleged or proved, and there is no showing that the Government intentionally delayed to gain some tactical advantage over appellees or to harass them. Appellees rely solely on the real possibility of prejudice inherent in any extended delay: that memories

---

[336] See Dickey v. Florida, 398 U.S. 30 (1970).

[337] 404 U.S. 307 (1971).

[338] *Id.* at 321–22.

[339] *Id.* at 325–36.

will dim, witnesses become inaccessible, and evidence lost. . . .
Events at the trial may demonstrate actual prejudice, but at
the present time appellees' due process claims are speculative
and premature.

Mr. Justice Douglas and Justices Brennan and Marshall concurred
in the result. They would rule that pre-arrest delay also fell within
the interdiction of the Sixth Amendment. But not here. As Mr.
Justice Douglas concluded:[340]

> I think a three-year delay even in that kind of case goes to
> the edge of a permissible delay. But on the bare bones of this
> record I hesitate to say that the guarantee of a speedy trial
> has been violated. Unless appellees on remand demonstrate
> actual prejudice, I would agree that the prosecution might go
> forward.

The Court, unlike its predecessors, and even joined by the most
ardent of the Warren Court members, refused to frame the kind
of prophylactic rule which had been so easily created for more
difficult situations. Left to the legislature, the answer might be: (1)
shorter statutes of limitation; (2) a burden on the prosecution to
show prejudice. But criminal defendants have, heretofore, essentially been clients of the Court; Congress is not likely, at least as
recently composed, to take on their defense in cases like this.

If the unwillingness in *Marion* to frame more stringent rules is
understandable, an equally unanimous opinion in *Barker v. Wingo*[341]
is less comprehensible, except that the case originated in the state
and not the federal courts. For there the inordinate delay was certainly the responsibility of the prosecution.

The *Barker* case grew out of a double murder allegedly committed by Barker and Manning. The killings occurred on 20 July
1958. Believing that it had a stronger case against Manning than
against Barker, and that it could not get a conviction of Barker
without Manning's testimony, the State brought Manning to trial
first. The Manning trial began in late October 1958; the first trial
ended in a hung jury; the second trial's conviction was reversed;
the third trial's conviction was reversed; a fourth trial resulted in a
hung jury; finally at a fifth trial Manning was convicted of one
murder and at a sixth trial he was convicted of the other. The latter
occurred in December 1962. In February 1963 the State moved to

---

[340] *Id.* at 335.   [341] 407 U.S. 514 (1972).

continue Barker's trial until 19 March, and at that time it moved for a continuance until June; it was continued again until September. At an October 1963 trial, Barker was convicted and sentenced to life imprisonment.

Mr. Justice Powell undertook "to set out the criteria by which the speedy trial right is to be judged."[342] After setting forth the facts, he turned to the abstract problems of the subject matter:[343]

> The right to a speedy trial is generically different from any of the other rights enshrined in the Constitution for the protection of the accused. In addition to the general concern that all accused persons be treated according to decent and fair procedures, there is a societal interest in providing a speedy trial which exists separate from and at times in opposition to the interests of the accused. The inability of the courts to provide a prompt trial has contributed to a large backlog of cases in urban courts which, among other things, enables defendants to negotiate more effectively for pleas of guilty to lesser offenses and otherwise to manipulate the system. In addition, persons released on bond for lengthy periods awaiting trial have an opportunity to commit other crimes. . . . Moreover, the longer an accused is free awaiting trial, the more tempting becomes his opportunity to jump bail and escape. Finally delay between arrest and punishment may have a detrimental effect on rehabilitation.
>
> If an accused cannot make bail, he is generally confined . . . in a local jail. This contributes to the overcrowding and generally deplorable state of those institutions. Lengthy exposure to these conditions "has a destructive effect on human character and makes rehabilitation of the individual offender much more difficult." At times the result may even be violent rioting. Finally, lengthy pretrial detention is costly.

He then went on to point out that delay may inure to the benefit of a defendant's case. "Finally, and perhaps most importantly, the right to a speedy trial is a more vague concept than other procedural rights."[344] The Court was also disturbed by the fact that the only judicial remedy for failure to afford a speedy trial was dismissal of the indictment. But this is really only a difference in degree from the exclusionary rule which will frequently have the same effect by preventing the use of the only cogent evidence available.

Mr. Justice Blackmun went on to say that two rules looking in different directions had become dominant. The one that fixed a

---

[342] *Id.* at 516.   [343] *Id.* at 519–20.   [344] *Id.* at 521.

period of time within which the defendant had to be brought to trial. The other to the effect that there was no bar to trial unless the defendant claimed the right to speedy trial, which otherwise would be deemed waived. The Court rejected "both of the inflexible approaches—the fixed period because it goes further than the Constitution requires; the demand-waiver rule because it is insensitive to a right which we have deemed fundamental. The approach we accept is a balancing test."[345]

The balancing test was to take into account four factors: "Length of delay, the reason for the delay, the defendant's assertion of his right, and prejudice to defendant."[346] In short, after a lengthy exegesis, the Court came out of the revolving door at the very place that it had entered it. These were the elements that the courts had long considered, usually with the result of finding the constitutional provision not violated, which was exactly what the Court did in the *Barker* case.

The question of speedy trial has thus been left to the discretion of trial judges until the legislature comes up with more rigid demands. The rigid rule that the Court thinks not implicit in the Constitution but indeed within the legislative competence is one that federal courts are adopting for themselves without legislative authority. As the opinion in *Barker* should indicate, there is some constitutional dubiety about the validity of such judicial legislation even if sponsored by the Chief Justice himself, unless the rule-making power of the courts is deemed equivalent to the legislative power of Congress. But who will say that these coordinate branches of government should not be deemed equal in their rule-making functions? Certainly not the Supreme Court.

E. JURIES

Still one more jury selection case alleging racial and sexual discrimination came before the Court last Term. *Alexander v. Louisiana*[347] was, nevertheless, a case with a difference. As Mr. Justice White said, for the entire seven-man Court:[348]

> This is not a case where it is claimed that there have been no Negroes called for service within the last 30 years, . . . only one Negro chosen within the last 40 years, . . . or no

---

[345] *Id.* at 529–30.

[346] *Id.* at 530.

[347] 405 U.S. 625 (1972).

[348] *Id.* at 629.

Negroes selected "within the memory of witness who had lived [in the area] all their lives." . . . Rather, petitioner argues that, in his case, there has been a consistent process of progressive and disproportionate reduction of the number of Negroes eligible to serve on the grand jury at each stage of the selection process until ultimately an all-white grand jury was selected to indict him.

The case was thus reduced from the general to the particular, perhaps on the way toward assuring actual Negro representation rather than the normal possibility of Negro representation on a jury. The statistical data was not sufficient to show discrimination, but it was sufficient to put the burden on the State to show that there was no discrimination:[349]

The progressive decimation of potential Negro grand jurors is indeed striking here, but we do not rest our conclusion that petitioner has demonstrated a prima facie case of invidious racial discrimination on statistical improbability alone, for the selection procedures themselves were not racially neutral.

By this, the Court meant that in the selection process, the cards representing potential jurors were identifiable as those of blacks and whites. "The racial designation on both the questionnaire and the information card provided a clear and easy opportunity for racial discrimination."[350] Thus, "although there is no evidence that the commissioners consciously selected by race," the statistics made it likely that they did so unconsciously. The analogy was drawn to *Avery v. Georgia*,[351] where different colored cards were used for blacks and whites. There, as here, proof of "specific discrimination" was "unnecessary." This is sufficient to put the burden on the State to explain the discrimination. "The State has not carried the burden in this case; it has not adequately explained the elimination of Negroes during the process of selecting the grand jury that indicted petitioner."[352]

The Court refused to go into the question whether the same standards would be applicable to the problem of discrimination by sex, although the statistical proof of exclusion of women was the same as that for blacks. The Court chose to "follow our usual custom of avoiding decision of constitutional issues unnecessary to the

---

[349] *Id.* at 630.

[350] *Ibid.*

[351] 345 U.S. 559 (1953).

[352] 405 U.S. at 632.

decision before us."[353] Mr. Justice Douglas took exception and would have ruled on the claim of exclusion of women: "A statutory procedure which has the effect of excluding all women does not produce a representative jury and is therefore repugnant to our constitutional scheme."[354] It is likely that, even without the passage of the Equal Rights Amendment, the conclusion reached by Justice Douglas will prevail.

There is some record evidence that mere statistical proof of disproportionate representation will not suffice to invalidate a jury selection system. Against a full-blown attack by Justices Douglas and Marshall, the Court declined review of a jury selection system that seemed to exclude blacks and Chicanos through the use of an intelligence test.[355] The absence of evidence of willful or conscious discrimination made the difference there that it could not make in *Alexander*.

So, too, did another memorandum order suggest a different attitude toward jury trials than that which prevailed when the jury was still regarded as the "palladium of justice." In *Resolute Insurance Co. v. Seventh Judicial District*,[356] the Court affirmed a decision that a jury trial is not a requisite in a bail forfeiture trial.

The real inroads on jury trial were made, however, in *Apodaca v. Oregon*[357] and *Johnson v. Louisiana*.[358] It will be recalled that in *Williams v. Florida*[359] the Court decided that the twelve-man jury was not a constitutional requisite. In *Apodaca* and *Johnson*, the Court contributed further to the serious debilitation of the jury system by holding that less than unanimous verdicts were not unconstitutional even in criminal cases.

The essential difficulty with the position taken by Mr. Justice White for four members of the Court—the Chief Justice, Justice Blackmun, and Justice Rehnquist, in addition to himself—lies in the proposition that a page of reason is worth a volume of history. The plurality opinion in *Apodaca* accepts as fact that the unanimous jury was thought to be required in eighteenth-century United States as it was at the common law of England. But it concludes that the

---

[353] *Id.* at 633. *Cf.* Jackson v. Indiana, 406 U.S. 715 (1972), discussed above in the text at note 329, where the Court followed the custom by ignoring it.

[354] 405 U.S. at 644.

[355] Donaldson v. California, 404 U.S. 968 (1971).

[356] 404 U.S. 997 (1971).

[357] 406 U.S. 404 (1972).

[358] 406 U.S. 356 (1972).

[359] 399 U.S. 78 (1970).

language of the Sixth Amendment is ambiguous—as it is—and that, because the legislative history of that Amendment shows the withdrawal of a specific proposal for unanimity in the course of its adoption, it is possible to say that the founders rejected this demand. The Court then shifts from the realm of history to that of "contemporary society."[360] It reasons that the nonunanimous jury can perform all the functions of a unanimous jury.

Thus, "the interest of the defendant in having the judgment of his peers interposed between himself and the officers of the State who prosecute and judge him is equally well secured."[361] There is no factual datum to support this proposition. The unanimous jury, it was said, really has nothing to do with the reasonable doubt standard; "the rule requiring proof of a crime beyond a reasonable doubt did not crystallize in this country until after the Constitution was adopted."[362] This may be true, but it doesn't respond to the fact that proof beyond a reasonable doubt that will satisfy all jurors is frequently likely to be a higher standard for proof than that which will satisfy less than a unanimous jury. Nor, say the four members of the Court, will the reduction in the demand for unanimity reduce the representativeness of a jury. But it will necessarily reduce the voice of the minority in the decision of criminal cases.

What are the benefits to "contemporary society" from the dilution of the meaning of the Sixth Amendment? A saving in time and money of some undetermined amount that is now necessary for the retrial of those whose juries refused unanimously to convict them.

Mr. Justice Powell in his concurring opinion[363] really rejects not the meaning of the Sixth Amendment as it has been understood during all our history, but rather the predicate of the earlier decision in *Duncan v. Louisiana*[364] that the Sixth Amendment is applicable in all its refinements to the States. On this ground, his position may indeed be well taken. And it demonstrates, almost as well as did *Williams*, that one price of the incorporation theory may be the watering down of the Bill of Rights protection against the national government, its original purpose and function, as well as a raising of the standards of the states. It may take the continued presence on the Court of Mr. Justice Powell and the four dissenters, all carry-

---

[360] 406 U.S. at 410.

[361] *Id.* at 411.   [363] *Id.* at 366.

[362] *Ibid.*   [364] 391 U.S. 145 (1968).

overs from the Warren Court, to protect the unanimous jury in federal cases.

Despite the tendency toward hyperbole in the dissenting opinions of Justices Douglas,[365] Brennan, [366] Stewart, [367] and Marshall,[368] they would seem to have the better of the argument on the law and the facts as to the meaning of the Sixth Amendment. On the question of the applicability of the Sixth Amendment to the states, they have only the precedent of *Duncan* on their side.

F. VOID FOR VAGUENESS

Although the "void-for-vagueness" label is frequently attached to a law with the substance of which the Court disagrees, the two statutes that were condemned in the 1971 Term on this ground clearly fell within the rationale for the existence of the rule. Two Florida statutes governing "vagrancy" were the subjects of invalidations.

In *Papachristou v. City of Jacksonville*,[369] Mr. Justice Douglas wrote a learned opinion for a unanimous Court. He traced the history of the Florida vagrancy law back to the English Statutes of Laborers[370] and their repressive functions. He invoked Luis Muñoz Marin's indorsement of "loafing" and Walt Whitman and Vachel Lindsay's poetic support of "wandering and strolling" and Henry Thoreau's philosophical justification of "walking" to show that the Florida statute authorized arrest for these innocent pastimes that were not vices but virtues.

It was lack of notice—on the assumption that the people are informed about the content of their regulatory laws—and, more important, undue license of the police to indulge their discretions and prejudices that demanded nullification of the law:[371]

> A presumption that people who might walk or loaf or loiter or stroll or frequent houses where liquor is sold, or who are supported by their wives or who look suspicious to the police

---

[365] 406 U.S. at 380. He was joined by Justices Brennan and Marshall.

[366] *Id*. at 395. He was joined by Justice Marshall.

[367] *Id*. at 397, 414. He was joined by Justices Brennan and Marshall.

[368] *Id*. at 399. He was joined by Justice Brennan.

[369] 405 U.S. 156 (1972). Justices Powell and Rehnquist did not participate.

[370] 23 Edw. III, c. 1 (1349); 25 Edw. III, c. 1 (1350); see Ledwith v. Roberts [1937] 1 K.B. 232.

[371] 405 U.S. at 171.

are to become future criminals is too precarious for a rule of law. The implicit presumption in these generalized vagrancy standards—that crime is being nipped in the bud is too extravagant to deserve extended treatment. Of course, vagrancy statutes are useful to the police. Of course, they are nets making easy the roundup of so-called undesirables. But the rule of law implies equality and justice in its application. Vagrancy laws of the Jacksonville type teach that the scales of justice are so tipped that even-handed administration of the law is not possible. The rule of law, evenly applied to minorities as well as majorities, to the poor as well as the rich, is the great mucilage that holds society together.

That the plea for tolerance of the style of living threatened by such statutes as this should have received the indorsement of all members of the Court is somewhat surprising. It is not the result that would have been expected to call forth separate opinions, but rather the form in which that result was justified. One wonders whether a religious sect endorsing "loafing" and "wandering and strolling" and "walking" would be able to earn the exemption from the compulsory education laws that was granted to the Amish because of their virtues of industry and productivity.[372]

Florida's state statute that closely resembled the Jacksonville ordinance was struck down in *Smith v. Florida*[373] on the basis of the *Papachristou* judgment. Cities and states facing urban problems not touched by Lindsay or Whitman or Thoreau will be faced with a difficult task if they hope to create a valid anti-vagrancy law directed toward restraining muggings and street-gang crime by preventing them rather than punishing the perpetrators. Whether they can do it at all is certainly a question that the Court will be called upon to answer after the newly tailored statutes are offered for judicial evaluation. Meanwhile, it is to be hoped that the police will not resort to that form of discretionary action that never receives judicial scrutiny at all.

G. RIGHT OF CONFRONTATION

Like other areas of the constitutional law governing state criminal procedure, the emerging doctrine about the right of confrontation was rather severely limited during the 1971 Term. In two opinions, both written by Mr. Justice Rehnquist for substantial

---

[372] See text *supra*, at notes 116–24.   [373] 405 U.S. 172 (1972).

majorities of the Court, earlier cases were straitjacketed so that further movement is unlikely.

In *Schneble v. Florida*,[374] it was *Bruton v. United States*[375] that received the limiting treatment. In both *Schneble* and *Bruton*, the defendant showed that a police witness testified as to the statement of a co-defendant who was not available for cross-examination by defendant because the co-defendant exercised his right not to take the stand. *Bruton* called for reversal of the conviction because of the use of this information at the trial. In *Schneble*, however, the Court, in some measure because of the admissions of the defendant, found that the testimony adduced indirectly from the co-defendant was of such small impact that its admission in evidence constituted harmless error. That the harmless error doctrine will grow as a means of containing the novel doctrines of the Warren Court in the criminal procedure field has long been anticipated. The resulting combination of prophylactic rules and harmless error doctrine will make each case *sui generis* with an additional and continuing burden on the Supreme Court to supervise the administration of criminal justice in the state courts.

Douglas, Brennan, and Marshall dissented, speaking through the junior member of their firm. They thought that the Court could not be sure that the jury accepted the defendant's admissions as true and, therefore, the co-defendant's statement could not be considered of small significance in the jury verdict. "Unless the Court intends to emasculate *Bruton* . . . or to overrule *Chapman* v. *California*[376] . . . sub silentio, then I submit that its decision is clearly wrong."[377]

The problems that derive from the variability of individual cases was demonstrated, too, in *Mancusi v. Stubbs*.[378] Stubbs was convicted of a felony in New York. He was sentenced as a second offender because of a Tennessee conviction for murder and kidnapping in a case in which the victims, a husband and wife, were both shot but the husband survived and testified against the defendant at the first trial. The conviction after the first trial was reversed because counsel had been appointed only four days before the trial began. At the second trial, the husband was unavailable as

---

[374] 405 U.S. 427 (1972).

[375] 391 U.S. 123 (1968).

[376] 386 U.S. 18 (1967).

[377] 405 U.S. at 437.

[378] 408 U.S. 204 (1972).

a witness because he had returned to Sweden and reestablished his domicile there. As a result, the husband's testimony at the first trial was read into the record of the second. On a petition for habeas corpus from the New York sentence on the ground of violation of Stubbs's right to confrontation, the lower federal court ruled in Stubbs's favor. New York resentenced Stubbs to the same sentence, this time resting on an earlier Texas conviction as the basis for a second-offender penalty.

When the case came to the Supreme Court on the Tennessee confrontation issue, it was urged that the question had been mooted by the resentencing. Only Mr. Justice Marshall bought this argument, although it is hard to understand why the Court should reach out for the issue when such a strong excuse was available to it for avoiding the question. Both Marshall and Douglas dissented on the merits, asserting that the use of the testimony at the earlier trial was inconsistent with the ruling in *Barber v. Page*.[379] In *Barber* the testimony of a federal prisoner had been utilized by way of transcript rather than by appearance as a witness. The Court had held that the state had not exerted itself sufficiently to secure the attendance of the witness at the second trial. Mr. Justice Rehnquist, for seven members of the Court, distinguished *Barber* on the ground that the witness here, residing in a foreign country, was unavailable to the state, there being no machinery available at that time for seeking his appearance in this country. That the state apparently made no effort to secure his appearance was not sufficient to constitute a violation of the right of confrontation.

Barber and *Bruton* were sufficiently discounted in these two 1971 Term decisions to make clear that the latitudinarian readings of the prophylactic rules heretofore forthcoming from the Supreme Court are not going to continue under the new regime.

H. CONFESSIONS

Two cases resulted in sustaining guilty verdicts which were obtained at trials utilizing defendants' confessions. The Court was divided in both so that the judgments depended in each case on a plurality of a single Justice.

In *Lego v. Twomey*[380] the question was the propriety of the procedure for determining the voluntariness of the confession. On a

---

[379] 390 U.S. 719 (1968).   [380] 404 U.S. 477 (1972).

preliminary hearing in an Illinois trial, the trial judge adjudicated the confession to be voluntary and admissible, although the evidence before him was in conflict. He purported to use a "preponderance of the evidence" rule in making his determination. At the trial, after the admission of the confession, the court instructed the jury generally on the burden of proof beyond a reasonable doubt that must be carried by the state, but did not present the issue of voluntariness of the confession for jury adjudication.

On the ground that the procedure was not intended to implement the presumption of innocence but only to assure a fair procedure for admission of confessions without determining the truth or falsity thereof, the majority of four Justices, Burger, Stewart, White, and Blackmun, speaking through Mr. Justice White, concluded that the burden of proof rule of *In re Winship*[381] was inapplicable. The procedure here comported with the requirements of *Jackson v. Denno*[382] and *Duncan v. Louisiana*[383] and did not require a resubmission to the jury of the question of the voluntary nature of the confession.

The dissent, written by Mr. Justice Brennan and joined by Justices Douglas and Marshall, rested largely on language from the concurring opinion of Mr. Justice Harlan in *In re Winship* to support the proposition that the standard for admissibility of a confession must be proof beyond a reasonable doubt that the defendant's utterance was voluntary. The opinion conceded that the higher standard would result in more guilty persons being exonerated. But it asserted that the cherished constitutional ideal of not convicting a person through his own words was worth the price of freeing some guilty persons.

In the second case, *Milton v. Wainwright*,[384] the five-man majority with the Chief Justice as its spokesman, fell back on the harmless error rule to avoid reversal of a conviction where the evidence in question was clearly constitutionally invalid. Here it was *Massiah v. United States*[385] that provided the reliance for petitioner's case. The defendant had talked to a policeman who was made his cellmate for purpose of eliciting the information from him that was ultimately adduced at trial. The Court found the evidence of

---

[381] 397 U.S. 358 (1970).

[382] 378 U.S. 368 (1964).   [384] 407 U.S. 371 (1972).

[383] 391 U.S. 145 (1968).   [385] 377 U.S. 201 (1964).

guilt, other than that secured by the policeman in the absence of counsel, "overwhelming . . . including no less than three full confessions that were made by petitioner prior to his indictment."[386] Even the Court, however, was unable to fathom why the policeman was planted in the cell when the case against petitioner was as clear as it was. "[W]e do not close our eyes to the reality of overwhelming evidence of guilt fairly established in the state court 14 years ago by use of evidence not challenged here; the use of the additional evidence challenged in this proceeding and arguably open to challenge was, beyond reasonable doubt, harmless."[387]

Nevertheless, there was at least a "reasonable doubt" in the minds of four of the Justices, for whom Mr. Justice Stewart wrote the opinion. In part, they were concerned that the other confessions were also tainted, even if not challenged. For them, the reason for the "plant" was obvious; in the absence of evidence that *Massiah* forbade, the case seemed to them to be a weak one.

Once again, one of the landmarks of the Warren Court was evaded rather than voided. The weakening of the authority of *Massiah* is evident even from the fact that the dissent relied principally on the principles of *Powell v. Alabama*[388] rather than squarely on *Massiah*. The majority didn't even trouble to distinguish the *Powell* case.

I. BREACH OF PROSECUTORIAL DUTY TO DISCLOSE

The duty of the prosecution to reveal information in its possession that would be of assistance to the defense is still one of comparatively undefined scope. For a while, it looked as if it might become one of the burgeoning rights that the Warren Court was anxious to foster. Last Term, the Court in one place seemed to be expansive in its reading, but in another it was niggardly.

In *Moore v. Illinois*,[389] the Court divided five to four, with an unusual combination in dissent, including Justices Douglas, Stewart, Marshall, and Powell. The defendant there contended that the prosecution had (1) concealed evidence that contradicted the testimony of one of its witnesses, and (2) had failed to reveal conflicts of pretrial investigation as to the identity of the defendant. The majority, speaking through Mr. Justice Blackmun, rejected the first

---

[386] 407 U.S. at 373.

[387] *Id.* at 377–78.

[388] 287 U.S. 45 (1932).

[389] 408 U.S. 786 (1972).

claim although reaffirming the principle of *Napue v. Illinois*,[390] on the ground that the allegedly unproduced evidence was not in fact contradictory of the testimony. It rejected the second claim, but again expressing adherence to precedent, this time *Brady v. Maryland*.[391] As to the latter the Court said:[392]

> The heart of the holding in *Brady* is the prosecution's suppression of evidence, in the face of a defense production request, where the evidence is favorable to the accused and is material either to guilt or to punishment. Important then, are (a) suppression by the prosecution after a request by the defense, (b) the evidence's favorable character for the defense, and (c) the materiality of the evidence.

The Court hints that the first two requirements were not met but it clearly decided that the element of materiality was totally absent here.

The dissent disagreed with the conclusion that the three elements were not present here. It conceded that the *Napue* argument alone would not be a basis for reversal, but somehow taken together with the *Brady* argument it adds that sufficient balance to satisfy the minority that the prosecutor willfully failed to produce data that would have materially aided defendant's cause.

In *Giglio v. United States*,[393] a unanimous Court, in an opinion by the Chief Justice, held it to be the duty of the prosecutor under the *Napue-Brady* standard to reveal that a government witness had been promised leniency in return for his testimony. While the problem was exacerbated here by the fact that the entire case turned on the testimony of the one witness, it is clear from the opinion that this obligation will be imposed on the prosecutor even where, as here, he did not personally know of the promised immunity.

J. RIGHT TO TRANSCRIPT

Just as the right-to-counsel concept was expanded to include cases of misdemeanor and lesser violations during the past Term, so, too, did the Court take the logical next step under the rule of *Illinois v. Griffin*[394] and extend the rule of free transcripts for in-

---

[390] 360 U.S. 264 (1959).

[391] 373 U.S. 83 (1963).   [393] 405 U.S. 150 (1972).

[392] 408 U.S. at 794–95.   [394] 351 U.S. 12 (1956).

digent defendants to misdemeanor cases. In *Mayer v. Chicago*,[395] moreover, the Court went further down the line than it had in *Argersinger v. Hamlin*[396] by covering appeals in cases in which the maximum punishment was a fine and no imprisonment. Chief Justice Burger's concurring vote was announced through a memorandum that reminded the Court that *Griffin* approved alternative records to full transcripts. And in *Britt v. North Carolina*[397] an alternative was in fact approved.

In *Britt*, Mr. Justice Marshall held that where a court reporter was available to read back his notes to the defense counsel and would have done so if asked, there was no error in refusing to make a full transcript available. For Mr. Justice Douglas, who wrote the dissent, and for Mr. Justice Brennan, who joined him, the alternative process was not an adequate substitute for a trial transcript. Whether the peculiarities of the case make it one of limited importance remains to be seen. The setting here was a small town where the reporter was well known to the lawyers and, presumably, was not too busy to afford them a reading of the notes. For most of our urban crime centers, this alternative to the *Griffin* transcript requirement is not likely to be available. Mr. Justice Blackmun's desire to dismiss the writ as improvidently granted suggests that his reading of the case does not promise much future use.

K. SENTENCING

For the most part, the problems of sentencing criminals are attributable not to judicial defalcation but to lack of information from the social sciences about the capacities of criminal sanctions either to deter crime or to rehabilitate delinquents. So long as no adequate data or remedies are available, the primary function of penal sentences is to exact retribution for injuries inflicted on society. And there remains the cyclical movement from the notion that the punishment should fit the crime to the notion that the punishment should fit the criminal. Equality of sentences in terms of the crime is on the upswing at the moment and this can be accomplished only by centralizing the control of punishment within each criminal

---

[395] 404 U.S. 189 (1971). See also Warden v. Jankowski, 404 U.S. 1010 (1972); Colbert v. California, 404 U.S. 1010 (1972).

[396] 407 U.S. 25 (1972), discussed in the text *supra*, at notes 310-17.

[397] 404 U.S. 226 (1971).

justice system. That accomplishment, however, would seem to be beyond the capacity of the judiciary to effect. If that goal is to be attained, legislative action will prove necessary. Thus, the central issues of criminal sentencing have not come to the courts. But questions of no small importance were brought to the Supreme Court for resolution, or at least decision, during the 1971 Term.

1. *Capital punishment.* The most noteworthy and surprising decisions of the Term were those that, for all practical purposes, invalidated existing laws imposing capital punishment. The decisions did not put the issue of capital punishment to rest once and for all because the rationales for judgment were anything but clear. They are tenuous not only for that reason but also because the Court was divided by five Justices to four and any change in personnel may have an effect on future determinations of the validity of new laws which most certainly will be forthcoming from both the state and national legislatures.

As prelude, the Court unanimously found that an appeal from a death sentence in California on federal grounds was mooted by the decision of the Supreme Court of California declaring the death penalty invalid in that jurisdiction under the terms of the California constitution.[398]

The major cases arose on a claim that the death penalty was violative of the Eighth Amendment's ban on cruel and unusual punishments. The five-man majority, determining that it was violative of the Eighth Amendment, wrote a per curiam opinon that said nothing more than that.[399] Then each member of the majority wrote his own opinion expressing the reasons why.

For Mr. Justice Douglas, the Eighth Amendment was violated for reasons that seemed more easily attributable to the Equal Protection Clause:[400]

> It would seem to be incontestable that the death penalty inflicted on one defendant is "unusual" if it discriminates against him by reason of his race, religion, wealth, social position, or class, or if it is imposed under a procedure that gives room for the play of such prejudices.

He was satisfied with the evidence that the penalty was exacted in just that discriminatory way. And his holding, therefore, would

---

[398] Aikens v. California, 406 U.S. 813 (1972).

[399] Furman v. Georgia, 408 U.S. 238 (1972).   [400] *Id.* at 242.

be as applicable to all criminal sanctions whether they could be labeled "barbaric" or not.

Mr. Justice Brennan's opinion was directed more precisely to the defects of the death sanction. His general thesis was:[401]

> At bottom, then, the Cruel and Unusual Punishments Clause prohibits the infliction of uncivilized and inhuman punishments. The State, even as it punishes, must treat its members with respect for their intrinsic worth as human beings. A punishment is "cruel and unusual," therefore, if it does not comport with human dignity.

This standard involved the application of four principles:

> The primary principle is that a punishment must not be so severe as to be degrading to the dignity of human beings. Pain, certainly, may be a factor in the judgment. The infliction of an extremely severe punishment will often entail physical suffering.[402]
>
> In determining whether a punishment comports with human dignity, we are also aided by a second principle inherent in the Clause—that the State must not arbitrarily inflict a severe punishment. This principle derives from the notion that the State does not respect human dignity when, without reason, it inflicts upon some people a severe punishment that it does not inflict upon others.[403]
>
> A third principle inherent in the Clause is that a severe punishment must not be unacceptable to contemporary society. Rejection by society, of course, is a strong indication that a severe punishment does not comport with human dignity. In applying this principle, however, we must make certain that the judicial determination is as objective as possible.[404]
>
> The final principle inherent in the Clause is that a severe punishment must not be excessive. . . . If there is a significantly less severe punishment adequate to achieve the purpose for which the punishment is inflicted . . . the punishment inflicted is unnecessary and therefore excessive.[405]

Brennan found that the death penalty as imposed in this country did in fact fall afoul of the general principle he asserted and each of the subordinate bases for that rationale.

Mr. Justice Stewart, rejecting the notion that retribution is not

---

[401] *Id.* at 270.

[402] *Id.* at 271.

[403] *Id.* at 274.

[404] *Id.* at 277.

[405] *Id.* at 279.

an appropriate basis for criminal sanction, essentially relied on the discrimination analysis set out in the other two opinions. "I simply conclude that the Eighth and Fourteenth Amendments cannot tolerate the infliction of a sentence of death under legal systems that permit this unique penalty to be so wantonly and so freakishly imposed."[406]

So, too, was Mr. Justice White taken by the capricious nature of the death penalty as it has been used in the several states. He would make it clear that he did "not at all intimate that the death penalty is unconstitutional per se or that there is no system of capital punishment that would comport with the Eighth Amendment."[407] For him it was the nature of the systems for imposing the death penalty that made it invalid. He saw these systems thus:[408]

> The narrower question to which I address myself concerns the constitutionality of capital punishment statutes under which (1) the legislature authorizes the imposition of the death penalty for murder or rape; (2) the legislature does not itself mandate the penalty in any particular class or kind of case (that is, legislative will is not frustrated if the penalty is never imposed) but delegates to judges or juries the decisions as to those cases, if any, in which the penalty will be utilized; and (3) judges and juries have ordered the death penalty with such infrequency that the odds are now very much against imposition and execution of the penalty with respect to any convicted murderer or rapist.

It remained for Mr. Justice Marshall to express, in the context of a historical review and functional analysis, what was essentially the approach of the humanist. The death penalty is, he said, although "should be" might be more accurate, "morally unacceptable."[409] And it is here that most of those who approve the conclusion of the Court will find themselves. One role of the Constitution is to help the nation to become "more civilized." A society with the aspirations that ours so often asserts cannot consistently with its goals, coldly and deliberately take the life of any human being no matter how reprehensible his past behavior. Perhaps the majority of our population does not display the sensitivity ascribed to it by Mr. Justice Marshall. And yet it seems appropriate to assume that they would were they as cognizant of the facts as they should be. Again,

---

[406] *Id.* at 310.   [408] *Id.* at 311.

[407] *Id.* at 310–11.   [409] *Id.* at 360.

if we have not come as far from the days when public hangings were a form of entertainment, the time has come when we should assume that our better natures are imminent if not immanent.

The disparity of views among the majority clearly invite legislatively compelled death sentences for particular crimes. And yet it should be expected that these five Justices, at least, will as readily reject the validity of the death penalty under so rigid a statute. *Noblesse oblige.*

The four dissenting Justices joined in the Chief Justice's opinion.[410] Protesting an abhorrence of the death penalty, except for "a small category of the most heinous crimes,"[411] the dissenters were convinced that neither history nor public opinion nor contemporary administration of the criminal justice system warranted this judicial intervention into the legislative realm. The four dissenting opinions met the separate arguments in the five majority opinions. But the reader gets the impression that the decisive element for each of the Justices was something above and beyond the logic and rhetoric that each of them used.

In the *Furman v. Georgia* decision the inevitable came to pass. The essential surprise is that it came to pass when it did. Earlier cases had afforded the majority Justices the same opportunities to justify the conclusion they reached, with the possibility of more support from the Justices who then sat on the bench and have since been replaced. If not then, why now? Perhaps they regarded this as the last opportunity for some time to come. Or perhaps it was the weight, as Mr. Justice Marshall pointed out, of up to six hundred lives to be saved or lost dependent on a judicial thumb directed upward or downward.

2. *Length of confinement.* Just as the Court imposed restraints on the pretrial commitment of a defendant because of alleged incapacities,[412] so too it carefully restrained postconviction extensions of time to be served even if under the rubric of "treatment." In *McNeil v. Director, Patuxent Institute,*[413] it was held that the prisoner, after serving his term, was entitled to the protection of those

---

[410] Mr. Justice Blackmun wrote an opinion for himself; Justices Powell and Rehnquist wrote opinions joined by the other three dissenters.

[411] *Id.* at 375.

[412] Jackson v. Indiana, 406 U.S. 415 (1972), see text *supra,* at note 329.

[413] 407 U.S. 245 (1972).

procedures required for indefinite commitments and could not be detained because he refused to cooperate with the psychiatrists who wanted to examine him for purposes of determining whether he was a defective delinquent. And, in *Humphrey v. Cady*,[414] the Court assured the defendant of his postsentence constitutional procedures and his right to assert them where, again, the state was seeking to confine him "for a potentially indefinite period"—this time as a "sex deviate." In both cases the opinion was written by Mr. Justice Marshall for unanimous courts, although Douglas wrote his own concurring opinion in *McNeil* setting forth the defendant's right to remain silent under the Fifth Amendment.[415]

L. PRIVILEGE AGAINST SELF-CRIMINATION

The Court finally got around to resolving the long-mooted question of the required scope for an immunity statute in order to compel testimony in the face of a claim of the Fifth Amendment privilege. In *Kastigar v. United States*,[416] the question determined was the validity of the federal immunity statute, 18 U.S.C. §§ 6002–03. Mr. Justice Powell held the statute constitutional in an opinion for five of the seven participating members of the Court.

The question was stated concisely:[417]

> This case presents the question whether the United States Government may compel testimony from an unwilling witness, who invokes the Fifth Amendment privilege against compulsory self-incrimination, by conferring on the witness immunity from use of the compelled testimony in subsequent criminal proceedings, as well as immunity from use of evidence derived from the testimony.

The opinion marched to its answer. The historical origins of both the privilege and immunity grants were recited. The argument that no immunity grant should survive the test of the Fifth Amendment

---

[414] 405 U.S. 504 (1972).

[415] In still another postsentence case, involving commitment as a defective delinquent, the Court dismissed a writ of certiorari as improvidently granted. Mr. Justice Douglas would have decided that detention as a "defective delinquent" should require proof beyond a reasonable doubt. In Haynes v. New York, 404 U.S. 804 (1971), the Court found no substantial federal question presented by a sentence for "addiction," which was (1) directed by the court; (2) proved by a preponderance of the evidence; (3) with a longer term than for similar categories; and (4) with no credit for time served.

[416] 406 U.S. 441 (1972).   [417] *Id*. at 442.

was quickly rejected on the basis of precedent.[418] The principle that the immunity grant must be coextensive with the privilege was accepted. And the Court concluded that "use immunity" satisfied this standard. *Murphy v. Waterfront Commission* was both distinguished and used as the prime support for the opinion:[419]

> The issue before the Court in *Murphy* was whether New Jersey and New York could compel the witnesses, whom these States had immunized from prosecution under their laws, to give testimony that might be used to convict them of a federal crime. Since New Jersey and New York had not purported to confer immunity from federal prosecution, the Court was faced with the question what limitations the Fifth Amendment privilege imposed on the prosecutorial powers of the Federal Government, a nonimmunizing sovereign. After undertaking an examination of the policies and purposes of the privilege, the Court overturned the rule that one jurisdiction within our federal structure may compel a witness to give testimony which could be used to convict him of a crime in another jurisdiction. The Court held that the privilege protects state witnesses against incrimination under federal as well as state law, and federal witnesses against incrimination under state as well as federal law. . . . The Court emphasized that this rule left the state witness and the Federal Government, against which the witness had immunity only from the *use* of the compelled testimony and evidence derived therefrom, "in substantially the same position as if the witness had claimed his privilege in the absence of a state grant of immunity."

It was conceded that *Murphy* did not decide the question presented to the Court in *Kastigar*. But *Murphy* and *Counselman v. Hitchcock*[420] were the two precedents nearest the question, although *Counselman* was concerned with a statute that the Court had construed to require transactional immunity. Use immunity was all that the Constitution required because its scope is as broad as that of the privilege, especially when it is emphasized that the burden of proof is on the government in proceeding against an immunized witness to demonstrate that the evidence proffered was not derived from his compelled disclosures:[421]

---

[418] Brown v. Walker, 161 U.S. 591 (1896); Ullman v. United States, 350 U.S. 422 (1956).

[419] 406 U.S. at 456–57.

[420] 142 U.S. 547 (1892).   [421] 406 U.S. at 460.

This burden of proof, which we reaffirm as appropriate, is not limited to a negation of taint; rather, it imposes on the prosecution the affirmative duty to prove that the evidence it proposes to use is derived from a legitimate source wholly independent of the compelled testimony.

The conclusion, on the analogy to the exclusionary rule in the confession cases, naturally followed:[422]

There can be no justification in reason or policy for holding that the Constitution requires an amnesty grant where, acting pursuant to statute and accompanying safeguards, testimony is compelled in exchange for immunity from use and derivative use when no such amnesty is required where the government, acting without colorable right, coerces a defendant into incriminating himself.

We conclude that the immunity provided by 18 U.S.C. § 6002 leaves the witness and the prosecutorial authorities in substantially the same position as if the witness had claimed the Fifth Amendment privilege. The immunity therefore is coextensive with the privilege and suffices to supplant it.

Mr. Justice Douglas, in dissent, relied on *Counselman* for the proposition that only transactional immunity could satisfy the demands of the Fifth Amendment. For Douglas, as for Mr. Justice Marshall, who also dissented, "use immunity" was not an enforcible standard and would, in any event, be counterproductive:[423]

As MR. JUSTICE MARSHALL points out . . . it is futile to expect that a ban on use or derivative use of compelled testimony can be enforced.

It is also possible that use immunity might actually have an adverse impact on the administration of justice rather than promote law enforcement. A witness might believe, with good reason, that his "immunized" testimony will inevitably lead to a felony conviction. Under such circumstances, rather than testify and aid the investigation, the witness might decide he would be better off remaining silent even if he is jailed for contempt.

In addition to this point of practicality as to the inutility of the "use immunity" rule, Mr. Justice Marshall protested the analogy drawn between the Fifth Amendment and the exclusionary rule:[424]

The Constitution does not authorize police officers to coerce confessions or to invade privacy without cause, so long as no

---

[422] *Id.* at 462.   [423] *Id.* at 467, n.2.   [424] *Id.* at 471.

use is made of the evidence they obtain. But this Court has
held that the Constitution does authorize the government to
compel a witness to give potentially incriminating testimony,
so long as no incriminating use is made of the resulting evidence. Before the government puts its seal of approval on such
interrogation, it must provide an absolutely reliable guarantee
that it will not use the testimony in any way at all in aid of
prosecution of the witness. The only way to provide that guarantee is to give the witness immunity from prosecution for
crimes to which his testimony relates.

. . . If an unconstitutional interrogation or search were held
to create transactional immunity, that might well be regarded
as an excessively high price to pay for the "constable's blun-
der." An immunity statute, on the other hand, creates a framework in which the prosecuting attorney can make a calm and
reasoned decision whether to compel testimony and suffer the
resulting ban on prosecution, or to forego the testimony.

The sufficiency of "use immunity" to validate federal immunity
statutes[425] was also established for state statutes affording the same
limited immunity.[426] In the *Zicarelli* case, the Court addressed one
more argument, but refused to deal with it. The argument was that
the immunity secured from the state, while sufficient under *Murphy*
to protect against prosecutions by the national and other state governments, would not protect against prosecution by a foreign sovereign. The Court found that there was no evidence in this case of
any potential contest with a foreign government. That question
would be dealt with when and if it arose.

So, too, the Court need not concern itself with the question
whether a state statute did in fact create use immunity or transactional immunity. That was a question on which the judgment of
the state courts would be final.[427]

The Court, although seriously divided, did decide that the privilege against self-crimination was violated by a Tennessee procedure
that barred the defendant from taking the stand in his own defense
unless he did so before any other evidence was introduced by him.[428]

---

[425] See, in addition to *Kastigar*, United States v. Cropper, 406 U.S. 952 (1972);
United States v. Korman, 406 U.S. 952 (1972).

[426] Zicarelli v. New Jersey Investigating Comm'n, 406 U.S. 472 (1972). See also
Elias v. Catena, 406 U.S. 952 (1972); Catena v. New Jersey Investigating Comm'n, 406
U.S. 952 (1972); Annaloro v. New Jersey Investigating Comm'n, 406 U.S. 952 (1972).

[427] Sarno v. Illinois Crime Comm'n, 406 U.S. 482 (1972).

[428] Brooks v. Tennessee, 406 U.S. 605 (1972).

Mr. Justice Brennan, joined by Justices Douglas, White, Marshall, and Powell, held: [429]

> Although the Tennessee statute does reflect a state interest in preventing testimonial influence, we do not regard that as sufficient to override the defendant's right to remain silent at trial. This is not to imply that there may be no risk of a defendant's coloring his testimony to conform to what has gone before. But our adversary system reposes judgment of the credibility of all witnesses in the jury. Pressuring the defendant to take the stand, by foreclosing later testimony if he refuses, is not a constitutionally permissible means of ensuring his honesty. It fails to take into account the very real and legitimate concerns that might motivate a defendant to exercise his right of silence. And it may compel even a wholly truthful defendant, who might otherwise decline to testify for legitimate reasons, to subject himself to impeachment and cross-examination at a time when the strength of his other evidence is not yet clear.

In the second part of the opinion for the Court, Mr. Justice Brennan asserted that the deprival of the right to time the defendant's appearance on the stand was a deprivation of due process because it interfered with the "guiding hand of counsel" to which defendant was entitled. It was on this ground that Mr. Justice Stewart joined the Court's judgment.

The Chief Justice and Mr. Justice Rehnquist each wrote a dissenting opinion in which the other joined and both were joined by Mr. Justice Blackmun. The dissenters thought the Tennessee statute bad but not unconstitutional. The fact that only one other jurisdiction indulged this practice did not bespeak its unconstitutionality. Nor did they think that the even-handed demand that both prosecuting witnesses and defendants speak first or forever hold their peace invaded the due process right to counsel.

The Court also reversed summarily a judgment in which a defendant's failure to take the stand had been the subject of comment by the prosecutor in violation of *Griffin v. California*,[430] even though the defendant had made no objection to this misbehavior by the prosecution.[431]

Neither the Tennessee case nor the immunity cases seem surprising in themselves. Taken together, however, there is revealed an

---

[429] *Id.* at 611–12.

[430] 380 U.S. 609 (1965).   [431] Camp v. Arkansas, 404 U.S. 69 (1971).

ambivalence on the part of the new Court about the privilege against self-crimination. The strangeness derives from the appearance of being willing to swallow the camel of limited immunity but straining at the gnat of ordering the presentation of defense witnesses. Why Justices Stewart, White, and Powell were in the majority in all cases affords the kind of mystery that is so tantalizing to those who would simplify analysis of judicial behavior.

M. WITHDRAWAL OF GUILTY PLEAS

A movement toward reality came last Term in the Court's recognition in *Santobello v. New York*[432] of the important role of plea-bargaining in the administration of criminal justice. In that case, the defendant had withdrawn pleas of not guilty and entered a guilty plea on the representation by the prosecutor that he would make no recommendation on sentence. When the time for sentence arrived, a new prosecutor did recommend the maximum sentence which the Court imposed, although it purported to do so without regard to the prosecutorial recommendation. Thereupon defendant sought and was denied the right to withdraw his guilty plea.

The Supreme Court, through the Chief Justice, asserted that the state was required to keep its bargain. The bargain was that between the state and the defendant and not merely between the individual prosecutor and the defendant. On the question whether the remedy should be specific performance by a new sentencing procedure to be decided by a different judge and without benefit of prosecutorial recommendation or the remedy of withdrawal of the plea, the Court left the answer to the state court.

Mr. Justice Douglas, who provided the fourth vote for a four-man majority, wrote a concurring opinion, arguing that as between the alternatives of new sentence and withdrawal of plea, the state court should rely heavily on the expressed choice of the defendant.

Justices Brennan, Stewart, and Marshall, speaking through the last, insisted that the defendant should have an absolute right to withdraw his plea where the state has broken its contract.

In still another state case, the Court denied the right to withdraw a plea after sentence.[433] The Court, through Mr. Justice Brennan, thought that defendant's claim unsubstantial. For the majority, as for the lower courts, there was no showing that the defendant's

---

[432] 404 U.S. 257 (1971).   [433] Dukes v. Warden, 406 U.S. 250 (1972).

lawyer's "alleged conflict of interest affected [defendant's] plea."[434] Mr. Justice Stewart agreed, but reasserted the position that where the request to withdraw the plea is made before sentence and a reason is given, the withdrawal should be permitted without going into the "merits" of the reason for withdrawal. The two dissenting Justices, Douglas and Marshall, suggested that the burden was the state's to show prejudice to it by withdrawal after sentence and urged that, because of defendant's continued assertion of his own innocence, plus the possibility of conflict of interest, the withdrawal of the plea should have been permitted.

The guilty plea is the means by which the criminal justice system survives the ever increasing burden of cases. Whether the plea-bargaining process should be conducted by the parties alone or by the parties and judges, as in civil pretrial, is still an unanswered question. But the fact is clear that plea-bargaining must be formalized to a greater extent than it has been and the recognition by the Court in *Santobello* of the contractual nature of the arrangement may move the Court toward a rationalization of the presently eclectic process.

N. RIGHTS OF PRISONERS

The crowded qualities of our jails and prisons, a direct consequence of the increased and increasing crime rate, is reflected as are most of our social problems, in the business of the High Court. The prison population certainly constitutes a large and discrete class in American society. It is to be expected that the status of the class will be in for redefinition in both the courts and the legislatures.

The infamous Attica riots and their suppression brought to the Court a preliminary motion for a stay in a case asserting class rights to the protection of the *Miranda v. Arizona*[435] rule for prisoners under inquiry as participants in the uprising.[436] Mr. Justice Douglas dissented from the denial of the stay and sought to have the case put on the Supreme Court's docket without awaiting decision in the court of appeals. For him there was no doubt about the right of the prisoners to the protections of *Miranda*. The entire Court was in accord that prisoners must be given access to legal materials that they might need to advance their legal arguments, whatever they

---

[434] *Id.* at 257.   [435] 384 U.S. 436 (1966).

[436] Inmates of Attica Correctional Facilities v. Rockefeller, 404 U.S. 809 (1971).

might be.[437] And in *Haines v. Kerner*,[438] the Court reversed the dismissal of a complaint alleging injuries by reason of disciplinary confinement while in prison. But the Court also found no substantial federal question in the attack on the constitutionality of a state statute immunizing the state from suit by one prisoner for injuries inflicted on him by a fellow prisoner.[439]

Certainly the most important case in this area was the decision affording parolees the right to hearing on the questions involved in parole revocation. The Court, in *Morrisey v. Brewer*,[440] spoke through the Chief Justice. There were, it seemed, two separate and separable questions for resolution. First, the question—essentially a factual one—whether the parolee had indeed violated the terms of his parole. Second, whether if in fact he had been a parole violator, the parole should be revoked.

The hearing on the question of parole violation was required to be conducted by an independent and impartial official. The constitutionally demanded procedural requirements were itemized:[441]

> With respect to the preliminary hearing before this officer, the parolee should be given notice that the hearing will take place and that its purpose is to determine whether there is probable cause to believe he has committed a parole violation. The notice should state what parole violations have been alleged. At the hearing the parolee may appear and speak in his own behalf, he may bring letters, documents, or individuals who can give relevant information to the hearing officer. On request of the parolee, persons who have given adverse information on which parole revocation is to be based are to be made available for questioning in his presence. However, if the hearing officer determines that the informant would be subjected to risk of harm if his identity were disclosed, he need not be subjected to confrontation and cross-examination.

The hearing officer would then be required to make a summary of the hearing and a determination whether there is probable cause to hold the parolee for a parole board determination of the question of parole revocation. While the Court comes down hard for informality and for the proposition that findings of fact and con-

---

[437] Younger v. Gilmore, 404 U.S. 15 (1971); Cruz v. Hauck, 404 U.S. 59 (1971).

[438] 404 U.S. 519 (1972); see also Piper v. Hauck, 404 U.S. 1055 (1972).

[439] Pinson v. California, 404 U.S. 804 (1971).

[440] 408 U.S. 471 (1972).   [441] *Id.* at 486–87.

clusions of law are not to be expected, this report would certainly
be expected to approximate such formalities.

In the absence of a finding of probable cause, the parolee presumably could not be remanded to custody pending determination
of his parole revocation; presumably the parole board hearing on
revocation could occur whether or not the parolee was in custody,
but if he is in custody the hearing should be a reasonably prompt
one, within two months.

The Court then proceeded, after denying its authority or intention to write a code of procedure for the states, to write a code of
procedure for the states:[442]

> Our task is limited to deciding the minimum requirements of
> due process. They include (a) written notice of the claimed
> violations of parole; (b) disclosure to the parolee of evidence
> against him; (c) opportunity to be heard in person and to pre-
> sent witnesses and documentary evidence; (d) the right to
> confront and cross-examine adverse witnesses (unless the hear-
> ing officer finds good cause for not allowing confrontation);
> (e) a "neutral and detached" hearing body such as a traditional
> parole board, members of which need not be judicial officers
> or lawyers; and (f) a written statement by the factfinders as to
> the evidence relied on and reasons for revoking parole. We
> emphasize there is no thought to equate this second stage of
> parole revocation to a criminal prosecution in any sense. It is
> a narrow inquiry; the process should be flexible enough to con-
> sider evidence including letters, affidavits, and other material
> that would not be admissible in an adversary criminal trial.
>
> We do not reach or decide the question whether the parolee
> is entitled to the assistance of retained counsel or to appointed
> counsel if he is indigent.

Mr. Justice Brennan would seem to have had no doubt of the
right to retained counsel, but conceded that appointed counsel was
an open issue.

Mr. Justice Douglas had his own code to be followed:[443]

> I do not prescribe the precise formula for the management
> of the parole problems. We do not sit as an ombudsman, tell-
> ing the States the precise procedures they must follow. I would
> hold that so far as the due process requirements of parole revo-
> cation are concerned:
>
> (1) the parole officer—whatever may be his duties under
> various state statutes—in Iowa appears to be an agent having

---

[442] *Id.* at 488–89.   [443] *Id.* at 499–500.

some of the functions of a prosecutor and of the police

(2) the parole officer is therefore not qualified as a hearing officer

(3) the parolee is entitled to a due process notice and a due process hearing of the alleged parole violations including, for example, the opportunity to be confronted by his accusers and to present evidence and argument on his own behalf; and

(4) the parolee is entitled to the freedom granted a parolee until the results of the hearing are known and the parole board —or other authorized state agency—acts.

Needless to say, Douglas's formulation would grant rights to the parolee of substantially greater proportions than did the majority of the Court.

Certainly this judgment opens a whole new package of business for the courts. First will be the cases to determine whether the federally created standards have in fact been met in particular cases. Then will come the plethora of cases seeking review on the merits of parole revocation, which whatever the standard of review will be numerous and time-consuming.

O. CONCLUSION

Crime continues to eat away at the vitals of American life, with both the criminals and the police contributing to the garrison society. The Supreme Court is in the unenviable position of not being able to do much about it, except to attempt to assure procedures that are fair to the accused—and those who might be accused—and not so destructive of the administration of criminal justice as to destroy whatever efficacy that system may have. The Court is neither so hard-nosed nor so soft-headed about this part of its business as its critics would have it. Certainly, the new Court is not as receptive as it had been in recent years to the presumption—rebuttable certainly—that defendants are right and prosecutors are wrong, although some Justices still display such a predilection. Nor can it be said that the opposite presumption is being indulged by other Justices. There does seem to be a new reluctance by the Court vastly to expand constitutionalization of state criminal procedure. The reliance both on doctrines of federalism and on experience suggests that the states will be allowed more freedom of movement than in the past, perhaps with the hope that the national system can teach better by example than by precept.

VIII. ENVIRONMENT

Ecology is the science that is concerned with the relationship of plants and animals, including the human animal, to their environment. It is also a subject that is more and more becoming a concern of government and, therefore, of the courts. Scientists have not afforded quick solutions to the problems recently acknowledged; sloganeers have quick solutions but they don't work; economists, or at least classical economists tell us to let the market make the decisions. What the courts will tell us is still largely a matter for the future. In the 1971 Term, the Supreme Court preferred avoidance to decision, thereby, perhaps, displaying the better part of wisdom.

Lake Carriers' Ass'n v. MacMullan,[444] brought the question whether the Michigan Water Pollution Control Act was invalid. The suit to enjoin its enforcement had been dismissed by the trial court as: (1) seeking an advisory opinion; (2) requiring the invocation of the abstention doctrine. The Supreme Court, through Mr. Justice Brennan, announced that the case was appropriately justiciable by declaratory judgment, but that abstention from federal jurisdiction until the state courts had acted was proper: "[W]e are satisfied that authoritative resolution of the ambiguities in the Michigan law is sufficiently likely to avoid or significantly modify the federal questions . . . to warrant abstention."[445] The Court "intimate[d] no view on the merits of appellants' claims."[446] The Chief Justice and Mr. Justice Powell, however, thought that the federal trial court should have decided the case on the merits.

The Court also declined jurisdiction over an original action filed by the state of Washington against the major American automobile manufacturers for their failure to provide adequate antipollution devices.[447] The Court properly decided that it was not a good tribunal to hear the evidence and resolve the factual problems involved. Mr. Justice Douglas's opinion for a unanimous Court recognized that its ability to manage its ever growing appellate docket would be seriously impaired if it were to assume jurisdiction over original antitrust suits like the one proffered them by the state of Washington. The Justice did take the opportunity, however, to acknowledge the evils of air pollution and to abominate them.

So, again, in *Sierra Club v. Morton*[448] the Court held that it was

---

[444] 406 U.S. 498 (1972).   [445] *Id.* at 512.   [446] *Ibid.*

[447] Washington v. General Motors Corp., 406 U.S. 109 (1972).

[448] 405 U.S. 727 (1972).

not called upon to address the issues because the Sierra Club lacked standing to maintain the action for an injunction against the development of skiing facilities by the national government in Mineral King Valley of the Sequoia National Forest. In this case, however, the Court was closely divided. Mr. Justice Stewart's majority opinion spoke for himself, the Chief Justice, and Justices White and Marshall. To those who expected a continuation of the expansion of the standing concept, the Court's position sounded strange:[449]

> The requirement that a party seeking review must allege facts showing that he is himself adversely affected does not insulate executive action from judicial review, nor does it prevent any public interests from being protected through the judicial process. It does serve as at least a rough attempt to put the decision as to whether review will be sought in the hands of those who have a direct stake in the outcome. That goal would be undermined were we to construe the APA to authorize judicial review at the behest of organizations or individuals who seek to do no more than vindicate their own value preferences through the judicial process.

Although one of the predicates of some of the Warren Court's most important judgments was that trees don't vote, Mr. Justice Douglas would give them representation in courts if not in legislatures. In an opinion redolent with the rhetoric of some of his books, he announced that he would give standing to anyone who purported to speak for "the land ethic." Justices Brennan and Blackmun, in their opinions, also chose to rely on the nature of the subject matter as that which gives rise to a need for unusual measures to bring the judiciary into the resolution of these problems. They appeared to concede that on the basis of precedent,[450] the majority was right. But they preferred to rely on John Donne's much abused dictum,[451] which somehow could be read to require judicial answers to problems that are resolvable in terms of private predilections.

---

[449] Id. at 740.

[450] Data Processing Service v. Camp, 397 U.S. 150 (1970); Barlow v. Collins, 397 U.S. 159 (1970); Flast v. Cohen, 392 U.S. 83 (1968).

[451] " 'No man is an Iland, intire of itselfe; every man is a peece of the Continent, a part of the maine; if a Clod bee washed away by the Sea, Europe is the lesse, as well as if a Promontorie were, as well as if a Mannor of thy friends or of thine owne were; any man's death diminishes me, because I am involved in Mankinde; And therefore never send to know for whom the bell tolls; it tolls for thee.' Devotions XVII." 405 U.S. at 760, n.2. Here, at last, then, is the rationale for judicial declaration of the unconstitutionality of the Vietnam War.

The opinions promise that when ecological issues do come before the Court, there will be no want of emotional commitment to Nature, its idealization, and its idolization, especially from its eminent fishermen and mountain climbers. In the one case decided on the merits, however, the Court affirmed a ruling that the standards for an atomic energy plant framed by the AEC preempted state law seeking to establish "higher" standards as well as lower ones.[452] Justices Douglas and Stewart dissented.

The Court otherwise declined a stay of the Alaskan waters atomic explosion[453] and declined to review the validity of the FPC evaluation of the Storm King Project on the Hudson River.[454]

These decisions of the 1971 Term are surely but prologue to what promises to be a lengthy and complex judicial drama.

IX. CONSUMERISM

Consumerism like ecology is a word with recently developed connotations, especially for the judicial arena. In both, pressure groups are supplying the litigating power, for they have learned from recent experience to choose the courts over the legislatures as the more friendly forums. Whether, in the long run, that will prove to have been a wise choice remains to be determined. In the 1971 Term, the gains have proved meaningful but not exciting. To a large degree the Court has not responded to the demands so far placed upon it to effect "the new property" as a constitutional concept.

In *Lindsey v. Normet*,[455] an attack on the Oregon Forcible Entry and Wrongful Detainer Statute proved unavailing. The statute provided for trial on a notice of eviction not later than six days after the complaint is filed unless security for the rent is posted by the tenant. Further, it precluded raising the issue of the landlord's nonperformance in the maintenance of the premises as a defense. And it required that in the event of a tenant appeal from an adverse judgment, the tenant post twice the value of the rent expected to accrue during the period of appeal, with forfeiture of the bond in the event of affirmance.

---

[452] Minnesota v. Northern States Power Co., 405 U.S. 1035 (1972).

[453] Committee for Nuclear Responsibility v. Schlesinger, 404 U.S. 917 (1971).

[454] New York v. F.P.C., 407 U.S. 926 (1972); Scenic Hudson Preservation Committee v. F.P.C., 407 U.S. 926 (1972); Sierra Club v. F.P.C., 407 U.S. 926 (1972).

[455] 405 U.S. 56 (1972).

The first two provisions were sustained against claims of denial of due process and equal protection. The double bond and forfeiture provision was held to violate the Equal Protection Clause because it discriminated against appellants in eviction cases. The opinion for the Court was written by Mr. Justice White, who was joined by the Chief Justice and Justices Stewart, Marshall, and Blackmun. In short compass, the Court ruled that "we cannot declare that the Oregon statute allows an unduly short time for trial preparation";[456] and that the legislative ban on raising landlord delinquency as a defense is not invalid because the "tenant is not foreclosed from instituting his own action against the landlord and litigating his right to damages or other relief in that action."[457] "The Constitution has not federalized the substantive law of landlord-tenant relations."[458]

Once more the attacking forces had sought to shift to the state the burden of proof of validity on the Equal Protection Clause issue by the "fundamental interest" argument. The Court rejected the approach:[459]

> . . . the Constitution does not provide judicial remedies for every social and economic ill. We are unable to perceive in that document any constitutional guarantee of access to dwellings of a particular quality or any recognition of the right of a tenant to occupy the real property of his landlord beyond the term of his lease, without the payment of rent or otherwise contrary to the terms of the relevant agreement. Absent constitutional mandate, the assurance of adequate housing and the definition of landlord-tenant relationships are legislative, not judicial, functions.

The Court went on in terms that will surely be shocking to the adherents of the new jurisprudence. For the Court suggested that the landlords' property rights might themselves be protected by the Constitution.

Mr. Justice Douglas dissented on the merits and Mr. Justice Brennan called for abstention, a doctrine of which he has become fond in more recent years.

Certainly the plaintiff in *D. H. Overmyer Co. v. Frick Co.*[460] was not the kind of consumer that "consumerism" is all about. The

---

[456] *Id*. at 65.

[457] *Id*. at 66.

[458] *Id*. at 68.

[459] *Id*. at 74.

[460] 405 U.S. 174 (1972). See also Osmond v. Spence, 405 U.S. 971 (1972).

Court held that enforcement of a cognovit note, providing for confession of judgment, did not violate the Constitution. The cognovit note in question, however, was negotiated at arm's length between two corporations each represented by counsel. Thus, as Mr. Justice Blackmun said for the Court:[461]

> Overmyer does not contend here that it or its counsel was not aware of the significance of the note and of the cognovit provision. Indeed, it could not do so in the light of the facts. . . .
> We therefore hold that Overmyer, in its execution and delivery to Frick of the second installment note containing the cognovit provision, voluntarily, intelligently, and knowingly waived the rights it otherwise possessed to prejudgment notice and hearing, and that it did so with full awareness of the legal consequences.

That the result was dependent on the facts was made doubly clear. The Court left open the questions of the validity of cognovit notes in other circumstances:[462]

> 1. Our holding necessarily means that a cognovit clause is not, *per se*, violative of Fourteenth Amendment due process. . . .
> 2. Our holding, of course, is not controlling precedent for other facts of other cases. For example, where the contract is one of adhesion, where there is great disparity in bargaining power, and where the debtor receives nothing for the cognovit provision, other legal consequences may ensue.
> 3. Overmyer, merely because of its execution of the cognovit note is not rendered defenseless. It conceded that in Ohio the judgment court may vacate its judgment upon a showing of a valid defense. . . .

Justices Douglas and Marshall, put further emphasis on the requirement of knowing waiver and the right to have a default judgment vacated on evidence sufficient to prevent a directed verdict, which was the standard in Ohio as they understood.

Indeed, the strictures on cognovit notes in *Overmyer* speak more loudly than the affirmance of the judgment. When a cognovit note judgment was again affirmed in *Swarb v. Lennox*,[463] it was again based on "understanding and voluntary consent." The disagreement within the Court went only to the failure of the Court to test the validity of a portion of the Pennsylvania statute relating only to

---

[461] 405 U.S. at 186–87.

[462] *Id.* at 187-88   [463] 405 U.S. 191 (1972).

nonappealing parties. The Court held that the cognovit note statute could not "be applied to the class of Pennsylvania residents who earn less than $10,000 annually and who enter into non-mortgage credit transactions, unless prior to the judgment it is shown that they voluntarily and knowingly executed such instruments purporting to waive trial and appeal."[464] Mr. Justice Douglas wanted the rule extended to mortgage transactions and to those earning more than $10,000 annually. He was alone, however, in seeking that declaration in this case. But surely, apart from the arm's length transaction of the *Overmyer* type, the classification in terms of income or nonmortgage transaction seems unlikely to survive future attack.

In *Lynch v. Household Finance Corp.*,[465] the Court struck down the barriers to an attack in the federal courts on prejudgment wage garnishment. The plaintiff was a wage-earner who had had her savings account garnished under the Connecticut statute that authorized "summary pre-judicial garnishment at the behest of attorneys for alleged creditors."[466] Mr. Justice Stewart writing for a bare majority of a seven-man Court held that the action was proper under 42 U.S.C. § 1983 and 28 U.S.C. § 1343(3), the substantive and procedural provisions of a civil rights act. The trial court's ruling that the statute justified suit for "personal" rights but not for "property" rights was rejected. "This Court has never adopted the distinction between personal liberties and proprietary rights as a guide to the contours of § 1343(3) jurisdiction. Today we expressly reject that distinction."[467]

Speaking more generally, in Holmesian terms, Mr. Justice Stewart concluded:[468]

> Such difficulties indicate that the dichotomy between personal liberties and property rights is a false one. Property does not have rights. People have rights. The right to enjoy property without unlawful deprivation, no less than the right to speak or the right to travel, is in truth a "personal" right, whether the "property" in question be a welfare check, a home, or a savings account. In fact, a fundamental interdependence exists between the personal right to liberty and the personal right in property. Neither could have meaning without

---

[464] *Id.* at 206.

[465] 405 U.S. 538 (1972). See also Weddle v. Director, Patuxent Institution, 405 U.S. 1036 (1972); Roberts v. Harder, 405 U.S. 1037 (1972).

[466] 405 U.S. at 539.   [467] *Id.* at 542.   [468] *Id.* at 552.

the other. That rights in property are basic civil rights has long been recognized. [Citing John Locke, John Adams, and Blackstone.] Congress recognized these rights in 1871 when it enacted the predecessor of §§ 1983 and 1343(3). We do no more than affirm the judgment of Congress today.

Whether Congress did indeed recognize these as "civil rights" in 1871 except for those who had been deprived of them because of their former status as slaves is not quite so clear as the Court would have it. Whatever its original meaning, the statute is no longer so restricted, any more than the Fourteenth Amendment has been so restricted.

Nor did 28 U.S.C. § 2283, which bars injunctions against state court proceedings, except under specified conditions, preclude this action.[469] Garnishment in Connecticut was an extrajudicial process to which the federal statute did not apply. No resolution of the issues on the merits was made here, but the shadows on the garnishment process were deep and deepened further when the Court held invalid the ancient remedy of replevin for reasons that would equally apply to Connecticut garnishment.

The condemnation of replevin came in *Fuentes v. Shevin*.[470] The Court was divided here exactly as it had been in *Lynch*, with the same spokesmen, Stewart for the majority and White for the dissenters. Plaintiffs again were among the less affluent. They were purchasers of consumer goods on conditional sales contracts. The Florida and Pennsylvania statutes both allowed for creditors, without any judicial proceeding, to secure a prejudgment writ of replevin by application to a court clerk, which writ had to be executed by the sheriff. The parties seeking such a writ did have to post a bond for twice the value of the property, which could be repossessed by the purchaser if he in turn posted a bond for double the property value.

Distinguishing *Overmyer*, and rejecting history, the Court ruled:[471]

> We hold that the Florida and Pennsylvania prejudgment replevin provisions work a deprivation of property without due process of law insofar as they deny the right to a prior opportunity to be heard before chattels are taken from their

[469] Justices White and Blackmun and the Chief Justice dissented only on the § 2283 issue.

[470] 407 U.S. 67 (1972).   [471] *Id*. at 96.

possessor. Our holding, however, is a narrow one. We do not question the power of a State to seize goods before a final judgment in order to protect the security interests of creditors so long as those creditors have tested their claim to the goods through the process of a fair prior hearing.

The radiations of the opinion are likely to be broad, except that the Court was without the participation of Justices Powell and Rehnquist, who might turn a minority into a majority. The minority made three points. First, that the case should not have been heard in the federal forum. Second, that the nature of the transactions almost assured that no action would be taken by creditors to repossess property except where default had in fact occurred. Third, that the opinion of the Court would be evaded by specific contractual provisions, to bring the case within the protection of *Overmyer*, or by self-help, or by proof sufficient in an uncontested hearing or even a contested one. Finally, Mr. Justice White fell back on the experience of the draftsmen of Article 9 of the Uniform Commercial Code as evidence of the error of the majority opinion.

Hidden in the dissent is a consideration that creates so many of the problems for consumerism. The result of the reforms may well be a price increase for all consumers, a sharing of the risk not by seller and buyer, but among buyers. The dissent put it that "the availability of credit may well be diminished or, in any event, the expense of securing it increased."[472] Here, indeed, is the monkey wrench that might ruin the machinery.

The next Term or the one after that might well tell a different story when the Court tests its seven-man divided judgments on a Court fully manned. Even in the 1971 Term, the Court decided that the requirement of a deposit by public utilities from those who could not otherwise establish their credit reliability was not invalid under the Equal Protection Clause.[473]

X. Legislative Powers and Privileges

Whatever lip service the Court paid to the legislative authority, it was in the 1971 Term as in the past less than receptive to claims made by legislatures and legislators who were parties litigant before the Court.

---

[472] *Id.* at 103.

[473] Wood v. Public Utility Comm'n of California, 404 U.S. 931 (1971).

In *Groppi v. Leslie*,[474] the Court unanimously and quickly struck down the Wisconsin legislature's determination of contempt for interruption of its proceedings two days before the contempt citation. In an opinion by the Chief Justice, the Court held that the contemnor was deprived of due process of law for lack of notice and opportunity to be heard on the question of his guilt. It was the lack of immediacy of the sanction that proved its defect. The Wisconsin legislature hesitated and lost:[475]

> At a very early stage in our history this Court stated that the legislative contempt power should be limited to "[t]he least possible power adequate to the end proposed." *Anderson* v. *Dunn*, 6 Wheat., at 231; *In re Oliver*, 333 U.S., at 274. While a different result might well follow had the Wisconsin Assembly acted immediately upon the occurrence of the contemptuous conduct and while the contemnor was in the chamber, or nearby within the Capitol building, as in [*Ex parte*] *Terry* [128 U.S. 289 (1888)], we conclude the procedures employed in this case were beyond the legitimate scope of that power because of the absence of notice or any opportunity to respond.

Certainly this much can be said for the Court's conclusion: It was imposing no more rigid a restriction on the state legislature than it had been imposing on the lower judiciary.

It was Congress before the bar of the Supreme Court in two other cases. *United States v. Brewster*[476] came to the Court under the now defunct Criminal Appeals Act from a judgment dismissing an indictment for constitutional defects. The defendant was charged with accepting bribes in exchange for using his office as a senator to further the programs of the bribers. His defense, successful in the trial court, was that Article I, § 6 granted immunity to national legislators: "[F]or any Speech or Debate in either House, they shall not be questioned in any other Place."

The Court, in an opinion by the Chief Justice, gave a narrow reading to the constitutional immunity and to the earlier decision that was appellee's chief reliance, *United States v. Johnson*.[477] The Clause was narrowed by rejecting the historical analogy to the privileges of members of Parliament. The reason was that our national legislature, unlike the Parliament, is not "the supreme au-

---

[474] 404 U.S. 496 (1972).

[475] *Id.* at 506–07.

[476] 408 U.S. 501 (1972).

[477] 383 U.S. 169 (1966).

thority" but only a "coordinate branch."[478] Moreover, our history did not reveal attempts by the executive branch to impose the kind of sanctions that had occurred in English history. That this happy result might be due to the fact that the Clause in question was assumed to have the same reading that the English constitution affords was not suggested. Nevertheless, it was the English experience that resulted in the inclusion in the Constitution of the safeguards for this "coordinate branch."

Johnson was narrowed thus:[479]

> *Johnson* thus stands as a unanimous holding that a Member of Congress may be prosecuted under a criminal statute provided that the Government's case does not rely on legislative acts or the motivation for legislative acts. A legislative act has consistently been defined as an act generally done in Congress in relation to the business before it. In sum, the Speech or Debate Clause prohibits inquiry only into those things generally said or done in the House or the Senate in the performance of official duties and into the motivation for those acts.

Johnson held nothing of the sort, of course, whatever inferences might be derived from the dicta. But, since congressmen have been known to abuse their privileges, the Court would read those privileges narrowly. And, since Congress may abuse its privileges, the danger of executive abuses were, somehow, thought to be decreased.

Nor could it be left to Congress to discipline its own members:[480]

> We do not discount entirely the possibility that an abuse might occur, but this possibility, which we consider remote, must be balanced against the potential danger flowing from either the absence of a bribery statute applicable to Members of Congress or a holding that the statute violates the Constitution. As we noted at the outset, the purpose of the Speech or Debate Clause is to protect the individual legislator, not simply for his own sake, but to preserve the independence and thereby the integrity of the legislative process. But financial abuses, by way of bribes, perhaps even more than Executive power, would gravely undermine legislative integrity and defeat the right of the public to honest representation. Depriving the Executive of the power to investigate and prosecute and the Judiciary of the power to punish bribery of Members of Congress is unlikely to enhance legislative independence. Given the disinclination of each House to police these matters, it is under-

---

[478] 408 U.S. at 508.

[479] *Id*. at 512.   [480] *Id*. at 524–25

standable that both Houses deliberately delegated this function
to the courts, as they did with the power to punish persons
committing contempts of Congress.

The Chief Justice concluded with what must be obvious to all: [481]

> Taking a bribe is, obviously no part of the legislative process
> or function; it is not a legislative act. . . . And an inquiry in the
> purpose of the bribe "does not draw into question the legisla-
> tive acts of the defendant member of Congress or his motives
> for performing them." [*Johnson v. United States,*] 383 U.S. at
> 185.

The three dissenting Justices found the result not so easy, indeed
impossible, to reach. Mr. Justice Brennan's opinion, in which he
was joined by Mr. Justice Douglas, was strong both on history and
precedent. And, ultimately, on principle: [482]

> I yield nothing to the Court in conviction that this repre-
> hensible and outrageous conduct, if committed by the Senator,
> should not have gone unpunished. But whether a court or only
> the Senate might undertake the task is a constitutional issue of
> portentous significance which must of course be resolved un-
> influenced by the magnitude of the perfidy alleged. It is no
> answer that Congress assigned the task to the judiciary in en-
> acting 18 U.S.C. § 201. Our duty is to Nation and Constitution,
> not Congress. We are guilty of a grave disservice to both Na-
> tion and Constitution when we permit Congress to shirk its re-
> sponsibility in favor of the courts. The Framers' judgment was
> that the American people could have a Congress of indepen-
> dence and integrity only if alleged misbehavior in the perfor-
> mance of legislative functions was accountable solely to a
> member's own House and never to the executive or judiciary.
> The passing years have amply justified the wisdom of that
> judgment. It is the Court's duty to enforce the letter of the
> Speech or Debate Clause in that spirit. We did so in deciding
> *Johnson.* In turning its back on that decision today, the Court
> arrogates to the judiciary an authority committed by the Con-
> stitution, in Senator Brewster's case, exclusively to the Senate
> of the United States. Yet the Court provides no principled
> justification, and I can think of none, for its denial that *United
> States* v. *Johnson* compels affirmance of the District Court.

Mr. Justice White's dissent was joined by Justices Douglas and
Brennan. For him, too, there was exclusive jurisdiction over the

---

[481] *Id.* at 526.   [482] *Id.* at 550.

alleged misconduct in the house of Congress to which the member belonged: [483]

> I return to the beginning. The Speech or Debate Clause does not immunize corrupt Congressmen. It reserves the power to discipline in the Houses of Congress. I would insist that the Houses develop their own institutions and procedures for dealing with those in their midst who would prostitute the legislative process.

The *Brewster* case was, in turn, the predicate for *United States v. Gravel*,[484] where the Court was again divided by a single vote, but this time with the participation of the two new Justices. Strangely, it was Mr. Justice White who shifted to make the majority of five with Mr. Justice Stewart moving into dissent.

This case grew out of the Pentagon papers fiasco, which also gave us *New York Times v. United States*,[485] among other landmarks. Despite the fact that the papers, or most of them, have been widely published, both in the press and in book form, the challenge here arose out of still one more publication, that by Beacon Press of the "Gravel edition." There were no additional materials in this version. Nevertheless, the federal grand jury in Boston sought to subpoena one of Senator Gravel's aides to discover the alleged wrongdoings that must have occurred in arranging for this publication. The principal question raised in the case, then, was whether the Speech or Debate Clause afforded immunity to a senator's aide as well as to the senator himself. In *Gravel*, the Court held that the legislator's protection would be incomplete if not afforded to the actions of his aides as well. But, the Court went on, the legislator's immunity is limited to "legislative acts," as was stated in *Brewster*. And the question what is a legislative act is to be answered not by the legislature but by the judiciary. Arranging for the publication and dissemination of the Pentagon papers was not a legislative act, nor, apparently, was the securing of the data for the senator's own use and subsequent publication. The propriety of the Court of Appeals' ban on grand jury inquisition of Gravel's aide, Rodberg, was therefore limited, said Mr. Justice White: [486]

> Focusing first on paragraph two of the order, we think the injunction against interrogating Rodberg with respect to any

---

[483] *Id.* at 563.

[484] 408 U.S. 606 (1972). See Note *supra*, at 181.

[485] 403 U.S. 713 (1971).

[486] 408 U.S. at 627–28.

act, "in the broadest sense," performed by him within the scope of his employment, overly restricted the scope of grand jury inquiry. Rodberg's immunity, testimonial or otherwise, extends only to legislative acts as to which the Senator himself would be immune. The grand jury, therefore, if relevant to its investigation into the possible violations of the criminal law and absent Fifth Amendment objections, may require from Rodberg answers to questions relating to his or the Senator's arrangements, if any, with respect to republication or with respect to third party conduct under valid investigation by the grand jury, as long as the questions do not implicate legislative action of the Senator. Neither do we perceive any constitutional or other privilege that shields Rodberg, any more than any other witness, from grand jury questions relevant to tracing the source of obviously highly classified documents that came into the Senator's possession and are the basic subject matter of inquiry in this case, as long as no legislative act is implicated by the questions.

Perhaps Justices Burger, White, and Rehnquist found it hard to avoid the inheritance from their years of prosecutorial authority in the Department of Justice.

Mr. Justice Stewart dissented both on substantive and procedural grounds. There was one question resolved that he thought was no part of the case:[487]

> The Court today holds that the Speech or Debate Clause does not protect a Congressman from being forced to testify before a grand jury about sources of information used in preparation for legislative acts. This critical question was not embraced in the petitions for certiorari. It was not dealt with in the written briefs. It was addressed only tangentially during the oral arguments. Yet it is a question with profound implications for the effective functioning of the legislative process. I cannot join in the Court's summary resolution of so vitally important a constitutional issue.

Stewart saw competing interests that should be resolved differently from the way in which the Court chose to resolve them.[488]

> Under the Court's ruling, a Congressman may be subpoenaed by a vindictive Executive to testify about informants who have not committed crimes and who have no knowledge of crime. Such compulsion can occur, because the judiciary has traditionally imposed no limits on the grand jury's broad investigatory powers; grand jury investigations are not limited

---

[487] *Id.* at 629–30.   [488] *Id.* at 631–32.

in scope to specific criminal acts, and standards of materiality and relevance are greatly relaxed. But even if the Executive had reason to believe that a member of Congress had knowledge of a specific probable violation of law, it is by no means clear to me that the Executive's interest in the administration of justice must *always* override the public interest in having an informed Congress. Why should we not, given the tension between two competing interests, *each* of constitutional dimensions, balance the claims of the Speech or Debate Clause against the claims of the grand jury in the particularized contexts of specific cases? And why are not the Houses of Congress the proper institutions in most situations to impose sanctions upon a Representative or Senator who withholds information about crime acquired in the course of his legislative duties?

Thus did Mr. Justice Stewart attempt to reconcile his position in *Brewster* with the conclusion he would reach in *Gravel*. He did not point out, as he might have done, that the privilege contended for was one that is waivable by the house of Congress affected. Applications have been made—and some have succeeded—to secure permission for the courts to secure data that falls within congressional privilege.

Mr. Justice Douglas used his opinion for an attack on the classification procedures of the executive, on the Executive Privilege which unlike the legislature's Speech or Debate privilege, finds no basis whatsoever in the Constitution, and for asserting the right of the Beacon Press to publish the Pentagon papers free from grand jury inquiry.

It remained for Mr. Justice Brennan, speaking for himself, and Justices Douglas and Marshall to defend at large the congressional privilege that was at the heart of the case. Does dissemination of information about the state of the nation and its governmental enterprises constitute protected legislative activity? He had no doubt that it did:[489]

> The dialogue between Congress and people has been recognized, from the days of our founding, as one of the necessary elements of a representative system. We should not retreat from that view merely because, in the course of that dialogue, information may be revealed that is embarrassing to the other branches of government or violates their notions of necessary secrecy. A Member of Congress who exceeds the bounds of

---

[489] *Id.* at 661–62.

propriety in performing this official task may be called to answer by the other Members of his chamber. We do violence to the fundamental concepts of privilege, however, when we subject that same conduct to judicial scrutiny at the instance of the Executive. . . . The Nation as a whole benefits from the congressional investigation and exposure of official corruption and deceit. It likewise suffers when that exposure is replaced by muted criticism, carefully hushed behind congressional walls.

For the three Justices represented in Mr. Justice Brennan's opinion, the necessary protection also extends to the securing of data by Congress, so that its sources of information should be similarly privileged:[490]

I would go further, however, and also exclude from grand jury inquiry any knowledge that the Senator or his aide might have concerning how the source himself first came to possess the Papers. This immunity, it seems to me, is essential to the performance of the informing function. . . . In any event, assuming that a Congressman can be required to reveal the sources of his information, . . . that power of inquiry, as required by the Clause, is that of the Congressman's House, and of that House only.

The partnership between the Executive and the Judiciary has in recent years contributed to the decline of the powers of a feckless Congress. The Term was marked by continued expansion of executive and judicial authority and decline of legislative power. The *Gravel* case was, therefore, within the mainstream of recent constitutional movement. Prerogative may yet be a word that, with the aid of the Court, will be returned to its original meaning, at some great cost to our democratic institutions.

XI. Constitutional Miscellany

A. THE COMMERCE CLAUSE

Crandall v. Nevada[491] held unconstitutional a head tax on passengers leaving the state of Nevada. It was from this acorn that grew the burgeoning doctrine of "the right to travel." *Evansville Airport v. Delta Airlines*[492] sustained the validity of a head tax on passengers leaving an Indiana airport, most of them for out-of-state destinations. The distinction between the taxes, on which the difference

---

[490] *Id.* at 663–64.   [491] 6 Wall. 35 (1868).   [492] 405 U.S. 707 (1972).

in result appeared to rest, was that the Indiana tax was to be used for the furtherance of airport operations. Mr. Justice Brennan, writing for seven members of the Court, said the tax was valid because it did not discriminate against interstate commerce in transportation; because the tax reflected "a fair if imperfect approximation of the use of facilities for whose benefit they are imposed";[493] and because the exemptions from the tax were within the legislative prerogative, however much they destroyed the argument of a charge measured by use. The failure to tax incoming passengers was excused by a strange concept of judicial notice:[494]

> It is not unreasonable to presume that passengers emplaning at an airport also deplane at the same airport approximately the same number of times. The parties in [the Indiana case], for example have stipulated that the number of passengers emplaning and deplaning at Dress Memorial Airport in 1967 were virtually the same.

Ergo, they are the same passengers?

It is surprising that only Mr. Justice Douglas dissented. Certainly he made the more plausible argument on the basis of precedent.

The states generally did well in the Court in the 1971 Term against attacks on the constitutionality of taxes allegedly violative of the Commerce Clause. A gross receipts tax on interstate transportation within the state was held valid,[495] as was a gross receipts tax on a General Motors Assembly plant that was assembling cars for out-of-town delivery,[496] and a franchise tax on an interstate carrier.[497] Nor did the Commerce Clause prove a better weapon against a state milk marketing order[498] or a state requirement of modern spark arresters,[499] although in both cases the claim was that federal legislation preempted state laws.

B. GOVERNMENT EMPLOYEES

Special treatment of government employees was singled out for attack in several cases. The Court generally sustained the power of

---

[493] *Id.* at 717.   [494] *Id.* at 719.

[495] United Air Lines v. Porterfield, 407 U.S. 917 (1972).

[496] General Motors Corp. v. Los Angeles, 404 U.S. 1008 (1972).

[497] United Air Lines v. Michigan, 404 U.S. 931 (1971).

[498] United Dairy Farmers Corp. v. Milk Control Comm'n, 404 U.S. 930 (1971).

[499] Chicago, M., St. P. & P.R. Co. v. Washington, 404 U.S. 804 (1971).

a government to treat its own employees in a different manner than nongovernment labor. Thus, the ban on strikes by postal employees was affirmed in *Postal Clerks v. Blount*.[500] And states were afforded similar rights in *Lawson v. Board of Education of Vestal School Dist.*[501] and *Kiernan v. Lindsay*.[502] *Lawson* was concerned with the propriety of sanctions for violating the rule, *Kiernan* with questions of federal jurisdiction over the claim. A ban on police living outside the city in which they were employed[503] and one on paying a state salary to a professor who also held a local or state office[504] were held not to raise substantial federal questions.

C.   LICENSING

Attacks on the validity of state licensing requirements were again issues that came to the fore in the 1971 Term. In *Latham v. Tynan*,[505] the Court reapplied its rule that a driver's license could not be suspended because the licensee had been involved in an accident before a hearing showing fault on his part.[506] But a state could, without raising a substantial federal question, deny licenses for practicing professions to applicants not satisfying examination criteria.[507]

D.   TAXATION

In addition to constitutional challenges under the Commerce Clause, the Court dealt with other attacks on the validity of state and local taxation. The use of different dates for apportionment of different vehicle taxes raised no substantial federal question under the Equal Protection Clause.[508] Nor did the failure of a state to allow a deduction on state income taxes for federal income tax payments.[509] The same disposition occurred where the charge was that the review afforded property tax assessments was inadequate

---

[500] 404 U.S. 802 (1971).

[501] 404 U.S. 907 (1971).   [502] 405 U.S. 1000 (1972).

[503] Detroit Police Officers Ass'n v. City of Detroit, 405 U.S. 950 (1972).

[504] Anderson v. Calvert, 405 U.S. 1035 (1972).

[505] 404 U.S. 807 (1971).

[506] See Bell v. Burson, 402 U.S. 535 (1971), on which the Court relied.

[507] Eger v. Florida State Board of Dentistry, 404 U.S. 988 (1971); Toczauer v. State Board of Registration, 406 U.S. 913 (1972).

[508] Midwest Freight Forwarding Co. v. Lewis, 406 U.S. 939 (1972).

[509] Kawitt v. Mahin, 405 U.S. 907 (1972).

and the standards applied by the assessor differed from property to property.[510] And, if parking fines are regarded as a form of taxation—certainly they are a form of revenue—in this category too is the New York case making either the lessor or lessee of an offending vehicle liable for parking fines.[511]

E. ORIGINAL JURISDICTION

The Court engaged in its anachronistic function of fixing boundaries between two states in *Nebraska v. Iowa*.[512] And it ruled that the escheat of Western Union funds should be to the state of the creditor on the unpaid money orders or, where that could not be determined, to the state of the corporate domicile, *i.e.*, New York.[513] Three dissenting Justices thought that the corporate domicile rule resulted in a windfall to New York and that a better alternative would be to presume that the creditor was domiciled where the transaction was entered into. Clearly the issue must be resolved by one arbitrary formula or another, for escheat is a windfall to whichever state receives it.

F. REAL PROPERTY

The Court affirmed a judgment that a Nebraska law was valid that barred a nonresident alien from inheriting real property, absent treaty provisions to the contrary, and providing for escheat unless the land were located within three miles of the corporate limits of a city.[514] This distinction between urban and nonurban property seems to belie whatever reason the state may have for the noninheritability rule. But it is a relic of the bygone days of an agricultural society.

The Court also held that no substantial federal question was presented by a zoning law that made an illegal structure a nuisance per se subject to demolition;[515] by a state law requiring subdividers to dedicate a portion of their land to park or recreational uses or pay a fee in lieu thereof;[516] by a law providing for confiscation by

---

[510] Hawaiian Land Co. v. Director of Taxation, 405 U.S. 907 (1972).

[511] Kinney Car Corp. v. City of New York, 404 U.S. 803 (1971).

[512] 406 U.S. 117 (1972).

[513] Pennsylvania v. New York, 407 U.S. 206 (1972).

[514] Shames v. Nebraska, 408 U.S. 901 (1972).

[515] Hershberger v. City of Troy, 404 U.S. 804 (1971).

[516] Associated Home Builders v. City of Walnut Creek, 404 U.S. 878 (1971).

eminent domain of "blighted property";[517] and by a statute requiring jury trial in eminent domain proceedings.[518]

Certainly any of these cases could have risen to the status of one resolved by full opinions. But the Court had more on its plate than it could masticate. And some issues must be disposed of by memoranda orders or resolved by alternative tribunals.

XII. NONCONSTITUTIONAL CASES

The cases heretofore discussed by no means exhaust the list of difficult issues resolved by the Court in the 1971 Term. The usual abundance of nonconstitutional issues of no small importance were also dispatched by the Court in a virtuoso display of work not heretofore exhibited. These cases admittedly are of more interest to specialists than to the constitutional lawyer or political scientist. And yet their resolution is intrinsically necessary to the maintenance of a government of laws. It is necessary that an ultimate judicial arbiter dispose of them; it is not necessary that that arbiter be the Supreme Court. A catalogue of these decisions is all that is attempted here.

Labor Board and other labor law cases were plentiful.[519] In the closely decided cases, the Warren Court remnants were dominant. The antitrust, merger, and trade practice cases were also prominent.[520] The closest division here came in the baseball case, with Stewart and White casting their deciding votes in favor of the

---

[517] Levin v. Township Committee, 404 U.S. 803 (1971).

[518] Maryland Community Developers v. State Road Comm'n, 404 U.S. 803 (1971).

[519] N.L.R.B. v. Plasterers' Local Union No. 79, 404 U.S. 116 (1971); N.L.R.B. v. Nash-Finch Co., 404 U.S. 138 (1971); Allied Chemical Workers v. Pittsburgh Plate Glass Co., 404 U.S. 157 (1971); N.L.R.B. v. Scrivener, 405 U.S. 117 (1972); N.L.R.B. v. Burns International Security Services, 406 U.S. 272 (1972); Norfolk & Western Ry. v. Nemitz, 404 U.S. 37 (1971) (ICC); Trobvich v. United Mine Workers, 404 U.S. 528 (1972) (LMRA); Iowa Beef Packers, Inc. v. Thompson, 405 U.S. 228 (1972) (FLSA); Andrews v. Louisville & N. R. Co., 406 U.S. 320 (1972) (RLA); Operating Engineers v. Flair Builders, 406 U.S. 487 (1972) (arbitration of labor contract).

[520] Hawaii v. Standard Oil Co., 405 U.S. 251 (1971) (antitrust; standing of state); Ford Motor Co. v. United States, 405 U.S. 562 (1972) (merger); United States v. Topco Associates, Inc., 405 U.S. 596 (1972) (antitrust); Flood v. Kuhn, 407 U.S. 258 (1972) (baseball antitrust); Port of Portland v. United States, 408 U.S. 811 (1972) (ICC; rail merger); F.T.C. v. Sperry & Hutchinson Co., 405 U.S. 233 (1972) (FTC, § 5); California Motor Transport v. Trucking Unlimited, 404 U.S. 508 (1972) (Clayton Act); United States v. Pfizer, 404 U.S. 548 (1972) (antitrust; affirmed by equally divided Court).

continued exemption of baseball from the Sherman Act. Only precedent was on the side of the decision; common sense was not.

In the tax cases,[521] the Chief Justice and Justice Stewart were in the majority in every case. The Government was the petitioner in each case, suggesting the inaccessibility of the Court to taxpayers. But the Court came down on the tax collector's side in only two of the four cases. The Court was not closely divided in any of the admiralty cases,[522] not even those involving the rights of longshoremen. But in two of the three conscientious objector cases decided by full opinion, the Court majority was by a single vote and the other was an avoidance of decision.[523]

There were also two FPC jurisdiction cases resolved in favor of the agency's authority;[524] three securities cases;[525] and two unanimously decided questions of federal jurisdiction;[526] an Indian partition case;[527] a Tort Claims Act suit for damages for sonic boom, resolved against the claimant;[528] an ICC case,[529] a class of cases which never should burden the Court's dockets; and a habeas corpus case.[530]

---

[521] United States v. Generes, 405 U.S. 93 (1972); United States v. Mississippi Chemical Corp., 405 U.S. 298 (1972); Commissioner v. First Security Bank of Utah, 405 U.S. 394 (1972); United States v. Byrum, 408 U.S. 125 (1972).

[522] McClanahan v. Morauer & Hartzell, Inc., 404 U.S. 16 (1971); Chevron Oil Co. v. Huson, 404 U.S. 97 (1971); Victory Carriers, Inc. v. Law, 404 U.S. 202 (1972); Atlantic Coast Line R. Co. v. Erie Lackawanna R. Co., 406 U.S. 340 (1972); M/S Bremen v. Zapata Off-Shore Co., 407 U.S. 1 (1972). See also Scrap Loaders, Inc. v. Pacific Coast Shipping Co., 404 U.S. 1035 (1972); Pacific Coast Shipping Co. v. Ryan, 404 U.S. 1035 (1972); Lykes Bros. S.S. Co. v. Chaoris, 404 U.S. 1009 (1972).

[523] Fein v. Selective Service System, 405 U.S. 365 (1972) (4-3); Strait v. Laird, 406 U.S. 341 (1972) (5-4); Parisi v. Davidson, 405 U.S. 34 (1972) (7-0). See also Blatt v. Local Board § 116, 405 U.S. 1014 (1972); St. Clair v. Selective Service Local Board #35, 405 U.S. 1014 (1972); Joseph v. United States, 404 U.S. 820 (1972); Rosengart v. Laird, 405 U.S. 908 (1972); McGarva v. United States, 406 U.S. 953 (1972).

[524] F.P.C. v. Florida Power & Light Co., 404 U.S. 453 (1972); F.P.C. v. Louisiana Power & Light Co., 406 U.S. 621 (1972).

[525] Superintendent of Insurance v. Bankers Life & Casualty Co., 404 U.S. 6 (1971); S.E.C. v. Medical Committee for Human Rights, 404 U.S. 403 (1972); Reliance Electric Co. v. Emerson Electric Co., 404 U.S. 418 (1972).

[526] Grubbs v. General Electric Credit Corp., 405 U.S. 699 (1972) (removal); Brunette Machine Works, Ltd. v. Kockum Industries, Inc., 406 U.S. 706 (1972) (aliens).

[527] Affiliated Ute Citizens of Utah v. United States, 406 U.S. 128 (1972).

[528] Laird v. Nelms, 406 U.S. 797 (1972).

[529] United States v. Allegheny Ludlum Steel Corp., 406 U.S. 742 (1972).

[530] Picard v. Connor, 404 U.S. 270 (1972).

A criminal gun-regulation statute was construed to require a relationship to interstate commerce for each element of criminality, with the Chief Justice and Mr. Justice Rehnquist dissenting.[531] And the Chief Justice was in dissent in two other cases construing a federal criminal law where the Court was divided by a single vote.[532]

The Court divided five to three in a Wunderlich Act case[533] and five to four in a series of cases concerned with bankruptcy,[534] patents,[535] the "act of state doctrine,"[536] and the FTC's CATV regulations,[537] These are demonstration enough that the nonconstitutional cases are frequently as difficult of resolution as are the constitutional decisions.

XIII. Conclusion

This record of the most recent chapter in the Court's history is as long as it is not only because of the loquaciousness of the writer but because of the extraordinary amount of business that the Court dispatched in its third year under the chairmanship of Chief Justice Burger. The 1971 Term was the busiest in history but promises to be eclipsed by the 1972 Term. The Court is not likely to be able to maintain this pace if it is not succored from the vast number of cases that can come before it for resolution. Certainly some of them would better be assigned to other tribunals and some even left for correction by the legislature.

In addition to its judicial tasks, the Justices are called upon—and generously respond—to perform all sorts of extracurricular chores they would do better to eschew. The profession, instead of asking the Justices to engage in speechmaking and other ceremonial functions, would do well to urge them to husband their energies for the tasks assigned to them. There are enough inherent factors that inter-

[531] United States v. Bass, 404 U.S. 336 (1971). See also Crow v. United States, 406 U.S. 945 (1972); Mullins v. United States, 404 U.S. 1008 (1972); Synnes v. United States, 404 U.S. 1009 (1972); Taylor v. United States, 404 U.S. 1009 (1972); Wiley v. United States, 404 U.S. 1009 (1972); Madril v. United States, 404 U.S. 1010 (1972).

[532] United States v. Campos Serrano, 404 U.S. 293 (1971) (18 USC § 1546); Gelbard & Parnes v. United States, 408 U.S. 41 (1972) (18 USC § 1826 (a)).

[533] S. & E. Contractors, Inc. v. United States, 406 U.S. 1 (1972).

[534] Caplin v. Marine Midland Co., 406 U.S. 416 (1972).

[535] Deepsouth Packing Co. v. Laitram Corp., 406 U.S. 518 (1972).

[536] First Nat. City Bank v. Banco Nacional de Cuba, 406 U.S. 759 (1972).

[537] United States v. Midwest Video Corp., 406 U.S. 649 (1972).

fere with proper judicial functioning. An enlarged staff threatens to bureaucratize the Court and to destroy the confidentiality necessary to open exchanges of views between the Justices.

The 1971 Term, like its two predecessors, will be remarked for the change of direction that has been brought about by its new members. Continuity with the Warren Court jurisprudence is not a duty but only a necessity. The necessity is not to follow precedent blindly, but to explain the reasons for departure from it and to justify, again by reason rather than personal predilection, the results reached in every case. This the Burger Court will be unable to do if it lacks the time and tools to do it. The Court must be protected, by legislation if necessary, from its overgenerous impulses to spend its time on cases that are not worthy of it and on nonjudicial tasks that are not properly its business.